ANGLO-NORMAN WARFARE

STUDIES IN LATE ANGLO-SAXON
AND ANGLO-NORMAN
MILITARY ORGANIZATION AND WARFARE

In Memory
OF
Reginald Allen Brown

ANGLO-NORMAN WARFARE

STUDIES IN LATE ANGLO-SAXON
AND ANGLO-NORMAN
MILITARY ORGANIZATION AND WARFARE

EDITED BY

Matthew Strickland

THE BOYDELL PRESS

This collection first published 1992 by The Boydell Press

The Boydell Press is an imprint of Boydell & Brewer Ltd
PO Box 9, Woodbridge, Suffolk IP12 3DF, UK
and of Boydell & Brewer Inc.
PO Box 41026, Rochester, NY 14604, USA

ISBN 0 85115 327 5 hardback
ISBN 0 85115 328 3 paperback

British Library Cataloguing-in-Publication Data
Anglo-Norman Warfare : Studies in Late Anglo-Saxon and
Anglo-Norman Military Organization and Warfare
I. Strickland, Matthew
355.00942
ISBN 0–85115–327–5
ISBN 0–85115–328–3 pbk

Library of Congress Cataloging-in-Publication Data applied for

The paper used in this publication meets the minimum requirements
of American National Standard for Information Sciences –
Permanence of Paper for Printed Library Materials, ANSI Z39.48–1984

Printed in Great Britain by
St Edmundsbury Press Ltd, Bury St Edmunds, Suffolk

CONTENTS

ACKNOWLEDGEMENTS

The articles in this volume are reprinted by permission, and were first published as listed below.

N. Hooper, 'The Housecarls in England in the Eleventh Century', *Anglo-Norman Studies*, vii, 161–76 (© N. Hooper 1984, 1985)

N. Hooper, 'Some Observations on the Navy in Late Anglo-Saxon England', *Studies in Medieval History presented to R. Allen Brown*, ed. C. Harper-Bill, C. Holdsworth and J. Nelson (Woodbridge), 203–213 (© N. Hooper 1989)

M. Chibnall, 'Military Service in Normandy before 1066', *Anglo-Norman Studies*, v, 65–77 (© M. Chibnall 1982, 1983)

J. C. Holt, 'The Introduction of Knight Service in England', *Anglo-Norman Studies*, vi, 89–106 (© J. C. Holt 1983, 1984)

J. O. Prestwich, 'War and Finance in the Anglo-Norman State', *Transactions of the Royal Historical Society*, 5th ser., iv, 19–43 (© Royal Historical Society 1954)

M. Chibnall, 'Mercenaries and the *Familia Regis* under Henry I', *History*, lxii, 15–23 (© The Historical Association 1977)

J. O. Prestwich, 'The Military Household of the Norman Kings', *English Historical Review*, xcvi, 1–37 (© Longman Group Limited London 1981)

R. A. Brown, 'The Status of the Norman Knight', *War and Government in the Middle Ages*, ed. J. Gillingham and J. C. Holt (Woodbridge), 18–32 (© R. A. Brown 1984)

J. Gillingham, 'William the Bastard at War', *Studies in Medieval History presented to R. Allen Brown*, ed. C. Harper-Bill, C. Holdsworth and J. Nelson (Woodbridge), 141–158 (© J. Gillingham 1989)

R. A. Brown, 'The Battle of Hastings', *Proceedings of the Battle Conference on Anglo-Norman Studies*, iii, 1–21 (© R. A. Brown 1980, 1981)

J. Bradbury, 'Battles in England and Normandy, 1066–1154', *Anglo-Norman Studies*, vi, 1–12 (© J. Bradbury 1983, 1984)

J. Gillingham, 'Richard I and the Science of War in the Middle Ages', *War and Government in the Middle Ages*, ed. J. Gillingham and J. C. Holt (Woodbridge) 78–91 (© J. Gillingham 1984)

M. J. Strickland, 'Securing the North: Invasion and the Strategy of Defence in Twelfth-Century Anglo-Scottish Warfare', *Anglo-Norman Studies*, xii, 177–198 (© M. J. Strickland 1989, 1990)

M. Bennett, 'Wace and Warfare', *Anglo-Norman Studies*, xi, 37–58 (© M. Bennett 1988, 1989)

J. Gillingham, 'War and Chivalry in the *History of William the Marshal*', *Thirteenth Century England. Proceedings of the Newcastle upon Tyne Conference*, ii, 1–14 (© J. Gillingham 1987, 1988)

INTRODUCTION

A collection of articles on the organization and conduct of war in eleventh and twelfth century England and Normandy needs little justification.[1] For the effects of war and its diverse dictates permeated the very fabric of society at every level, from the king, the supreme war leader, to the peasantry who bore the brunt of the ravaging and economic attrition which so dominated the prosecution of war itself.

If the obverse of royal seals portrayed the king as *rex sacerdos*, seated in majesty, the reverse, with an armed equestrian figure, stressed his equally fundamental role as *dux*. Personal prowess in arms, such as displayed by William Rufus or Richard I, greatly augmented the prestige of a king, but skill as a strategist and tactician, as a besieger and commander in the field was a vital prerequisite for political success. Irrespective of the growing sophistication of Anglo-Norman administration, the exercise of power never moved far beyond the ability to field and fund an effective fighting force and to construct and adequately garrison the chain of castles on which depended both internal security and defence from external attack. Anglo-Norman kings might not have mounted a major military expedition inexorably every year as the Carolingians had done at the height of their power,[2] but there was scarcely a year without some campaigning, and the needs of defence, particularly on the Norman border, were ever present, with the concomitant expenditure on supplies, wages and building. And if fiscal resources were the 'sinews of war', then the need to generate ever increasing sums for the war chest was the fundamental dynamic behind the expansion of Anglo-Norman government.

In his role as warleader, the king or duke was but *primus inter pares* of a nobility whose *raison d'être* was war; in the traditional schema of the three orders of *oratores*, *bellatores* and *laboratores*,[3] the aristocracy was defined first and foremost by its military function. The costly equipment of the heavily-armoured knight necessary to fulfil this role was itself symbolic of rank and status. The military households of both rulers and lords formed one of the most fundamental

---

[1] I would like to express my thanks both to Bill Zajac for saving me from many errors of style, and to Dr Fiona Watson for frequent rescue from my cloud of technical unknowing in word-processing.

[2] L. Halphen, *Charlemagne et l'empire Carolingien* (2nd ed., Paris, 1949), 167; 'La guerre est pour les Francs une institution nationale . . . Les annalistes relèvent commes des années exceptionelles celles où l'on ne s'est point battu. Chaque année par conséquent, tout subject de l'Empire peut être requis de prendre les armes au premier appel'. See also F. L. Ganshof, 'L'armée sous les Carolingiens', *Ordinamenti militari in Occidente nell'alto Medioevo*, 2 vols. (*Settimane di Studio del Centro Italiano di studi sull'alto Medioevo*, Spoleto, 1968), i, 109–30; *idem, Frankish Institutions under Charlemagne*, tr. B. and M. Lyon (Brown, 1968; repr. New York, 1970), 58–68; J. F. Verbruggen, 'L'armée et la stratégie de Charlemagne', *Karl der Grosse: Lebenswerk und Nachleben*, ed. W. Braunfels (Dusseldorf, 1965), I, 420–36.

[3] G. Duby, *Les trois ordres ou l'imaginaire du féodalisme* (Paris, 1978), trans. A. Goldhammer, *The Three Orders* (Chicago, 1980).

of political and social institutions, while the basis of land tenure, in the first generation of the conquest at least, was directly linked to the provision of knight service. Aristocratic culture was suffused with the values of a warrior élite, reflected most forcefully in *chansons de geste* like the *Song of Roland*[4] or *Raoul de Cambrai*,[5] but equally visible in the more courtly Arthurian romances of Chrétien de Troyes.[6] Among the troubadours, Bertran de Born's paean of praise for the joys of war stands in relative isolation,[7] but his *planh* or lament for Henry, the Young King, eldest son of Henry II, is typical of a genre extolling chivalric values,[8] and even the language of love could adopt the similes and metaphors of warfare.[9] The castle, the fortified dwelling of a lord, epitomized the fusion of domestic, administrative and military facets of noble life,[10] while two of the aristocracy's principal pastimes, hunting[11] and the tournament[12] (the latter increasing in popularity and importance from the second quarter of the twelfth century), were closely linked to training for war.

But it was not only the secular nobility that was concerned with war. At a theological level, the Church had long concerned itself with attempting to reconcile the teachings of Christianity to the realities of defensive or aggressive war, and the concomitant need to define the status of the warrior in society by such means as just war theory, penitentials and a developing crusade ideology.[13] The Peace and Truce of God had tried to proffer some degree of protection to the most vulnerable elements of society, the clergy and the peasantry, and to circumscribe knightly aggression, a concern which was reflected in the subsequent (and largely

---

[4] *The Song of Roland*, tr. G. Burgess (Harmondsworth, 1990) provides an accesible new translation, with an appendix containing much of the French text.

[5] *Raoul de Cambrai*, ed. and trans. S. Kay (Oxford, 1991). There is an earlier translation by J. Crosland, *Raoul de Cambrai: an Old French Epic* (London, 1926), and a partial translation in *The History of Feudalism*, ed. D. Herlihy (New Jersey and Sussex, 1979), 131–176. Cf. *William Count of Orange. Four Old French Epics*, ed. G. Price (London, 1975).

[6] *Chrétien de Troyes: Arthurian Romances*, tr. W. W. Kibler and C. W. Carroll (Harmondsworth, 1991).

[7] '*Be.m platz lo gais temps de pascor*', ed. and trans. in A. R. Press, *An Anthology of Troubadour Lyric Poetry* (Edinburgh, 1985), 158–163.

[8] '*Si tuit li dol e.lh plor e.lh marrimen*', *Troubadour Lyric Poetry*, 168–171.

[9] See, for example, Bernard de Ventadour's *Lo rossinhols s'esbaudeya*, where the poet begs his lady for a truce and peace (*Troubadour Lyric Poetry*, 72–75), or the similar sentiments of Girault de Borneil, more graphically expressed:

> Lady, as when a castle is besieged by grim barons, when the siege engine topples the towers – and the catapult and the mangonel – and the onslaught is so fierce from every side that neither cunning nor guile avails them, and the suffering and the cries are so terrible of those within who are in such great anguish, does it not seem and appear to you that there's need for them to cry mercy? In the same way, I humbly cry mercy of you, good lady, noble and worthy (*Can lo glatz e.l frechs e la neus, Troubadour Lyric Poetry*, 134–7).

[10] See *inter alia*, R. A. Brown, *English Castles* (2nd ed., London, 1976) and N. J. G. Pounds, *The Medieval Castle in England and Wales: A Social and Political History* (Cambridge, 1990).

[11] For a general study of hunting in the middle ages see J. Cummins, *The Hawk and the Hound. The Art of Medieval Hunting* (London, 1988).

[12] On the tournament see J. R. V. Barker, *The Tournament in England, 1100–1400* (Woodbridge, 1986), and R. Barber and J. R. V. Barker, *Tournaments* (Woodbridge, 1989).

[13] P. Contamine, *La Guerre au moyen âge* (Paris, 1980), tr. M. Jones, *War in the Middle Ages* (Oxford, 1984), 260–302, and for relevant bibliography, 355–60.

unsuccessful) attempts by the Church to prohibit the tournament and the employment of *routiers*.[14]

Such efforts sprang not simply from ideology but pragmatism, for in *tempus gwerrae* itself, a combination of wealth and lack of effective protection made the lands, chattels and personnel of the Church liable to widespread spoliation. Knights might seize estates, plunder treasuries and strip reliquaries, exact forced labour and dues in kind from the peasantry on ecclesiastical lands, turn churches and abbeys into makeshift castles, or even immolate them by accident or design. Yet the relationship between warriors and ecclesiastics was far more complex than the simple polarity of aggression in war and benefaction in peace.[15] A deep if unsophisticated piety manifested itself among the knighthood in numerous ways in war itself; in the blessing of standards and weapons, many of which carried religious inscriptions; in confession, absolution and receipt of the sacrament prior to battle, which might also be preceded by fasting, almsgiving or some other act of purifcation; in the use of relics, hallowed banners and the invocations in war-cries of God or his saints; and in votive offerings or endowments in thanksgiving for victory.[16]

The aristocratic nature of many of the higher clergy, moreover, tended to blur distinctions between ecclesiastics and the knighthood; for while warrior prelates such as Odo of Bayeux, Geoffrey of Coutances, Henry of Blois and Philip of Beauvais, who bore arms in contravention of canon law, were always in a minority, many more by virtue of their territorial holdings and position of high political as well as spiritual responsibility were the builders or custodians of key castles. Bishop Gundulf of Rochester, who was William I's master of works on the White Tower and was commissioned by Rufus to rebuild Rochester castle in stone,[17] was only exceptional in that he was the actual architect of such works. In addition, bishops and abbots might not only command the service of many enfeoffed knights but might have a substantial military household. The potential conflict of interests this might engender was dramatically revealed in the debate over Stephen's seizure of the Le Poer bishops in 1139, though the problem of the military implications of ecclesiastical temporalities and the role of leading churchmen as administrators and commanders in war was never satisfactorily solved.[18] The imagery of war even penetrated the cloister; Anselm's sermons contained

---

14 For a good introduction to the Peace movement see H. E. J. Cowdrey, 'The Peace and Truce of God in the Eleventh Century', *Past and Present*, xlvi (1970), 42–67, and G. Duby, 'Laity and the Peace of God', *The Chivalrous Society*, tr. C. Postan (London, 1977), 123–133; cf. C. Holdsworth, 'Ideas and Reality: Some Attempts to Control and Defuse War in the Twelfth Century', *The Church and War*, ed. W. J. Sheils (*Studies in Church History*, xx, Oxford, 1983), 59–78.

15 C. Harper-Bill, 'The Piety of the Anglo-Norman Knightly Class', *Anglo-Norman Studies*, ii (1979), 63–77.

16 Contamine, *War in the Middle Ages*, 296–302, offers a useful summary of these themes, which are discussed further in M. J. Strickland, *The Conduct and Perception of War under the Anglo-Norman and Angevin Kings* (Cambridge, forthcoming).

17 M. Ruud, 'Monks in the World: The Case of Gundulf of Rochester', *Anglo-Norman Studies*, xi (1988), 248.

18 There is to my knowledge no specific study of the role of Anglo-Saxon or Anglo-Norman ecclesiastics in warfare itself, whether as commanders or as actual warriors, but in general see F. Prinz, *Klerus und Krieg im früheren Mittelalter. Untersuchungen zur Rolle der Kirche beim Aufbau der Königsherrschaft* (Stuttgart, 1971), and E. Hehl, *Kirche und Krieg im 12. Jahrhundert. Studien zu kanonischem Recht und politischer Wirklichkeit* (Stuttgart, 1980).

frequent military analogies, the liturgy itself might be couched in terms of the war against sin and evil, while monastic writers such as Orderic Vitalis regarded Norman monasteries as the spiritual castles of the duchy, manned by the true *militia Christi*.[19]

It was, however, the third order, the peasantry and burgesses, upon whom the realities of war weighed most heavily, whether in terms of taxation, the effects of debased coinage and the requisitioning of supplies and labour dues, or as the main targets of the chevauchée. At its most fundamental, war was about the procurement or destruction of crops, vineyards and livestock. An attack upon an opponent's peasantry disrupted his revenues and highlighted his inability to defend his own, thereby undermining the status of his lordship. Not, however, that such elements of society were always the *imbellis* – mere passive victims of war. For although the medieval footsoldier before the fourteenth century has been undeservedly neglected by historians, it is clear that infantry drawn from the peasantry or urban communities played a significant role in the warfare of the eleventh and twelfth centuries.[20]

Given such an all-pervading influence of war on medieval society, the term 'military history' becomes something of a misnomer.[21] For while legitimate enough in itself (and both too widespread and too useful to be discarded), the phrase still all too often carries the pejorative overtones of a narrow and myopic discipline very much on the fringes of mainstream historiography; a world where endless campaign narrative or the minutiae of tactics and equipment are the impoverished substitute for significant analysis and 'big ideas', and one which is at best the preserve of retired colonels, and at worst of academics with a suppressed militaristic bent. If such a misconception has been the unfortunate (and perhaps not wholly justified) legacy of works in the genre of Sir Charles Oman or Lt Colonel A. H. Burne,[22] then equally it is a myth that should have long been dispelled by the writings of such as Michael Howard, Geoffrey Parker, Phillipe Contamine, Maurice Keen and John Keegan,[23] to name but a few exponents of an area of study as diverse as it is fundamental.

---

[19] Harper-Bill, 'Piety of the Anglo-Norman Knightly Class', 65, 75–6; M. Chibnall, 'Feudal Society in Orderic Vitalis', *Anglo-Norman Studies*, i (1978), 36 and n. 6. Cf. B. H. Rosenwein, 'Feudal War and Monastic Peace: Cluniac Liturgy as Ritual Aggression', *Viator*, ii (1971), 129–57.

[20] The best general discussion of the medieval infantryman prior to the Hundred Years War is that given by J. F. Verbruggen, *The Art of Warfare in Western Europe during the Middle Ages (from the Eighth Century to 1340)* (Amsterdam and New York), especially 99–184, an abridged translation of his *De Krijkunst in West-Europa in de Middeleeuven (IXe tot begin IXe eeuw)* (Brussels, 1954), while for the Anglo-Norman period see J. H. Beeler, 'The Composition of Anglo-Norman Armies', *Speculum*, xl (1965), 398–414. Most attention has focused on the archer, for example R. Hardy, *Longbow. A Social and Military History* (London, 1976); J. Bradbury, *The Medieval Archer* (Woodbridge, 1985); J. Manley, 'The Archer and the Army in the Late Saxon Period', *Anglo-Saxon Studies in Archaeology and History*, iv (1985), 223–35.

[21] For an excellent and provoking discussion on the nature of 'military history' see J. Keegan, *The Face of Battle* (Harmondsworth, 1976), 13–77.

[22] See, for example, C. W. C. Oman's *The Art of War in the Middle Ages, AD 378–1485*, 2 vols. (London, 1924; repr. Ithaca, 1960, and Oxford, 1991) and A. H. Burne, *The Battlefields of England* (London, 1950); *idem, More Battlefields of England* (London, 1952).

[23] See, *inter alia*, M. Howard, *Studies in War and Peace* (London, 1970); *War in European History* (London, 1976); *War and the Liberal Conscience* (London, 1978); *The Causes of War and Other*

As regards the middle ages, moreover, the potential and importance of treating war in a broader social context had been amply demonstrated considerably prior to Contamine's widely-acclaimed *War in the Middle Ages* by a number of scholars principally concerned with the Hundred Years War.[24] There have, however, been few comparable studies for the eleventh and twelfth centuries, and, despite a resurgence of interest in the period, the number of monographs dealing specifically with warfare remain surprisingly small.[25] The majority of work has been predominantly institutional, centered on Anglo-Saxon and Anglo-Norman military organization and concerned with war only in so far as it relates to questions of obligation and tenure.[26] Equally, despite the burgeoning of castle studies, the secondary literature on siege and the role of the castle in war scarcely reflects the dominance which castles exercised in contemporary warfare.[27] For a treatment of

Essays (London, 1982); G. Parker, *The Army of Flanders and the Spanish Road* (London, 1972); *The Thirty Years War* (London, 1984); *The Military Revolution: Military Innovation and the Rise of the West* (Cambridge, 1988); P. Contamine, *Guerre, état et société à la fin du moyen âge: Études sur les armées des rois de France, 1337–1494* (Paris, 1972); *La France au XIVe et XVe siècles: Hommes, mentalités, guerre et paix* (London, 1981); *War in the Middle Ages* (London, 1984); *Guerre et société en France, en Angleterre et en Bourgogne, XIVe – XVe siècles* (ed. with M. Keen) (Lille, 1991); M. Keen, *The Laws of War in the Later Middle Ages* (London, 1965); *Chivalry* (Yale, 1984); J. Keegan, *The Face of Battle* (Harmondsworth, 1976); *Soldiers: A History of Men in Battle* (London, 1985); *The Mask of Command* (Harmondsworth, 1988); *The Price of Admiralty* (London, 1989).

24 For example K. Fowler (ed.), *The Hundred Years War* (London, 1971); C. T. Allmand (ed.), *Society at War. The Experience of England and France During the Hundred Years War* (Edinburgh, 1973); J. Barnie, *War in Medieval Society. Social Values and the Hundred Years War, 1337–99* (London, 1974). See also P. Pieri, 'Sur les dimensions de l'histoire militaire', *Annales*, xviii (1963), 625–638, and P. Contamine, 'L'histoire militaire et l'histoire de la guerre dans la France médiévale depuis trente ans', *Actes du Ce Congrès national des Sociétés savantes, Paris 1975, Section de philologie et d'histoire jusqu'à 1610* (Paris, 1977), I, 71–93.

25 The two best general works on medieval warfare, Verbruggen, *The Art of Warfare*, and Contamine, *War in the Middle Ages*, contain much of value, but are perforce broader survey works covering a wide chronological span, a qualification which applies equally to works on the nature and development of chivalry, such as R. Barber, *The Knight and Chivalry* (London, 1970; repr. 1974), J. Flori, *L'essor de la chevalerie* (Geneva, 1986), and Maurice Keen's magisterial *Chivalry* (Yale, 1984). J. H. Beeler's *Warfare in England, 1066–1189* (Ithaca and New York, 1966) is essentially a chronological survey of campaigns, but contains some useful chapters on military organization; his subsequent *Warfare in Feudal Europe, 700–1200* (Ithaca and London, 1971), however, is a broad and somewhat ephemeral survey.

A welcome addition to the literature on pre-Conquest armies is R. P. Abels' *Lordship and Military Obligation in Anglo-Saxon England* (Berkley and Los Angeles, 1988), and see also *idem*, 'Bookland and Fyrd Service in Late Anglo-Saxon England', *Anglo-Norman Studies*, vii (1985), 1–25. A useful and diverse collection of essays on aspects of Anglo-Saxon warfare is provided by *Weapons and Warfare in Anglo-Saxon England*, ed. S. C. Hawkes (*Oxford University Committee for Archaeology*, Monograph no. 21, Oxford, 1989), and see R. Abels, 'English Tactics, Strategy and Military Organization in the Late Tenth Century', *The Battle of Maldon, AD 991*, ed. D. Scragg (Oxford, 1991), 143–155. Cf. N. Lund, 'The Armies of Swein Forkbeard and Cnut: *Leding* or *Lið*', *Anglo-Saxon England*, xv (1986), 105–18.

26 See, for example, C. Warren Hollister, *Anglo-Saxon Military Institutions on the Eve of the Norman Conquest* (Oxford, 1962); *idem, The Military Organization of Norman England* (Oxford, 1965); F. M. Stenton, *The First Century of English Feudalism* (Oxford, 2nd ed., 1961); R. A. Brown, *Origins of English Feudalism* (London, 1973).

27 The detailed study of R. Rogers, *Latin Siege Warfare in the Twelfth Century* (D.Phil. thesis, Oxford, 1984) remains as yet unpublished, but see now J. Bradbury, *The Medieval Siege* (Woodbridge, 1992).

strategy, tactics and the nature of war in Anglo-Norman England and Normandy, moreover, one searches in vain for any single work to match in scope and quality R. C. Smail's excellent *Crusading Warfare, 1097–1193*.[28]

But if there has been a paucity of monographs, much valuable and wide-ranging work on the organization and conduct of warfare has appeared in article form. It was with this in mind that Dr Marjorie Chibnall and Dr Richard Barber suggested that a compilation of articles pertaining to warfare might be drawn from *Anglo-Norman Studies*, since the Battle Conference, under the aegis of the late Allen Brown, the doyen of Norman military matters, has been a principal forum for the discussion and promotion of the study of Anglo-Norman (and earlier) warfare among its many other ecclesiastical, political and cultural concerns. To provide a more focused volume, however, it was decided to adopt a wider remit to bring together some of the best articles on the subject, drawn not simply from *Anglo-Norman Studies* but from a variety of journals and *Festschriften*.

The object of the resulting compilation is to furnish both scholars and students with a collection of essays which are not only fundamental to the study of late eleventh and twelfth century warfare, but which also serve to place the conduct and organization of war in a broader social, political and cultural context. The castle, which played so integral a part in Anglo-Norman warfare, is to be the subject of a companion volume.

The articles collected here fall into two broad sections; the first concerned with questions of organization and the nature of forces, the second with the conduct of war itself. Any such selection must by its very nature be subjective, and doubtless others would have chosen differently. I am particularly conscious that some areas of study that pertain directly to warfare, such as that of logistics,[29] or of arms, armour and equipment[30] are not represented here. This is not to imply these topics are in any sense peripheral; such sins of omission, which are hopefully remedied

---

[28] R. C. Smail, *Crusading Warfare, 1097–1193* (Cambridge, 1956, repr. 1978). Equally, while predominantly an administrative and political analysis, F. M. Powicke's *The Loss of Normandy, 1189–1204. Studies in the History of the Angevin Empire* (Manchester, 1913, repr. 1963) still remains the best study of the Angevin defences and war-effort from 1194 to 1204.

[29] The study of logistics has been a noticeable growth area in Anglo-Norman military studies. See, for example, C. Gillmor, 'Naval Logistics and the Cross-Channel Operation', *Anglo-Norman Studies*, vii (1984), 105–131, and *idem*, 'The Logistics of Fortified Bridge Building on the Seine under Charles the Bald', *Anglo-Norman Studies*, xi (1988), 87–106; B. S. Bachrach, 'Some Observations on William the Conqueror's Horse Transports', *Technology and Culture*, xxv (1985), 505–31; *idem*, 'Some Observations on the Military Administration of the Norman Conquest', *Anglo-Norman Studies*, viii (1985), 1–26. Cf. E. M. C. van Houts, 'The Ship List of William the Conqueror', *Anglo-Norman Studies*, x (1987), 159–184.

[30] On which see I. Peirce, 'Arms, Armour and Warfare in the Eleventh Century', *Anglo-Norman Studies*, x (1987), 237–258; D. Nichol, *Arms and Armour of the Crusading Period, 1050–1350*, 2 vols. (New York, 1988); H. Ellis Davidson, *The Sword in Anglo-Saxon England* (Oxford, 1961); *Weapons and Warfare in Anglo-Saxon England*, ed. S. C. Hawkes (*Oxford University Committee for Archaeology*, Monograph no. 21, Oxford, 1989); Ewart Oakeshott, *The Sword in the Age of Chivalry* (London, 1964); *idem*, *The Archaeology of Weapons* (London, 1960); *idem*, *Records of the Medieval Sword* (Woodbridge, 1991); R. H. C. Davis, 'The Warhorses of the Normans', *Anglo-Norman Studies*, x (1987), 67–82 and *idem*, *The Medieval Warhorse: Origin, Development and Redevelopment* (London, 1989). It was originally intended to include Matthew Bennett's '*La Règle du Temple* as a Military Manual, *or* How to Deliver a Cavalry Charge', *Studies in Medieval History Presented to R. Allen Brown*, ed. C. Harper-Bill, C. J. Holdsworth and J. Nelson (Woodbridge, 1989) in this selection, but this has now appeared as an appendix to *The Rule of the*

by the inclusion of a select bibliography, are purely the result of the dictates of space. Similarly, I have deliberately avoided the vexed question of the continuity (or otherwise) of Anglo-Norman feudalism; the diversity of scholarly opinion and the complexity of the issues involved merit a separate and extended treatment which falls outside the remit of this volume.

Nevertheless, two important articles relating to knight service are included which embrace wider issues. In 'Knight-Service in Normandy before 1066', Marjorie Chibnall explores the varied and often loosley defined nature of tenure and service in pre-Conquest Normandy, pointing to the widespread absence of features that were later to become standard, such as imposed quotas of knights, forty days unpaid service, castle guard, reliefs and other feudal incidents such as wardship and marriage.[31] While knights, military households and fiefs are much in evidence, it seems that the performance of castle-guard and military service was probably the outcome of individual agreements between lord and vassal, or even a reflection of earlier Carolingian obligations. Systematization of service, she argues, only came later as a result of the military demands of the conquest itself and in imitation of the more logical system that William I was able to create *de novo* in a conquered land.

If Chibnall demonstrates the embyronic nature of knight service on the eve of the Conquest, J. C. Holt's paper 'The Introduction of Knight Service in England' explores the origin and development of knight-service principally through an analysis of the 1166 *Cartae Baronum*.[32] Re-confirming Round's thesis that the crown had imposed arbitary, decimally-based quotas of knight-service on its tenants-in-chief at an early date, probably from the first decade of William I's reign but at the very latest by the end of the eleventh century, Holt demonstrates how the size of the quotas, whether decimal or random, was directly linked to the history of the descent of tenancies-in-chief. Up to the latter years of Rufus's reign, argues Holt, the Norman kings were able to construct baronies *de novo* from the lands of Anglo-Saxon tenants, royal demesne and early forfeitures on which they could impose artificial decimal quotas. Thereafter, however, most escheated land (and because of the frequency of rebellion between 1088 and 1106 there was much which came into the king's hands) was already in the possession of tenants performing specified amounts of service established by their former, now dispossessed, lords. This made the imposition of an artificial quota far harder. In some instances, a new, decimal *servitium debitum* was levied on a reconstructed fee, in others the quotas remained random and were reflected as such in the 1166 *Cartae*.

Significantly modifying Round's conclusions, however, Holt stresses the fundamental point that most baronies were not established at a stroke, but were the composite products of accretion over many years. Thus the knight service quotas

---

Templars: The French Text of the Rule of the Order of the Knights Templar, translated and introduced by J. M. Upton-Ward (Woodbridge, 1992).

[31] Cf. E. Zack Tabuteau, 'Definitions of Feudal Military Obligation in Eleventh-Century Normandy', *On the Laws and Customs of England: Essays in Honor of Samuel E. Thorne*, eds. M. Arnold *et al.* (Chapel Hill, North Carolina, 1982), 18–59.

[32] On the *cartae* see T. K. Keefe, *Feudal Assessments and the Political Community under Henry II and his Sons* (University of California Press, 1983), and *English Historical Documents* II, ed. D. C. Douglas (London, 2nd ed., 1981), 968–981, for a selection of these 'charters of the barons' in translation with a useful introduction to this vital source for Anglo-Norman feudalism.

of some tenants-in-chief were not static, but were re-adjusted to reflect the terri-torial enlargement (or otherwise) of a barony, while in the case of new baronies service was imposed *ab initio*; and in both cases the assessments were in decimal quotas. But whatever the origin of quotas, argues Holt, at no stage can one envisage the king's marshal actually totting up in fives and tens the contingents brought to the host by tenants-in-chief. For whereas knight service quotas may well have been imposed by William I in England and later by Henry II in Ireland in order to guarantee a minimum level of defence for newly conquered lands, the size of individual barons' retinues brought to the muster must in practice have depended on the exegencies of time and place.

If studies such as those of Chibnall and Holt have done much to refine our perception of knight-service as an obligation, then it is the work of J. O. Prestwich which has served to set the still more fundamental question of the military effec-tiveness of the feudal host in its true perspective. In a classic article, 'War and Finance in the Anglo-Norman State', Prestwich effectively demonstrated that the Anglo-Norman kings relied heavily on stipendiary knights, not just in the excep-tional circumstances of the early years of the Conquest, but throughout the reigns of William I, Rufus and Henry I. The unstable political climate made it imperative to have as the mainstay of armies knights unaffected by the conflicting ties of loyalty that rent the Anglo-Norman nobility during the many outbreaks of rebel-lion and civil war between 1066 and 1154.[33] As Prestwich notes, commenting on the treaty of 1101 by which Henry I hired 1000 Flemish knights from Robert, count of Flanders, in return for an annual pension of £500, 'it is significant that a time when the total *servitium debitum* of England did not produce more than 5,000 knights, Henry should have been arranging for the service of 1,000 knights from one external source alone'.[34]

It was, moreover, the ever increasing pressure of war finance which, argues Prestwich, was the driving force behind Norman administrative reform initiated by Rannulf Flambard and Roger of Salisbury, which may also, he hints cautiously, have lain behind the earlier Domesday *descriptio* of 1086, and which goes far to explain the extent of the fiscal exploitation of patronage witnessed by the 1130 Pipe Roll. Nothing could illustrate more forcefully the extent to which society might be affected by war, not simply by the passage of armies, the economic impact of hostilities, direct taxation and currency debasment, but at a far more fundamental level by moulding and directing the very instruments of government and administration.

The evidence of Henry I's contracts with the count of Flanders led Prestwich to suggest that the indenture of knights for wages and expenses, which had long thought to be a development of the fourteenth century and so called 'bastard feudalism', was already common at the beginning of the twelfth century and possibly even earlier. This theme has more recently been taken up by David Crouch, who argues that the often posited opposition between 'feudalism', whereby aristocratic power was based on ties established by the distribution of fiefs, and 'bastard feudalism', whose essence was the creation of ties of depend-

---

[33] Cf. S. Brown, 'Military service and Monetary Reward in the Eleventh and Twelfth Centuries', *History*, ccxl (1989), 20–38.
[34] Prestwich, 'War and Finance', below, 69.

ence other than by those of tenure (principally the indenture for wages or annuities) is a chimera.[35] He rejects the view which suggests that a society based on the honour (integral and extensive baronial estates) was superseded by one based on the affinity (waged retainers): such a model not only over-estimates the importance of enfeoffment in the Anglo-Norman period, but ignores the fact that retaining for wages and expenses (*stipendia et donativa*) was widespread among magnates as well as the king, with affinities and indentures visible from the 1140s if not earlier.[36] By the 1190s, William Marshal's following emerges as a 'classic "bastard feudal" affinity': ties of land tenure were peripheral in the formation of his household, whose members were attracted to his service by wages, grants of office and his ability to procure royal patronage.[37]

The enfeoffment of knights in post-Conquest England was a popular method of maintaining a military force only because, as later in Outremer and Ireland, there was an initial – but only temporary – surplus of land for re-distribution, and by 1135 the granting of fiefs was a rarity. But even so, enfeoffment 'was no more than one among a number of alternative ways of contracting or sub contracting for a military retinue'.[38] Just as earls and other great Anglo-Saxon lords had maintained followings of stipendiary warriors, so Norman lords hired knights for their own households which were in effect microcosms of the *familia regis*, the military household of the Norman kings.[39]

It has long been realized that throughout the Anglo-Saxon period, warriors of the household of the king and his great magnates had formed the core of royal fighting forces, though largely due to the dictates of the sources, attention has been focused on the Anglo-Scandinavian housecarls, the *corps d'elite* of kings from Cnut to Harold II. In two closely related articles, 'The Housecarls in the Eleventh Century' and 'Some Observations on the Navy in Late Anglo-Saxon England', Nicholas Hooper examines these late Anglo-Saxon stipendiary forces in detail, providing a definitive analysis of the nature and organization of the housecarls, and contrasting them with the *lithsmen*, the warriors who manned the hired fleet in royal service upto 1050, and who were paid for by the *heregeld*.

It was these latter forces and not the housecarls, argues Hooper, which represented a permanent military force, capable of operating as well on land as at sea.

---

[35] See the debate between D. Crouch, D. Carpenter and P. R. Coss, 'Bastard Feudalism Revised', *Past and Present*, cxxxi (1991), 165–203, especially 165–176.

[36] 'Bastard Feudalism Revised', 169, 173–77.

[37] D. Crouch, *William Marshal: Court, Career and Chivalry in the Angevin Empire, c. 1147–1219* (London, 1990), 157–68.

[38] 'Bastard Feudalism Revised', 169.

[39] The *Vita Herluini*, for example, provides a vivid glimpse of the *familia* of Gilbert of Brionne (*The Life of Herluin, Abbot of Bec* by Gilbert Crispin, in J. Armitage Robinson, *Gilbert Crispin Abbot of Westminster* (Cambridge, 1911), 87–91, translated in R. A. Brown, *The Origins of English Feudalism* (London, 1973), 114–117), while Orderic Vitalis recalls how Mabel of Bellême tried to bankrupt St Évroul by demanding hospitality for her retinue of 100 knights, and gives a famous description of the *familia* of Hugh of Avranches (*The Ecclesiastical History of Orderic Vitalis*, ed. and trans. M. Chibnall, 6 vols. (Oxford, 1969–80), II, 54–55, III, 216–217). Similarly, in its depiction of the household of William of Tancarville and later that of the Marshal himself, the *Histoire de Guillaume le Maréchal* shows the maintenance of knights on a considerable scale (S. Painter, *William Marshal: Knight-errant, Baron and Regent of England* (Johns Hopkins, 1933), 16–25; Crouch, *William Marshal*, 133–149).

The housecarls by contrast should be seen less as a standing army than as the kind of household warriors found constituting the retinue of any great lord; to distinguish markedly between Beowulf's retainers, King Alfred's thegns, Bryhtnoth's *heorthwerod* at Maldon, the household knights of Norman lords and rulers and, to take up Crouch's thesis, the 'affinities' of the later middle ages, is to impose essentially artifical and anachronistic categorization on warriors who alike served and fought for '*stipendia et donativa*'.

For the post-Conquest period, two articles, the first by Marjorie Chibnall, 'Mercenaries and the *Familia Regis* under Henry I', the second by J. O. Prestwich, 'The Military Household of the Norman Kings', give substance to Prestwich's earlier suggestion that under the Anglo-Norman kings, the *familia regis* 'supplied the standing professional element, capable of fighting independent actions, and for a major campaign, providing the framework into which other forces could be fitted'.[40]

Concentrating on the operations of the *familia regis* in Normandy under Henry I and drawing heavily on the evidence furnished by Orderic Vitalis, Chibnall shows that the king's mounted household troops were highly trained and mobile, and significantly comprised not just knights but also *servientes*, some of whom were mounted archers. Serving as standing and substantial garrisons in key castles, yet capable of being quickly drawn together to form a small but highly professional field army, these forces played a vital military role in Henry I's defence of the duchy. Prestwich in turn examines the role of the *familia* in the campaigns of William I, Rufus and Henry I, demonstrating how in a period where it was very much the exception to field a force containing over 4–500 knights, Henry I's military household contributed at least as high a proportion of cavalry to the royal armies as the household of Edward I was to do during the latter's Welsh and Scottish wars.

But as Prestwich strikingly demonstrates, the *familia* was more than just a military force: it was a vital political institution. Its commanders were men of great power, intimate with the king. It served as a vehicle through which men could rise to prominence and favour, thereby forging strong traditions of service and ensuring continuity of personnel and policy. Its officers served as sheriffs, justices, ambassadors or as other important royal agents and membership of it brought together representatives of the 'old aristocracy' such as Robert of Beaumont and 'new men' like Nigel d'Aubigny. Equally, it could serve as a vehicle for political rapprochement: not a few of its members were cadets of families who had suffered desseisin following revolt, serving with a hope of partial or full restoration of lands. Above all, service in the *familia*, whether in arms or administration, created vital bonds of loyalty between the monarch and an important element of his nobility, a particularly vital function at a time when the tournament was embryonic and the creation of secular orders of chivalry distant indeed.

The knights of the *familia regis* were of varied social composition, though its mainstay were the *juvenes* or aristocratic 'youths' about whom Duby has written so perceptively.[41] Some were elder sons from good families, seeking gainful

---

[40] Prestwich, 'Anglo-Norman Feudalism and the Problem of Continuity', in *Past and Present*, xxvi (1963), 50–51.
[41] G. Duby, 'Youth in Aristocratic Society', in *The Chivalrous Society*, ed. C. Postan (London, 1977), 112–22.

employment and military reputation during their fathers' lifetime, others were
landless younger sons, though often of high birth, supporting themselves by their
wages and the profits of ransom and hoping to win an heiress or receive a fief as a
reward. Their numbers were swelled by stipendiary knights of lesser birth (*milites
gregarii*) owning only their equipment,

As its title implies, the question of status forms the heart of Allen Brown's 'The
Status of the Norman Knight', a wry but impassioned reassertion of the social as
well as military dominance of the professional mounted warrior and for the
elevated status of knighthood. Refuting the demotion by such as Sally Harvey[42] of
the majority of Anglo-Norman knights to the rank of well-to-do peasants, he
argues that collectively, pre-Conquest ducal charters reveal 'an aristocracy of
warrior knights', and that the term *miles* had been adopted by some of the greatest
nobles well before 1066 and even as early as 965. Brown equally rejects the
would-be distinction between lowly 'fighting knights' and lords who were but
nominally knights and who saw little active service; as he rightly emphasizes, this
was an age when the greater one's nobility, the greater one's military participation
in the field was expected to be. If this was true of the age of the Black Prince,
Thomas of Woodstock and Henry of Derby, it was equally if not more true of the
eleventh and twelfth century. Not that there was a lack of distinction in terms of
lineage and wealth among the knightly class itself, but that the fundamental
distinction was always between members of this class and the peasantry, between
the *bellatores* and the *inermes*. Both the lord's household and the fief (which only
supplemented and never supplanted service in the household) were the crucial
mechanisms by which the warriors achieved the wealth to meet the great cost of
horses and equipment and the leisure necessary to maintain a high level of
professionalism.

This proficiency in arms was geared to a single end – the successful prosecution
of warfare. Thus if the study of military obligation, tenure and organization,
particularly that of the *familia regis*, has significantly altered our view of the
nature of the forces available to a commander, we should beware of neglecting
strategy, tactics and the nature of war itself. As John Gillingham has commented,
'most recent historians have been so busy getting their armies into the field that
they have left themselves little room in which to consider what they did once they
were there'.[43] It is surely a fallacy to dismiss the study of strategy, tactics and
methods of prosecuting war as dry and essentially irrelevant military science
when such issues so fundamentally reflect the nature of the society that produces
them. Nowhere is this more true than for the period in question, when the
aristocracy was a social élite because it was a military élite. No study of Anglo-
Norman aristocratic culture and society can be complete without the recognition
of the extent to which warfare and the associated virtues of a warrior nobility –
notions of honour and shame, loyalty, prowess and largesse – dominated contemporary perceptions and preoccupations.

The second section of this collection therefore focuses on how war was actually
fought, bringing together for the first time a group of articles which encapsulate
the latest approaches to the interpretation of medieval warfare. Three closely

[42] S. Harvey, 'The Knight and the Knight's Fee in England', *Past and Present*, xlix (1970).
[43] J. Gillingham, 'Richard I and the Science of War in the Middle Ages', below 196.

related articles by John Gillingham examine what he has justifiably called 'the science of war' through the study of the generalship of William I, Richard I and William Marshal, taking up the fundamental point constantly stressed by Allen Brown that the Anglo-Norman knights 'were professionals through and through'. In a concerted re-evaluation of the quality and sophistication of medieval generalship, his main theme is that pitched battle was an exceptional event, fraught with physical but above all political risk, which the majority of commanders attempted to avoid wherever possible. Instead, it was siege and the ravaging of an opponent's lands which constituted the norm of warfare: at its most fundamental, war was about the control of a region's supplies.

Gillingham's analysis of William I's campaigns up to 1075, of Richard I's victory over Saladin at Arsuf in 1191, and of the military acumen of William Marshal all serve to highlight the caution and skill of the best medieval commanders. In 'Securing the North', I have tried to demonstrate how the military imbalance caused by the superiority of Anglo-Norman armies in terms of knights, equipment and training made the avoidance of battle by Scottish forces a virtual necessity, and to examine the resulting strategies of defence and attack in Anglo-Scottish warfare.

Such approaches do not attempt to deny the significance of battle itself, but rather to contextualize it. Thus an appreciation of the rarity of pitched battle highlights still further the exceptional events of 1066, the year of Fulford, Stamford Bridge and Hastings, and the phenomenal challenges facing Harold Godwineson. Equally, Gillingham's suggestion that Hastings was in all probability the first major battle in which William had been the principal commander throws the events of 14 October itself into an intriguing new focus.

Allen Brown's account of Hastings is included here both as a classic and near-definitive analysis of this great battle, and to illustrate the nature of one of the few major engagements in this period for which we have a relative abundance of material.[44] Many would perhaps question Allen Brown's deeply held conviction that the victory of William's knights over the Anglo-Danish housecarls and Saxon infantry symbolized not only a clash of cultures and military traditions, but also an inevitable triumph of a brave new 'feudal' European order over a retrospective and outmoded Anglo-Saxon state, a fossilized relic echoing the old Carolingian world order.[45] Such a clear-cut view seems no longer tenable in the light of the wealth of recent scholarship on every aspect of the Conquest, much indeed emanating from the *Proceedings* of the Battle Conference itself. In military terms, while it seems indisputable that Harold was outmanoeuvred, there was nothing inevitable about the outcome of the battle, despite the fact that Harold was hampered by considerable disadvantages: the loss of many of his best troops at

[44] Compared, of course, to the wealth of sources for battles of the Hundred Years War such as Crécy or Agincourt the sources for Hastings are meagre indeed, but no other battle in England or Normandy is so well documented either during the Anglo-Saxon period or until the accounts of Bouvines in 1214.

[45] A view expressed most forcibly, for example, in R. A. Brown, 'The Norman Conquest', *TRHS*, 5th ser., xvii (1967). Cf. *idem*, *Origins of English Feudalism*, 41: 'The differences in composition and therefore in the tactics of the two armies point to the differences of the two societies which then met in arms, and militarily at Hastings, as in so many other ways, the Old World went down before the New.'

Stamford Bridge, a long forced march (which may have left behind any missile arm he possessed), and being taken by surprise before his army was properly arrayed and with part of it not yet on the field. Few would deny the professionalism and discipline of the Franco-Norman knights, epitomized in their use of the tactic of the 'feigned retreat', or of the tactical effectiveness of combining cavalry with a strong force of archers, but one must resist the temptation of judging the efficiency of Anglo-Saxon military organization and methods of fighting by the outcome of a single battle, fought in exceptional circumstances and itself a 'near-run thing'.

Nevertheless, though there will doubtless continue to be divergent views as to questions of continuity or innovation in military organization and tenure pre- and post-Conqest, Allen Brown surely remains correct in his equally firmly held view that Hastings saw the clash of two very different techniques of combat; though the Bayeux Tapestry shows Harold's housecarls and the Norman knights to have used very similar equipment, the former fought on foot and the latter on horseback as their principal mode of combat. This is not the place to discuss further the hoary question of 'the horsing of the Saxons',[46] still less that of the couched lance.[47] The arguments which Brown adduced at length[48] to refute the stimulating but ill-founded thesis of Richard Glover that the Anglo-Saxons actually fought as cavalry,[49] to my mind at least, still hold good against the more recent assertions of R. H. C. Davis, who, in his recent studies of the medieval warhorse, argued that because one can adduce considerable evidence for the breeding and training of quality horses in England prior to 1066, the Saxons must have fought from horseback.[50] There is no doubt that Anglo-Saxons made widespread use of the horse for both agriculture and domestic and military transport, or that horses and harness were high-status objects among the nobility. Yet there remains not one piece of unequivocal evidence that elements of Anglo-Saxon armies fought from the saddle as trained cavalrymen in the way in which their Franco-Norman knightly opponents clearly did by 1066.[51] Had they done so, it is inconceivable that the Saxon horsemen would not have taken full advantage of their position on Senlac ridge to sweep the Normans before them with a cavalry charge.

[46] To adapt the title of J. H. Clapham's 'The Horsing of the Danes', *EHR*, xxv (1910), 287–293.
[47] D. J. A. Ross, 'L'originalité de 'Turoldus': le maniement de la lance', *Cahiers de civilisation médiévale*, vi (1963), 127–38; J. Flori, 'Encore l'usage de la lance . . . La technique du combat chevaleresque vers l'an 1100', *Cahiers de civilisation médiévale*, xxxi (1988), 213–40.
[48] R. A. Brown, *Origins of English Feudalism*, 34–43.
[49] R. Glover, 'English Warfare in 1066', *EHR*, lxvii (1952).
[50] R. H. C. Davis, 'The Warhorses of the Normans', *Anglo-Norman Studies*, x (1987), 67–82; idem, *The Medieval Warhorse: Origin, Development and Redevelopment* (London, 1989); idem, 'Did the Anglo-Saxons Have Warhorses?', *Weapons and Warfare in Anglo-Saxon England*, ed. S. C. Hawkes (Oxford University Committee for Archaeology, Monograph no. 21, Oxford, 1989), 141–144.
[51] It was a relief to find this conclusion shared by Nick Hooper, 'The Anglo-Saxons at War', *Weapons and Warfare in Anglo-Saxon England*, 200: 'In a skirmish or a pursuit, as in that which followed the battle of Brunanburgh, it is likely that the English were capable of fighting from horseback. What set them apart from the Franks and the Normans was their lack of specific cavalry tactics, which consisted of a close order charge with spear and sword. . . To argue that the English could on occasion fight from horseback is not the same as saying they were trained in the tactics of specialized horse soldiers.' My own prejudices on the subject stem from M. J. Strickland, 'The Anglo-Saxons and the Warhorse' (unpublished Cambridge B.A. dissertation, 1982).

Although he was writing a century after the events at Hastings, it is significant the Anglo-Norman poet Wace, when coming to record traditions concerning the battle as part of his *Roman de Rou*, noted specifically that the Anglo-Saxons were ignorant of cavalry tactics. The value of Wace and of vernacular poetry for the study of eleventh and twelfth century warfare is the subject of Matthew Bennet's 'Wace and Warfare', providing a valuable parallel to John Gillingham's examination of war and chivalry in the *Histoire de Guillaume le Maréchal*, and demonstrating how careful examination can yield much information not simply on logistics, strategy and tactics, but on contemporary perceptions of warfare.[52]

Warriors' perceptions of themselves, both as individuals and as groups, are inextricably bound up with how they fight and with whom.[53] Methods of combat, moreover, not only dictate tactics, but also the composition of armies, which in turn reflects the institutions a society develops to raise the necessary kinds of troops. Herein lies the real value of the hoary debate about the Anglo-Saxons and the warhorse, and of greater importance, the overall significance of the (properly contextualized) study of tactics. In 'Battles in England and Normandy, 1066–1154', Jim Bradbury not only re-emphasizes the enormous risks which large-scale engagements entailed and the desire of most medieval commanders to avoid pitched battle wherever possible, but also provides a valuable survey of the tactics employed by Anglo-Norman armies. From Tinchebrai, 1106, to Lincoln, 1141, there was a significant emphasis on the role of dismounted knights, usually assuimg a defensive position and sometimes supported by archers – features which prefigure the formations adopted by English armies during the Hundred Years War, though Bradbury is right to point to the continued importance of mounted elements, either on the flanks or in reserve.

In questioning Hollister's view that it was the Normans' experience at Hastings which in large part accounts for these tactical developments, Bradbury raises the intriguing and as yet still underdeveloped topic of the transmission and cross-fertilization of military ideas, whether in terms of stategy, tactics or behaviour in war. Thus, for example, the campaigns of David I of Scotland reveal how Anglo-Norman concepts of chivalric behaviour, assimilated by the king through his Anglo-Norman *mesnie*, could be juxtaposed with the more extreme behaviour of his native troops, while at the battle of the Standard, 1138, David's original disposition of his forces was clearly influenced by the successes of his brother-in-law Henry I at Tinchbrai and Brémule.[54] Nevertheless, though Bradbury adduces Frankish precedents for knights dismounting to fight on foot *in extremis*, the context of these measures does not convincingly correspond to the majority of the Anglo-Norman engagements in which units of knights dismounted. It is difficult to divorce so consistent an adoption of defensive tactics post 1066 from the

---

[52] For a similar exercise undertaken in regard to Wace's contemporary Jordan Fantosme, see M. J. Strickland, 'Arms and the Men: War, Loyalty and Lordship in Jordan Fantosme's *Chronicle*', *Medieval Knighthood IV. Papers from the fifth Strawberry Hill Conference, 1990* (Woodbridge, 1992).

[53] For changing perceptions of the nature of the enemy and of conduct in war see M. J. Strickland, 'Slaughter, Slavery or Ransom?: The Impact of the Conquest on Conduct in Warfare', *Medieval England VI: Proceedings of the 1990 Harlaxton Symposium on Eleventh Century England*, ed. C. Hicks (Stamford, 1992), 41–59.

[54] Strickland, *Conduct and Perception*, ch. 7.

enormous efforts it took the Norman army to dislodge the Saxon infantry from the ridge at Hastings.

In conclusion, it may be hoped that this collection of articles will not only be of use to students and scholars as a work of reference, but will also serve to illustrate the diversity of approaches to the study of medieval warfare, and to re-emphasize the central significance of war to the society of the eleventh and twelfth centuries.

THE HOUSECARLS IN ENGLAND IN THE ELEVENTH CENTURY

Nicholas Hooper

In comparison with the Norman Conquest the submission of England to a foreign conqueror fifty years earlier has seemed of lesser significance. Major changes have been difficult to identify and several apparent innovations prove to have antecedents in the later tenth century. Cnut's employment of Englishmen in positions of power and the eventual re-establishment of the English royal house have served to obscure the effects of the long and unsuccessful wars against England's Scandinavian attackers. One innovation which there is no difficulty in attributing to the period after 1016 is the introduction of a body of men called housecarls. In this paper I shall review the established interpretation of the housecarls and then suggest that it is mistaken and that a new explanation is required.

After 1016 the materials for Old English history begin to include references to men called housecarls, both in groups and as individuals. Although the housecarl appears to have been a dependant of the king or earls there is no explanation of his status or duties. The term is derived from two Old Norse words meaning house and man or servant.[1] This emphasises the dependent status of the housecarl but brings little further enlightenment. In the narrative sources housecarls are encountered as warriors, and on one occasion as tax-collectors, in addition to members of households. In other written records they are found as landowners. In these circumstances help has been sought from Scandinavian sources of the twelfth and thirteenth centuries, in particular the *Lex Castrensis sive curie*. The most complete account of the housecarls was compiled by L. M. Larson. It is upon this work that the accepted interpretation is based and Larson's arguments were followed in their entirety by Hollister in his work on Old English military organisation.[2] Before proceeding it will be necessary to summarise what Larson said of the housecarls and their organisation. His account was drawn from two versions of the *Lex Castrensis* preserved in the later twelfth-century works of the Danes Sven Aggeson and Saxo Grammaticus (which will be discussed below).

In 1018 Cnut paid off the host which had won England for him, retaining in his service the crews of forty ships.[3] This body consisted of some three to four thousand men organised into a royal guard of a splendour hitherto unknown in the North. Its members, the aristocratic and the brave, were distinguished by the possession of

---

[1] J. Bosworth and T. N. Toller, *An Anglo-Saxon Dictionary*, Oxford 1898, s.v. *hus-carl*. The argument presented in this paper is developed further in my forthcoming London PhD thesis on Old English military organisation.
[2] L. M. Larson, *The King's Household in England before the Norman Conquest*, Madison 1904; C. W. Hollister, *Anglo-Saxon Military Institutions on the eve of the Norman Conquest*, Oxford 1962, 9-19; T. Oleson, *The Witenagemot in the reign of Edward the Confessor*, London 1955.
[3] This summary is based on Larson, *King's Household*, 153-71, and *Canute the Great*, New York and London 1912, 131-5.

swords whose hilts were chased with gold. Cnut drew up for this body a set of regulations with the purpose of promoting a spirit of friendship and the maintenance of good order and fitting behaviour in the king's hall. When they dined in the king's presence housecarls sat in order of precedence, determined by nobility of birth or martial prowess, and minor misdemeanours were punished by demotion to a lower place. Failure to care properly for a comrade's horse was one such offence. Anyone convicted of three petty crimes was sent to the foot of the table where none of his fellows was to communicate with him. Housecarls were also free to pelt the offender with gnawed bones. Crimes were tried in the assembly of the housecarls (*huskarle-steffne*) under the presidency of the king, who was also subject to their discipline. The murder of a fellow was punished by the sentence of *niðing* (a form of outlawry) and exile or by death. Treason (*crimen majestatis*) was met with by the confiscation of property and death. The king provided daily board and entertainment in addition to a monthly wage, and the contract of employment could be dissolved only on the last day of December.

The laws tell that Cnut was the first to contravene them when in anger he slew a member of the guard. It assembled and pardoned him, but Cnut fined himself for his crime. Monetary compensation for the murder or injury of a housecarl was not introduced until the early twelfth century. Additional information shows that the housecarls were heavily and richly armed.[4] Some possessed homes and estates but the guard as a whole was distributed between the court and garrisons in the principal towns of the kingdom. Thus the housecarls established in England by Cnut formed a standing army and law-bound guild.

In drawing up his household regulations Cnut was influenced by the rules of the Jomsvikings, the household codes of the kings of Norway and canon law. Indeed, the remnants of the Jomsvikings followed Swein and Cnut to England after their defeat by the Norwegians Hakon and Eric. The rules of this pirate brotherhood established in the fortress of Jom in Pomerania bear little relationship to those of the housecarls. Membership was restricted to men between the ages of eighteen and fifty, each man swore to avenge his fellows, women were not permitted in the camp, absences were restricted to three days and all news was to be taken directly to the commander. When these rules were ignored and discipline became slack, disaster struck and the Jomsvikings met defeat off the coast of Norway.

Larson thought that the Jomsvikings did not play the dominant role in influencing Cnut. He admitted that the housecarl rules as they survive were set down some four to five generations after the time to which they claim to relate. Nevertheless, Sven Aggeson recalled that his grandfather had been tried as a housecarl in the early part of the twelfth century, and Larson argued that early English evidence confirms the existence of the corps of housecarls and their sophisticated organisation in eleventh-century England. This has not been doubted by historians who have written subsequently. From 1016 until 1066 the kings of England had at their disposal a guard which was also a standing army of mercenary warriors paid from the proceeds of the *heregeld* or Danegeld. The grant of lands to members of the guild did little to affect its corporate identity or its readiness for war. Hollister wrote of

a unique, closely-knit organisation of professional warriors who served the kings of England from Cnut to Harold Godwineson and became the spearhead

---

[4] Worcester, i, 195, *EHD* i (2nd edn 1979), 318; *Lex Castrensis sive Curie* in M. C. Gertz, *Scriptores Minores Historiae Danicae Medii Aevi*, Copenhagen 1917-18, i, 64-93, chapters x, xi.

of the English army ... the most highly trained and battle-ready force available to the English monarchs. Many of the housecarls were landowners, yet they remained essentially mercenary troops ...[5]

To Stenton also the housecarls remained professional soldiers. It was no longer the custom that they lived with the king at all times. Many had received grants of estates where they lived, some lived on fifteen acres of royal land in Wallingford, perhaps a sole reference to strategically placed garrisons. 'But wherever he might live, the housecarle was available for instant service in the event of war.'[6] Since Larson wrote further evidence has been unearthed which may seem to support his case. Four great viking camps in Denmark with circular ramparts and regular layouts have added substance to the story of the Jomsvikings. They have been associated with the armies assembled by Swein and Cnut for the conquest of England, and have emphasised the training and discipline of these forces.[7]

Such an organisation would represent a considerable accretion to royal power in time of peace as well as war. It would give to the king a freedom of action unlike that enjoyed by any earlier English monarchs. It would also make England unique among European states in possessing a standing army, although such a concept can be reconciled with the precocious development of late Old English government. One may ask, however, how much freedom of action did a king like Edward the Confessor possess in his political dealings? Where, in the crisis of 1051, was this corps of professional warriors ready for instant service? In fact, we are told that Edward relied upon the military aid that the loyal earls could bring and was powerless to act until their arrival. If the evidence for the accepted interpretation of the housecarls is examined, it will be found that there are flaws in the argument.

Larson's case depended on being able to demonstrate that the late twelfth-century laws of the Danish housecarls could be seen at work in England before the Norman Conquest. He argued that two passages in the Anglo-Saxon Chronicle reveal the operation of the court of the housecarls. In 1049 Swein, the black sheep of the sons of Earl Godwine, treacherously murdered his cousin Earl Beorn. The C chronicle, which had already shown an interest in the dealings of Swein,[8] reports King Edward's reaction:

> *ond se cing þa ond eall here cwaedon Swegen for niðing.*
> (and the king and all his host declared Swein a scoundrel.)[9]

Larson, in the company of many historians, took the word *here* to mean a host of Danes, that is the housecarls, and *niðing* to be the sentence of their court as described in the *Lex Castrensis*. 'When we consider the crime, the court and the verdict, it becomes clear that we have here a formal act of the house-carle-gemot,' he concluded. For this crime to have been tried in the court of the housecarls Beorn must have been 'one of the chiefs of the royal guard'.[10] Although Larson did not add this, Swein must also have been a member of the guild.

5 Hollister, *Military Institutions*, 12.
6 F. M. Stenton, *Anglo-Saxon England*, 3rd edn, Oxford 1971, 582.
7 For example, E. John, 'War and Society in the tenth century: the Maldon Campaign', *TRHS* xxvii, 1977, 175-6.
8 *ASC* C 1046.
9 *ASC* C 1049; C. Plummer, *Two of the Saxon Chronicles Parallel*, Oxford 1892-9, reissued 1952, i, 171.
10 Larson, *King's Household*, 165.

The second example of housecarl justice follows the account of the armed defiance of the king by Godwine and his sons in 1051. There are two different accounts in the Anglo-Saxon Chronicle. The version in the D chronicle first:

they advised the exchange of hostages, and *they issued summonses for a meeting* at London (*setton stefna ut*); the folk (*folc*) throughout all this northern province, in Siward's earldom and Leofric's and elsewhere, were ordered to go there ... and Earl Swein his other son was outlawed. Then it did not suit him to come to defend himself against the king and against the force (*here*) that was with the king. Then Godwine went away by night, and next morning the king held a meeting of his council and he and all the army (*here*) declared him an outlaw, and all his sons with him.[11]

The E chronicle has much the same story.

Then the king and his councillors decided that there should be a meeting of all the councillors a second time at the autumnal equinox, and the king *ordered the force to be called out* (*bannan ut here*) both south of the Thames and in the north, all the best of them. Then Earl Swein was declared an outlaw and Earl Godwine and Earl Harold were ordered to come to the meeting as quickly as ever they could make the journey ... Then Godwine asked for safe-conduct and hostages, so that he could come to the meeting, and leave it without being betrayed ... but he was refused hostages and granted five days' safe-conduct to leave the country.[12]

Once again the word *here* allegedly refers to the housecarls and the use of *stefna* for the court recalls the *huskarlesteffne* of the *Lex Castrensis*. Larson wrote: 'everything considered, it is hard to escape the conclusion that the *here* was the corps of housecarles and that this body was an organisation with extensive jurisdiction over its own membership'.[13] We must imagine that the earls were all members of the housecarl guild, even those who were of English origins.

The argument here turns on what Larson thought was the use of technical vocabulary. In each case the evidence is weak. Firstly, the sentence of *niðing*. There is no doubt that this was a punishment of Norse rather than Old English derivation, and Swein Godwineson richly deserved the loss of legal status which it entailed. However, it is unlikely to have found its way into Old English legal usage from laws which Cnut drew up for his household. The word occurs in two other legal contexts. On neither occasion may it be associated with a housecarl tribunal. Two twelfth-century collections of English laws make 'nithing's word' the punishment for *wælreaf*, robbing the dead of their arms or clothes. This crime required the oaths of forty-eight full-born thegns in compurgation. The *Leges Henrici Primi* make no mention of *niðing*, but outlawry is recorded as the punishment for despoiling the dead.[14] In 1088 William Rufus called to arms 'everyone who was not a scoundrel (*unniðing*) ... French and English, from town and country'. William of Malmesbury used the Latin *nequam* to translate *niðing*.[15] There is nothing about the use of *niðing* in 1049

---

[11] *ASC* D 1052 (=1051), Plummer, *Two Chronicles*, i, 175.
[12] *ASC* E 1048 (=1051), Plummer, *Two Chronicles*, i, 174-6.
[13] Larson, *King's Household*, 167.
[14] Bosworth and Toller, *Dictionary*, s.v. *niðing*. F. Liebermann, *Die Gesetze der Angelsachsen*, Halle 1903-16, i, 392-3; L.J. Downer, *Leges Henrici Primi*, Oxford 1972, paras 83.4, 4a, 83.5 and p. 405.
[15] *ASC* E 1087 (=1088); *De gestis regum*, ii, 362.

which shows the implementation of the *Lex Castrensis* in England. In England and Scandinavia it was a penalty which entailed loss of legal status and the protection of the law.

Second, the use of the word *here*. There was a time when this was normally employed in the Anglo-Saxon Chronicle to describe Danish hosts. English forces were described as *fyrd*. This usage is found in the accounts of the wars of Alfred and Edward the Elder, but it was a convention which ceased to be observed after that time. In the eleventh-century annals of the Chronicle *here* and *fyrd* were often employed as synonyms. For example, in 1066 Harold led a host described both as *here* and *fyrd*.[16] It is unlikely, then, that the use of *here* in 1049 and 1051 refers to a specifically Danish body and to the royal housecarls sitting as a court. Why Godwine and his sons were judged by an armed force of some kind may be explained by reference to the circumstances in which they were tried. In 1049 a fleet had been assembled at the request of the emperor and then kept under arms in anticipation of a Viking descent. In 1051 both sides had raised armed forces in an atmosphere of threatened civil war. It was the *here*, the levy which the king had called out from throughout the kingdom, which would have to implement the royal will. The phrase *bannan ut here* is not significant in the way that Larson suggested, and the D chronicle account employs the more neutral phrase *biddan ut folc*. Edward used the truce with Godwine during September to call out a levy of those who owed military service to the crown and were prepared to support the king.

This is an interpretation which finds support in the language chosen in the Latin account of these events in the *Chronicon ex chronicis*, which is very close to the D chronicle here. In addition, the author has much extra information concerning the Danes in England. He wrote of how Edward collected a greater army (*exercitus*) from throughout Mercia and Northumbria: the *exercitus* of Godwine began to melt away, he fled by night, and the king and all the *exercitus* with him condemned the earl and his sons. The translator of this chronicle read no special meaning into the use of *here*.[17]

Lastly there is the use of *stefn*. As a noun it was used in the construction *setton stefna ut to Lundene*, where it may take the Scandinavian sense 'summons, citation'.[18] An alternative explanation might be from one of the Old English meanings, 'a fixed time', hence 'they fixed times for coming to London'.[19] The verb *stefnian*, 'to summon', occurs in the Chronicle for 1051 and again for 1093, where William Rufus called Malcolm III of Scotland to his court at Gloucester.[20] Nowhere is *stefn* or one of its forms employed as the name for a court. While the Norse sense of the word may have found its way into English in the aftermath of the conquest of 1016, it may also be the result of an earlier borrowing. The form *rad-stefn* appears in a backward-looking treatise associated with Archbishop Wulfstan and consequently datable to the first two decades of the eleventh century.[21]

---

16 *ASC* C, D 1066, Plummer, *Two Chronicles*, i, 197-8. Cf. *ASC* C, D 1055, C 1056, and H. G. Richardson and G. O. Sayles, *The Governance of Medieval England*, Edinburgh 1963, 55.
17 Worcester, i, 206, *EHD* ii, 207. R. R. Darlington and P. McGurk, 'The *Chronicon ex Chroniciis* of "Florence of Worcester" and its use of sources for English history before 1066', *ante*, v, 193-4.
18 Bosworth and Toller, *Dictionary*, s.v. *stefn* (third entry).
19 E. Classen and F. E. Harmer, *An Anglo-Saxon Chronicle*, Manchester 1926, Glossary s.v. *stefn, settan*.
20 *ASC* E 1093, Plummer, *Two Chronicles*, i, 227.
21 Bosworth and Toller, *Dictionary*, s.v. *stefn*, where the definition given under *rad-stefn* is

Parallels drawn from English evidence suggest that in the Anglo-Saxon Chronicle the terms *here*, *niðing* and *stefn* were not used in a precise technical manner, the key to the understanding of which lies in the *Lex Castrensis*. Moreover, this coincidence in the use of *here* and *niðing* in the 1049 annal, and *here* and *stefn* in that for 1051 is not met with again, even though it might be expected. Earls were outlawed and exiled on several occasions in the period 1016-1066.[22] Where the Chronicle goes into any detail, which it does rarely, the terminology employed is vague – the decisions were made before *witenagemot* or 'all the people who were assembled there'.[23] It is perhaps more significant that when Godwine and his sons were restored to power in 1052, and it was the turn of Edward's followers to be outlawed, we are told that this was in *witenagemot* and that Edward had with him a host and his fleet.[24] In another version they were received back to favour in a great meeting, 'and all the earls and all the best men that were in this land were in that meeting'.[25] The meeting in which Godwine exculpated himself for his part in the killing of Alfred ætheling was also said to consist of 'the ealdormen and more important thegns of almost the whole of England' (*principibus . . . ministris*).[26] It is rarely safe to argue from silence, and the annals for 1049 and 1051 do appear to represent a departure from what might be considered normal English legal practice. Nevertheless, when the background to these events is considered and the terminology employed is put in an English context, Larson's demonstration that the *Lex Castrensis* may be seen to have operated in eleventh-century England falls.

What is the authority of the *Lex Castrensis* itself? It survives in three recensions. One is in the two manuscripts of the *Brevis Historia regum Dacie*, completed 1185-1202 by the otherwise unknown Danish nobleman Sven Aggeson.[27] Another is in the tenth book of the *Gesta Danorum* by Saxo Grammaticus, an almost equally anonymous Danish cleric.[28] The third is a vernacular text of the fifteenth century whose composition may be dated to the early thirteenth century.[29] The three are not independent versions of a single text. Sven said that he had translated a vernacular record set down by Archbishop Absalon after consultation with his nursling Cnut VI (1182-1202). Their purpose was to preserve the traditional laws by which the king's household was kept in order and which were in danger of being forgotten. Tradition linked the composition of these laws with Cnut the Great. Saxo took this Latin translation as his exemplar, but he made significant alterations to it. The final recension, far from being the vernacular original, is a composite translation made from the two earlier versions. There is much in the *Lex Castrensis* which there is no reason to doubt that Cnut may have wished to promulgate in order to discipline his cosmopolitan household. Grounds do exist, however, for suspecting the motives of Absalon, Sven and Saxo in preserving a set of laws and attributing them to an im-

rejected; also T. N. Toller, *An Anglo-Saxon Dictionary Supplement*, Oxford 1921, s.v. *rad-stefn*.
[22] Thorkell (1021), Swein (1047), Ælfgar (1055, 1058); also the important Danish thegn (he is never called housecarl) Osgod Clapa, 1046.
[23] *ASC* C 1055, E 1055.
[24] *ASC* C, D 1052, Plummer, *Two Chronicles*, i, 180-1, where the king's host is *fyrd*.
[25] *ASC* E 1052.
[26] Worcester, i, 195, *EHD* i, 318.
[27] M. C. Gertz, *Scriptores Minores Historicae Danicae Medii Aevi*, i, 64-93.
[28] *Saxo Grammaticus Danorum Regum Heroumque Historia Books X-XVI*, ed. E. Christiansen, British Archaeological Reports International series 84, Oxford 1980, i, books x-xiii.
[29] For the *Witherlax raet* see T. Riis, 'Hirdlovgivningen hos Saxo og Sven Aggeson', *Saxostudier*, ed. I. Boserup, Copenhagen 1975, 143-7.

portant figure in Danish history. Absalon was a remarkable man – he had been
brought up with Valdemar I (1157-82) and identified himself entirely with the
interests of the Crown. He was a warrior, builder of fortresses, reformer, defender
of the interests of his family and zealous promoter of the royal power.[30] Sven and
Saxo knew each other and both were servants of Absalon.[31] In view of the con-
nections between the Danish monarchy, Absalon and the chroniclers Sven and Saxo,
their reasons for wishing to set down these household rules may be questioned. In
late twelfth-century Denmark the housecarls were a noble elite, 'the central administrative institution of the country, comprising the supreme political court and civil
service as well as the royal bodyguard'.[32]

We do not know how much of Absalon's original record was set down by Sven,
or how much truth there was in either version, although there seems little need to
reject the code out of hand. Sven wrote that his grandfather had been tried before
the housecarl court in the time of King Nicholas (1104-34), but this does little to
establish the *Lex Castrensis* as the work of Cnut, nearly a century earlier. The inclusion of *crimen maiestatis* shows that Sven was capable of innovation.[33] Saxo
introduced important changes. The punishment laid down for petty offenders,
being pelted with bones, was removed and replaced by a provision from the Rule
of the Temple. Brothers were to maintain a spirit of harmonious co-operation and
those guilty of serious offences were to be set apart.[34] Here there is an example of
the reduction in severity of a punishment unbecoming to a noble elite and the use
of a popular and contemporary work. Saxo introduced the principle of witness into
the prosecution of serious crimes, as Cnut VI had in 1200. His introduction of greatly
increased compensation for such offences also reflected contemporary feeling.[35]
Finally, the *Lex Castrensis* reveals the influence of canon law. Cnut may have introduced this influence as a result of his Christianity or his exposure to Old English
law, as Larson suggested.[36] It seems equally possible, and more appropriate, that
Sven and Saxo breathed in the atmosphere of their patron's household. Indeed, it
has been suggested that the Latin employed by Saxo betrays a legal training, perhaps
gained in the schools of Paris, England or Germany.[37]

While it is possible, then, that the *Lex Castrensis* does contain accurate memories
of a guild law established in England by Cnut for his household, this is far from
likely given the circumstances in which Sven and Saxo composed their versions.
Christiansen compared the Danish laws with the Norwegian *Hirdskra* (laws to regu-
late the royal bodyguard):

30 See E. Christiansen, *The Northern Crusades: the Baltic and the Catholic Frontier 1100-1525*,
London 1980, 58-9, for a thumbnail sketch of Absalon.
31 Sven wrote that his comrade (*contubernalis*) Saxo was rewriting his work and improving the
style. See H. E. Davidson and P. Fisher, *Saxo Grammaticus' History of the Danes*, Woodbridge
1979-80, ii, 9-11; Christiansen, *Saxo*, i, 153.
32 Christiansen, *Saxo*, i, 155.
33 Adam of Bremen also received information on Danish history from a king, Swein Estrithson,
who was Cnut's nephew. He refers neither to a standing army nor a guild of housecarls established
by his uncle. See F. J. Tschan, *The Archbishops of Hamburg-Bremen by Adam of Bremen*, New
York 1959, 90ff.
34 Christiansen, *Saxo*, i, 38, 200 n.135.
35 Christiansen, *Saxo*, i, 39-40, 202 n.141; 42-3, 205 n.152.
36 Larson, *King's Household*, 167.
37 P. W. Nielsen, 'Den Typiske Saxo-saetning', *Saxostudier*, ed. Boserup, 67-75.

the *hirdskra* seldom invokes the past ... the chapters on military service ... are more detailed and practical than anything in the Danish codes ... This is a code for use, rather than ornament or study, and by comparison Saxo's *Lex Castrensis* seems to be related to wider programmes of political and legal reform, rather than to the immediate problems of discipline at court.[38]

In the two earlier recensions of the *Lex Castrensis* we appear to see the foundation of a royal attempt to increase control over the nobility of the kingdom. If this is true, Saxo or his masters were not satisfied with the initial work by Sven (or Absalon). Saxo's changes served to increase royal control over the housecarls as well as to keep the *Lex Castrensis* up to date with the legislation of Cnut VI. In this context the attribution of the rules to Cnut the Great may echo his reputation as a law-maker, but also represents an attempt to win respect for contemporary regulations and modifications to them.

It has already been noted that the rules attributed to the Jomsvikings bear little relationship to those found in the *Lex Castrensis*. Historians have been drawn to compare the housecarls with the Jomsvikings for a number of reasons. One is that both groups seem to be sworn brotherhoods of men dedicated to lives of war. The rules of the Jomsvikings, as related in the versions of the saga, are very brief and probably have no historical foundation. It is doubtful that the saga contains anything of historical value, and attempts to trace the descendants of Palna-Toki, the leader of this mythical pirate band, in England do not convince.[39] In one version of the saga the survivors of the brotherhood followed Swein to England where they were established at London and the unidentified *Slessvik*. Thorkell the Tall's brother Heming was the commander of the latter of these fleets, each of which consisted of sixty ships and observed Palna-Toki's regulations.[40] The testimony of the saga is unacceptable here. The last three chapters have been condemned as 'late and worthless' and 'legends of the wildest type'.[41] There is no evidence that the Jomsvikings came to England or that the important Thorkell the Tall was ever a member of the brotherhood.[42]

Nevertheless, there is solid evidence which has given substance to the Jomsviking legend. Four great camps discovered in Denmark, with their circular ramparts, axial streets and regular pattern of identical houses, have suggested barracks occupied by communities organised on Jomsviking lines. It has been suggested that these fortresses were occupied by men dedicated to lives of war, held in readiness for the descent upon England.[43] There certainly is a suggestion in the sources that Æthelred and England were confronted by a well organised enemy led by kings or important Danish magnates. Their hosts were large and able to stay in the field for considerable lengths of time. In 1013 Swein's host seems not to have plundered until it crossed

[38] Christiansen, *Saxo*, i, 155.
[39] For Palna-Toki, A. S. Napier and W. H. Stevenson, *The Crawford Collection of Early Charters and Documents*, Oxford 1895, 144 and Plummer, *Two Chronicles*, ii, 181. For doubts about the Jomsvikings, Plummer, *Two Chronicles*, ii, ix, and Gwyn Jones, *A History of the Vikings*, Oxford 1968, 127, 130, 360.
[40] The last three chapters of the Saga are printed by A. Campbell, *Encomium Emmae Reginae*, Camden 3rd ser. lxxii, 1949, 87-93; see also 73-82 for Thorkell in history and legend.
[41] Campbell, *Encomium*, 74, 91. Larson, *King's Household*, 155-6, accepted the story.
[42] Campbell, *Encomium*, 73-4.
[43] John, 'War and Society', 175-6, P. H. Blair, *Introduction to Anglo-Saxon England*, Cambridge 1956, 93-4.

Watling Street and left the land of those who had submitted to him.[44] We can accept that the Danish forces were well organised, however, without inventing communities of Jomsvikings. While the four fortresses at Trelleborg, Aggersborg, Fyrkat and Nonnebakken are signs of a potent royal authority they do not need to be seen as barracks. At Fyrkat women and children were buried in the cemetery and a careful analysis of the finds has shown that some of the houses were used for storage and for metalworking. The dating of the finds points to the reign of Harald Bluetooth, which is confirmed by the dendrochronological date of 980 for the foundation of Trelleborg. Many uses have been suggested for the fortresses: barracks, royal centres for the collection and storage of dues, fortified palaces, refuges for use during attacks by German or Baltic raiders, or garrisons to bolster Harald's new authority over Denmark. Their construction may have contributed to his deposition by his son in the 980s. Not all of these uses are likely, but in view of their early date and short lives it is difficult to accept that they should be associated with Swein's conquest of England, still less with Cnut's.[45]

What I hope to have demonstrated is that although Larson's argument has seemed attractive and the pieces of evidence appeared to fit neatly together, the hypothesis is weak. The strength of the argument is illusory. But if we do not accept this interpretation what is to be made of the housecarls in England? First, in rejecting the evidence for a guild bound by elaborate regulations which are preserved in late twelfth-century Danish works, I do not deny that the English housecarls possessed some form of corporate identity. On several occasions the king's housecarls are met with as a group: at the translation of the remains of Ælfheah in 1023; witnessing a private agreement of the 1050s as *eallra þaes kynges huscarlan*; dwelling on plots of land in Wallingford; with Queen Emma at Winchester in 1035.[46] It is also possible that the remarkable list of men with Scandinavian names who were commemorated in the Thorney *Liber Vitae* represent Cnut's military following.[47] They appear in the list after the king and his earls, but without title or rank. This is the crux of the problem: were the housecarls members of a unique organisation, law-bound guild and standing army, or were they more like the usual households of tenth and eleventh-century England? I shall suggest that we should follow the latter interpretation.

First, the law-bound guild. It has been shown above that the *Lex Castrensis* has little or no authority for the England of Cnut the Great. Furthermore, there is no reference in Cnut's laws or in post-Conquest legal collections to such a body. This may not seem especially significant, particularly as Cnut's lawcodes consist largely of a rehearsal of earlier Old English laws. Nevertheless, the absence of any reference

44 *ASC* C, D, E 1013 appears to suggest this. S. Keynes, *The Diplomas of King Æthelred 'the Unready' 978-1016*, Cambridge 1980, 221-6, for the Danish hosts of this period.
45 O. Olsen and H. Schmidt, *Fyrkat. En jysk Vikingeborg I: Borgen og bebyggelsen*, Copenhagen 1977, has English summaries 205-22, and gives a good survey of the literature. E. Roesdahl, *Fyrkat. En jysk Vigingeborg II: Oldsagerne og gravpladsen*, Copenhagen 1977, 185-207, discusses the finds. I follow Roesdahl in preference to Olsen. Also, D. Wilson, *Civil and Military Engineering in Viking Age Scandinavia*, London 1978, and 'Danish kings and England in the late tenth and early eleventh centuries — economic implications', *ante*, iii, 1980. Trelleborg date — *Medieval Archaeology* xxiv, 1980, 275-8.
46 Osbern, *Historia de Translatione Corporis S. Elphegi a Lundonia a Cantuariam*, in H. Wharton, *Anglia Sacra*, London 1691, ii, 143-7; A. J. Robertson, *Anglo-Saxon Charters*, Cambridge 1939, no. 115; *Domesday Book*, i, 56a; *ASC* E 1035.
47 D. Whitelock, 'Scandinavian Personal Names in the *Liber Vitae* of Thorney Abbey', reprinted in *History, Law and Literature in Tenth and Eleventh Century England*, London 1981, 136, suggests these men may have been the following of one of Cnut's earls. Cf. p.57 above.

to the housecarls and their laws in these sources further weakens the claim that they possessed an exclusive set of regulations. After all, any code which covered the king, earls and a substantial body of men, and also withdrew them all from the normal jurisdiction of hundred, shire and royal courts, might be expected to have made some impact upon the legal records.[48]

Second, the mercenary standing army. There is little doubt that housecarls received payment. Domesday Book records of the four Dorset boroughs that they gelded for forty-five hides, '*scilicet ad opus huscarlium*' four and a half marks of silver.[49] Two sources of confusion exist here. When Cnut paid off his victorious army he retained with him the crews of forty vessels. This does not appear to have anything to do with the housecarls and is instead to be connected with the fleet of *liðsmenn*. This originated in the reign of Æthelred who took into his service Scandinavians in groups and as individuals. In 1012 he employed Thorkell the Tall and forty-five ships of his fleet, which had been plundering in England since 1009, and he had employed Pallig earlier in the reign.[50] To pay for Thorkell's fleet the *heregeld* had been instituted and it was this tax which paid for the *liðsmenn* until both were abolished in 1051. The size of the fleet fluctuated: by the end of Cnut's reign it was down to sixteen ships, in 1040 Hardecnut paid sixty or sixty-two vessels and thirty-two in the following year, while Edward paid for fourteen in 1049 and five in 1050.[51] This was the mercenary force which bolstered Cnut's position in England and helped him to dominate the North Sea. In 1035 they played a role in the succession, putting their weight behind Harold Harefoot.[52]

The receipt of payment makes of the housecarls neither a standing army nor mercenaries. All early medieval monarchs needed to have around them men of military age in order to perform a variety of duties, of which fighting was only one. In general we possess very little evidence about such households. Bede tells us something about the court of Edwin,[53] and we are exceptionally well informed about the young knights of Henry I's household.[54] Of Anglo-Saxon monarchs we know most about the household of Alfred. In his will the king referred to payments to the men 'who serve me'. His biographer Asser records that Alfred paid a sixth of his revenues each year to his 'fighting men and likewise to his noble thegns who lived at the royal court in turns, serving him in various capacities'.[55] If a prince was to maintain fitting

[48] The Old Norse word *Þingemannis*, which appears in the *Leges Henrici Primi*, ed. Downer, para. 15.1, seems to apply to the fleet. *Þingemannalið*, used in the Jomsviking saga supplement, Campbell, *Encomium*, 92-3, has the same meaning. See next paragraph for the *liðsmenn*.
[49] *Domesday Book*, i, 75a. The figures are for all four boroughs together.
[50] *ASC* C, D, E 1012, 1013; Campbell, *Encomium*, 74-5. For Pallig, *ASC* A 1001. St Olaf appears to have aided Æthelred in 1014, *EHD* i, 333.
[51] *ASC* D 1052 (=1051); Worcester, i, 204. *ASC* C, D 1040, E, F 1039 (=1040); E, F 1040 (=1041); C 1049, E 1047 (=1050); D 1052 (=1051).
[52] *ASC* E 1036 (=1035), Plummer, *Two Chronicles*, i, 159.
[53] *Bede's Ecclesiastical History of the English People*, eds B. Colgrave and R. A. B. Mynors, Oxford 1969, ii, 9.
[54] M. Chibnall, 'Mercenaries and the *familia regis* under Henry I', *History* lxii, 1977, 15-23. The *Constitutio Domus Regis* (c.1136) does not deal with the household knights. See C. Johnson, F. E. L. Carter and D. Greenaway, *Dialogus de Scaccario. The Course of the Exchequer by Richard, Fitz Nigel*, Oxford rev. ed. 1983, xlix-lii, 128-35. For later Old English household officers see Keynes, *Diplomas*, 158-61.
[55] F. E. Harmer, *Select English Historical Documents*, Cambridge 1914, 18; S. D. Keynes and M. Lapidge, *Alfred the Great. Asser's 'Life of King Alfred' and other contemporary sources*, Harmondsworth 1983, 106, and W. H. Stevenson, *Asser's Life of King Alfred*, Oxford reprinted 1959, 86-7.

dignity and keep around him a retinue he would have to provide food and lodging, entertainment and, by this time, a monetary stipend. The difference between payments to individual *milites* who served in the king's household, unmarried men without estates, and the wages of mercenary bands such as Thorkell the Tall's fleet, the army of Stephen's adherent William of Ypres and the *routier* bands employed by the Angevin monarchs is clear. The housecarls are not called mercenaries in any of the sources. References to *stipendiarii* and *solidarii* are either to the *liðsmenn* or are intended to show that Harold was so unpopular that only hirelings would follow him to meet William in 1066.[56]

Consequently there is no evidence that housecarls formed a paid standing army. In receiving wages they were no different from many other household warriors. The problem of housecarl garrisons remains to be discussed. Stenton suggested on the basis of a single entry in Domesday Book that housecarls were used to garrison strategical points: in Wallingford King Edward possessed 'fifteen acres where housecarls used to dwell'.[57] It is true that invading armies crossed the Thames at Wallingford, in 1013 and 1066, but there were more strategic points in the kingdom. While it is difficult to know precisely what to make of this entry in Domesday Book it is by no means certain that the housecarls who lived on royal land in Wallingford were performing garrison duty. Vinogradoff relied instead on the evidence of the payments made by the Dorset boroughs *ad opus huscarlium* and suggested that the men described as *butsecarls* also formed garrisons, in Hastings and Sandwich. Oleson added the possibility that *burgware* should also be taken to mean garrison.[58] I discuss both *butsecarls* and the role of fortified places in England at this time in my thesis. One simple observation may be made here. If this suggested network of garrisoned towns did indeed exist before 1066 it impeded William's advance not at all. It seems more likely that *butsecarls* were a naval force of some kind particularly associated with what were later known as the Cinque Ports. *Burgware* is more appropriately interpreted as the Old English word for the inhabitants of a town. They could defend their homes if the need arose but it was upon them that the defence of English towns depended in the eleventh century, rather than upon housecarls and *butsecarls* acting as garrisons.

This brings me to my first conclusion. The housecarls represent Cnut's household followers. They were sometimes described in England by the use of a Norse term because many of them would have been of Scandinavian origins.[59] In most respects they differed little from the *milites* of other princely households, whether they were described as thegns, *chevaliers* or housecarls in the appropriate vernacular. Households such as these must have been disciplined in some way, but there were already laws which would serve for this purpose. The laws of Cnut repeat Alfred's injunctions against betrayal of a lord and fighting in the royal hall. Cnut also enjoined obedience on all men, English and Danish.[60] Equally, the existence of some sort of sworn association need not excite especial interest. A reference to the 'sworn housecarls'

---

56 *Solidarii*, Worcester, i, 204; *stipendiarii*, *De gestis regum*, i, 282. Larson, *King's Household*, 163, Hollister, *Military Institutions*, 14, assume that the references are to mercenaries.

57 *Domesday Book*, i, 56a; Stenton, *Anglo-Saxon England*, 582.

58 P. Vinogradoff, *English Society in the Eleventh Century*, Oxford 1908, 19-22; Oleson, *Witenagemot*, 168-9.

59 The witness-lists of Cnut's charters contain a mixed bag of names, English and Scandinavian. Of the former, some seem to be men who witnessed the later diplomas of Æthelred. The names of men who were clearly Cnut's northern followers do not dominate in position or numbers.

60 Alfred 4, 7; II Cnut 57, 59, 83, in *EHD* i, 409-10, 463, 467.

needs to be set against some of the surviving Old English guild laws. The regulations of the Cambridge thegn's guild refer to the 'oath of true loyalty' and concern, among other matters, pursuance of blood-feud by the guild and payment of compensation for contraventions of its rules.[61] The term housecarl, then, should be interpreted as a general one for members of a household. It was in this vein that Osbern described Cnut's housecarls when explaining their part in the translation of Ælfheah's remains. Osbern derived his information from an eyewitness, and his gloss on housecarl sounds like the explanation given by his informant. They were the *milites* of Cnut's household, *'quos lingua Danorum Huscarles vocant'*.[62]

There is no room here for either a standing army or the Danish *Lex Castrensis*. Turning now to the place of the housecarls in Old English society, Stenton wrote that their personal status was very similar to that of the thegns. However, 'the force as a whole was set apart from other men by the severity of its discipline, its elaborate constitution, and its intimacy with the king'. He recognised that they were granted lands by their lords, king and earls, but 'they formed a distinctive element in English society. Like the knighthood which superseded them, they were specialised for war as was no other class'.[63] Reason has been given to reject the notions of an elaborate constitution and a standing army. There is no doubt that the housecarls who lived at court, like the English thegns who served Cnut, were ready for instant service. It is difficult to maintain that those who were granted estates remained in some way more ready for war than their neighbours the thegns and the king's thegns.

We do not know how many housecarls received grants of land between 1016 and 1066. Domesday Book lists twenty-two individuals as housecarls of king and earls, two men simply as housecarls and one unnamed man as 'a housecarl of earl Waltheof'. A few more men are named as housecarls in writs and a single charter. On the whole, however, the sources name very few landholders as housecarls and are often incon-sistent. The earliest reference to a housecarl is in a charter of 1033. The recipient of Cnut's grant was described as 'faithful thegn' (*fidelis minister*).[64] In an endorsement, copied into the cartulary in Old English, the donee was described as King Cnut's *huskarle*. This man may have been in England with Cnut from the beginning of the reign, for a man of this name attests three charters as *minister*.[65] A housecarl about whom rather more is known is Urk. As thegn (*minister*) he attested charters between 1033 and 1045, and also received lands in Dorset from Cnut and Edward. In a writ dated to between 1053 and 1058 he was addressed as the king's housecarl.[66] This

[61] *EHD* i, 340, verse 5 of the 'Tøgdrapa' on King Cnut by Thorarin Loftunga; 604-5, the Cam-bridge thegn's guild.
[62] Wharton, *Anglia Sacra*, ii, 146. See for Osbern, T. D. Hardy, *Materials for British History*, RS 1862, i, part 2, 621-2; R. Southern, *St Anselm and his biographer*, Cambridge 1963, 250; A. Gransden, *Historical Writing in England, c.550-c.1307*, London 1974, 127-8. Osbern's repu-tation is low but this explanation does sound as if it may have been given to him by Dean Godric.
[63] Stenton, *Anglo-Saxon England*, 412; *The First Century of English Feudalism 1066-1166*, 2nd edn, Oxford 1961, 120-2.
[64] P. H. Sawyer, *Anglo-Saxon Charters. An Annotated List and Bibliography*, London 1968 (hereafter cited as S), no. 969. It was copied into the twelfth-century Sherbourne cartulary. While it is not always safe to assume that *minister* = thegn, there appears to be no problem here. See Keynes, *Diplomas*, 94-5, 149, 158-62.
[65] S956 (A.D. 1019), S961 (1024) and S975 (1035).
[66] Attestations: S969 (1033), S975 (1035), S993 (1042), S999 (1043), S1010 (1045). Grants to Urk: S961 (1024), S1004 (1044). F. E. Harmer, *Anglo-Saxon Writs*, Manchester 1952, no. 1. No. 2 in the same collection concerns the rights of his widow Tole to bequeath their lands to St Peter's, Abbotsbury; *EHD* i, 606-7, is a record of Urk's guild at Abbotsbury.

is evidence that no special title was employed for housecarls in Latin documents before the Conquest, in either charters or their witness-lists. The word *miles* was employed in a few documents but it cannot be linked with housecarls.[67]

Greater ambiguity is found in Domesday Book and narrative sources. Of the twenty-five housecarls mentioned in the former twenty-one are found in the shires which have been identified as comprising circuit three of the Survey.[68] Even here there was no consistency in the use of housecarl. A man described in one place as housecarl was elsewhere a thegn of the king or an earl, a freeman or sokeman or was given no title at all. A single example will suffice. Azor, the son of Toti, held two and a half hides in Buckinghamshire. In this entry he was a housecarl of King Edward. A further twelve entries relate to his holdings of a total of thirty-six hides. For ten of these entries Azor's name was given without qualification. In one he was the man of Queen Edith and in another he was King Edward's thegn.[69] By 1086 the Domesday scribes probably had little interest in the exact status of the Englishmen who had held before 1066, but such differences as these suggest two things. One is that the commissioners were given information which was inconsistent. The other is that the English juries who provided this information were rather vague on the difference between housecarl and thegn.[70]

A similar ambiguity is found in the narrative sources. Two accounts of Earl Siward's Scottish expedition of 1054 give different descriptions of the losses which he suffered.

Also many fell on his side both among English and Danes . . .	But his son Osbern and his sister's son Siward and some of his housecarls and also some of the king's were slain there . . .[71]

Again, in the accounts of the Northumbrian revolt of 1065, a similar difference may be observed.

All the thegns of Yorkshire went to York and killed there all Tostig's housecarls that they could find . . .	All the thegns in Yorkshire and in Northumberland came together and outlawed the Earl Tostig and killed the men of his household, and all they could get at, both English and Danish . . .[72]

The *Chronicon ex Chronicis* appears to combine features of both accounts. On the first day of the revolt two of Tostig's Danish housecarls were killed as they attempted to escape ('Florence' gives their names as Amund and Ravensuart). On the next day

---

67 S1005 (1044) where the first seven thegns are called *miles* and the remaining eight *minister*. In S1003 (1044) and S1019 (1049) some of the men called *miles* have become *nobilis*. But in most charters they are all called *minister*.

68 Middx, Herts., Bucks., Beds., and Cambs. See R. Welldon Finn, *An Introduction to Domesday Book*, London 1963, 38-9.

69 *Domesday Book*, i, 152b (housecarl), 151b (*homo reginae Eddid*), 152b (*teinus regis Edwardi*), 143, 144b, 146b, 147b, 149b, 150b (no title).

70 The concentration of housecarls in this region is unlikely to have anything do with the proximity of London. Housecarls are not found in Surrey, nor around other royal centres such as Winchester and Gloucester.

71 *ASC* C 1054, D 1054.

72 *ASC* C 1065, D 1065, E 1064 (=1065). In the last passage (D, E) Whitelock rendered *hiredmenn* as 'bodyguard'. I have preferred 'the men of his household'.

they killed two hundred men from his household (*curia*).[73] This variety in terminology gives the impression that the term housecarl was not applied to a well-defined and unique body of men. On the contrary, it was simply one of a number of possible words for a member of a royal or noble household.

The use of a phrase like 'English and Danish' in one source where another employs housecarl brings to mind three Worcester leases from the 1040s and 1050s. In each it is declared that the lease was made with the witness of 'all the thegns in Worcestershire, both English and Danish'.[74] Worcestershire is not a place which is likely to have seen much Danish settlement in the tenth century. The Danish thegns of these leases probably received lands in the West Midlands after 1016, and we are informed about some of the ways in which they acquired them in Hemming's cartulary. One newcomer was Sigmund the Dane, a *miles* of Earl Leofric who coveted land which belonged to the monks of Worcester, 'as the men of his race are wont to do'.[75] The word housecarl appears neither in Hemming's work nor in the Worcestershire Domesday Book, yet as a Danish retainer of one of Cnut's earls it would clearly have been an appropriate description for Sigmund. Also from Worcestershire is the example of Richard son of Scrob. In a writ of the early 1060s one of those addressed was Richard, King Edward's housecarl. In another writ from the same time Richard's name was unqualified by any title.[76] Richard was one of Edward's Norman companions who had received land in Worcestershire. He seems not to have been expelled in 1052, although it is unknown whether he was settled in the West Midlands that early.[77] He may have been the son of an Englishman who accompanied Edward in his Norman exile but he can scarcely have been the member of a military guild such as Larson described. He was, however, of foreign extraction if his name is anything to go by.[78] A final example comes from Domesday Book again. In 1066 a Buckinghamshire vill was held by four men called thegns. The entry went on to list their names: Aluuinus, Eduuinus, Almar and Thori the housecarl of King Edward.[79]

These examples seem to add up to make a case for the argument that housecarl was used to describe a landholder who was of Danish, or in the case of Richard foreign, origin. Of the group of four thegns listed above only Thori had a name

---

[73] Worcester, i, 223.

[74] S1394, S1406, S1409. They are printed in Robertson, *Anglo-Saxon Charters*, nos. 94, 111, 112, dated 1042-55. A similar phrase occurs in a charter of Æthelred: 'all the thegns who were gathered there from far and wide, both West Saxons and Mercians, Danes and English' (S939, *EHD* i, 580; see Keynes, *Diplomas*, 161-2).

[75] T. Hearne, *Hemingi Chartularium Ecclesie Wigorniensis*, Oxford 1723, 251, 264-5; *Domesday Book*, i, 174, 176b, 242b (Simund *danus*). I am grateful to Dr A. Williams for access to her forthcoming paper,'"Cockles amongst the Wheat": Danes and English in Mercia in the first half of the eleventh century'.

[76] Harmer, *Anglo-Saxon Writs*, nos. 116-17. Richard was not called housecarl in Domesday Book.

[77] Worcester, i, 210.

[78] Richard is a name of continental origin, O. von Feilitzen, *The Pre-Conquest Personal Names of Domesday*, Uppsala 1937. Scrob seems to have been an Old English nickname or Old Norse personal name, derived from a nickname (G. Tengvik, *Old English Byenames*, Uppsala 1938, 224-5; E. Ekwall, *The Concise Oxford Dictionary of English Place Names*, 3rd edn, Oxford 1947, s.v. Shrewsbury; E. Bjorkman, *Zur Englischen Namenkunde*, Halle 1912, 72). Richard's father may have taken a Norman wife and his own name may have come from her family. He probably married a Norman, the daughter of Robert the Deacon, Worcester, i, 210. I am grateful to Christopher Lewis for this information.

[79] *Domesday Book*, i, 147b (*ACHECOTE*); for similar entries see 152 and 164.

which was not English, and he was described as both thegn and housecarl.[80] Indeed, of all the examples of named men described as housecarls some eighty-seven percent have names which are of Old Norse origin. The inconsistency with which these men were identified as housecarls suggests that this racial distinction may have been the only difference between English thegn and Danish housecarl, and even that was not observed very frequently. This means that when we encounter the term housecarl in English sources it should be interpreted in two ways. As the member of a household, of king or earl, it represents no more than the men who served all early medieval monarchs in a variety of capacities and are known, according to circumstances, as thegns, knights or housecarls. As landowners housecarls may only be distinguished from English thegns on racial grounds, and this distinction was observed infrequently in the sources. The two functions were not distinct, of course, and it is probable that men close to the king alternated between living at court and on their estates.

It is time to debunk the housecarls. Larson thought that Scandinavian evidence from the twelfth century could be employed to illuminate the status and activities of the housecarls in England between 1016 and 1066. Compelling evidence suggests that the *Lex Castrensis* has more to do with attempts to increase royal power over late twelfth-century Denmark than with a genuine desire to record laws originally drawn up by Cnut soon after 1016. As a famous and successful warrior he doubtless attracted to his service men from far and wide, and it is likely that such a cosmopolitan body was disciplined in some way. If we make use of the English evidence alone we find that Cnut was served by a mixed body of Scandinavians and English. It is unlikely that Cnut granted lands to his followers until he felt safe in his new acquisition, but when he did they took their place alongside the community of English landholders. A pertinent example is that of Urk. He is encountered as housecarl in the 1050s, although he attested the charters of Cnut and his son. But as early as 1024 he was the recipient of land in Dorset. This settling of personal followers, if that is what the grant to Urk represents, would have increased Cnut's influence in the shire communities.[81] There is no evidence, however, that the housecarls were any more specialised for war than their English neighbours. Even in the early years of his reign, when we may assume that Cnut kept around him a large body of retainers, the English were also well versed in war after a generation spent fighting the Danes, and not always without success.

The housecarls did not form a distinctive element in Old English military organisation, a standing army and a law-bound guild. Those who held land must have been indistinguishable from their neighbours, and together with their tenants the thegns and housecarls formed the shire hosts. Those who lived at their lord's side are also unlikely to have differed from English thegns, although together they may have possessed an edge over the countrydwellers. As retainers they may have had greater *esprit de corps* and superior arms and training. They most likely received a stipend for their services. This does not make a standing army. The status and function of the housecarls and thegns were identical — Hardecnut's use of his own housecarls to collect tax in 1041 was abnormal, for he had only just entered England as an invader.[82] All were expected to possess the arms appropriate to their station,

80 See von Feilitzen, *Personal Names*.
81 See note 66 above.
82 *ASC* C, D 1041.

to exercise their military prowess and to fight for the king when summoned. In rejecting the traditional view of the housecarls we make the English defeat at Hastings more understandable, and in some measure increase the reputation of the men who did fight alongside Harold in 1066.

For some reactions to this paper and further development of some of its themes, see Nicholas Hooper, 'Military Developments in the reign of Cnut', in A. R. Rumble ed., *The Reign of Cnut* (Leicester, forthcoming).

SOME OBSERVATIONS ON THE NAVY IN
LATE ANGLO-SAXON ENGLAND*

Nicholas Hooper

'Lo, it is nearly 350 years that we and our fathers have inhabited this most lovely land, and never before has such terror appeared in Britain as we have suffered from a pagan race, nor was it thought that such an inroad from the sea could be made.'[1] Thus wrote Alcuin to Æthelred, king of Northumbria, following the Viking raid on the monastery of Lindisfarne in 793. At first sight his shock seems misplaced. The English had come to Britain as seaborne raiders before they began to settle and conquer. It would appear unlikely that they were unaware other races could use the sea in the same way. And yet in Northumbria and Kent at least, important monasteries occupied exposed coastal sites, as if the sea was truly a highway for traders and travellers alone. Subsequent generations learned the need to take precautions against attack from the sea. Allen Brown has always expressed surprise at the way in which late Anglo-Saxon kings were able to raise fleets at 'the drop of a hat'. It is the intention of this paper to re-examine some aspects of naval organisation in the late Anglo-Saxon state.

Every schoolboy used to know that the founder of the Royal Navy was Alfred. The *Anglo-Saxon Chronicle* does not make this claim for him when it describes his new model ships under the year 896,[2] but it has not always been noticed that there are references to English naval activity before this. Some versions of the *Chronicle* note that the West Saxons opposed the Vikings by sea as early as 851, and Alfred's first recorded voyage, in the summer of 875, ended in victory over a small flotilla. Two further successes are recorded for Alfred in 882 and 885, although in the latter year a West Saxon defeat at sea is mentioned too.[3] The vital information missing is how Alfred and his predecessors raised and manned the ships mentioned in the annals. The tone of the passage describing the 'new vessels' suggests they were the king's ships, for among the casualties were a king's reeve and *geneat*, perhaps a member of Alfred's household. The annals for

* I wish to take this opportunity to register my thanks to Allen for the way in which he inspired me to study medieval history in my first weeks at King's. The evidence for the eleventh century has been discussed by C. Warren Hollister, *Anglo-Saxon Military Institutions on the eve of the Norman Conquest*, Oxford 1962, chapters I and VI. This paper is intended in part as a modification of some of his conclusions.

[1] *EHD* i (2nd edn., 1979), 842.

[2] *ASC* 896; C. Plummer, *Two of the Saxon Chronicles Parallel*, Oxford 1892–9, reissued 1952, i, 90–1. Quotations from *ASC* are taken from *EHD* with some changes.

[3] *ASC* 851 (A and Asser omit the information that King Athelstan and Ealdorman Ealhhere were in ships), 875, 882, 885; Plummer, *Two Chronicles* i, 64–5, 74–5, 76–9.

875 and 882 point in the same direction. The presence of Frisians among the West Saxon dead in 896 also suggests these were Alfred's ships and that he had bought in naval expertise. A late source hints that he might also have employed Danes to man his ships.[4] The 885 fleet was from Kent, however, and so may have been raised from the people of the region.

Whatever method Alfred used to provide these vessels they appear to have been few in number and of only limited value. The *Chronicle* references show them making coastal patrols and dealing with small Viking flotillas, on one occasion carrying war into Danish East Anglia, although significantly this was followed by defeat. It was only during the tenth century that the West Saxon fleet became larger and more effective in projecting the authority of its kings into Scotland, the Irish Sea and across the Channel. In the time of Edgar, it was noted, 'nor was there fleet so proud nor host so strong that got itself prey in England'.[5] In the eleventh century too English ships exerted power on the seas as Æthelred employed them in the Irish Sea again and against Normandy, Cnut used them in Sweden and Norway and their services were requested by the Emperor Henry III and Swein of Denmark[6] – these in addition to the defence of England from seaborne invasion, a task which was performed with mixed success. In the eleventh century England was successfully invaded on several occasions. From this time we are fortunate to possess a considerable amount of information on the ways in which these naval forces were raised. In examining this evidence it is proposed to consider the stipendiary element first and then the ships provided by the nation.[7]

We have already come across Frisians in Alfred's employment, and it seems likely that some of the 'foreigners . . . and harmful people' attracted to England by Edgar were employed by him in keeping the seas.[8] There is more substantial evidence from the eleventh century. In 1001 Æthelred already had Scandinavians in his employment, for Pallig, who is said to have been the brother-in-law of Swein of Denmark, deserted with 'the ships he could collect', despite his pledges to the king and the gifts of lands and gold and silver he had received.[9] Subsequently the Danish chieftain Thorkell the Tall joined Æthelred with forty-five ships of the 'immense raiding army' which had already been ravaging

---

[4] What W. H. Stevenson, *Asser's Life of King Alfred*, Oxford 1904, printed as chapter 50c of his reconstruction of the *Life* was taken from a thirteenth-century St Alban's chronicle. It puts Alfred's decision to build 'longships' under 877 and refers to the crews as *piratis*. Plummer, *Two Chronicles* ii, 111–12, assumed them to have been Frisians. That Alfred might have employed Scandinavians is suggested by the presence of 'Vikings' in his household, and of 'someone of Viking parentage' in his monastery at Athelney (Asser cc. 76, 94 in *Alfred the Great. Asser's 'Life of King Alfred' and other contemporary sources*, ed. and trans. Simon Keynes and Michael Lapidge, Harmondsworth 1983, 91, 103).

[5] *ASC* DE 975; Plummer, *Two Chronicles* i, 121.

[6] *ASC* 911 [recte 910], 934, 1000, E 1025 [recte 1026], CDEF 1028, D 1048 [recte 1047], CD 1049, CD 1054, DE 1063; Plummer, *Two Chronicles* i, 96, 106, 133, 157, 166–7, 184–5, 190–1; Flodoard's *Annals* s.a. 939, printed in *EHD* i, 344–5; Jumièges, 76–7.

[7] For earlier accounts of the stipendiary forces see Hollister, *Military Institutions*, chapter I.

[8] *ASC* DEF 959; Plummer, *Two Chronicles* i, 114–15; see also P. H. Sawyer, *From Roman Britain to Norman England*, 1978, 127.

[9] *ASC* A 1001; Plummer, *Two Chronicles* i, 132.

England since August 1009, and which reportedly received the huge payment of £48,000 before dispersing in 1012. The terms of their service were that Æthelred was to feed and clothe them, in return for which they would defend England.[10] This agreement did not prevent them from taking their own measures in the following year. In their entries for 1051 MS D of the *Chronicle* and 'Florence' of Worcester's chronicle refer to the abolition of the tax known as the *heregeld* in, respectively, the thirty-ninth and thirty-eighth year since Æthelred established it to pay the 'Danish soldiers' (*solidarii*). Since this refers to 1012 or 1013 it is clear that Thorkell's fleet, which was waiting for payment and supplies at Greenwich in 1013, is meant.[11] It may have been the same force which received £21,000 at Greenwich in 1014. However, when Æthelred returned from his refuge in Normandy in 1014 he seems to have had a new Scandinavian ally, the Norwegian Olaf Haraldsson.[12]

When Cnut became king he employed his own ships: in 1018 forty ships of the fleet which conquered England, falling to sixteen vessels by the end of the reign. This figure was maintained by his successor Harold Harefoot, but Harthecnut brought some sixty ships with him in 1040 and still had thirty-two of them in service the following year. The last references to the hired fleet concern its end. Edward paid off nine out of fourteen crews in 1049 and the remainder in 1050. It was after this that the *heregeld* was abolished, demonstrating the close relationship between the hired fleet and this tax. The rate of pay was eight marks a rowlock, probably with the higher sum of twelve marks to a steersman. The rates of pay make it possible to calculate that there were some eighty men to each of these ships,[13] a figure which receives confirmation from 'Florence' of Worcester's description of a ship and eighty very heavily armed warriors presented to Harthecnut by Godwine in 1040.[14] The fact that the men paid off in 1050 took the ships with them suggests that the vessels were their own. The *lithsmen* do not reappear in English history, although it is by no means certain that the *heregeld* was not reinstituted before 1066. The advantages of possessing such a force may not, in Edward's opinion, have outweighed the potential threat they represented to his own freedom of action.[15]

This fleet represented a permanent military force in a way that the housecarls

---

[10] *ASC* CDE 1012; Plummer, *Two Chronicles* i, 143.

[11] *ASC* D 1052 [recte 1051]; Plummer, *Two Chronicles* i, 173 and Worcester i, 204; *ASC* CDE 1013; Plummer, *Two Chronicles* i, 144.

[12] *ASC* CDE 1014; Plummer, *Two Chronicles* i, 145. Olaf's support is implied by the skaldic verse of Otar the Black in *EHD* i, 333. The identity of the forty ships Ealdorman Eadric defected with in 1014 is unknown.

[13] *ASC* CDE 1018, CD 1040, E 1039 [recte 1040] (62 ships), E 1040 [recte 1041], C 1049, E 1047 [recte 1050], C 1050; Plummer, *Two Chronicles* i, 154, 160–3, 171–2. M. K. Lawson, 'The Collection of Danegeld and Heregeld in the reigns of Aethelred II and Cnut', *EHR* xcix, 1984, 721–2, 737–8.

[14] Worcester i, 195.

[15] For the possibility that *heregeld* was levied after 1051 see Frank Barlow, *Edward the Confessor*, 1970, 106 n.5, and 102 for the political potential of the *lithsmen*. The belief that they were taken on again after 1051 (Hollister, *Military Institutions*, 17–18) rests on a mistaken interpretation of *lið in ASC* C 1066 (Plummer, *Two Chronicles* i, 197) where it means no more than 'troops' or 'force'. It is used in this sense several times in the accounts of 1052 and 1066.

did not. The distinction is an important one. The fleet is referred to in the *Chronicle* by the name *lithsmen* (or the variants *litsmen* and *litsmanna*) which seems to mean men of the fleet or army (the difference may not have been important in the eleventh century). They are presumably the royal vessels referred to in 1049 when Earl Godwine commanded a squadron of two of the king's ships, captained by his sons Harold and Tostig, and forty-two of the people's ships. In peacetime too they could be an influential body. During the limbo which followed the death of Cnut in 1035 the *lithsmen* in London were among those who chose Harold Harefoot to rule. Queen Emma held Winchester with Earl Godwine and Harthecnut's housecarls, but this was not sufficient to prevent Harold becoming full king.[16] It may be that he did not trust the *lithsmen* which led Harthecnut to entrust his housecarls with the collection of tax in 1041. Elsewhere I have argued that the housecarls should not be seen as a standing army but as the sort of household following which princes commonly maintained.[17] It is in comparison with the *lithsmen* that this distinction becomes important, for we know that they were paid wages and possibly based at London as a body. There is no evidence that they received grants of land, as housecarls certainly did, and it is suggestive that the *lithsmen* could be paid off *en masse* where housecarls as landowners are found in England beyond 1066. This is not to deny that housecarls did have 'some of the functions of a standing army',[18] but if we are looking for such a force in eleventh-century England then the evidence makes it necessary to see it in the *lithsmen*. It is interesting, moreover, to note the relationship of some earls to the *lithsmen*. When Beorn was murdered by Swein Godwineson in 1049 it was his 'friends and *lithsmen* from London' who retrieved the body. As Harold, Tostig Godwineson and Beorn himself had captained royal ships that year, it is possible that they had official duties with the *lithsmen*, even that they were reckoned members of the fleet.[19]

In addition to *lithsmen*, the *butsecarls* ('boatmen') have been identified as another mercenary force on the strength of a passage in Domesday Book. This notes that when the king went on an expedition he had from Malmesbury 'either twenty shillings to feed his boatmen (*ad pascendos suos buzecarlis*) or he took one man from each honour of five hides'.[20] Against this must be set the significant link between Hastings, Romney, Hythe, Dover and Sandwich, which were later the 'head ports' of the Cinque Ports, and the use of the term in the *Chronicle*. The link is clear in the account of 1052. On his return from exile in Flanders Earl Godwine 'enticed all the men of Kent and all the *butsecarls* from the district of Hastings' and many more besides. Later Godwine and Harold 'went towards

[16] *ASC* E 1046 [recte 1049], E 1036 [recte 1035]; Plummer, *Two Chronicles* i, 168, 159.
[17] N. Hooper, 'The housecarls in England in the eleventh century', *Battle* vii, 161–76.
[18] James Campbell, 'Some Agents and Agencies of the Late Anglo-Saxon State', *Domesday Studies*, ed. J. C. Holt, Woodbridge 1987, 201–18, at 203–4. Compare Mr Campbell's suggestion that 'housecarl' meant *domesticus miles* with my own that housecarls 'differed little from the *milites* of other princely households, whether they were described as thegns, *chevaliers* or housecarls' ('Housecarls', 171).
[19] *ASC* E 1046 [recte 1049]; Plummer, *Two Chronicles* i, 168. Barlow, *Edward the Confessor*, 100, suggests that Beorn commanded them.
[20] *DB* i, 64v. Hollister, *Military Institutions*, 12–19.

Sandwich and kept on collecting all the *butsecarls* they met, and so they came to Sandwich with an overwhelming force.' The 'E' manuscript does not refer to *butsecarls* but lists the ports from which they took ships, and presumably their crews, as Pevensey, Dungeness, Romney, Hythe, Folkestone and Sandwich.[21] In 1066 Tostig also took *butsecarls* from Sandwich, 'some willingly and some unwillingly', before proceeding northwards, After his defeat by Earls Edwin and Morcar they deserted, leaving him with twelve small ships (*snaccum*) of his original force of sixty vessels.[22] Domesday Book gives added significance to these references as it records that Dover, Sandwich and Romney had received privileges in return for naval services. At Dover the duty owed was fifteen ships each with twenty-one men for fifteen days, *ad custodiendum mare*.[23]

The interpretation that these *butsecarls* were mercenary garrisons appears to strain the evidence. A more natural reading of the *Chronicle* and Domesday Book than Hollister's leads to the conclusion that *butsecarls* were the inhabitants of the maritime towns of Kent and Sussex, some of whom owed naval service to the king and whose obligations would later lead to the Cinque Ports organisation. But others among them were doubtless ready to join in ventures for personal gain. Whether Edward made a bargain with these towns when he paid off the *lithsmen* in 1051, as Murray suggested, or the service is older, cannot be answered. Hollister's objection to this explanation, on the grounds that not all naval mercenaries were paid off in 1051, has already been shown to be based on a mistaken reading of the *Chronicle*.[24] What is clear is that by the time of Edward the Confessor the crown was taking advantage of the ships of its subjects for naval service. If this interpretation of the *butsecarls* is to be accepted it is necessary to explain the identity of those at London late in 1066 who wished to raise Edgar the Ætheling to the throne. They were perhaps part of the fleet Harold is reputed to have sent to blockade Hastings after the Norman landing and which did not return to their ports because of William's harrying.[25] This is also the only element of Old English naval forces which can be traced after the Conquest. William I used *butsecarls* against Ely in 1071 and his son William set

[21] *ASC* C, E 1052; Plummer, *Two Chronicles* i, 178–9.

[22] *ASC* C, D 1066; Plummer, *Two Chronicles* i, 196–7.

[23] Dover, *DB* i, 1r; Sandwich, *ibid.* i, 3r, 'renders to the king the same service as Dover'; Romney, *ibid.* i, 4v, 10v, 'service at sea'; Hythe had the same exemption from payment of customary dues as Romney, although there is no reference to naval duties (A. Ballard, *An Eleventh-Century Inquisition of St Augustine's, Canterbury*, British Academy Records of Social and Economic History iv (1920), 20. From the Sussex borough of Lewes the king could send his men *ad mare custodiendum*, although if he did not join them 20s were collected 'from all the men . . . and this money had those who were in charge of the arms in the ships' (*DB* i, 26r). This is an obscure reference – does it mean the king's ships or those of Lewes? Hastings is practically ignored in Domesday Book but its ships captured two of Swein Godwineson's vessels in 1050 (*ASC* D 1051 [recte 1050]; Plummer, *Two Chronicles* i, 170). Maldon, in Essex, also owed one ship to the king (*DB* ii, 48). See in general Hollister, *Military Institutions*, 115–23.

[24] See n. 15 above. K. M. E. Murray, *The Constitutional History of the Cinque Ports*, Manchester 1935, 25–6. In his discussion of butsecarls and the Cinque Ports (*Military Institutions*, 18 and 116–22) Hollister does not notice the close link between them.

[25] Worcester i, 228; *Gesta Guillelmi*, 180. Vengeance was taken at Romney and Dover burned by the Normans (*ibid.*, 210–12).

them to guard the sea when he heard of Duke Robert's intended invasion, although they deserted him.[26]

Butsecarls and *lithsmen* represented only a fraction of English naval resources in the eleventh century. Much more impressive is the organisation which raised a fleet from the English kingdom. This is sometimes called *scipfyrd*, although in Old English this meant any naval force. The earliest reference to it may be in 992 when it was 'decreed that all the ships that were any use should be assembled in London'.[27] The decision of 1008 to build a new fleet was probably taken because the existing vessels were decayed beyond repair. The work was done all over the country, 'a warship (*scegth*) from three hundred hides and ten, and a helmet and mailcoat from eight'.[28] An indication of the number of ships collected at Sandwich the following year is that Brihtric's squadron contained eighty vessels.[29] No more is heard of the ship-levy until the reign of Edward the Confessor. The great fleet (*scyphere*) Edward stationed at Sandwich in 1049 included a Mercian contingent which was soon stood down. The ship service of Wessex must have been Earl Godwine's squadron of forty-two of the people's vessels (*landes manna scipa*).[30] Another fleet at Sandwich in 1052 consisted of forty small vessels (*snacca*), according to the 'C' and 'D' versions of the *Chronicle*. This might indicate that it was raised in a different way, perhaps from the ports of the south-east. The 'E' version, however, records that the ships returned to London for relief crews and earls to command them. This suggests that the ships were indeed the national ship-levy. Shortly after this the king and his loyal earls had fifty ships at London.[31] The last recorded muster of the ship-levy was in 1066 when Harold summoned a fleet which slowly assembled at Sandwich, but appears to have been positioned at the Isle of Wight as the threat was from Normandy rather than the north. It held station for up to four months throughout summer and harvest until, on 8 September, 'the provisions . . . were gone' and the fleet was sent home.[32]

This narrative raises many questions, some of which it is possible to answer. The gathering of ships in 992 suggests that the organisation already existed, indeed that the ships had been built long enough before then for decay to be a problem. The working life of medieval vessels is not known. The *Chronicle* describes the Danes in 896 using the ships they had built 'many years before'. The tenth-century ship found in Kent is thought to have had a life of some twenty years. This may suggest that Edgar established these arrangements, and

---

[26] Worcester ii, 9, 48 (Simeon of Durham and Roger of Howden follow him in this usage).

[27] Another fleet was assembled in 999, *ASC* CDE 992, 999; Plummer, *Two Chronicles* i, 127, 133.

[28] *ASC* CDE 1008; Plummer, *Two Chronicles* i, 138. The law-code V Æthelred, from the same year, exhorts the supplying of ships so that they may be ready after Easter, and the associated VI Æthelred adds that the penalty for damaging a 'warship of the people' was reparation and a fine (*EHD* i, 445, §27 and n. 8). The *ASC*'s figure is usually emended to 300 hides.

[29] *ASC* CDE 1009; Plummer, *Two Chronicles* i, 138.

[30] *ASC* CD 1049, E 1046 [recte 1049]; Plummer, *Two Chronicles* i, 166–9.

[31] *ASC* CDE 1052; Plummer, *Two Chronicles* i, 177–81.

[32] *ASC* C 1066; Plummer, *Two Chronicles* i, 196. The length of time the fleet was out suggests it returned to London for relief crews half-way through its service (see below).

in later years there was a tradition that he had maintained a powerful fleet. It is no more than a tradition and the details are apocryphal, yet there is no evidence to refute the suggestion that the fleet as it existed in the eleventh century owed its organisation to Edgar.[33] The importance of Sandwich (on several occasions) and the Isle of Wight (in 1066, but possibly also in 1022) as mustering points has been seen.[34] The several references to fleets assembling at London, or returning there at the end of a campaign, make it possible to suggest tentatively that London was a naval base of some sort, perhaps where ships could be beached above the bridge.

The way in which these ships were provided by the people of England appears at first straightforward. In 1008 the *Chronicle* says that districts of uniform size were responsible for building ships. As Bishop Æthelric declared to Ealdorman Æthelmær that his bishopric (Sherborne) had lost thirty-three hides of 'the three hundred that other bishops had for their shire' and so was not receiving the full amount of 'ship-scot', it is likely the *Chronicle's* figure of three hundred and ten hides is corrupt.[35] The most famous example of an ecclesiastical endowment of three hundred hides is Worcester. It seems impossible to maintain that the charter by which Edgar established a triple hundred for Bishop Oswald is genuine.[36] Not all the privileges claimed in this charter were spurious, however. According to Domesday Book Worcester did have three hundred hides at Oswaldslow where 'no sheriff can have any claim . . . and if any portion of them was leased to any man, for the service to be done to the bishop for it, he who held that land on lease could not . . . retain the land beyond the completion of the term agreed between them, or betake himself anywhere with that land'. There is no reference here to a ship, but one of the estates of Oswaldslow was held by four *liberi homines* rendering sake and soke, churchscot and burial dues, military service and *nauigia* ('ship-service').[37] That the bishop did supply a ship to the royal host is confirmed by a reference in Hemming's cartulary to 'Eadric, who was in the time

[33] *ASC* 896; Plummer, *Two Chronicles* i, 90. *The Graveney Boat: a tenth-century find fron Kent*, ed. V. Fenwick, British Archeological Reports, British ser. 53, 1978, xix. For Edgar's fleet, *De gestis regum*, 177–8 and Worcester i, 143–4. The naval element of Edgar's coronation ceremony (*ASC* DE 972 [recte 973]; Worcester i, 142–3) must be seen in this context.

[34] Cnut took his ships to the Isle of Wight in 1022 for no recorded reason (*ASC* CDE 1022; Plummer, *Two Chronicles* i, 154–5). For Sandwich, see Hollister, *Military Institutions*, 125. In the eleventh century it occupied a strategic site: its now silted-up bay formed a safe anchorage in the sheltered lee of Thanet from which ships could move north, along the channel of the Stour into the Thames estuary; move south and west along the coast of Wessex; or stay put to intercept fleets from Scandinavia.

[35] P. H. Sawyer, *Anglo-Saxon Charters. An Annotated List and Bibliography*, 1968 (*hereafter cited as* S), no. 1383; printed F. E. Harmer, *Anglo-Saxon Writs*, Manchester 1952, no. 63. The date is 1001 × 1012 (D. Whitelock, *Anglo-Saxon Wills*, Cambridge 1930, 141, 144f., prefers 1002). The MS reads *scypgesceote* for which Harmer suggested 'contribution to supply a ship'.

[36] E. John's attempts to produce a genuine version of this charter, S 731 (*Land Tenure in Early England*, Leicester 1960, 113–26 and 162–7) have been widely rejected. N. P. Brooks, 'Anglo-Saxon Charters: the work of the last twenty years', *Anglo-Saxon England* iii, 1974, 229, notes that 'beyond all reasonable doubt . . . this charter is a compilation of the twelfth century and . . . no part of it can reasonably be used as evidence for the tenth'. It is worth adding that the terms *naucupletio* and *scypfylleth* seem to be unique to this document while *scipsocn* occurs only in twelfth-century contexts.

[37] *DB* i, 172v, 173 ('Bisantune').

of King Edward, the steersman of the bishop's ship, and the leader of the same bishop's army in the king's service'.[38]

The *Chronicle* entry for 1008 and the twelfth-century *Leges Henrici Primi* imply that the organisation to supply ships covered the whole kingdom. According to the latter every county was divided into these areas, which it calls 'ship-sokes' (*sipessocna*).[39] Although these arrangements can have been little more than a century old by the time Domesday Book was made, and were still in use up to the Conquest itself, they have left remarkably little trace. This may indicate that they were a lot less regular than has been assumed or that they were rapidly modified as a result of bargains between subjects and kings during the eleventh century. Moreover, none of the examples which have been collected refer to ship-service north of the Humber. It is possible that the organisation was never extended into the kingdom of York.

Most evidence for naval service is ecclesiastical. Despite the evidence of Bishop Æthelric's declaration, no other episcopal endowments are as distinctive as Worcester's. The Sherborne ship-soke is probably to be seen in the head manors of three hundreds held in 1086 by the bishop of Salisbury, whence the bishopric had been moved, although only 228 hides were to be found there.[40] The bishop of Dorchester also possessed three hundreds which have been seen as strongly reminiscent of a ship-soke.[41] Pershore abbey held three hundreds until Edward gave two to Westminster.[42] The bishop of Winchester did not hold the whole of Taunton hundred, but the men of it were under his jurisdiction and had to go 'on military service with the bishop's men', which may represent a trace of a composite ship-soke.[43] Lastly, there is the list of men for a ship from St Paul's. While the memorandum does not account for sufficient men to crew a vessel of sixty or so oars (*see below*) it is presumably to the bishop's warship that it refers.[44]

Another indication of a ship-soke, or at least of ship-service, is reference to a steersman. We have seen that the Worcester ship and contingent were commanded by Eadric the steersman. In the same county another steersman, Thorkell, held in 1066 an estate which King Edward had given to Westminster. It is likely he commanded a warship owed by Westminster from the two hundreds it had received from Edward. As these two had been held by Pershore, with a third which the house still had, this probably represents the Pershore ship-soke. In Norfolk Eadric, *rector navis regis Edwardi*, was the tenant of St Benet of Holme for Horning. After the Conquest he was outlawed to Denmark.[45] A

---

[38] *DB* i, 173v; T. Hearne ed., *Hemingi Chartularium Ecclesiæ Wigorniensis*, Oxford 1723, i, 80.

[39] *Leges Henrici Primi*, ed. L. Downer, Oxford 1972, 97.

[40] *VCH Dorset* iii, 124, 132, 145. The bishop later held all three hundreds.

[41] *VCH Oxfordshire* vii, 2.

[42] *DB* i, 174v and *VCH Worcestershire* i, 175, 259, 299, 304–5.

[43] *DB* i, 87v and *VCH Somerset* i, 442.

[44] A. J. Robertson, *Anglo-Saxon Charters*, 2nd edn., Cambridge 1956, 144–5, 389–92. The list accounts for 45 men. It may be incomplete, or the remaining men may have been found in some other way. It is even possible, although unlikely, that the bishop of London's ship was smaller than others which are known.

[45] *DB* ii, 200 and *VCH Norfolk* ii, 122.

context is provided for this story by the fourteenth-century chronicle of St Benet attributed to John of Oxenedes, according to which the abbot was entrusted with the defence of the coast by Harold and was forced to seek refuge in Denmark by William. The story is late but not implausible. Eadric also appears as a benefactor in a spurious charter in the St Benet cartulary, where he is described as *sciresman*, surely a misreading for steersman.[46] The only other steersman I have been able to trace is 'Ulfech' (Wulfheah), King Edward's steersman, who is not recorded holding of an ecclesiastical institution. As his land was held by Countess Judith in 1086 he may have been a tenant of Tostig and captain of the earl's vessel.[47]

Among the laity there are fewer references to the organisation for levying ships. The eighteen Domesday hundreds of Buckinghamshire were arranged in six groups of three, perhaps as early as 1086, and so may reflect lay ship-sokes. Pipe Rolls refer to ship-sokes in Warwickshire in the twelfth century. However, here the association between three hundred hides and ship-sokes breaks down. Of the three Warwickshire ship-sokes identified in Pipe Rolls only Knightlow consisted of three hundreds, but it cannot be established how many hides were there. Kineton contained four hundreds and Hemlingford one. Few hundreds did in fact consist of a round one hundred hides. Some were very much smaller and others a great deal larger. In the case of Buckinghamshire each of the groups of hundreds contained more than three hundred hides, and the Aylesbury group consisted of four hundred.[48] This must have complicated the organisation of ship service and made it impossible to spread the burden evenly. A further complication were towns, which did not fit in consistently. Some served with the surrounding land, for example Stamford as twelve-and-a-half hundreds *in navigio*, Bedford as half a hundred 'by land and sea' and Exeter as five hides.[49] Others had made special arrangements: Leicester provided four horses for carrying service to London if service was by sea, Warwick furnished four sailors (*bat suein*), Colchester 6*d* from each house annually and Maldon provided a ship.[50]

There are, moreover, references to a tax for ships rather than the actual provision of vessels. Thus Bishop Æthelric's memorandum complains that it is the contributions to the ship-scot that he has lost, and a writ of William I refers

[46] *Chronica Johannis de Oxenedes*, ed. H. Ellis, RS 1859, 291, 293; F. M. Stenton, 'St Benet of Holme and the Norman Conquest', *EHR* xxxvii, 1922, 227, 233. I have not consulted the manuscript, only J. R. West, ed., *The Eleventh- and Twelfth-Century sections of Cott. MS. Galba E.ii. The Register of the Abbey of St Benet of Holme*, Norfolk Record Soc. ii–iii, 1932, 2–5 (= S 1055).

[47] *DB* i, 217v and *VCH Bedfordshire* i, 258.

[48] *PR 16 Henry II*, PRS xv, 1892, 90, '*sipe socha de Cnichtelawa, sipe socha de Chinton*'; *PR 21 Henry II*, PRS xxii, 1897, 94, '*sipe socha de Humeliford*' (H. M. Cam, 'Early Groups of Hundreds' in *Liberties and Communities in Medieval England*, Cambridge 1944, 91–6). This suggests that a complete level of organisation of resources could exist leaving practically no trace in eleventh-century documents. For Buckinghamshire, *VCH Buckinghamshire* i, 225–6. I am grateful to Jim Bradbury for his figures.

[49] Stamford, *DB* i, 336v; Bedford, *ibid.* i, 209; Exeter, *ibid.* i, 100.

[50] Leicester, *DB* i, 230; Warwick, *ibid.* i, 238; Colchester, *ibid.* ii, 107; Maldon, *ibid.* ii, 48. Hollister notes (*Military Organisation*, 115 n. 2) that the Maldon ship served for forty days in the twelfth century.

to the day when 'most recently in the time of King Edward a tax was taken to build ships'.[51] Hollister's suggestion is that some ship-sokes commuted 'their obligation of providing a ship by paying a sum of money instead. Ship-scot may have replaced the actual ship-building obligation over large areas of inland England.'[52] The effort of constructing a national fleet was a great one, as calculation of the resources required to raise a fleet in Normandy in 1066 has shown, and the necessary ship-wrights can only have been found in coastal districts.[53]

The bequests of ships to religious and lay communities in the reign of Æthelred II suggests that the rich shouldered some of this burden. At some time in the reign the thegn Æthelhelm bequeathed a *scegth* to the Ramsey community. Archbishop Ælfric of Canterbury left three ships, the best with sixty helmets and mailcoats to the king, another to the people of his diocese and a third to Wiltshire where he had formerly been bishop. Bishop Ælfwold of Crediton also left Æthelred a *scegth* of sixty-four oars, 'all ready except for the rowlocks',[54] Perhaps the most significant of these examples is Æthelhelm's ownership of a ship of which he could dispose in his will. It implies that while the kingdom was organised to pay for ships and to provide their crews, the actual ownership of vessels could be vested in individuals. This opens a further possibility, that part of the cost could be offset by employing the vessels for personal gain when they were not required for war.

The necessity of providing crews remained, however. Hollister has demon- strated that the obligation to serve in the host covered service by both land and sea and that the same men performed both services. At the rate of service given in the Domesday survey of Berkshire, that is one man from five hides, a crew of sixty men would be provided from three hundred hides. The Domesday passage also sets the term of service at two months. This explains why Edward's fleet returned to London for relief crews in 1051, and how Harold was able to keep a fleet on the south coast until early September in 1066.[55] The size of the crew is confirmed by the equipment Archbishop Æthelhelm included in the vessel he bequeathed to the king, although the sixty-four oars of the Crediton ship warns against imposing uniformity where it is not to be expected. If the ships provided by the ship-sokes were likely to have been of different sizes, we should not press too closely the link between sixty men and three hundred hides. Reality is untidy whereas historians sometimes look too hard for patterns. What exactly a *scegth* was is not clear. The term is of Scandinavian origin and meant 'longship'. The gloss, *scapha, vel trieris, litel scip vel sceigth* is contradictory and the explanation that 'evidently it was the shape, not the size, which was the distinguishing feature of

[51] Hemming i, 78.
[52] Hollister, *Military Institutions*, 114–15.
[53] C. M. Gillmor, 'Naval Logistics of the Cross-Channel Operation, 1066', *Battle* vii, 105–31.
[54] S 1487, Whitelock, *Wills*, no. 13, dated 975–1016; S 1488, Whitelock, *Wills*, no. 18, dated 1003 × 1004; S 1492, A. S. Napier and W. H. Stevenson, *The Crawford Collection of Charters and Documents*, Oxford 1895, no. 10, *EHD* i, no. 122.
[55] Hollister, *Military Institutions*, 104–8; *DB* i, 56v.

the *scegþ'* appears wide of the mark.[56] Nevertheless, the evidence that the normal English warship of the late tenth and eleventh century had some sixty oars takes us back to Alfred's ships at the end of the ninth century.

The naval resources of men and money available to the rulers of England in the eleventh century were several and considerable. They are powerful testimony to the control these kings had over their subjects, and to the cooperation they had from them. Yet in defence they were inadequate. There were three successful takeovers of England in the first seventy years of the century, by Cnut, Harthecnut and William.[57] Moreover, on a lesser scale the returns from exile of Godwine in 1052 and Ælfgar in 1055 could not be prevented, although Tostig was eventually driven off in 1066. Nor was it possible to prevent Viking raids.[58] William did not employ Old English methods against the Scandinavian invasions, real or projected, of 1069–70 and 1085 due partly to the destruction of the indigenous military resources during the Conquest. But as a successful invader, poacher turned gamekeeper, he may have understood the problems of defending an island, problems which were to recur to English kings for four more centuries. The fleets which Æthelred and Edward mustered at Sandwich were essentially a deterrent to invasion. The chance that they would actually intercept an enemy fleet at sea and fight was remote. The available resources were most successfully employed in projecting English power abroad. Within the British Isles the last success of the Old English fleet came in 1063 when Harold led ships from Bristol (presumably the ship-service of the shires around the Severn) to north Wales.[59] When it came to preventing invasions, raids on the coasts of England or landings by invaders with support within the kingdom, medieval naval technology had no answer in the eleventh century as in the fifteenth.[60]

[56] Whitelock, *Wills*, 137.
[57] A fourth was attempted in 1058 by Magnus of Norway, although it is dismissed by the chronicler; cf. Stenton, *Anglo-Saxon England*, 560.
[58] *ASC* C 1048; Plummer, *Two Chronicles* i, 166, when the fleet was called out after the attack.
[59] *ASC* D 1063; Plummer, *Two Chronicles* i, 191.
[60] I am thinking of C. F. Richmond, 'English Naval Power in the Fifteenth Century', *History* lii (1967), 1–15.

MILITARY SERVICE IN NORMANDY BEFORE 1066

Marjorie Chibnall

In the half-century that has elapsed since C. H. Haskins published his *Norman Institutions* a number of documents and studies relating to the subject of early Norman military service have appeared. Few scholars who have looked closely at the subject would now accept the clear and persuasive hypothesis Haskins then put forward; indeed he himself, with his keen critical sense and respect for sources, would probably have been one of the first to wish to modify it, had he been writing at the present day. But because his views have crept in an over-simplified form into general histories, to be repeated and exaggerated, the whole question of possible changes after the Normans came to England has tended to become distorted by wrong assumptions about their earlier customs in Normandy.

Haskins looked at the feudal obligations of Norman abbeys and bishoprics in the 1172 returns and, starting from the fact that only the older foundations (though not all the older foundations) owed such service, argued plausibly enough that fixed quotas must have been imposed in ducal Normandy, probably (in spite of the slight anomaly of Saint-Evroult, founded in 1050) at least as early as the reign of Robert the Magnificent.[1] He did not, in fact, explicitly argue that all the later accepted incidents of knight service − forty days a year at the vassal's own expense, castle-guard, reliefs, aids, wardships − existed in their final form at so early a date. But others have certainly assumed that this was so. Henry Navel, for example, saw the obligations of feudal service as fixed and unchangeable over a long period; in discussing the vavassors of Le Mont-Saint-Michel he asserted that the military service owed to the abbey after it acquired certain properties c.1024 must have been imposed in its entirety by the duke at an earlier date, because 'we know how difficult it was for a lord to impose fresh services on a vassal at this period'; yet his proof consists of a case occurring in 1157, over a hundred years later.[2] Even Powicke set the seal of approval on the general hypothesis when he wrote: 'Before 1066 the Norman dukes were able to regard their country as divided for the most part into a number of knights' fees . . . The grouping of warriors was symmetrical and was evidently imposed from above'.[3] And as recently as 1979 Eric John alleged, in an article published in the *English Historical Review*, that in pre-Conquest Normandy feudal service was limited to forty days, offering as proof only that 'all the text-books tell us so'.[4] It seems, then, that the time has come to look again with care both at the original hypothesis and at the assumptions that have been built upon it.

Wrong assumptions, of course, are by no means universal. We have had for over

[1] C. H. Haskins, *Norman Institutions*, Harvard Historical Studies, xxiv, 1925, 5-30.
[2] H. Navel, 'Les vavassories du Mont-Saint-Michel', *Bulletin de la Société des Antiquaires de Normandie*, xlv, 1938, 149-51.
[3] F. M. Powicke, *The Loss of Normandy*, 2nd edn 1961, 40.
[4] Eric John, 'Edward the Confessor and the Norman succession', *EHR*, xciv, 1979, 241-67.

twenty years now, in the edition of Marie Fauroux, a collection of early ducal charters,[5] the need for which was emphasised by Haskins himself. Their evidence has not been overlooked: D. C. Douglas used it to some purpose,[6] and so did Jean Yver. Yver, indeed, was most explicit in his address to the Spoleto conference in 1968: citing Douglas, he suggested that perhaps the Norman feudal and military system was developed only after the conquest of England, in imitation of the more logical order that William had been able to impose in a conquered country. In support of this, he noted that the words *fevium*, *fevum*, *feodum*, *feudum*, do not appear to become widespread in Normandy before the middle of the eleventh century, and that there is scarcely a mention of *feudum militis* or *feudum loricae* except in charters that are suspect or at least tampered with later. In the ensuing discussion A. Marongiu added his complete agreement with what he called 'the important assumption, fundamental yet at the same time surprising' that in Normandy before the conquest there were no true fiefs.[7]

To many this may now seem obvious; but it is a point of departure for examining the nature of what might for convenience be called pre-feudal military obligations in early eleventh-century Normandy, and attempting to reinterpret the evidence used by Haskins. For Normandy was full of vassals and mailed knights; the basic fighting unit was in practice the *conroi*, usually of some multiple of ten men; there were castles manned by vavassors and knights, and courts held by some lords for their vassals; from the 1040s sub-vassals even are beginning to be discernible. Yet there is no clear proof of any general system of military quotas imposed from above; or of an accepted norm for feudal services and obligations, legally enforceable on the initiative of either side in a superior ducal court – and this surely is a necessary corollary for any accepted general norm. It is at least arguable that the services owed were either relics of older, Carolingian obligations, or the outcome of individual life contracts between different lords and their vassals, and that their systematisation was the result only of the intense military activity of the period of the conquest, and the very slow development of a common law in the century after it.

In the pre-1066 ducal charters collected by Marie Fauroux the word *feudum* or one of its variants occurs half-a-dozen times: in one charter whose terminology has been characterised as 'suspicious' by Jean Yver;[8] in a notice actually written just after the conquest referring to a grant by bishop John of Avranches to his bishopric of certain lands together with the service of five knights (this is the first reference to the 'honour of Saint-Philbert');[9] and four times in charters from the period 1050-1066, referring to single small 'fees' of land or churches or tithes held by laymen or canons of Norman magnates, not of the duke.[10]

One must, of course, be careful not to assume that the *feudum* itself is not there because the language has not yet caught up with it. The concepts familiar to the writers of charters were the precarial gift, the *beneficium*, and the hereditary tenure, the *alodium*; what is crucial is the date when – in Maitland's words – 'the *beneficium*

5 Marie Fauroux, *Recueil des actes des ducs de Normandie (911-1066)*, 1961.
6 D. C. Douglas, *William the Conqueror*, London 1964, 96-8.
7 Jean Yver, 'Les premières institutions du duché de Normandie', *I Normanni e la loro espansione in Europa nell'alto medioevo*, Settimane di studio del Centro italiano di studi sull'alto medioevo, xvi, Spoleto 1969, 334-7, 591.
8 Yver, 335 n.84; Fauroux, no. 208.
9 Fauroux, no. 229; for Saint-Philbert see below, p.73.
10 Fauroux, nos. 120, 165, 183, 213.

and *alodium* met in the *feodum*'.[11] Maitland, however, did not attempt to put it before the mid-eleventh century, and Robert Carabie put it decidedly later.[12] Both terms occur here and there in the early charters. Gilbert Crispin (1046-66) conveys to the abbey of Jumièges the *beneficium* of Hauville, which he had obtained from his lord, the duke, by fighting for him.[13] Gifts to Saint-Georges-de-Boscherville include six acres from 'the men who hold Anxtot as a *beneficium*'.[14] Duke William himself, before 1040, grants – or restores – to Fécamp a miscellany of lands and men: 'in the Cotentin one of my knights called Alfred with all his land, and another called Anschetil with his land, Borel and Modol with their whole alod ... also Godebold the knight and all his brothers, with the whole of their alod, but not the *beneficium* which they hold in Le Talou and in the Pays de Caux'.[15] In another early charter (1043-8) Roger I of Montgomery confirms a grant to Jumièges by Geoffrey, one of his vassals, of an alod which Geoffrey held in the village of Fontaines, 'for which he did service to me because that alod was within my sway'; in return for this the abbot and Geoffrey gave Roger of Montgomery a horse worth 30 livres and a hauberk worth 7 livres.[16]

The tenures, then, are loosely defined; the men are clearly visible. There are knights (*milites* and *equites*) and vavassors in plenty in these charters. In 1050-66 Roger of Clères, with the consent of his lord Ralph of Tosny, grants Saint-Ouen various lands with their churches and tithes, reserving only the reliefs of the vavassors and one guard service a year.[17] Ralph the Chamberlain grants Saint-Georges-de-Boscherville everything he holds in Manneville, in church, lands or meadows, 'without the knights'.[18] Robert Bertram grants Saint-Ouen '40 acres of land, and two peasants, and the tithe of his mares, and two knights, namely Goscelin and Osbern'.[19] Osbern d'Ectot, on becoming a monk at Saint-Ouen, grants 'ten acres of meadow, and fisheries ... and the churches and tithes of Ectot, and part of the wood, and seven knights at Grainville, and the vineyards of Giverny ...'[20] Other vavassors and knights are granted, with and without land. At times one is reminded of passages in Domesday Book, where men commend themselves in different ways to their lords, and the land may or may not go with them.

There is no clear pattern; most of the grants are, naturally, to religious houses, in whose archives the records were preserved. Most refer to a single benefice, or perhaps to a group of brothers holding an *alodium*. On the rare occasions when the term *honor* is used it is usually exactly equivalent to *beneficium*.[21] Occasionally a larger unit is just discernible: the grant of Roger of Clères (1050-66) was witnessed by *homines ipsius honoris*.[22] And on the eve of the conquest (1063-6) Odo Stigand

[11] F. Pollock and F. W. Maitland, *A History of English Law*, 2nd edn, Cambridge, 1968, i, 72.
[12] R. Carabie, *La propriété foncière dans le très ancien droit normand*, Bibliothèque d'histoire du droit normand, Caen 1943, 237-8.
[13] Fauroux, no. 188.
[14] Fauroux, no. 197, p.383.
[15] Fauroux, no. 94.
[16] Fauroux, no. 113, 'Is itaque Goisfredus alodum possidebat in villa que dicitur Fontanas, et inde michi serviebat pro eo quod ipse alodus in mea ditione manebat'. Geoffrey had become a monk at Jumièges with Roger's consent.
[17] Fauroux, no. 191 (c.1050-1066).
[18] Fauroux, no. 197, p.383.
[19] Fauroux, no. 205 (1051-1066).
[20] Fauroux, no. 210 (1055-1066).
[21] e.g. Fauroux, nos. 122, 197, 234 (a later charter containing details of earlier donations).
[22] Fauroux, no. 191, 'homines etiam ipsius honoris ... testes fuerunt'.

made a grant to Saint-Martin d'Écajeul which the church was to hold 'as freely as his other vassals (*barones*), and as he had received his *honor* from the duke of the Normans'.[23] Both charters are evidence of the existence of large honours where sub-vassals had received grants of land. But they are not evidence of imposed quotas, or of stereotyped contracts.

The language of the early Norman chroniclers implies the social structure one would expect from the charters. Dudo of Saint-Quentin twice goes into some detail on oaths of fealty. There is the famous agreement between Rollo and Charles the Bald at Saint-Clair-sur-Epte, confirmed by mutual oaths, when Rollo is said to have placed his hands between those of the king, and the king to have granted him the land between Epte and the sea 'in alodo et in fundo' – that is, 'as his patrimony, by hereditary tenure'.[24] Whatever may have taken place in 911, this is likely to have been the relationship between duke and king which would have seemed appropriate in Dudo's day; the fealty implies vassalage on the Carolingian pattern, and it is still too early for any attempt to force it into a pattern of developed feudal homage. Dudo's description of the fealty sworn to young William Longsword belongs to the same world; the Breton count and the magnates of Normandy all swore fealty and vowed to fight for him against neighbouring peoples without further specification.[25] There is no convincing evidence that anything more precise was ever undertaken in the early years of the eleventh century, when Dudo wrote.

The language of William of Poitiers and William of Jumièges, who both wrote a few years after the conquest, is only very slightly more feudal. William of Jumièges calls the county granted to William of Arques a *beneficium*, and uses the same term to describe two or three grants of castles by the duke.[26] Mounted knights (*milites*) are particularly numerous in the long-term garrisons of castles. Neither writer ever calls anyone a vavassor; but William of Poitiers divides the *milites* into those of some standing (*mediae nobilitatis*) and the rank and file (*gregarii*);[27] and William of Jumièges distinguishes between the *milites* and the *stipendiarii* in castle garrisons.[28] If both were elements in household troops, which is perfectly possible, the former were probably vassals or the sons of vassals, and the latter fighting men bound by a less formal oath, serving purely for wages. Neither writer ever suggests that military service was owed to the duke by any Norman abbey; and it is worth noting inciden-tally that before 1066 there is no charter or chronicle evidence for the exaction of homage from any Norman abbot for the temporalities which might be granted by investiture.[29]

On the other hand, the charters show that there were a number of knights settled on the lands of some of the older Norman abbeys, and that some kind of unspecified

23 Fauroux, no. 222.
24 Dudo, 168-9. Carabie, 239, stresses that the meaning is most probably tenure with full hereditary right and not, as it has often been interpreted, full possession in contrast to tenure in fee.
25 Dudo, 182.
26 Jumièges, 119, 101.
27 *Gesta Guillelmi*, 232.
28 Jumièges, 140, 142.
29 There is one example from the year 1059 of the abbot of Saint-Julien de Tours kissing the duke's knee when he received investiture *cum baculo* of a property near Bavent, which had been granted to him, subject to the duke's permission, by one of the duke's exiled vassals. The compli-cated transaction is described in Fauroux, no. 142. But this concerns an isolated property, trans-ferred by a vassal to an abbey outside Normandy, and even then the ceremony is slightly archaic.

service might be due to those abbeys; moreover a few references in later chronicles give some indication of the forms that service might take. Several monasteries, notably Jumièges, Saint-Wandrille and Fécamp, suffered considerable spoliation of their lands by their hereditary patron and protector, Duke Robert the Magnificent, who was anxious to make provision for his vassals during the years when military needs were pressing and his respect for the Church barely perfunctory.[30] The years immediately after 1028 have been characterised as the years of the great usurpations. His later reconciliation with the Church involved a partial restoration of some of the plundered estates, and this continued during the minority of his son William. One of Robert's charters restoring Argences, Heudebouville, Maromme and other territories to Fécamp states that he had applied them to the uses of his *militia* – his military dependents. Among these dependents was one Haimo, who had been rewarded for his service with a grant of Ticheville, a property of Saint-Wandrille. In this case provision was made for Haimo to be compensated elsewhere when Ticheville was restored to the abbey.[31] Sometimes intruding occupants remained on the land. When Richard restored to Fécamp the lands at Arques, Tourville and Saintigny, which made up a vicomté, he stipulated that the abbot should grant the vicomté to Goscelin son of Heddo, who had a claim to it; and Goscelin subsequently distributed some of the lands to his own men.[32] It was always possible for the duke to retain some rights to the service of his men in his acts of restitution. So there is a possible alternative to Haskins' hypothesis that military quotas must have been imposed early because they affected only the older abbeys. Only the older abbeys had held estates long enough for them to have been secularised and restored with sitting military tenants.

And here the case of Saint-Evroult is particularly valuable. Though much of the evidence comes from the early twelfth century and is recorded in slightly anachronistic language, some facts can be checked against the abbey's re-foundation charters; and one crucial fact is that the act of 1050 was a re-foundation. A Merovingian monastery had existed on the site, and though no traces of regular life and only ruined buildings remained, the ecclesiastical origins of some of the secularised estates had not been forgotten. Some of those in the Hiémois had been absorbed by the vicomtes of the Hiémois and other lords, of whom Heugon was one. If Orderic's account of the early history of the patrons of his abbey is correct, Giroie, a vassal of William of Bellême, obtained properties in the region of Saint-Evroult by right of his deceased betrothed, a daughter of Heugon, with the consent of Duke Richard, round about 1026.[33] Also, St Peter's church, which was part of the scattered monastic complex of the first abbey, was in the fee of Bocquencé, and at some date before the restoration Baudry the German, who had come to Normandy to serve Duke Richard, was settled on it. The family tree is not entirely clear; but Baudry, one of Duke William's archers, possibly the son of the original Baudry, was settled there in 1050 with his brother Viger as a vassal of one of Giroie's grandsons, Arnold

30 See, for example, L. Musset, 'La vie économique de l'abbaye de Fécamp sous l'abbatiat de Jean de Ravenne (1028-1078)', *L'Abbaye bénédictine de Fécamp*, Ouvrage scientifique du xiiie centenaire, Fécamp 1959-60, i, 78.

31 F. Lot, *Études critiques sur l'abbaye de Saint-Wandrille*, Paris 1913, 61-2; the agreement was that the land was to be restored within three years even if Haimo had not been compensated within that time.

32 L. Musset, 'Actes inédits du xie siècle', *Bulletin de la Société des Antiquaires de Normandie*, lii, 1952-4, 32-6.

33 Orderic, i, 11-13; ii, 22-4, 34-6; iii, xv-xviii.

of Échauffour, who gave the land to the new abbey. The brothers, according to Orderic, were unwilling to accept the monks as their lords; and when Robert of Grandmesnil succeeded the gentle Thierry of Mathonville as abbot in 1059 he took effective action. He handed them back, apparently with their land, for life to Arnold of Échauffour. Arnold, Orderic relates, piled all kinds of services on them, and forced them and their men to perform guard duties in his castles of Échauffour and Saint-Céneri. As a result they begged the abbot to take them back, and it was arranged that Baudry and his men and the land of Bocquencé should be restored to the monks, who in return gave Arnold a magnificent war-horse they had just received from Engenulf of Laigle. Baudry did homage to Abbot Robert, promised that he and his men would submit to the abbot's justice, and asked that 'his honour should never again be alienated from the lordship of the monks'. If Orderic gave the names correctly, the transfer of homage had not lasted long, for Abbot Robert was driven into exile only two years after taking office. 'To this day,' concluded Orderic, writing in the early twelfth century, 'Baudry and his son Robert after him have done military service for the land of Bocquencé to the abbot alone.'[34]

Orderic may occasionally have used technical terms more appropriate to his own day than to the mid-eleventh century; but at least his story of the acquisition of Bocquencé and of Cullei (Rabodanges), the second of the abbey's later military fees, is entirely consistent with the foundation charters, which is more than can be said for some of the charters attributed to Henry I. According to the foundation charter, precisely cited by Orderic, Hugh of Grandmesnil gave Cullei to the monks 'at the request and with the consent of the lords of the vill, who held it as an alod (*quorum alodium erat*)'.[35] This means that they held it by hereditary tenure, and Orderic gives no further information about its later history. But one of the abbey's early charters describes how Samson of Cullei confirmed the gifts of his ancestors to the monks, promising to give himself and all his possessions to the abbey at his death, and received in return a horse from Abbot Roger of Le Sap (1091-1123).[36] Two royal charters of doubtful authenticity carry on the story, progressively converting the tenure of Cullei into a stereotyped knight's fee.

The more reliable of Henry I's charters on the subject confirms the grant of Cullei by the abbot and monks to Nigel of Aubigny, to hold of them in fee and inheritance, on condition that he perform at their summons and on their behalf the service of one knight, which was owed for it.[37] There are already some doubtful features in the wording of this charter, and the alleged confirmation charter of 1128 contains some even more suspicious passages. Haskins judiciously observed that 'there are some difficulties with regard to it'. As it stands in the version printed in *Gallia Christiana* allegedly from a lost original, it runs:

> I grant also to them the whole vill of Cullei ... by gift of ... Robert and Hugh of Grandmesnil, which is one knight's fee; and another knight's fee of

34 Orderic, ii, 80-5.

35 Orderic, ii, 32, 'Terram uero de Cueleio dedit Hugo petentibus sponte dominis eiusdem uillae, quorum alodium erat'. Cullei is now Rabodanges.

36 *Orderici Vitalis Ecclesiasticae Historiae libri tredecim*, ed. A. Le Prévost, Société de l'Histoire de France, 1838-55, v, 193-4.

37 Le Prévost, v, 200-1; *Regesta*, ii, no. 1595. The charter survives in the thirteenth-century cartulary of Saint-Evroult, and there are some suspicious features in the wording, especially in the witness clause beginning, 'Testibus me ipso . . .'. In its present form it may be a later recording of a grant made orally to Nigel. The date is not later than 29 July, 1129.

the gift of William Giroie, which is between Touquettes and the vill of Villers and is called Bocquencé, of the fee of Montreuil; and which my father William (with the consent of Thierry the first abbot ... and Robert and Hugh of Grandmesnil and William Giroie their uncle, the founders of the abbey) constituted a barony for the service of him and his heirs in all his expeditions throughout Normandy, in such a way that Richard of Cullei and Baudry son of Nicholas, the knights to whom Abbot Thierry gave these two knight's fees in inheritance to hold of him, with the assent of my father William, shall be obliged to perform this service, each one for his fee with horses and arms at his own expense, and his heirs after him, whenever the abbot of Saint-Evroult is summoned by me, and they by the abbot.[38]

If the language of the charter for Nigel of Aubigny is to some extent that of Henry I towards the end of his reign, this is the language of the reign of Henry II. Neither is the language of 1050, though some of the facts recorded are near enough to the truth to have deceived Haskins. Yet the second charter is quite incompatible with what Orderic had to say about the transfer of Baudry's service to Arnold of Échauffour in the time of Abbot Robert. And if we may accept that Orderic's undertaking to write the history of his abbey received impetus from Henry I's visit to Saint-Evroult at Candlemas, 1113, when the monks sought confirmation of their properties and privileges,[39] then his history is likely to contain as true an account of conditions up to that date as he could ascertain from sources then in existence. The cartulary copies of the foundation charters of Saint-Evroult have certainly been tampered with; the election clauses were interpolated at a later date, probably in the 1130s.[40] The process of interpolating Henry I's later charters may have begun at the same time and continued into the reign of his grandson, to bring them into line with what was becoming customary. If the history allegedly recorded in these later, suspicious charters, was true and not interpolated history, why had Orderic nothing to say about it? And why did he say that Baudry of Bocquencé fought only for the abbey? Haskins' interpretation of the more probable truths in these documents is not the only one that fits the few known facts.

In 1050, when Saint-Evroult was founded in a marcher region where war was endemic, knights and vavassors were fairly numerous on lands that came into the possession of the abbey. The lords of Bocquencé had certainly been military dependants of the duke; the same may have been true of the lords of Cullei, who had come to hold the land alodially under the Grandmesnil. The abbey undoubtedly had its own knights. When William Giroie, old and blind, went to visit his kinsmen in south Italy to collect gifts for the abbey he was accompanied by a dozen of the abbey's knights, who gave him escort. He himself and all but two of the knights died of the fevers of Italy; when one of the two survivors misappropriated the abbey's wealth entrusted to his care he was brought to justice in the abbot's court and condemned to forfeit his land until he made amends.[41] If the abbot did not need knights for castle-guard, he needed them for his own protection, and particularly for escort service. Land could be given and service retained; it is possible that the dukes still had a claim to service from one or two of the knights of Saint-Evroult from an earlier

[38] Haskins, 11-14; *Gallia Christiana*, xi, instr. 204-10.
[39] See Orderic, i, 32.
[40] Orderic, i, 66-75.
[41] Orderic, ii, 58-65.

period of vassalage. Baudry of Bocquencé had been the duke's archer. We know nothing of Richard of Cullei, but Samson of Cullei may have been his son; the gift of a horse and the provision for the reversion of the land, suggests that he may have been a knight who was allowed to hold the property from the abbey for his lifetime, and was equipped to serve the abbot. Though there is no evidence of service being exacted on behalf of the duke when the land was given, ducal claims may have remained dormant and finally been satisfied in the course of the next century by the progressively more feudal arrangements recorded in interpolated royal charters and in the returns for 1172. By that time Saint-Evroult was recognised as a barony, owing the service of two knights; and in the registers of Philip Augustus they were charged against the fees of Cullei and Bocquencé.[42] Whether the arrangements crystallised before the death of William I or − as I think more likely − in the late 1120s or 1130s, they cannot have existed with anything like their final precision before the Norman conquest.

Military service, though variable at all levels, weighed more heavily on lay vassals and even on bishops than on any of the abbeys. These men, in any case, kept up substantial military households for their own protection; and though Duke William aimed at keeping as many of the castles of the duchy as possible in his own demesne under castellans appointed by him, a number of castles − especially in the marcher regions − fell into private hands and remained there.[43] I have already mentioned that Arnold of Échauffour held castles at Échauffour and Saint-Céneri; and there were others in this region at Pont-Échanfray and Moulins-la-Marche, where the duke attempted to assert his authority with only partial success. Some vassals were certainly forced into service in these castles, though hired knights provided some of the garrisons, together with a good stiffening of the châtelain's own brothers and sons.[44] Any evidence that the duke exacted a minimum period of service is sadly lacking; service was governed by need, and household troops and more casual mercenaries were both prominent. Much has been made of Orderic's statement that Guy, count of Ponthieu, was only released from prison after his capture at Mortemer in 1054 on condition that he did homage and promised to give the duke military service every year at his command, with a hundred knights.[45] But even if the figure is correct, the transaction reads more like a treaty of peace and alliance with a neighbouring lord than a record of the normal relations of the duke with his Norman vassals.

That knights would tend to become organised in groups of five or ten was, in the long run, inevitable; it was a fact of military tactics. Chroniclers' accounts of battles in this period were vitiated because they used a language that had been perfected to describe infantry engagements, and was not really adapted to cavalry warfare. They write of lines, columns, squadrons, wedges and so forth with a fine variety of phrase; but not until the vernacular became the language of narrative does the *conroi* clearly emerge from the classical verbiage.[46] Mounted knights were trained as far as possible

---

42 *The Red Book of the Exchequer*, ed. Hubert Hall, RS 1896, ii, 626; Haskins, *Norman Institutions*, 12.
43 See J. Yver, 'Les châteaux forts en Normandie', *Bulletin de la Société des Antiquaires de Normandie*, liii, 1955-6, 42-63 for a discussion of castles in the reign of William the Conqueror.
44 See, for example, *Gesta Guillelmi*, 54; the case of Arnold of Échauffour, above, p.00; Fauroux, no. 117.
45 Orderic, iv, 88-9.
46 See Orderic, i, 104; J. F. Verbruggen, *The Art of Warfare in Western Europe during the Middle Ages*, trans. Sumner Willard and S. C. M. Southern, Amsterdam, 1977, 16-17.

in small groups of five or ten, combined in larger units under their *magistri militum*.[47] A number of explanations might be offered for Orderic's statement that, when William fitzOsbern (as regent of Normandy) was summoned to accompany King Philip of France in the disastrous expedition of 1071 against Robert the Frisian, he rode off gaily with only ten knights as though he were going to a tournament.[48] It may mean that ten was the fixed quota obligation owed by the duke of Normandy to the king of France; but alternatively it may mean that ten was the minimum team that a knight of substance would put into the field for a tournament. Charles the Good, count of Flanders, who could have mustered many vassals with their contingents, was said by Galbert of Bruges to keep his knights in training by engaging in tournaments in Normandy or France, with 200 knights.[49]

On the eve of the conquest, or just after, we find the first charter reference to a fief on which five knights were settled, so that the tenurial corresponded with the tactical unit. The place is a charter of Duke William for the church of Avranches, recording a complicated family transaction by which John, bishop of Avranches, arranged for the transfer to his bishopric after his death of part of his own personal inheritance.[50] The Norman episcopate (with the solitary exception of the see of Rouen) was filled at this date with members of the highest Norman aristocracy, who were prepared to use their family lands to provide for the needs of their sees, and whose reconstruction of their bishoprics — as the history of Geoffrey of Coutances and Odo of Bayeux abundantly illustrates — was as military as it was pastoral.[51] John of Avranches had made a gift of half his territory of Vièvre (now Saint-Philbert); his nephew Robert contested this, and was finally bought off by the payment of ten pounds; the commendation of five knights to the bishop was allowed, with the stipulation that after the death of Bishop John the knights should hold their land as a fee of the bishop of Avranches. In 1172 the bishop of Avranches owed the duke of Normandy the service of five knights from the honour of Saint-Philbert; and it is very likely that a promise of service may have been made c.1066 when the gift was confirmed and recorded. At this date military needs were particularly pressing; it was necessary for the duke to know the military resources available both for his expedition and for the defence of the duchy he was leaving behind. The commendation of knights settled on the lands of laymen to a prince of the church would be more acceptable if their swords would remain available for the needs of the duke no less than those of the bishop. I would suggest that it is only at this date, in the thick of the preparations for the great expedition to England, that the widespread obligations of vassalage began to be more clearly systematised as obligations to provide at least a minimum contingent for the ducal armies in Normandy. If the lands of knights had passed into the possession of the Church the men might still be held to a duty of serving the duke, and the responsibility for producing them could be put upon their lord.

---

[47] J. F. Verbruggen, 'La tactique des armées de chevaliers', *Revue du Nord*, xxix, 1947, 163-4, cites examples of groups of 30 or 40 combattants, though the size of the *conroi* might vary.
[48] Orderic, ii, 282.
[49] Galbert of Bruges, *The Murder of Charles the Good*, trans. James Bruce Ross, New York/Evanston/London 1967, ch. 4.
[50] Fauroux, no. 229.
[51] See D. C. Douglas, 'The Norman episcopate before the Norman Conquest', *Cambridge Historical Journal*, xiii, 101-15; J. Le Patourel, 'Geoffrey of Montbray, bishop of Coutances 1049-1093', *EHR*, lix, 1944, 129-61; David R. Bates, 'The character and career of Odo, bishop of Bayeux (1049/50-1097)', *Speculum*, 1, 1975, 1-20.

The relation of these commended knights to their land is a very complex one. A great deal of the land of Normandy was held by hereditary tenure, and was regarded as an inalienable patrimony; but many of the holders were vassals, and benefices were for life.[52] This apparent contradiction can be explained by the facts that benefices were granted for past service; that a feudal vassal might occasionally be moved from one benefice to another; and that any inheritance, whilst passing by customary family law (a law that was slowly crystallising into *parage*), would not necessarily give the best share to the man most capable of bearing arms.[53] Once lordship and feudal service became so important that the lord's influence on the choice of an heir among the kindred became greater than the influence of the kindred, the benefice and alod could be said to have met in the fief. There is a twilight period when the process of determining the heir, and the nature of his claim to any particular fief, were matters of custom, not of right. In early ducal Normandy the kindred of a minor sometimes acted as guardian; only gradually did the lord assume this function.[54] Henry I, winning the support of his vassals of Norman birth by his coronation charter, would scarcely have agreed that the children of widows should be in the guardianship of their mother or another relative unless this had still been customary in Normandy no less than in England as late as 1100.[55] But his practice of taking money from the chosen guardian shows that the lord's right was making headway.[56] Hereditary right was rooted in the patrimony, and in time this combined with military needs to produce feudal customs. And it was only when feudal custom became feudal law that the lawful incidents could be defined with precision.

There is no clear evidence of the amount of feudal service that would have been regarded as reasonable in early ducal Normandy; if any theories had existed they would have been tempered by the harsh necessities of a struggle for survival and the lure of the spoils of war. Orderic has a story of how, during King William's difficult campaigns in Yorkshire and the West Midlands in the winter of 1069-70, the men of Anjou, Brittany and Maine complained and wished to go home. The king made no concessions; and when the army was disbanded at Salisbury and the men had received their rewards he kept back those who had wished to desert, and made them serve an extra forty days as a punishment.[57] If Orderic took all his facts from William of Poitiers, this would be a nearly contemporary tradition; but although the passage

---

52 The complexities of the situation are well illustrated in the *Vita Herluini* of Gilbert Crispin, which describes how, after Herluin had withdrawn from Count Gilbert's service and forfeited what he held of the count, he still had twenty knights among his own men. See J. Armitage Robinson, *Gilbert Crispin, Abbot of Westminster*, Cambridge 1911, 87-90, and the discussion by Christopher Harper-Bill, 'Herluin, abbot of Bec, and his biographer', *Studies in Church History*, ed. Derek Baker, xv, 1978, 15-16.
53 See R. Génestal, *Le parage normand*, Caen 1911; John Le Patourel, *The Norman Empire*, Oxford 1976, 264. J. Yver, *Égalité entre héritiers et exclusion des enfants dotés*, Paris 1966, 106 ff. has described the rapid crystallisation of custom in Normandy before the end of the eleventh century, even though rules of law were not formulated until the twelfth.
54 R. Génestal, *La tutelle*, Caen 1930, however, considers that in Norman custom the lord had rights of wardship earlier than in French custom, and that in any case the rights of the duke were more extensive than those of another feudal lord.
55 William Stubbs, *Select Charters*, 9th edn, Oxford 1921, 118, 'Et terrae et liberorum custos erit sive uxor sive alius propinquorum qui justius esse debebit'.
56 Henry I's dealing with the four orphan children of Walter of Auffay shows how the rights of lord and kindred were kept in balance; he entrusted the wardship to the boys' uncle, who paid for the privilege. Orderic, iii, 258-61.
57 Orderic, ii, 234-7.

has some statements in common with the *Liber Eliensis* which also used the lost text of William of Poitiers for these campaigns, the figure of forty days is peculiar to Orderic; and he wrote in the middle of Henry I's reign, when forty days service was an accepted norm for many vassals.[58] In any case, the men were malcontents from outside the duchy, not Normans. The implication seems to be that those who served under the ducal banner might expect to serve as long as they were needed, or take the consequences. For loyal service the rewards might be great.

As for the other obligations, they seem to have depended on individual contracts and to have been variable, both before the conquest and for some time afterwards; some indeed were never standardised. Baudry of Bocquencé had to meet different demands for castle guard from his two lords. The first aid 'pour fille marier' taken by a Norman king in England was Henry I's aid for his daughter Matilda's marriage in 1109, and it was assessed on the hide, not the fee; there is no evidence that it was collected in Normandy.[59] As late as 1133 the Bayeux Inquest produced a statement on the obligations of the bishop's knights.[60] The bishop was entitled to receive from the fief of each knight a relief consisting of a hauberk and stirrup, or fifteen livres; each knight in addition owed an aid of 20s. if the bishop had to go to Rome on the business of his church, and an aid of an unspecified amount for rebuilding the cathedral church if necessary, or rebuilding the houses of the city if they were burnt. These obligations were clearly tailor-made for the bishopric, and were different from those appropriate for a lay lord with daughters to marry or sons to knight. They may very well have been fixed during the period when Odo was most active in building up the wealth and strength of his bishopric some time in the later part of the reign of William I. The duty of support if he went to Rome on the business of his church does not seem realistic before the 1070s at the earliest; although any Norman might undertake a south Italian adventure under guise of pilgrimage in the early eleventh century, constant recourse to Rome on ecclesiastical business was not a characteristic of the Norman church until considerably later, when reform began to bite. When Odo was arrested in 1082 he was accused of trying to take knights to Rome to further his own ambitions, but that was hardly the business of the see.[61] On the other hand some of the obligations might have been found in other lordships; the relief of fifteen livres in silver, which ultimately became standard in Normandy and remained so for a considerable period, may already have been customary in many honours.[62]

Whatever the terms of individual contracts, feudal obligations were enforceable

[58] As late as 1172, however, there are indications that the length of service was not entirely uniform; see *The Red Book of the Exchequer*, ii, 643, 'De honore comitis Mortonii per Ricardum Silvanum, xxix milites et dimidium et octavam partem; ad servitium Regis, per manus Comitis, ad marchiam per xl dies ad custum eorum, deinceps ad custum Regis vel Comitis. Et Comiti serviebant prout debebant'.

[59] Huntingdon, 237, 'Rex cepit ab unaquaque hida Angliae iii solidos'; *ASC* E, *sub anno* 1110, 'This was a very severe year in this country because of taxes that the king took for the marriage of his daughter'. Various churchmen, including the bishops of Lincoln and Norwich, the abbots of Battle and Abingdon and the prior of Spalding, secured writs stating that this aid was not to impair the exemptions granted to some of their lands, or introduce new customs (*Regesta*, ii, nos. 942, 946, 959, 963, 964, 968).

[60] *Antiquus cartularius ecclesiae Baiocensis*, ed. V. Bourienne, Société de l'Histoire normande, 1902-3, 19.

[61] *De gestis regum*, ii, 334; Orderic, iv, 40; *Liber monasterii de Hyda*, ed. E. Edwards, RS 1866, 296.

[62] H. Navel, 'L'enquête de 1133 sur les fiefs de l'évêché de Bayeux', *Bulletin de la Société des Antiquaires de Normandie*, xlii, 1935, 57.

in honorial courts. There seems little doubt that such courts existed in ducal
Normandy before 1066, though it is not easy to separate formal judicial proceedings
from general business. The court was a place for the meeting of lords and vassals for
various activities, including knightly sports and the discussion of matters of common
interest. Witness lists of charters indicate that grants were sometimes made in such
assemblies.[63] Chroniclers writing in the first generation after the conquest certainly
believed that pleas were heard and judgements enforced in them. Gilbert Crispin's
Vita Herluini describes a debate on whether Herluin should have been deprived of
his lands for failure to carry out a mission on behalf of his lord, Count Gilbert of
Brionne, and implies that it took place in the lord's court.[64] Somewhat later, Orderic
recorded proceedings in the court of Saint-Evroult, allegedly in the time of the first
two abbots. The knight Anquetil of Noyer, who had misappropriated the treasures
he was supposed to carry back from Italy, was summoned to judgement in the court
of Saint-Evroult and condemned to lose what Orderic, in the language of 1120, calls
'the whole fief he held from Saint-Evroult', but which appears to have included a
third of the bourg of Saint-Evroult which he held as his inheritance from his father.[65]
Orderic may be less than clear on the precise legal condition of Anquetil's land, and
like Gilbert Crispin he may have read back into the earlier period the more formal
procedures of his own day. But it is difficult to doubt the existence and competence
of the courts whose proceedings both chroniclers described.

Much is obscure in the history of honorial courts in the eleventh century; and
the diffuculties of interpreting the evidence continue well into the twelfth. Charters
no less than chronicles used anachronistic language, and were themselves liable to
later interpolation. The cartulary copy of Henry I's charter to Saint-Evroult, confirming the grant to Nigel of Aubigny of Cullei to hold in fee of the abbey, contains
detailed arrangements about jurisdiction in these words: 'In order to secure the relief
of the land and the royal services or dues granted to the abbey of Saint-Evroult by
me or my heirs, the abbot and monks shall have the right of exercising jurisdiction
in that vill as often as they find necessary; and if Nigel or his heirs attempt to impose
any customs on the knights or other men of the vill beyond those which of right are
owed to the abbot and monks of Saint-Evroult, and if the men bring any plea arising
out of this, the abbot and monks shall bring him to justice in that vill until suitable
penalties have been exacted; similarly for all forfeitures and other penalties which
Nigel may incur against the monks.' I have shown that there are suspicious features
in the wording of this charter, parts of which may even have been interpolated after
the reign of Henry I.[66] But, taking it together with Orderic's narrative, we may safely
conclude that the monks of Saint-Evroult were exercising jurisdiction as a matter of
course over their vassals in the third decade of the twelfth century, and that they
had held a court of some kind to deal with failure to perform service even before
1066, in the lifetime of the first abbot.

Moreover, anachronistic language shows the way in which feudal law was developing, and may indicate the realities that had underlain earlier customs. The
development was slow. But as the duke came to have a defined interest in the military
obligations of his sub-vassals, the workings of the honorial courts became a matter
of direct concern to him. To a certain extent it is true, as Professor Milsom has clearly

[63] Fauroux, no. 191.
[64] Armitage Robinson, 90.
[65] Orderic, ii, 62-5.
[66] Le Prévost, v, 200-1; and see above, p. 70 n.37.

demonstrated, that the feudal courts were a law unto themselves; there was at first no regular procedure of appeal from them to a higher court.[67] Nevertheless the ducal power was held in reserve, and might, in the course of time, intervene and guarantee the smooth workings of the honorial courts. By the end of Henry I's reign feudal service, with all its incidents, was becoming precisely defined, and custom was hardening into law. As a consequence of this, the residual power of the ducal court soon became a reality for enforcing customary law. But this is a far cry from the tangle of incipient feudal customs, partly built up from below, that had existed in Normandy during the period before William the Bastard became William the Conqueror of England.

[67] F. M. Stenton, *The First Century of English Feudalism*, 2nd edn, ch. 2; S. F. C. Milsom, *The Legal Framework of English Feudalism*, Cambridge 1976, especially 183-6.

THE INTRODUCTION OF KNIGHT SERVICE IN ENGLAND*

J. C. Holt

The *cartae baronum* submitted to King Henry II in 1166 are a curiously neglected source in English history. Edited by Thomas Hearne in 1728[1] and by Hubert Hall in 1896[2] they were one of the bases of J. H. Round's paper on the Introduction of Knight Service published in 1891.[3] Yet they have not been re-examined systematically in recent discussions of Round's famous thesis. Perhaps Round has seemed to squeeze them dry. Perhaps the *cartae* have not seemed particularly relevant to the lines which have been followed by Round's critics, for they provide only ancillary evidence in the debate about local 'continuity' between thegnly and knightly estates, and, since they were composed a century after the Norman Conquest, they seem to leave room for the argument that the quotas of knight-service of the late twelfth century arose, not artificially from some act of government, but through gradual growth in the century following the Conquest. Yet the *cartae*, with the Pipe Rolls, are the fundamental source for this whole field of study. They establish the size of many quotas of military service, whether by direct statement or by permitting computation; they illustrate the attitudes both of the Crown and its tenants-in-chief towards military service; and they lead to questions about military service to which there is still no satisfactory answer. It is with the *cartae*, therefore, that this paper is first concerned.

Round's chief concern was to correlate the *cartae* with the information on scutage in the Pipe Rolls of Henry II. The present objective is to correlate the information of both the *cartae* and the Pipe Rolls with the history of feudal tenements. For it is obvious enough that the military burdens laid on the tenants-in-chief of the Crown were bound to bear the mark of forfeiture, escheat, marriage, sale and all the other accidents, genealogical, economic, and political, which might befall in the descent of a great estate. Round was not concerned with this within the context of his argument, and for good reason; for he set out to refute the notion that the military service of the Norman period 'developed in unbroken continuity from Anglo-Saxon obligations'.[4] To that end the establishment of the existence of an unrelated, artificial system of military tenure was sufficient; and he scarcely paused to consider whether that apparently artificial system might itself be a result of gradual growth, not over the years of the Conquest itself, but in the century which followed. The

* I am indebted to Professor C. Warren Hollister and Professor T. K. Keefe for commenting on an earlier version of this paper.
1 *Liber Niger Scaccarii*, ed. Thomas Hearne, Oxford 1728.
2 *The Red Book of the Exchequer*, ed. H. Hall, RS 1896.
3 'The Introduction of Knight Service into England', *EHR* vi, 1891, 417-43, 625-45, vii, 1892, 11-24; reprinted in J. H. Round, *Feudal England*, London 1909, 225-314 from which all references below are taken.
4 Round, 234.

evidence to the contrary, which placed responsibility firmly on the shoulders of William the Conqueror, seemed to him both clear and certain. However, Round had rejected 'continuity' through the front door only to leave the back unbarred; for a historian approaching the evidence of the Pipe Rolls and the *cartae* independently will at once be struck by the number of examples which do not seem to fit Round's hypothesis, either because the service seems to be random, quite unrelated to the units of fives and tens on which Round's arguments depended, or because the tenant-in-chief does not seem to know what his quota was.[5] Now it is these instances which underpin the argument that quotas emerged gradually in the century following the Conquest.[6] Round noted some of them, but asserted that they 'are quite insufficient to overthrow the accumulated array of evidence on the other side and some of them are, doubtless, capable of explanation'.[7] This is the starting point of the present argument.

The *cartae* are not easy to deploy effectively. Some of the barons who made returns seem to have been uncertain about what was required. Henry II had apparently asked three questions:[8]

1. How many knights were enfeoffed by the death of Henry I? (The old en-feoffment.)
2. How many knights have been enfeoffed since the death of Henry I? (The new enfeoffment.)
3. How many knights remain on the demesne? That is how many knights was the tenant-in-chief to supply from his own resources in order to fulfil the service quota or *servitium debitum*?

A number of barons confused the second and third questions by recording that the new enfeoffment had taken place on the demesne, and a few confused the old enfeoffment in 1135 with the service due. Disentangling such misunderstandings is relatively easy where the transcripts of the *cartae* in the Black Book and the Red Book of the Exchequer present the whole or most of the original text. In many cases, however, they simply include lists of fees under the formal headings of old enfeoffment, new enfeoffment and demesne, categories which may be misleading in view of the confusion revealed by some of the complete returns.

There is one further essential difficulty which cannot be circumvented. The *cartae* only reveal the service quota if it was directly stated or if it exceeded the sum of the old and new enfeoffment; in the latter case it can be calculated by simple addition of the old and new enfeoffment and service due on the demesne. Where there is no statement of the quota, and no genuine service recorded on the demesne, then the quota cannot be computed from the *cartae*. In some cases it can be established from the payments of scutage recorded in the Pipe Rolls of 1159, 1161, 1162 and 1165. But if that proves impossible then it is unlikely to be established at all, since later scutages were based not on the quota, but on the new or old enfeoffment. There are nearly forty tenancies-in-chief, numbering five knights' fees or more, where the sum of the old and new enfeoffments either exceeds, or coincides with, the quota

---

5 H. G. Richardson and G. O. Sayles, *The Governance of Medieval England*, Edinburgh 1963, 88-90.
6 In addition to Richardson and Sayles, see Frank Barlow, *William I and the Norman Conquest*, London 1965, 107-9; D. J. A. Matthew, *The Norman Conquest*, London 1966, 127-8.
7 Round, 257.
8 Round, 236-46; F. M. Stenton, *The First Century of English Feudalism*, 2nd edn, Oxford 1961, 137-9.

and where no service is stated to have lain on the demesne. They include the earl-doms of Arundel, Cornwall, Gloucester, Buckingham, Norfolk and Clare, and the great honours of Port, Belvoir, Wallingford and Eye.

In some of these cases it may be that the old or the total enfeoffment approxi-mates to or coincides with the quota.[9] There is also a handful of examples where later evidence seems to provide a hint of what the quota had been; for instance, in 1213 Earl Roger Bigod fined with King John to secure a reduction of service from 125¼ knights, a figure based on the old enfeoffment which was the usual basis of assessment for the Bigod fee, to sixty,[10] which is a typical figure for the larger honours established in the generation of the Norman Conquest. But all this is infer-ence, and in all that follows, at least as regards the analysis of quotas, almost all these baronies have been left out of account. The random service which they rendered does not disprove Round's hypothesis; nor does it give support to some alternative argument that quotas arose from the gradual accumulation of precedent. In these cases there is no evidence that quotas had ever been established; it is equally true that if they had, the information would not reveal them.

The remaining baronies, totalling some 150, may be categorised in two different ways. The first may be defined by the quota, which is represented either by a small number, up to five, or by multiples of fives and tens, or by some quite random num-ber. Now there is no need to found the decimal quotas in Round's *constabularia*. What matters is that such quotas must in general represent an arbitrary system of service. Precedents do not accumulate in fives and tens. Anglo-Saxon tenements of five hides certainly survived into the Norman period; some, a few, became knight's fees;[11] but no convincing argument has yet been produced to equate the decimally based quotas of the Norman period with the decimally arranged hides or the duo-decimally arranged carucates of the Anglo-Scandinavian kingdom.[12] There is no satisfactory escape from the conclusion that the decimal quotas were imposed. The random quotas in contrast could simply have grown. Indeed one of the objects of this paper is to show how they grew.

A second, more complex set of categories is concerned with the history of the tenancies-in-chief simply as property. Some baronies enjoyed a relatively smooth passage from the Conquest to the reign of Henry II, descending directly in the male line, undisturbed by political disaster or the fortunes of civil war, unaffected by the financial consequences of excessive enthusiasm for the Crusade, monastic endow-ment, lavish building, or the accumulation of estates. Some baronies had a more chequered history, broken by division among heiresses or the succession of a col-lateral, or a disputed claim sometimes coinciding with civil war. Some escheated to the Crown, temporarily or permanently, because of default of heirs or the treason of the tenants. Many baronies of the twelfth century were not at first tenancies-in-chief at all; they began as undertenancies of the great lordships of the Norman

9 The knights' fees reported from the honour of Eye in 1166 totalled 80, but there is nothing in the return to indicate that that was the *servitum debitum* (*Red Book*, 411).

10 *Pipe Roll 13 John*, 2.

11 Marjory Hollings, 'The Survival of the Five-Hide Unit in the Western Midlands', *EHR* lxiii, 1948, 453-87.

12 See the difficulties encountered by Hollings, 475-60 and by John, 158-9, and the comments thereon of J. O. Prestwich, 'Anglo-Norman Feudalism and the problem of continuity', *Past and Present* 26, 1963, 43-4. Compare the comment of Helena M. Chew, *The English Ecclesiastical Tenants-in-Chief and Knight Service*, Oxford 1932, 6-7 on F. W. Maitland, *Domesday Book and Beyond*, Cambridge 1897, 160.

period — Mortain, Bayeux, Montgomery, Lancaster — and emerged as holdings in chief only when the mesne lordship had disappeared through reversion to the Crown. Others were late creations, established long after the influences which had determined the initial pattern of enfeoffment had lost impetus. Others were Marcher lordships and hence had special, localised military functions. Yet others were reconstituted holdings, motley concoctions manufactured out of bits and pieces from other estates.

These categories have been distinguished more sharply than a close examination of individual estates might sometimes warrant. Nevertheless, artificial though they are, they established a point of great importance. The less disturbed the descent of an estate the more likely it is to have a decimal quota. The more difficult its descent, the less likely it is to have a decimal quota. The decimal quota goes with the normal, the random with the abnormal. This contrast is by no means obvious from a casual glance at the known *servitia*, for the decimal quotas come from baronies which illustrate almost the whole range of 'accidents' affecting the descent and homogeneity of feudal tenancies. It is only when approached through the history of the tenancies that it stands out sharply and clearly.

Much the largest single group of baronies with known quotas descended relatively undisturbed as tenancies-in-chief in the male line from the time of the Domesday Survey to the reign of Henry II. Of these, nearly thirty in all, the Vere barony of Hedingham paid scutage on thirty-one fees in 1162[13] and the Giffard barony of Elston (Wiltshire) apparently owed a quota of nine;[14] all the rest had decimal quotas.[15] Of the Domesday tenancies-in-chief with known quotas which descended unimpaired in the female line, a group of fifteen, only three had random quotas in 1166; the Peche barony of Great Bealings or Great Thurlow (Suffolk) returned twelve,[16] the barony of Aveley (Essex) seven and a half[17] and the Marmion barony of Tamworth probably twelve;[18] all the rest had decimal quotas.[19] Of the Domesday tenancies-in-chief with known quotas which descended unimpaired and without dispute through collaterals, a relatively small group of three, there was no exception to the general pattern.[20] Even where rebellion led to escheat, and the temporary or final dispossession of a family, an honour was still likely to return a decimal quota so long as it was not dismembered. Hence the Lacy honour of Pontefract was assessed

---

[13] *Pipe Roll 8 Henry II*, 71. Compare *Pipe Roll 14 Henry II*, 39, *Pipe Roll 6 Richard*, 37, *Pipe Roll 13 John*, 124. The total of fees returned in 1166 was 29 1/8 (*Red Book*, 352-3).

[14] *Pipe Roll 8 Henry II*, 14, *Red Book*, 245.

[15] Benington, Blankney, Cainhoe, Cavendish, Caxton, Crich, Eton, Hastings, Craon, Helion Bumpstead, Horsley, Kentwell, Norton, Pleshey, Poorstock, Rayne, Richard's Castle, Rothersthorpe, Stafford, Tarrington, Tattershall, Thoresway, Tutbury, Weedon, West Dean, Whitchurch, Wolverton, Wormegay.

For convenience of reference, here and throughout, I have used the classification of I. J. Sanders, *English Baronies: a study of their origin and descent 1086-1327*, Oxford 1960.

Limitation of space prevents me from including a full apparatus. I have restricted detailed references to particular cases or to supplementing information both on the descent of estates and military service which is summarised in Sanders.

[16] *Red Book*, 366-7.

[17] *Red Book*, 353; *Pipe Roll 14 Henry II*, 38.

[18] *Pipe Roll 11 Henry II*, 18. On the origins of the Marmions as lords of Tamworth see GEC, viii, 505-6. The descent of Tamworth probably also involved collateral succession.

[19] Blagdon, Brattelby, Chipping Warden, Dudley, Hockering, Hooton Paynel, Kempsford, Malton/Alnwick, Lewes, Nether Stowey, Okehampton, Trowbridge.

[20] Bywell, Castle Cary (?), Monmouth. But see also Tamworth in n.18 above. Okehampton also descended to collaterals as well as through heiresses. See GEC, iv, 308-9.

at sixty,[21] and so also were the Mowbray honour of Thirsk[22] and the great fee of Tickhill,[23] all of which underwent escheat in the century after the Conquest. Holderness, confiscated in turn by the Conqueror, by Rufus and by Henry I, nevertheless retained its integrity and rendered a service of twenty knights in 1168.[24] In all, more than twenty baronies out of a total of nearly thirty which escheated temporarily to the Crown, or which seem to have suffered some un-explained break in descent and yet retained their unity, returned a decimal quota on performed service equivalent to a decimal quota.[25] As a group they are less uniform than those which descended easily in the male line, but the decimal quota was nevertheless preponderant.

The main source of random quotas lay elsewhere. Most important of all in terms of numbers are those baronies of the late twelfth century, nearly fifty in all, which had emerged from undertenancies of the great lordships of the first Norman settle-ment. In many instances direct continuity between the initial undertenancy and the later barony can be demonstrated without much difficulty, both as regards the holding and its tenancy. The same is sometimes true of the service, and hence this, when it emerges as a 'baronial' quota in the relative light of day of the late twelfth century, reflects the policies of the early tenants-in-chief rather than of the Crown. The most obvious instance is that of the 'fees of Mortain' which were assessed by the Exchequer at two-thirds of a normal fee.[26] They cannot have been anything but the creation of Robert, Count of Mortain, or of his son, William. Many of them, indeed the majority, carried decimal quotas.[27] This is also true of some of the Shropshire baronies which were first established by Roger of Montgomery, or by his son Robert of Bellême.[28] In contrast, only a few of the Kentish baronies which originated in fiefs held of Odo, Bishop of Bayeux, returned a decimal quota: the Talbot/Mountchesney barony of Swanscombe, which owed thirty,[29] the baronies of Chilham and Patricksbourne, each of which owed fifteen[30] and the Arsic barony

---

21 For the breaks in the descent of Pontefract see W. E. Wightman, *The Lacy Family in England and Normandy*, Oxford 1966, 66-73. For the quota see *Red Book*, 421-4.

22 I take the 60 fees *de antiquo feodo* to stand for the *servitium* (*Red Book*, 420). On the descent of Thirsk and its associated lordships see *Charters of the honour of Mowbray*, ed. Diana E. Greenway, London 1972, xxi-xxiv.

23 *Pipe Roll 7 Henry II*, 38, *Pipe Roll 8 Henry II*, 34. On the descent of the honour see *The Cartulary of Blyth Priory*, ed. R. T. Timson, Thoroton Society, Record Ser. xxvii, xxviii, 1973, cxv-cxl.

24 For the confiscation and descent of the lordship see Barbara English, *The Lords of Holder-ness 1086-1260*, Oxford 1979, 6-16; for the *servitium*, see *Pipe Roll 14 Henry II*, 90, *Pipe Roll 18 Henry II*, 62.

25 Returning decimal quotas in 1166 or performing decimal service apparently equivalent to the quota: Barnstaple, Bourn, Bradninch, Cogges, Curry Malet (?), Great Weldon, Great Torring-ton, Holderness, Little Dunmow, Little Easton, Odell, Patricksbourne, Pontefract, Shelford, Southoe, Stansted Montfichet, Stanton le Vale, Thirsk, Tickhill, Totnes(?), Winterbourne St Martin. Apparently carrying non-decimal quotas: Berkhamstead, Cottingham, Haughley, Salwarpe, Lavendon. In the case of Haughley there may have been a quota of 50. The enfeoff-ment of 80 in the honour of Eye could possibly coincide with a quota.

26 *Red Book*, 232; Sir Paul Vinogradoff, *English Society in the eleventh century*, Oxford 1908, 52-4; C. Warren Hollister, *The Military Organisation of Norman England*, Oxford 1965, 44-6.

27 Cardinham (20 fees of Walter Hay, *Red Book*, 261), Chiselborough 10, Hatch Beauchamp 20, Odcombe 15. For further comment on the fee of the Surdeval family see below, pp. 96-7.

28 Castle Holgate probably 5 (*Red Book*, 275), Cause 5, Wem probably 5 (*Book of Fees*, 144).

29 *Red Book*, 195-6.

30 *Red Book*, 191-2, 197; and probably also Peverel of Dover (*Pipe Roll 33 Henry II*, 209).

of Cogges which owed ten.[31] The remaining quotas were either three, or a multiple of three, or some apparently quite random number.[32] In all these cases, what determined the pattern of enfeoffment initially is now largely lost to view, but the tendency of the pattern to vary from one honour to another is clear and beyond question: the obvious conclusion is that the Norman tenant-in-chief was himself responsible. It is not impossible, of course, that the service was adjusted when such an undertenancy became a tenancy-in-chief. But, if so, it is apparent that such an intrusion was insufficient to eradicate the characteristic features of the fees of Mortain, for example, and it is likely in general that neither William Rufus nor Henry I would want, or be in a position to re-order the service of tenants who sided with them against the great rebel lords. As a category, therefore, this group of baronies is of considerable interest. It reflects the remarkable loyalty of the undertenants to the Crown and the increasing security of tenure which their loyalty achieved.[33] It also suggests that these quotas at least were established at an early date: before Odo's final forfeiture of 1088 for the tenancies of his barony, before 1102 at the very latest for the baronies which stemmed from the honour of Roger of Montgomery and before 1104, in some cases probably earlier, for the fees of Mortain.[34]

This group of baronies is partly overlapped by another: the Marcher lordships. The records of the late twelfth and early thirteenth centuries reveal the existence along the northern and Welsh borders of estates graced with the title and status of baronies from which military service was *sui generis*, designed to meet the special circumstances of border warfare. The Northumbrian baronies were created in the main by Henry I; a few may have originated before 1100, either in grants from Rufus or as undertenancies of the Norman earldom of Northumbria.[35] Styford and Mitford had a quota of five; Bywell returned sometimes five, sometimes thirty;[36] the rest carried random quotas, all of them except the Vesci barony of Alnwick which returned twelve, of less than five.[37] The pattern is similar further west in Cumbria. Here all the early holdings, whether established by the first lord of Cumbria, Ranulf Meschin, or by Henry I, were held by the render of cornage; it was only gradually in the course of the twelfth century and in the reign of John that this was converted to knight-service, and then the quotas were small and random.[38] Some of the Welsh Marcher lordships likewise lay outside any formal pattern. At Wigmore, in the late thirteenth century, the Mortimers claimed to hold by the service of two knights in time of war in Wales and of one knight in time of war in England.[39] At Oswestry in 1166 the fitz Alans held by the service of ten knights *in exercitu et chevalcia* within the county of Shropshire and, 'as the old men testify' of five knights outside the county.[40]

---

[31] *Pipe Roll 7 Henry II*, 26.

[32] Allington probably 3 (*Red Book*, 197). Chatham either 12 or 14 (*Pipe Roll 11 Henry II*, 106, *Red Book*, 191), Folkestone probably 21 (*Red Book*, 615-16), Pont probably 12 (*Red Book*, 618), West Greenwich probably 24 (*Red Book*, 617). The above figures largely depend on the castle-guard owed at Dover. For Ros, in contrast, there is a firm statement of 7 (*Red Book*, 197).

[33] For further comment see J. C. Holt, 'Feudal Society and the Family in early medieval England; I. The Revolution of 1066', *TRHS* v, 32, 209-12.

[34] For further discussion of some of the tenancies of Mortain see below, p.103.

[35] William E. Kapelle, *The Norman Conquest of the North*, London 1979, 191-200.

[36] *Red Book*, 437-8; *Pipe Roll 8 Henry II*, 52, *Pipe Roll 14 Henry II*, 172, *Book of Fees*, 201.

[37] *Book of Fees*, 200-3. The figures here depend on the returns to the Inquest of 1212.

[38] J. C. Holt, *The Northerners*, Oxford 1961, 91-2; Kapelle, 212; *Book of Fees*, 197-9.

[39] *Cal. I.P.M.*, iv, 235.   [40] *Red Book*, 274.

Baronies which were originally under-tenancies and the Marcher lordships account for a very large proportion of the random quotas of service. The remainder come largely from baronies which escheated for a time to the Crown and from baronies which were seriously reconstructed. True, an escheated barony might retain a decimal quota if there were no serious delapidation. But any estate which did not descend in the direct line of adult heirs was to some degree at risk. Estates which underwent wardship or descended through heiresses or through collaterals, and even more those estates which escheated through default of heirs or treason, were vulnerable, a prey to litigation, to the greedy eye of powerful neighbours, most of all to the Crown's exercise of patronage. Consider the fate of the Domesday holding of the Picard, Arnulf de Hesdin, which Round touched on in his paper on the origins of the Stewarts.[41] Arnulf's sons died without heirs; one was probably hanged by Stephen at Shrewsbury in 1138; and the estates, centred on Wiltshire and Gloucestershire, were divided respectively between two daughters, Maud and Aveline. A quota, either for Maud's portion or the whole estate, was still recorded under Henry II; it was assessed at forty in 1165.[42] Even so, Maud's grandson, Pain of Montdoubleau, submitted a confused *carta* in 1166: seven fees of the honour had got into the hands of Geoffrey de Vere during the reign of Henry I; Earl Patrick of Salisbury had received twenty fees in marriage with Pain's aunt, and had also taken a further fee by war which was now in the hands of Alfred of Lincoln.[43] Indeed it would be quite impossible to construct a quota for this barony but for the assessment of 1165. For the other portion of the estate which Aveline took by marriage to the fitz Alans of Oswestry, there is no such saving evidence. In 1166 William fitz Alan returned a *carta* which is among the most insistent and idiosyncratic in distinguishing between the enfeoffment and the quota. Nevertheless, in accounting for his Wiltshire fee all he could do was to list knights fees, which totalled eight and a half, and then add: 'We are not certain what service is owed to the King from this holding which belonged to Arnulf de Hesdin'.[44] Yet a quota there must in all probability have been for the other division of Arnulf's Domesday holding still carried one. The obvious conclusion to be drawn from William's *carta* is that it was no longer possible to trace it. It is also noteworthy that William fitz Alan expected an estate which he defined by reference to its Domesday tenant, dead before the end of the eleventh century, to have carried one.

Other baronies present similar stories. William son of Reginald de Ballon's was but briefly reported in his *carta* in language still reflecting the pathos of the dispossessed:

William son of Reginald performs the service of one knight from his demesne. Hamelin de Ballon, his grandfather, was enfeoffed of the old feoffment to perform the aforesaid service. He has been deprived of Great Cheverell on the order of the lord king and of the honour of Abergavenny for which he owes service, if the lord king so pleases. He has no-one enfeoffed of the new enfeoffment.[45]

The estates of Roger of Berkeley were undergoing similar decomposition. Berkeley itself had just been lost to Robert fitz Harding. In his *carta* Roger reported two and a half fees of the old enfeoffment on which some of the service had been lost. He then added five fees and a number of hides from which further service had

---

[41] *Studies in Peerage and Family History*, London 1907, 116.
[42] *Pipe Roll 11 Henry II*, 74. [43] *Red Book*, 297-8.
[44] *Red Book*, 274. [45] *Red Book*, 281.

been lost; some of these were in dispute with Maurice son of Robert fitz Harding.[46] From this report the Exchequer plumped for a service of seven and a half fees in 1168 and subsequent assessments.[47] What it had been earlier it is impossible to say. Robert fitz Harding, in contrast, the new tenant with a clear commitment and a clean sheet, reported a quota of five for the honour of Berkeley in 1166.[48] The delapidated barony is one side of the coin; the reconstituted barony the other.

These two groups, especially the reconstituted baronies, are much the most illuminating of all. Up to a certain point it was possible for the Norman kings to act on a *tabula rasa*, to construct baronies from the lands of English tenants, from the royal demesne and from escheated estates of rebels, and to impose an artificial, decimal quota. After that point this became difficult if not impossible, for the escheats were occupied by enfeoffed knights owing specified amounts of service established by their dispossessed lords. The dividing line between the two, the point of balance, came in the reign of Rufus and Henry I, especially in the decade straddling the battle of Tinchebrai of 1106. This is well illustrated from the history of a number of Lincolnshire and Yorkshire baronies which were reaching their final form at this time. The Paynel fee, for example, was a conglomerate estate which included considerable additions to the lands which Ralph Paynell held at the time of Domesday Survey: in Lincolnshire, lands previously held by the Lacys which in 1086 had formed part of the barony of Odo of Bayeux, forfeited in 1088; and fees which Richard de Surdeval held of the honour of Robert, Count of Mortain.[49] Both these acquisitions probably came to Ralph by marriage.[50] Despite these diverse origins, and despite the complicated division of the barony among the Paynels it seems quite certain that the *servitium* came to the artificial total of forty-five in the 1160s: fifteen the responsibility of Robert de Gant;[51] fifteen the responsibility of William Paynel of Hooton Paynel;[52] and fifteen apparently already divided by 1124 between Hugh Paynel of West Rasen and Fulk Paynel of Drax.[53] How was such a total figure reached? It can scarcely be accepted as an accidental accumulation. It must therefore be that either the service due on the Paynel Domesday fief, plus the service on the new acquisitions, happened to come to forty-five, which seems too much of a coincidence; or the original service due on the 1086 holding was forty-five and the later additions carried no additional service, a process of augmentation which occurred in the case of some knights' fees, but at first sight seems most improbable in this case because of the extent of the additional tenancies; or the whole service of the Paynel fee was recast after the acquisition of the Lacy and Surdeval estates and their conversion to tenancies-in-chief following the forfeiture of Odo of Bayeux and the Counts of Mortain.

This last hypothesis requires us to accept a projection of the atmosphere of the Conquest into the period 1088-1106, with the King still constructing great fiefs and his leading subjects still ready to accept heavy feudal service. However, this can have

[46] *Red Book*, 292-3.
[47] *Pipe Roll 14 Henry II*, 123; *Pipe Roll 18 Henry II*, 121.
[48] He nevertheless reported that he was unable to obtain service from manors and fees still held by Roger of Berkeley (*Red Book*, 298).
[49] *Early Yorkshire Charters*, vols i-iii, ed. W. Farrer, Edinburgh 1914-16; vols iv-xii, ed. C. T. Clay, Yorkshire Archaeological Society, Record Ser., Extra Ser., 1935-65, vi, 56-62.
[50] *Early Yorkshire Charters*, vi, 4.
[51] *Early Yorkshire Charters*, vi, 33-4.
[52] *Early Yorkshire Charters*, vi, 41-2.
[53] *Early Yorkshire Charters*, vi, 8, 19.

been achieved only so long as there was the possibility of a clean sweep, only so long as the estates in question were not already in the possession of tenants holding by precise amounts of military service. If such tenants were firmly established then the perpetuation or establishment of an artificial quota would obviously be much more difficult. Compare the Paynel fee with the barony of Bourne which was granted by Henry I to Baldwin fitzGilbert de Clare within a decade or so of the point at which the Paynel barony was reaching its final form. Bourne included estates drawn from at least three Domesday fiefs, those of Oger the Breton, Godfrey of Cambrai and Baldwin the Fleming.[54] It could only have produced a conveniently round number of knights, if the lands had hitherto carried no service, or if the original service was now overridden, or if by coincidence the service came to a round figure. In fact it did not. The service of Bourne was $10^1/8$. That $^1/8$ does not simply represent a near miss at ten. $10^1/8$ is not only the service recorded in the 1166 return for the barony but also the service for which scutage was consistently charged thereafter.[55] In this instance assessment in round numbers was abandoned; instead the service was determined by the amount already due on the various fiefs which were thrown together to form the barony, plus any later enfeoffment. All this finds confirmation in the unusually diffuse and irregular *carta* which Hugh Wake submitted for his barony in 1166. Instead of accepting the usual distinction between old feoffment and new feoffment and service in demesne, he seems to have followed categories of his own: first the fees existing in the barony when it was created and secondly the subsequent feoffments of his predecessors, William de Rollos and Baldwin fitz Gilbert, and himself. The sum total was the service due. 'This is the service,' he submitted, 'whereby my predecessors in their day served King Henry I who gave them the lands and I owe you, as the lord who gave them to me, the service of my body when you wish to take it.'[56] This is quite different from the Paynel fee. Here the *servitium* is derived from the original and later constituents of a fief; there the *servitium* was apparently imposed on those constituents.

Neither the Paynel nor Bourne fees stand as isolated examples. On the side of Paynel there is also Trussebut. This barony consisted largely of the Domesday holding of Erneis de Burun. But Geoffrey fitz Pain, the tenant in the early twelfth century, held further lands in Beckering, Riby and elsewhere in Lincolnshire, some if not all of which were derived from the estates of Roger of Poitou forfeited in 1102.[57] The fee then was conglomerate in structure. Yet the *servitium* of the Trussebut fee was almost certainly 15 and if not that then 10.[58] Again the Brus fee comprised numerous lands in Yorkshire which were still the lands of the King in 1086, many more where Robert de Brus succeeded Robert Count of Mortain, many more still where Brus succeeded the Count's tenant, Richard de Surdeval, and also the small Domesday holding of William Taillebois in Lincolnshire:[59] once again a conglomerate structure, yet the service of the Brus fee was indubitably 15.[60] Other fees followed the pattern

54 *The Lincolnshire Domesday and the Lindsey Survey*, ed. C. W. Foster and T. Longley with intr. by F. M. Stenton, Lincoln Record Society xix, 1924, 162-4, 173, 196-7; *Facsimilies of early charters from Northamptonshire collections*, Northamptonshire Record Society iv, 1930, 19-20.
55 *Pipe Roll 14 Henry II*, 64; *Pipe Roll 2 Richard*, 90; *Pipe Roll 3 John*, 7, 9.
56 *Red Book*, 378-80.
57 *Early Yorkshire Charters*, x, 23-7.
58 *Pipe Roll 11 Henry II*, 50; *Pipe Roll 14 Henry II*, 90; *Early Yorkshire Charters*, x, 8.
59 *Early Yorkshire Charters*, ii, 16-19; *Lincolnshire Domesday*, 197, *Book of Fees*, 166.
60 *Pipe Roll 14 Henry II*, 90; *Red Book*, 434.

suggested by the example of Bourne. The Ros barony of Helmsley originated in the grants which Henry I made to Walter Espec, again from the forfeited estates of Robert Count of Mortain.[61] This was concurrent with the foundation of the Brus barony; indeed Robert Brus and Walter Espec were closely associated figures in the administration of the northern counties at this time. Yet while the Brus fee appears to have had an artificial *servitium*, the Ros fee certainly had not. The feoffment in 1166 was $5^{23}/24$ *de veteri* and $2^1/3$ *de novo*. Scutage was usually charged on $5^3/4$.[62] Nor was the Crown the only influence at work recasting the structure and service of tenancies-in-chief. The 1166 *carta* of the honour of Mowbray reveals yet another possible development. Here the knights of the honour presented the awkward number of 88 enfeoffed knights, but added that 60 were *de antiquo feodo* and that 28 had been added by Nigel d'Albini from the demesne.[63] Nigel acquired the barony in the reign of Henry I c.1109. But for the long memory of the knights of the honour we should not know what the original service had been or that the change of ownership had been accompanied by, or had led during Nigel's lifetime to, a considerable increase in the number of fiefs.

The consequences of forfeiture, accumulation and reconstitution were unpredictable. However, they contributed to many of the random *servitia* which appear in 1166. The honour of Miles of Gloucester, combining lands held in the previous generation by Walter of Gloucester and Bernard de Neufmarché, along with acquisitions from both Stephen and Matilda, returned 17 *de veteri* and $3^3/4$ *de novo* fees.[64] Cottingham, the remnant of the Stuteville estates seized after the capture of Robert de Stuteville before Tinchebrai and only restored to the family under Stephen, carried a quota of 8.[65] Marshwood, first established for the Mandevilles by Henry I, returned a quota of 11 plus some fractions of fees and one fee of Mortain.[66] In one important case the process whereby the random quota was achieved is clearly recounted. William d'Aubigny's *carta* runs as follows:[67]

This is the holding of William d'Aubigny, butler of the Lord King, of the gift of Henry [I] who gave him fifteen knights of the fee of Corbuchon. And later he gave him a fee of ten enfeoffed knights of the land of Roger Bigod with the daughter of Roger Bigod of his own hand. And later he gave him the service of Ralph son of Godric of twelve knights; and the service of Alfred de Athelburgo of two knights; and of Picot de Bavent of one knight; and the fee of Reiner *Sine Averio* of one knight; and the fee of William de Musterville of one knight.

These totalled 42 fees. William then outlined his father's and his own enfeoffments. As it happened the grand total, including the 10 fees held in mesne tenure of the Bigod fee, came to 75. That is a useful reminder that a decimal quota could sometimes be achieved at random, for this barony clearly originated in a succession of grants of enfeoffed knights. That could scarcely produce a decimal quota other than at second-hand or by accident.

61 *Early Yorkshire Charters*, x, 143-5.
62 *Red Book*, 432-3, 490; *Pipe Roll 6 Richard*, 163; *Pipe Roll 8 Richard*, 185.
63 *Red Book*, 420, 490.
64 David Walker, 'The "Honours" of the Earls of Hereford in the Twelfth Century', *Transactions of the Bristol and Gloucestershire Archaeological Society* lxxix, pt ii, 1960, 174-211; *Red Book*, 293-4.
65 *Early Yorkshire Charters*, ix, 5, 70-6; *Red Book*, 429.
66 *Red Book*, 219.   67 *Red Book*, 397-8.

Such an analysis of the relation between the quotas and the descent of baronies establishes one certain and central point: the decimal quotas were the more ancient. To dig down through the layers of evidence deposited by disturbed tenancies, to shift to one side the peculiar services of the Marcher baronies, to recognise that some layers in the record are the work not of the Crown but of tenants-in-chief, is to strip and lay bare the remains of a structure, much of it still surviving in 1166 in clear detail, in which quotas were based on a decimal system; that is on an artificial system, on an arbitrary system. Change was from the artificial to the random, not from the random to the artificial. Change occurred when something happened to disturb the normal descent of tenancies; and it was likely to occur only when that happened. If the hypothesis of gradual growth involves the view that there was some kind of debate about the service-quotas in the course of the twelfth century, either within baronies, or between barons and the Exchequer, a debate whereby in the end, through the accumulation of precedents, many quotas were settled on a decimal basis, then some evidence must be produced to establish a trend which seems to run clean against the demonstrable consequences of tenurial disturbance and quite contrary to the Exchequer's determination, from 1166 onwards, to move away from artificial quotas towards some more realistic assessment based on the number of knights enfeoffed. The obvious conclusion to be drawn from the evidence is that the quotas were mostly known and fixed by the end of the eleventh century at the latest.

There are other routes to the same end. The instances collected by Round of barons who in 1166 claimed tenure a conquestu[68] ought perhaps to be left out of the count; for these assertions are balanced on the other side by statements that quotas were unknown, or were confirmed only by reference to juries of knights of the fee; and in the last resort what these soldiers said either way is not certain evidence. But the division of their estates is. Between 1145 and the accession of Henry II the lands of William Paynel of Drax were divided between the two sons of his first marriage on the one hand, and his daughter by a second marriage and her husband, Robert de Gant, on the other. Despite opposed political allegiances, which led to conflicting grants by Stephen and Henry of Anjou, and despite the fact that one half was subsequently subdivided unequally between the two sons, each half returned the same quota of 15 in 1166.[69] Sometime before 1100 Joel of Totnes was established by William Rufus in the honour of Barnstaple. When Joel died before 1130 his lands descended to a childless son and then to two daughters married respectively to Henry de Tracy and Philip de Briouze. In 1165 their sons each accounted for the service of 25 knights.[70] William de Rames, lord of Rayne in Essex, who died before 1130, left his estates to two sons, Robert and Roger. Robert died without issue before 1142 and the lands were reunited, but when Roger died before 1159 they were split up once again. In 1159 each half of the original barony accounted for 9½ fees, but as each enjoyed a reduction of half a knight the quota of each half must have been 10, which one half had in fact returned in 1166.[71] Hardouin de l'Escalerie, the Domesday tenant of Caxton, Cambridgeshire, divided

---

68 Round, 295-6.
69 *Early Yorkshire Charters*, vi, 19, 32-3.
70 *Pipe Roll 31 Henry I*, 153; *Pipe Roll 11 Henry II*, 80.
71 J. H. Round, *Geoffrey de Mandeville*, London 1892, 399-404; *Pipe Roll 5 Henry II*, 5; *Liber Niger*, i, 240, which is superior to *Red Book*, 356-7.

his lands between two sons. In 1166 his grandsons each returned a quota of 15.[72] In all these cases only three explanations seem possible. One is that the quotas of the separate fragments of these baronies happened to coincide. A second is that equal quotas were imposed subsequently to the division of the baronies. A third is that an existing quota was divided when an estate was partitioned, and there can be little real doubt that this last is the most satisfactory explanation. If so, then the Paynel quota must have been settled before 1154; the Barnstaple quota, certainly, and the Rayne quota, probably, before 1130; and the quota for Caxton within a few years of the end of the eleventh century. The acquisition of the lands of heiresses provides evidence less strict in its implications, but pointing to the same conclusion. The *carta* which William de Roumare returned in 1166 made no distinction between the honour of Bolingbroke, the lands of the heiress Lucy, on the one hand, and the patrimony of the Roumare family in Hampshire and Wiltshire on the other. These estates had long been associated for Lucy's second husband, Roger son of Gerald de Roumare, who brought them together, died c.1097.[73] Yet in 1159 and in 1162 the Roumare patrimony was assessed separately at 20 fees.[74]

All this seems to lead on to a ready acceptance of Round's great thesis of 1891. But it is not quite so easy, for at the very core of Round's case there lay a simplification at once unacceptable and inaccurate. It is contained in his statement:

> I hold that ... [the tenant-in-chief's] military service was in no way derived or developed from that of the Anglo-Saxons, but was arbitrarily fixed by the king, from whom he received his fief, irrespectively both of its size and of all pre-existent arrangements.[75]

It is clear from the context that Round was not referring to any king, but to William the Conqueror. His statement was aimed in determined fashion against the notion of 'continuity', but it also conveyed the impression that the Conqueror, at one and the same time and in one and the same act, established both a barony and its service quota, and that impression has been a pervading influence ever since Round wrote. The difficulty, of course, is that although a quota might be established in a moment the honour to which it was attached could not. One of the curiosities of the historiography of Anglo-Norman feudal tenures is that this problem was recognised or at least dimly perceived long ago. Few apparently now read Stubbs' *Constitutional History* on the introduction of knight-service, yet the sixth edition of volume 1 appeared in 1897, six years after Round's famous paper, and Stubbs overcame his episcopal responsibilities and defied the onset of academic encrustation to the extent of making three amendments to the existing text. The first referred to Round's paper and accepted his distinction between the 'exaction of military service' and the 'carving out of the land into knights' fees'. The second amounted to a cautious acceptance of Round's main point:

> The early date at which the due service (debitum servitium) of feudal tenants appears as fixed goes a long way to prove that it was settled in each case at the time of the royal grant.

But that concession to the new view was followed immediately by a third amendment

---

[72] *Curia Regis Rolls*, v, 139-40; *Red Book*, 367-9.
[73] GEC, vii, 743-4.
[74] *Pipe Roll 5 Henry II*, 47; *Pipe Roll 8 Henry II*, 36.
[75] Round, 261.

to the old text — *'It must not however be assumed that this process was other than gradual.'*[76] Maitland also sank a probe into this central vagueness at the heart of Round's argument. He, like Stubbs, was convinced in principle, and agreed that 'We have good reason to believe that the Conqueror when he enfeoffed his followers with tracts of forfeited land defined the number of knights with which they were to supply him'. But he added a prescient footnote:

> This we regard as having been proved by Mr Round's convincing papers ... Sometimes when land came to the king by way of escheat and was granted out, new terms would be imposed on the new tenant; but, in the main, the settlement made in the Conqueror's day was permanent.[77]

That note, properly pursued, would have started several important questions to which Round's hypothesis gives rise. For the situation which he imagined, in which an honour created in its entirety was bestowed on a baron in return for a specified amount of military service, can have occurred but rarely. The land which the Conqueror used to endow his followers came to his disposal in successive lots: in 1066 the old royal estates of the Anglo-Danish royal house, the possessions of the family of Godwin and the lands of those who had fought and lost at Hastings; in 1069-71 the midland and northern estates of Earls Edwin and Morcar and their followers; in 1075 the East Anglian properties of Ralph Guader. Even along the southern English littoral, in Sussex, where the first baronies were established between 1067 and 1070, Mr Mason has convincingly demonstrated that there was extensive subsequent readjustment.[78] Further north the great baronies were built up even more obviously by miscellaneous acquisition. Count Alan of Brittany cannot have received many of his estates in Yorkshire before the fall of Earl Edwin in 1071; it is unlikely that he received the Lincolnshire and Norfolk estates of Ralph the Staller before the rebellion of Ralph Guader in 1075; the honour of Richmond was of composite origin.[79] So also was the honour of Chester. As recorded in Domesday it was a hotch-potch, made up of lands which had been held not only by English predecessors — Harold, Earl Siward, Earl Edwin, and Eadnoth the Staller, but also by Frenchmen — Walter of Dol, Ralph de Beaufou; and indeed in one estate Walter of Dol had been preceded in King William's time by Walter of Caen. As William Farrer noted, 'it is improbable that Earl Hugh obtained all the lands that he held in 1086 at the same time'.[80] Nor did the process of accretion end in 1086. It was continued after 1088 by the escheat and redistribution of the estates of Odo of Bayeux and of some of the lands of Robert, Count of Mortain; in 1095 by the escheat of the lands of Robert de Mowbray; and these were but the first of successive deprivations and redistributions continuing until after Tinchebrai. All this left its mark. The Bigod fee in Suffolk included manors which Roger Bigod had held of Odo of Bayeux at the time of Domesday.[81] So also did the Lacy fee in Yorkshire

---

76 W. Stubbs, *Constitutional History of England*, 6th edn, Oxford 1897, i, 284-5. Cf. 4th edn, 1883, i, 284-5.
77 F. Pollock and F. W. Maitland, *History of English Law*, Cambridge 1898, i, 258, 259 n.
78 J. F. A. Mason, *William the First and the Sussex Rapes*, Historical Association, Hastings and Bexhill Branch, 1966, 13-16.
79 *Early Yorkshire Charters*, iv, 2, 94-5, 117; *Lincolnshire Domesday*, 63-8; *Domesday Book*, ii, 144, 147, 148b; VCH *Norfolk*, ii, 10, 17; GEC, ix, 568-74; x, 783-4.
80 W. Farrer, *Honors and Knights' Fees*, ii, London 1924, 5-6.
81 VCH *Suffolk*, i, 392-3.

and other counties.[82] The Mowbray fee included over 100 carucates in Yorkshire, Lincolnshire and Nottinghamshire which Gilbert Tison had held at the time of the Survey.[83] Lands held by Erneis de Burun in 1086 are later found in the Mowbray, Trussebut and Paynel fees;[84] all three lordships had decimal quotas in 1166.

How were the decimal quotas established for such conglomerate baronies? There seem to be four obvious hypotheses. The first is that estates, as they were combined and redistributed during and after the Conqueror's reign, already carried service which happened in combination to produce decimal quotas. That demands excessive faith in coincidence; moreover, when such a process can be observed in the late twelfth century it clearly had the opposite effect of producing random quotas. A second possibility is that the quotas were not established until the end of the process of territorial agglomeration, and this too is unconvincing. There is clear evidence, too well known to require further discussion here, that William the Conqueror had imposed quotas on ecclesiastical tenants-in-chief by 1070/72.[85] Moreover, there appears to be no obvious explanation of why we should allow Rufus and Henry I to impose arbitrary quotas, but not William. Yet again the territorial flux did not cease at any one point in time. There was no occasion when Rufus or Henry could assume that all was at last ship-shape and ready for the establishment of the neat, artificial system much of which still survived in 1166. Finally, the process led increasingly away from decimal towards random quotas; this stage had already been reached when Henry I began to enfeof William d'Aubigny, his butler.[86]

This leaves two possibilities. One is that nothing was done to change the quota when new estates were added to an honour. The other is that the quota was recast, either in the Conqueror's time or later, as additions or changes were made to the estates of an honour, but recast within the system of arbitrary, decimal figures. These hypotheses are not mutually exclusive. Policy must have depended on the King's relations with a particular tenant-in-chief, perhaps on the size of a barony and its existing quota, on whether the accretion of estates came suddenly or as a more continuous trickle, on whether the lands were enfeoffed or not. Hence it is reasonable to assume in any particular case that the quota may have been either maintained or recast.

The evidence on this matter is very fragile. The first hint comes from two episcopal baronies: Thetford/Norwich, which has been carefully examined by Miss Dodwell;[87] and London, which was discussed by Round.[88] In each case the baronies carried decimal quotas, of forty and twenty respectively; and for Norwich the quota can be shown to have been established before 1111-13. In each case the Domesday Survey listed considerable acquisitions made by divers and sometimes devious means between 1066 and 1086, one at least of which in the case of Thetford/Norwich can scarcely have been held as a tenancy-in-chief before 1075.[89] In each case the acquisitions were listed separately from the other episcopal holdings. Those of Thetford/Norwich

---

[82] *Early Yorkshire Charters*, iii, 123, 125; Whiteman, 31-2.

[83] *Early Yorkshire Charters*, xii, 19-23.

[84] *Charters of the Honour of Mowbray*, xxii-xxiii; *Early Yorkshire Charters*, vi, 57; x, 23-4.

[85] The importance of the writ to Aethelwig, abbot of Evesham, which Round, 303-4, rightly emphasised, is not seriously diminished by Richardson and Sayles, 64-5.

[86] See above, p.98.

[87] Barbara Dodwell, 'The Honour of the Bishop of Thetford/Norwich in the late eleventh and early twelfth centuries', *Norfolk Archaeology* xxxiii, pt 2, 1963, 185-99.

[88] VCH *Essex*, i, 339.

[89] Eccles was recorded in Domesday Book as a tenancy held of Earl Ralph; Dodwell, 186.

are headed *terra de feudo*; those of London *feudum episcopi*.[90] Whatever is made of this, it seems clear that the Domesday commissioners were conscious of the problem created by territorial accretion, and in these cases they seem to be settling it by stating that the acquisitions were part of, not separate from, the service quota. An alternative, less acceptable hypothesis would be that these acquisitions *were* the whole fee, but this does not tally with the pattern of subenfeoffment. The gains were considerable. In the case of Thetford/Norwich Miss Dodwell noted that 'they radically altered the balance of properties . . .' and since they lay in south-east Norfolk 'cannot but have facilitated the later move [of the diocesan centre] to Norwich'.[91] But, whichever hypothesis is adopted, there is nothing definite to show whether territorial accretion affected the quota in these instances or not.

Some further light is shed on the problem by the break-up of the lands of Robert and William of Mortain, for their enfeoffments might still survive as small 'fiefs of Mortain' in the late twelfth century. It is certain that some of their estates in the north, which never seem to have been restored after Robert's rebellion of 1088, were incorporated in other baronies without any apparent effect on the quota or the rate at which fees were charged.[92] In many southern counties, in contrast, these accretions tended to figure as fees of Mortain additional to a separate quota charged at the full rate, and it may well be significant that charters to the monastery of Marmoutiers demonstrate that William of Mortain still had control of some of his Dorset estates in 1104-6.[93] The different treatment of the Mortain estates may then reflect the date at which they escheated: the earlier escheats being incorporated in existing or revised *servitia*; the later escheats leaving the characteristic increments to *servitia* in the form of fees of Mortain.

This problem is probably incapable of any general solution. However, it matters less than a more obvious point which Round's argument obscured. Whatever view is taken of the perpetuation or reconstruction of the original quotas it is clear that Rufus and Henry I still had the capacity to establish considerable territorial agglomerations, either *ab initio* or through reconstruction, which carried decimal quotas. The last obvious examples are the Redvers barony of Plympton which must have been established by 1107 and the Brus barony of Skelton which originated at about the same time. The first probably and the second certainly were assessed at fifteen knights.[94] Moreover, it seems probable that the main reason for moving away from such assessments toward random quotas is not to be found in any deliberate change in royal policy but in the fact that estates available for redistribution to deserving supporters were encumbered with sitting tenants. Now if this is so it necessarily reflects on the *rationale* behind the whole system. It has been argued with increasing force in the last two decades, most convincingly of all by J. O. Prestwich, that the Norman kings relied on long-term military service for pay and other rewards and that the service quotas were an unreal basis for the muster of an effective fighting

90 *Domesday Book*, ii, 11, 193.
91 Dodwell, 187.
92 *Early Yorkshire Charters*, ii, 11, 16, 19; vi, 57-8.
93 *Cal. Docs. France*, 1209.
94 On Skelton see above, p.97. The 15 owed from Plympton was the recognised service and apparently included Christchurch and the Isle of Wight, *Book of Fees*, 74. At the end of the twelfth century scutage was also paid on 45 fees which were not recognised, *Pipe Roll 6 Richard*, 171; *Pipe Roll 1 John*, 199. It may be that the break in the tenure of the honour in the reign of Stephen lies behind the discrepancy, GEC, iv, 309-12.

force.[95] What then was their function? It might easily be imagined that the Conqueror introduced the system simply because he could not conceive of land held freely on any other terms, and it is this escape-route which the present argument necessarily closes. For if, as Round argued, the quotas were established by the Conqueror, it follows that the quotas must have been reconsidered and confirmed or readjusted, and in some cases established *ab initio* by Rufus and Henry I. And few would be ready to accept the hazardous hypothesis that not just one, but all three, were acting in unquestioning, purposeless, absence of mind.

At this point the Pipe Rolls provide an invaluable cross-bearing. At first sight they seem to fit into a neat scheme in which tenants-in-chief either paid scutage or not, and in which the scutage was calculated *pro rata*, on the quota up to 1166 and thereafter on the old or new enfeoffment. The system of the Normans was apparently still in working order. But there is a difficulty, serious enough to wreck such a neat reconstruction. The implication of the Pipe Roll evidence is that men paid their full scutage, or none at all, and hence that they served with their full quota or not at all. Now there are many entries of quittances on only a part of the service due, but these are usually allocated to under-tenants, who had presumably given their service; indeed some of these under-tenants were themselves tenants-in-chief and can be shown on such occasions to have received quittances in that capacity also. But, these cases apart, the Pipe Rolls scarcely ever reflect the ordinary accidents of military organisation and campaigning. The record never mentions tenants-in-chief charged just on one or two fees, representing tenants who lay sick abed or had important engagements elsewhere. Now that must mean that the impression of the Pipe Rolls is unreal and unacceptable. And that in turn means that service in the field must have been acquitted not necessarily by the precise quota but by a reasonable turn-out acceptable to the King and his Marshal; and what that amounted to must have depended on many other factors: the interest of the tenant-in-chief in military matters, the period for which he and his men were ready to serve, and so on. In short, the earliest Pipe Rolls at first hide, but in fact imply, that feudal obligations were met as they were later, in the late twelfth and early thirteenth centuries, when service in the field was not precisely related to the quota or to the old or new enfeoffment.

If these arguments are correct they help to explain an unusual feature of the *cartae* of 1166. A considerable number of tenants-in-chief expressed ignorance of their quotas or reported some difficulty in establishing what it was: that they had had to enquire, for example, from juries or from the ancient men of the fee. In some cases these difficulties can be directly related to the history of the tenancy, but not in all. Earl Patrick of Salisbury reported his enfeoffment and quota of forty knights after enquiring from 'his honest and ancient men';[96] the 'ancient men' of the barony of Little Dunmow likewise informed Walter fitz Robert that his quota was fifty;[97] and Geoffrey de Mandeville consulted with the men of his fee to establish that his quota was sixty.[98] These statements, otherwise difficult to explain, fall into place if it is accepted that service need not have been performed at the level prescribed by the quota. For the common feature of the *cartae* quoted above is not that these

---

[95] J. O. Prestwich, 'War and Finance in the Anglo-Norman State', *TRHS*, 5th ser., 4, 19-43. Since feudal tenants often served for diverse forms of reward quite apart from their due service I have deliberately avoided the word 'mercenary'.
[96] *Red Book*, 239-40.
[97] *Red Book*, 348.
[98] *Red Book*, 347.

men had not served; if their absence from the earlier accounts from 1159 to 1165 can be taken at its face value, they had; but that they had not paid scutage. And if the payments of sums assessed against the knight's shield was the main practice keeping the quota alive, then it is probable that these men, and others who served regularly, had not been required to remember their quotas for a very long time. There need be no wonder that the memories of the ancients had to be searched.

Nothing has bedevilled the discussion of military service in Anglo-Norman England so much as the peculiar nature of the *cartae* and the related Pipe Roll evidence. In one aspect they are a living record, a revelation of a system of financial assessment still being hammered out and refined. In another aspect they are dead, an archaeological deposit left by the tenurial history of the previous century. The reality of the one should not be confused with the unreality of the other. The *cartae* were drawn up at a time when the pattern of enfeoffment was changing. Henry II continued old established quotas, but he never attempted to establish new baronies with large decimal quotas. Berkeley, with a quota of five, was an example from the first years of the reign and was probably determined by the fact that it had formed part of an already established barony. For the rest, Henry II was satisfied with small *servitia* which rarely exceeded one knight. Admittedly by this time, there was less opportunity for the Crown to redistribute property in the large-scale lavish manner of Rufus and Henry I. But Henry II made no obvious attempt to follow earlier practice, and the small baronies and quotas of his reign are better associated with the later enfeoffments of Richard and John. At least that was so in England. In Ireland it was different, for Henry II was to Ireland as the Conqueror had been to England, and Henry, who never established a single new barony with a quota of more than five in England, imposed a quota of a hundred on Leinster, sixty on Limerick, sixty on Cork and fifty on Meath.[99] At the same time the Norman aristocracy, heavily engaged in conspicuous expenditure on more comfortable stone-built castles in England, reverted to raising motte and baileys by the dozen in the newly subject land across the Irish sea.[100] The old system was dead, but could be resuscitated very rapidly if the circumstances required. And, as in England earlier, so in Ireland the system soon became unreal, overlain by scutage and paid service within not much more than a generation of the first settlement.

What then was the system? Is system even the right word? It seems to have amounted simply to this: that when, or perhaps before, the Conqueror in England or Henry II in Ireland granted large estates to their followers they wanted some guarantee that the recipients would contribute towards the successful maintenance of the conquest. Hence the imposition of quotas. Was it 'when' or 'before'? In Ireland it was 'when'; quota and endowment coincided. In England the quota could have come first, to be matched by territorial endowment as and when it became available. That is consistent with the indications that decimal quotas survived territorial accretion. There is no need to follow Round in imposing the practices of the twelfth century, in which specified service was performed for precisely defined tenure, on the crucial years immediately after the Conquest. The English quotas were large in comparison with those in Normandy, or in the case of Ireland in comparison with Henry II's enfeoffments in England, not because William was more powerful as king

99 J. Otway-Ruthven, 'Knight Service in Ireland', *Journal of the Royal Society of Antiquaries of Ireland*, lxxxix, 1959, 1-15.
100 H. G. Leask, *Irish Castles and Castellated Houses*, Dundalk 1964, 6-11: G. H. Orpen, *Ireland under the Normans*, Oxford 1911, i, 338-43; ii, map.

than as duke, or simply because Henry II wanted to bring the Norman adventurers in Ireland to heel, but because of the greater urgency in newly conquered lands. There is little to suggest that either William I or Henry II expected their vassals to stand in serried ranks of fives and tens to be told off by numbers from the right; military urgencies were likely to be too immediate for such strict accounting. At this preliminary stage too, as regards the conquest of England, there can have been little serious intention of using an army so raised for war on the continent; nor was there much possibility yet of exploiting the quotas as fiscal assessments. These emphases came in later generations, the result first of the wars among William's sons and then of the wide ranging interests of the Angevin kings. If the rigid accountancy of the late twelfth-century Exchequer is transferred from scutage to service and then from late twelfth-century service to late eleventh-century service the system looks woefully illogical and unsatisfactory. How could men serve both as tenants-in-chief and under-tenants, for example? And how could they fight in the field and defend their castles at one and the same time? But the system in its origin was real enough if viewed as a simple, rough-and-ready practical response to the hazards of conquest.

WAR AND FINANCE
IN THE
ANGLO-NORMAN STATE

By J. O. Prestwich, M.A.

READ 14 FEBRUARY 1953

'MONEY', wrote Richard FitzNeal in the preface to the Dialogue of the Exchequer, 'appears necessary not only in time of war but also in peace. In war it is poured out in fortifying castles, in soldiers' wages and in numerous other ways, depending on the nature of the persons paid, for the preservation of the kingdom.'[1] In time of peace, the Treasurer added, money was spent on charitable purposes; but it is clear from even the limited evidence of the Pipe Rolls of Henry II that expenditure on defence greatly exceeded that on charity.

This statement on the relations between war and finance made about 1179 raises the general problem which I wish to consider in this paper. Was Richard FitzNeal merely justifying himself and his book with a well-worn commonplace, appropriate for inclusion in a preface? Or was he calling attention to a change in the character of war and its demands upon revenue, a change which both reflected and conditioned a major transformation of society and government under Henry II and his sons?

Few historians are now prepared to commit themselves to clear, confident generalizations about this period; but it still appears to be the orthodox view that such a major transformation was taking place in these reigns. Indeed, it is precisely because the transition is so obvious to historians that they find generalization so difficult. Dr. A. L. Poole, writing of the late twelfth and early thirteenth centuries, has told us that 'already in this period a society based on tenures and services is beginning to pass into a society based on money, rents and taxes'; that 'the feudal levy had ceased to be an effective fighting force . . . It was superseded by an army chiefly composed of men paid to fight'; and that 'in the Pipe Roll

---

[1] *Dialogus de Scaccario*, ed. C. Johnson, p. 2.

of 1162 we have the earliest mention of *milites solidarii*.[1] More-over, the records of the reigns of Richard and John reveal the startling magnitude of the financial effort made in their wars, and allow us to trace in great detail the expenditure on paid troops, castles, foodstuffs, materials, weapons, ships and allies. The wages of soldiers, sailors and workmen absorbed a high proportion of this expenditure, though the payment of Richard's ransom and the subsidies to John's allies imposed a great additional strain. We can also follow in this period the ambitious attempts to organize a war economy: the direct taxation of incomes, price controls, import and export licences, the regulation and close supervision of certain industries, requisitioning, control of currency and credit and an expansion of borrowing, the organization of a national customs system, regulations against trading with the enemy and even the use of the black-list technique. It is only against this background of war finance that it is possible to understand the administrative expedients and the complicated interplay of ideas, interests and personalities which make up the political history of these years.

If we now look back to the first century following the Conquest, we find ourselves, it seems, in a very different and a much simpler world. Mr. Jolliffe, for example, when in an illuminating discussion of Magna Carta he turned back to this earlier period, observed that 'the military habit of the Normans and the comparative modesty of the wars of the first century after the Conquest enabled the monarchy to survive without putting any intolerable strain upon the generosity of its vassals'.[2] The demands of these modest wars were largely met by the system of knight-service and castle-guard, supplemented at need by the fyrd or militia. Round long ago taught us of the introduction of knight-service by the Conqueror. Vinogradoff spoke of the post-Conquest period as one in which 'society settled down on the basis of land tenure, and natural economy superseded for a time the "cash" system which had ruled the relations between the government of Canute or Edward the Confessor and its hired soldiers'.[3] Sir Frank Stenton, although warning us that the influ-

[1] *Obligations of Society in the XII and XIII centuries*, pp. 3–4, 52.
[2] J. E. A. Jolliffe, 'Magna Carta', *Schweizer Beiträge zur allgemeinen Geschichte*, x (1952), 95.
[3] *English Society in the Eleventh Century*, pp. 21–2.

ence of money on feudal relationships has often been underestimated, has emphasized that throughout this period 'the feudal
army remained the ultimate defence of the land', and that for over
sixty years after the Conquest the monarchy therefore 'depended
in the last resort on the loyalty of individual barons and the
knights of their honours'.[1] Professor Painter was even more cate-
gorical when he wrote of the Conqueror that 'even if there had
been sufficient resources to maintain an adequate hired army, the
fact that William and his men were deeply steeped in feudal
tradition would have made the adoption of such a military system
out of the question'.[2]

Vinogradoff's use of the phrase 'natural economy' in explaining
the system of unpaid service and restricted warfare suggests that
it may now be difficult to gain the support of economic historians
for this part of the argument. But the difficulty appears to be
verbal rather than substantial. Professor Postan, if I understand
his chronology correctly, suspects that there was an economic
slump at the time of the Conquest and holds that the late eleventh
and early twelfth centuries were a period 'in which landlords
happened to prefer fixed yield to fluctuating profits from rent and
cultivation' and explains this in terms of 'the general economic and
political insecurity of the age, which made it difficult for landlords to control production in their outlying estates, to exact
labour services and to move large quantities of agricultural produce across the country'.[3] Indeed, the interpretation of the evidence for military organization and the interpretation of the
evidence for economic trends support each other in an unusually
reassuring way. The first century of English feudalism when
military needs were largely met by unpaid service coincides with
a period when the volume of production and exchange was low.
The succeeding period when a bureaucratic state was able to
finance a war effort vastly greater in scale and different in kind
coincides with the rapid economic expansion of the thirteenth
century, defined as beginning in about 1180. Thus Richard Fitz-
Neal's remark about the pouring out of money in war, made just

[1] *The First Century of English Feudalism, 1066–1166*, pp. 50, n. 1, 214,
191.
[2] *Studies in the History of the English Feudal Barony*, p. 20.
[3] M. M. Postan, 'The Rise of a Money Economy', *Economic History
Review*, xiv (1944), 133, 129.

when England was passing into this new phase of development, shows that he had a sharp and even prophetic eye.

Nevertheless, it is worth while re-examining the evidence on war and finance in the Anglo-Norman period. One reason is that Richard FitzNeal himself intended his remark as a commonplace, made familiar and respectable by long practice. Writing of the period immediately following the Conquest, he says that coined money for the wages and rewards of knights was derived from pleas of the kingdom, from voluntary payments for privileges and from the urban communities; and he adds that this payment of troops persisted under the Conqueror's sons.[1] But it would be unwise to make much of this, for the Treasurer could make mistakes, and we have been warned that he is 'a very unsafe authority for anything that had happened more than a generation before his own time'.[2] Next there are the qualifications and silences of the scholars whom I have already quoted. Round was concerned with the introduction of knight-service, not with its enforcement; and he was only able to find three instances of the summoning of the feudal host.[3] Sir Frank Stenton similarly noticed the paucity of evidence for the actual performance of knight-service.[4] Both these scholars drew attention to the early evidence for the commutation of knight-service and castle-guard. And Vinogradoff pointed out that mercenaries were employed after the Norman Conquest, though he considered that the social importance of this expedient was not great.[5]

Another reason for re-examining the evidence is that, as Mr. McFarlane has pointed out, the origin of the practice of substituting paid for unpaid service remains untraced in detail; and indeed he left open the question whether even military service was ever wholly or mainly a matter of tenure.[6] Moreover, the orthodox account of the military organization of the Anglo-Norman state presents anyone seeking to understand the political history of the period with serious difficulties. If the field armies and garrisons were largely composed of tenants-in-chief and their knights performing their due service, then indeed the monarchy must have depended on the loyalty of these men. But

---

[1] *Dialogus*, p. 40. [2] V. H. Galbraith, *Studies in the Public Records*, p. 48.
[3] *Feudal England*, p. 305. [4] *Op. cit.*, pp. 168, 177. [5] *Op. cit.*, p. 15.
[6] K. B. McFarlane, 'Bastard Feudalism', *Bulletin of the Institute of Historical Research*, xx (1945), 162.

it is very difficult to find sufficiently strong grounds for this assumption in the accounts of the chroniclers. Nor is it easy to explain the outbreak and course of civil war in the reign of Stephen. Above all, it is peculiarly difficult to fit in what we know of financial policy and institutions under Rufus and Henry I. Perhaps the monkish writers grossly exaggerated the financial exactions of Rufus; and in any case money had to be found for granting the mortgage on Normandy and for the building of Westminster Hall. But for Henry I there is the solid and impressive evidence of the Pipe Roll of 1130.

Stubbs's calculation that the total sum accounted for in this year was £66,593, while in 1156 it was little over £22,000 and in 1189 only £48,781, cannot be taken as giving an accurate and complete account of the revenues of Henry I, Henry II and Richard I, but it at least indicates the formidable severity of Henry I's financial demands.[1] It is not easy to explain that severity on what has recently been called 'the feudal assumption that the Crown was an Anglo-Norman estate burdened with nothing but the Household expenses, the outlay of the great feasts, and an occasional foray into the Welsh border or Maine'.[2] For Henry I appears to have regulated and restricted the expenses of his household, and is even reported to have dropped the three great annual feasts held by the Conqueror and Rufus.[3] And if the troops for these occasional forays were largely provided by unpaid knight-service, only pointless avarice can have driven Henry to levy the great sums accounted for in 1130. Constitutional historians have unravelled the introduction and development of knight-service and thrown much light on the origins and structure of the Exchequer; but they have not shown how the working of these two institutions can be intelligibly related to each other in the Anglo-Norman period.

Yet to those who lived and wrote in this period these difficulties did not exist. William of Malmesbury commented on the Conqueror's avarice and added: 'But it will easily be excused, because it is impossible to rule a new kingdom without a great deal of

---

[1] *Gesta Regis Henrici Secundi* (R. S.), ii, pp. xciv, xcix.

[2] Jolliffe, *op. cit.*, p. 95.

[3] *Gesta Regum* (R. S.), ii. 335, 483, 487. Walter Map, *De Nugis Curialium* (ed. M. R. James), p. 219, refers to Henry's written regulations, and these survive in the *Constitutio Domus Regis* of *c*. 1136 (ed. C. Johnson in *Dialogus de Scaccario*).

money.' The Conqueror, he continued, 'for fear of his enemies, cheated his territories of money in order that with it he might either delay or even repel their attacks . . . and this shameful evil still endures and daily increases, vills and churches being subjected to payments'.[1] How then did the Conqueror spend this money? Largely, it seems, on paying and rewarding his troops. It was the Conqueror's generosity which attracted so many foreign knights to the cross-Channel enterprise.[2] A little later, probably in 1067, the Conqueror rebuked William FitzOsbern for wasting treasure by excessive expenditure on knights.[3] And in 1068 he called together his mercenary knights, *solidarios milites*, paid them liberally and allowed them to return across the Channel.[4] But they were required again for the winter campaign of 1069–70. William spent Christmas at York, completed the harrying of the north in January, and then crossed the Peak country to put down the Welsh and the men of Cheshire, Staffordshire and Derbyshire. During this arduous march the troops drawn from Anjou, Brittany and Maine sought to be released; but William held his forces together, and when he reached Salisbury he was able to reward his knights liberally.[5] This was probably late in March, for William went on to spend Easter, which fell on 4 April, at Winchester.

From what source were the knights rewarded? It can hardly be a coincidence that in mid-February the Conqueror had, according to the Worcester chronicler, ordered a search of all the monasteries of England and had transferred to his own treasury the money which the wealthier Englishmen had deposited in the monasteries. Indeed, the plan had been suggested by William FitzOsbern, notoriously solicitous for the financial interests of the knights.[6] It is interesting to notice that the Easter council of 1070 which the Conqueror attended was presided over by Bishop Ermenfrid; for this same Ermenfrid held a Norman council later in the year

[1] *Gesta Regum*, ii. 335–6.
[2] William of Poitiers, *Gesta Willelmi* (ed. J. A. Giles), p. 146.
[3] William of Malmesbury, *op. cit.*, ii. 314.
[4] Ordericus Vitalis, *Historia Ecclesiastica* (ed. Le Prevost), ii. 187.
[5] *Ibid.*, ii. 196–9.
[6] Florence of Worcester (ed. Thorpe), ii. 4–5. For other evidence of the seizure of treasure in the monasteries see *Annales de Wintonia* in *Annales Monastici* (R. S.), ii. 29, and *Historia Monasterii de Abingdon* (R. S.), i. 486, 493–4.

which ordered the restitution of goods pillaged from churches. Moreover, the penitential code drawn up in this council for all ranks of the army which had achieved the conquest makes it plain that that army was not regarded as being purely feudal in composition. It distinguishes between those whom William had armed on his own orders, those armed not on his orders, those who owed him service as a matter of duty and those who fought for hire.[1]

But the Conquest was the result of an exceptional military effort, achieved, it may be thought, by forces raised and financed in exceptional ways. During the first difficult and dangerous years tenants-in-chief found it necessary to keep their knights together and to pay them; but as conditions became more settled and secure these stipendiary knights were dispersed and quartered out on lands which they held in the familiar way. We have accounts of this process at Abingdon and Ely, for example.[2] And we know from a letter of Lanfranc that Ralph Guader's followers in the rebellion of 1075 were composed partly of Bretons who held lands in England, partly of landless men who served for pay.[3] The Conqueror's own son, Robert Curthose, complained that he was being treated as just such a landless knight when he told his father: 'I do not want to be always your mercenary. Sometime I want to have something of my own, so that I may give proper pay to my followers.'[4] And when the Conqueror put down the subsequent rebellion of Robert and his followers, he confiscated their lands and, with characteristic economy, applied the rents to the pay of the mercenaries he had employed in the campaign.[5] Again it was the exceptional emergency of threatened invasion in 1085 which led William to bring over from France the mercenary force which so impressed contemporaries by its size.[6] It is also hard to deny the exceptional character of the

[1] Wilkins, *Concilia*, i. 366. Sir Frank Stenton called attention to the interest of this document in *Anglo-Saxon England*, pp. 653–4.

[2] *Historia Monasterii de Abingdon*, ii. 3; *Liber Eliensis*, ed. D. J. Stewart, p. 275.

[3] Epistola xxxv (Migne, *Patrologia Latina*, cl. 534): 'Qui vero Rodulpho traditori, et sociis suis sine terra pro solidis servierunt.'

[4] Ordericus Vitalis, ii. 378.   [5] *Ibid.*, ii. 297.

[6] Florence of Worcester, ii. 18; William of Malmesbury, *op. cit.*, ii. 320; *Historia Monasterii de Abingdon*, ii. 11. Cf. Stenton, *First Century of English Feudalism*, pp. 149–50: 'In a great emergency the knight-service due to the king from his tenants in chief was obviously unequal to the defence of the land.'

Domesday *descriptio* and the Salisbury assembly of 1086, whatever may have been the purpose of the one and the exact composition of the other.[1] During the twenty years which followed
Hastings there were exceptional reasons why the Conqueror and
his tenants-in-chief should employ paid knights and exceptional
proceeds from loot and extortion to finance such practices. It is
therefore necessary to review the evidence for the succeeding
twenty years, from the making of the Domesday survey to the
battle of Tinchebrai.

William of Malmesbury has a revealing account of Rufus's
measures.

> At the very outset of his reign, fearing disorders, he had
> assembled knights, denying them nothing and promising more
> for the future. And so because he had energetically emptied his
> father's treasuries and limited revenues were left, his substance
> fell short; but he continued to be extravagant, for this had
> become second nature to him. He was a man who did not
> know how to beat down the price of anything or to get proper
> value in his dealings. Sellers sold to him at their own prices
> and knights fixed their own rate of pay.[2]

There was then a sellers' market for mercenaries in England.
Meanwhile Duke Robert was engaged in similar negotiations to
raise troops in Normandy. When his own treasures were exhausted, he raised more by selling territory to Henry.[3] The

---

[1] In recent discussions of the purpose of the Domesday Inquest the significance of *descriptio*, the contemporary and official term for the undertaking,
has not been emphasized. In Gregory of Tours and in official documents
of the Merovingian and Carolingian periods *descriptio* is used as the term
for assessment and enrolment for public taxation. Cf. Gregory of Tours,
Histoira Francorum, vi. 28: 'post congregatos de iniquis descriptionibus
thesauros', echoed by Robert of Hereford at the end of his note on the
Domesday *descriptio*: 'Et vexata est terra multis cladibus ex congregatione
regalis pecuniae procedentibus.' For other evidence see *Thesaurus Linguae
Latinae*, v. 665, and Dopsch, *Economic and Social Foundations of European
Civilization*, pp. 292, 377. *Descriptio* was also used to refer to the collection
of taxes. Cf. the charter of Adela, countess of Chartres, of 1109 cited by
Ducange, *s.v.* 'descriptio': 'Descriptionem pecuniae, quae consuetudinarie
tallia nominatur . . . fieri praeceperam.' Ralph of Diceto has an interesting
account of the *descriptio generalis* carried out by the *regii exactores* of Louis
VII of France in order to supply his army in 1173 (*Opera Historica*, R. S., i.
372).

[2] *Op. cit.*, ii. 368.   [3] *Ibid.*, ii. 468; Ordericus Vitalis, iii. 266–7.

financial power to raise paid troops was not even a monopoly of princes. In the autumn of 1090 the leading citizen of Rouen, Conan, arranged to hand over the city to Rufus and, we are told by Orderic Vitalis, employed his own great wealth to raise a considerable body of troops for use against Duke Robert.[1]

But it was Rufus's war expenditure which astonished and dismayed the chroniclers. In 1094 he is described as raising mercenaries on all sides in Normandy and showering gold, silver and lands on those whom he detached from Robert.[2] In 1095 he sent his brother Henry into Normandy with ample funds; and in the campaigns of 1097 and 1098 he spent lavishly on troops drawn from France, Burgundy, Brittany and Flanders, and on subsidies to Robert of Bellême.[3] Suger, a practical statesman with his own experience of the problems and methods of war finance, described Rufus in striking terms as 'that wealthy man, a pourer out of English treasures and a wonderful merchant and paymaster of knights (*mirabilisque militum mercator et solidator*)'.[4] It is revealing that just as William of Malmesbury used the words *commercium* and *mercimonium*, so Suger applied the term *mercator* to Rufus. For war was a trade and troops, castles and allies its merchandise.

The cost of war and policy was not limited to the payment of troops. 10,000 marks had to be raised when Robert pawned Normandy in 1096. Much, too, went on the construction and repair of castles; for, as Rufus reminded Hélie de la Flèche, masons and stone-cutters were anxious for monetary gain.[5] There was, too, a lively traffic in ransoms. Orderic explains Rufus's relative lack of success in the campaigns of 1097–8 by the fact that the French were stimulated by their handsome gains from ransoms.[6] According to Suger, the balance of payments on this account was wholly in favour of the French; for Rufus's knights when captured were so anxious for their wages that they speedily ransomed themselves, while the impecunious French captives suffered long imprisonment and were released only on condition

[1] Ordericus Vitalis, iii. 352.

[2] Florence of Worcester, ii. 34.

[3] Henry of Huntingdon, *Historia Anglorum* (R. S.), p. 218; Ordericus Vitalis, iv. 40, 45.

[4] Suger, *Vie de Louis VI le Gros*, ed. H. Waquet, p. 8.

[5] Ordericus Vitalis, iv. 38.

[6] *Ibid.*, iv. 21–4: 'quorum redemptionibus opimis egentes Franci ad dimicandum animati sunt'.

of doing homage to Rufus and swearing to fight against their own kingdom and king.[1]

Rufus's only mourners may have been the troops whom he had paid so well and the loose women, uncharitably linked with the mercenaries by the chroniclers.[2] But the mercenaries were not thrown into unemployment on Rufus's death, and there are indications that they were acquiring a recognized professional pride and standing. In the rebellion of 1102, Robert of Bellême handed over the castle and town of Bridgnorth to three of his captains, placing under them 80 mercenary knights. Henry I besieged Bridgnorth, detached the rebels' Welsh allies by bribes and promises, and then threatened that unless the garrison surrendered within three days, he would hang every man whom he took. The three captains and the burgesses agreed to surrender and, when the mercenaries refused to collaborate, cooped them up in a corner of the castle and admitted the royal forces. 'Then', says Orderic,

> the king, because the mercenaries had kept faith with their prince, as was proper, decreed that they should depart freely with their arms and horses. When the mercenaries came out through the crowds of besieging forces, they publicly lamented and bewailed the fact that they had been tricked by the fraud of the burgesses and captains; and before the whole army they laid bare the trickery of their associates, lest what had happened to them should bring other mercenaries into discredit.[3]

There are other examples which suggest that at this time the mercenaries' standard of loyalty to their paymasters compared favourably with that of vassals to their lords.[4] Valuable evidence of the value attached to mercenaries and of the numbers required is afforded in the remarkable Treaty of Dover of 10 March 1101. By this treaty Count Robert of Flanders agreed to make 1,000 knights available to Henry in England against invasion or rebellion, to produce 1,000 knights in Normandy or 500 knights

---

[1] Suger, *op. cit.*, p. 10: 'Anglie captos ad redempcionem celerem militaris stipendii acceleravit anxietas.'

[2] Ordericus Vitalis, iv. 90. Cf. William of Malmesbury, *op. cit.*, ii. 379.

[3] Ordericus Vitalis, iv. 173–5.

[4] E.g. the conduct of the captains of the garrison at Le Mans after the death of Rufus (Ordericus Vitalis, iv. 99–102).

in Maine.[1] In return, Count Robert was to receive an annual pension of £500. It is significant that at a time when the total *servitium debitum* of England did not produce more than 5,000 knights, Henry should have been arranging for the service of 1,000 knights from one external source alone. For the value of the *servitium debitum* was reduced not merely by the practical difficulties of mobilizing it for a campaign of any duration in the field and not merely by the rebellion of individual barons. It was reduced above all by the political concern of many barons who did follow the king with the consequences to themselves of a decisive royal victory.[2]

That baronial leaders understood the ease with which cash could be converted into military power is illustrated by an incident which occurred on 2 August 1100. On that day, directly after the death of Rufus, Henry rode hard for Winchester, conveniently close, and demanded the keys of the treasury. He was there confronted by another member of the hunting party, William of Breteuil, who had spurred on his horse even faster, and who put forward the claims of Duke Robert to the succession.[3] Who was William of Breteuil? Not, as historians have sometimes supposed, the treasurer[4]: he was the son of William FitzOsbern and brother of Roger, earl of Hereford, who had rebelled in 1075. William of Breteuil had joined Robert of Bellême and Robert Mowbray in the ineffectual demonstration of Robert Curthose against the Conqueror, had fought for Duke Robert in 1088 and had ransomed himself on three occasions for a total sum of £7,000.[5]

[1] The best text of this treaty is that printed by F. Vercauteren, *Actes des comtes de Flandre, 1071–1128*, no. 30. Although this is the first such treaty of which the text survives, William of Malmesbury suggests that similar arrangements had been made by the Conqueror and renewed by Rufus. See the discussion by Bruce D. Lyon in *English Historical Review*, lxvi (1951), 178–9.

[2] For attempts of baronial followers of the king to mitigate the consequences of a royal victory, or even to prevent such a victory, see Ordericus Vitalis, iii. 274–8 (1088) and iv. 174 (1102); *Gesta Stephani* in *Chronicles of the reign of Stephen*, etc. (R. S.), iii. 27–8 (1136), 42 (1138); John of Hexham, *Historia*, in Symeon of Durham (R. S.), ii. 291 (1138); Henry of Huntingdon, *op. cit.*, p. 287 (1153).

[3] Ordericus Vitalis, iv. 87–8.

[4] H. W. C. Davis, *England under the Normans and Angevins* (10th ed.), p. 118, described William of Breteuil as the treasurer, and was followe by A. L. Poole, *From Domesday Book to Magna Carta*, p. 115.

[5] Ordericus Vitalis, ii. 380, iii. 296, 336, 348, 413.

William of Breteuil's intervention of 2 August was the act not of
an official concerned for the due observance of legal formalities
but of a baron who understood that the treasure at Winchester
could be converted into military force for the mastery of England
and the recovery of Normandy. In the battle of Tinchebrai which
allowed Henry to recover control of Normandy, the role of the
hired contingents from Brittany and Maine was decisive.[1]

The heavy and sustained war expenditure of these years
between the Domesday survey and Tinchebrai was met in part
by developments in judicial and financial organization and in part
by irregular exactions which set up mounting political strains. Mr.
Southern has shown that the apparently undiscriminating abuse
heaped on Flambard by the chroniclers expresses not merely their
resentment of the spoliation of the church but also their recognition of specific administrative developments and a general plan.[2]
On one point William of Malmesbury has not received full
justice. His comment on Flambard that, as translated by Stubbs,
'whenever a royal edict went forth taxing England at a certain
sum, it was his custom to double it' reads like a loose generalization which cannot stand critical examination.[3] But William of
Malmesbury's own language makes it probable that he was
referring to the geld and not to all forms of taxation; and in 1096
the rate of geld was indeed double the normal rate. Moreover, if
the knight-service of the abbey of Ely was raised from forty to
eighty knights at this period there would be further ground for
the charge of doubling.[4] And perhaps too much has been made of
the fact that the word *scaccarium* does not appear in English
records before the reign of Henry I. Rufus's writ of 1095 ordering
the famous Worcester relief contains the clause *sicut per barones
meos disposui*,[5] and it seems probable that this refers to the central
board soon to be addressed as *barones mei de scaccario*.[6] But
despite the substantial continuity of men and methods in the
reigns of Rufus and Henry I, temporary concessions had to be

[1] Ordericus Vitalis, iv. 229–30; Henry of Huntingdon, *op. cit.*, p. 235.
[2] R. W. Southern, 'Ranulf Flambard and early Anglo-Norman administration', *Trans. R. Hist. S.*, 4th ser., xvi.
[3] *Ibid.*, p. 97.   [4] *Liber Eliensis*, ed. D. J. Stewart, p. 276.
[5] J. H. Round, *Feudal England*, p. 309.
[6] E.g. in the writ of Henry I cited by R. L. Poole, *The Exchequer of the
Twelfth Century*, p. 39, n. 4. A. L. Poole (*op. cit.*, p. 416) has called attention
to an earlier mention of the barons of the exchequer in 1110.

made in 1100. Flambard went to the Tower and lucrative practices were renounced in the coronation charter. How then did
Henry I finance the campaigns of the next few years? There are
no records to answer this question; but it is interesting that Robert
of Meulan advised Henry at this juncture to live on capital and
promises, and to promise even London or York if necessary.[1] For
it was after making similar concessions that Richard I lived
temporarily on capital and is reported to have said that he would
sell London itself if he could find a purchaser.[2]

After Tinchebrai it was both possible and expedient to reduce
the scale of war expenditure. William of Malmesbury said justly of
Henry that 'he preferred to fight with policy rather than with the
sword: he triumphed, if he could, without spilling blood; if he
could not, he spilt as little as possible'.[3] So successful was this
policy that whereas Rufus was mourned by the knights to whom
he had given full employment and high wages, Henry's peace was
hated by the knights of England, reduced thereby to a slender
diet.[4] Much of Henry's policy consisted in the skilful use of the
orthodox techniques of diplomacy. In addition he employed the
weapon of economic pressure. William of Malmesbury explains
that Henry's relations with Murchertach, the High King of
Ireland, were normally good, but that on one occasion Murchertach took an independent and insolent line. 'But soon', the
historian went on, 'he was brought to reason by the embargo declared on shipping and trade. For what would Ireland be worth
if goods were not shipped to it from England?'[5] Fortunately there
is a scrap of record evidence to support this statement, for the
Pipe Roll of 1130 shows that the burgesses of Gloucester rated
Henry's influence in Ireland sufficiently highly to justify their
offering him thirty marks for the recovery of money stolen from
them in Ireland.[6] And when the pretender to the English throne
was invested in 1127 with the county of Flanders, already
importing wool from England, the embargo on trade drove the
citizens of Bruges to rise against their count.[7] Another ingenious

[1] Ordericus Vitalis, iv. 112.
[2] Richard of Devizes in *Chronicles of the reign of Stephen*, etc., iii. 388.
[3] William of Malmesbury, *op. cit.*, ii. 488.   [4] *Ibid.*, ii. 540.
[5] *Ibid.*, ii. 484–5.   [6] *Pipe Roll 31 Henry I*, p. 77.
[7] Galbert of Bruges, *Histoire du meurtre de Charles le Bon*, ed. Pirenne,
p. 152.

measure was the planting of a Flemish settlement in Pembroke-
shire shortly after the Tinchebrai campaign, for Henry thereby
freed himself of a potential source of disorder in England and
provided himself with a method of restraining the Welsh less
dangerous than that of a marcher lordship.[1]

By these methods defence expenditure was reduced but not
abolished. The general comments of chroniclers show that, in their
view, Henry continued to employ mercenary troops as a regular
practice. William of Malmesbury tells us that Henry had been
familiar from his youth with the readiness of the Bretons to serve
for foreign pay, and that he, 'well aware of these characteristics,
spent much on the Bretons whenever he needed mercenary
knights, borrowing the faith of that faithless people with his
coins'.[2] Robert of Torigni, a well-placed observer, emphasizes
that even in the relative tranquillity of his last ten years Henry's
wealth allowed him to defend his frontiers with large forces of
knights whom he paid well and rewarded liberally.[3] Henry
remembered these mercenaries on his deathbed, ordering Robert,
earl of Gloucester, to pay them their wages and rewards from the
treasury at Falaise, recently replenished from England.[4] The use
of mercenaries was indeed a commonplace to the writers of this
generation. Orderic Vitalis described the monks who gained promotion as abbots by currying favour with lay authorities as
stipendiarii non monachi[5]; and Lawrence of Durham, explaining in
the preface to one of his poems that the poet, like other men,
required incentives, wrote of the farmer spurred on by the prospect of harvest, the pedlar by the motive of gain and the soldier
by thinking of his wages.[6]

[1] William of Malmesbury, *op. cit.*, ii. 477: 'ut et regnum defaeceret, et
hostium brutam temeritatem retunderet'.

[2] *Ibid.*, ii. 478.

[3] *Gesta Normannorum Ducum*, ed. J. Marx, p. 296.

[4] Ordericus Vitalis, v. 50. Robert of Torigni (*Chronicles of the reign of
Stephen*, etc., iv. 129) adds the information that Earl Robert removed the
bulk of this treasure, recently brought over from England.

[5] Ordericus Vitalis, ii. 225, where this phrase occurs in an elaborate comparison beginning 'Sicut Tironibus suae a principibus erogabantur stipendia
militiae, sic quibusdam coronatis pro famulatu suo dabantur a laicis episco-
patus et abbatiae . . .'

[6] Lawrence of Durham (Surtees Society, vol. lxx), p. 62. Cf. the provision
for 'conducticii uel solidarii uero uel stipendiarii' in *Leges Henrici Primi*
(Liebermann, *Die Gesetze der Angelsachsen*, i. 554).

On one of Henry's later campaigns we have information which, though fragmentary, is of particular interest when assembled. In the autumn of 1123 a powerful group of Norman barons, headed by Waleran of Meulan and Amaury de Montfort, planned rebellion in the interests of William Clito. The threat was the more formidable since it was backed by the resources of Fulk of Anjou and Louis of France. Against the rebels Henry, always nervous of treachery, employed mercenaries, drawn largely from Brittany: indeed, in this campaign he is said to have feared the treachery of his own men more than external attacks.[1] Henry's siege of Pontaudemer alone consumed six or seven weeks, though when it fell his Breton mercenaries were richly rewarded by the abundant loot.[2] On 25 March 1124 a group of the rebel leaders, including Waleran, rashly confident in themselves as the flower of the knighthood of Normandy and France, were captured by a superior force of Henry's mercenaries.[3] After this, resistance in Normandy quickly collapsed. In the summer of 1124 Henry planned a decisive stroke against Louis of France by persuading the emperor Henry V, his son-in-law and ally, to march on Rheims. Nothing more was achieved than a useful diversion of the French forces away from the Norman border, for the imperial army was too weak to risk moving beyond Metz. Henry I gave his son-in-law the characteristic advice to levy a tax.[4] He had already been applying that remedy in England. Because of the Norman rebellion heavy exactions were laid upon the people in England.[5] Two factors made these exactions the heavier to bear: a bad harvest, resulting in a famine, and a debasement of the currency which pushed prices still higher.[6] Against this background of unusual distress and heavy taxation it becomes possible to understand why the Anglo-Saxon chronicle singled out for particular mention the visitation of Ralph Bassett and his hanging of 'so many thieves as never were before' in Leicestershire in November 1124.

It also becomes possible to understand a little more clearly Henry's action in ordering the savage punishment of the English

[1] Symeon of Durham, ii. 274.   [2] *Ibid.*
[3] Ordericus Vitalis, iv. 456–8.
[4] Otto of Freising, *Chronicon*, vii. 16.
[5] Symeon of Durham, ii. 274–5.
[6] *Anglo-Saxon Chronicle*, a. 1124; Symeon of Durham, ii. 275.

moneyers, carried out under Roger of Salisbury at Christmas
1124. The English writers describe this as simply a punishment
of the moneyers who had issued coins below the proper standard
of fineness.[1] But Robert of Torigni gives a more detailed account.
During the Norman rebellion the English moneyers issued coins
of which scarcely a third was silver, the rest being tin. When
Henry's knights in Normandy received their wages in this currency and discovered that they could buy nothing with it, they
complained to the king; and it was for this reason that Henry
issued his savage orders to Roger of Salisbury.[2] The passage has
several points of interest. It supplies further evidence that the
continental campaigns were financed with English treasure; it
demonstrates the pressure which the mercenaries could bring to
bear on the king; and it illustrates the familiar technique of currency debasement in war finance. It is possibly significant that it
was in 1108, shortly after the Tinchebrai campaign, that Henry
found it necessary to take action against the clipping of the currency.[3] But a closer parallel is supplied by the substantial
exports of tin to La Rochelle in 1195, for Lady Stenton has suggested that this too was used to adulterate the coinage in which
Richard's troops were paid.[4] And there is the further parallel
between Henry I's recoinage of 1125 and that carried out by John
in 1205.[5]

But despite the temporary economic distress in England in
1123 and 1124, the English economy which supported the exactions of Henry I was neither primitive in its organization nor
running at a low level of production and exchanges during the
first four decades of the twelfth century. Vinogradoff's point about
the connexion between the existence of 'natural economy' and a
system of unpaid military service is a valid one; but no such
economy existed in England at this period. Nor is it easy to find
evidence for the view that conditions made it difficult for landlords to exact labour services and to move quantities of produce

[1] Symeon of Durham, ii. 281.

[2] *Gesta Normannorum Ducum*, p. 297.

[3] Florence of Worcester, ii. 57.

[4] Introduction to *Chancellor's Roll 8 Richard I* (Pipe Roll Society, N. S.,
vii), p. xix, where it is pointed out that some of Richard's continental pennies
contained only three parts silver to nine of alloy.

[5] See summary of the evidence in introduction to *Pipe Roll 7 John* (Pipe
Roll Society, N. S., vii) pp. xxvii–xxxii.

across the country. At Abingdon under Abbot Faricius, at Battle under Abbot Ralph, at Hereford under Bishop Geoffrey, at Lincoln under Robert Bloet, at Durham under Flambard and at Winchester under Henry of Blois there is evidence of enterprising management, the resumption of demesne lands, investment in improvements and a rapidly increasing revenue which supported the costs of greatly increased establishments of monks and canons, of lavish building programmes and of a higher and more civilized standard of living.[1] Nor does the evidence suggest that the long-distance transport of bulk produce by road or water was impossible or infrequent. Perhaps the references in the Anglo-Norman law-books to the special protection of roads and waterways prove little about the actual conditions.[2] It is more noteworthy that the timber for Abbot Faricius's building operations at Abingdon was brought from Wales by six wagons, each drawn by twelve oxen, the round trip taking six or seven weeks[3]; that a great bell cast in London for Durham was transported by road on a vehicle drawn by twenty-two oxen[4]; and that in 1121 Henry I cleared and deepened the Fossdyke, the canal linking Lincoln with Torksey, thus making possible the passage of shipping from the Wash to the Humber by inland waterways.[5]

There are frequent and revealing comments in William of Malmesbury's *Gesta Pontificum* on regional specialization in agriculture and on the organization and volume of trade. He describes the fertile orchards of the Vale of Gloucester and the volume of shipping handled by Bristol[6]; he stresses the predominantly pastoral economy of Cheshire and its dependence on trade with Ireland[7]; and he dwells on the importance of London as a centre of international trade and as a food market.[8] Moreover, the

[1] For Abbot Faricius, see *Historia Monasterii de Abingdon*, ii. 44–159, 286–90; for Abbot Ralph, *Chronicon Monasterii de Bello*, pp. 51–9; for Bishop Geoffrey, William of Malmesbury, *Gesta Pontificum* (R. S.), p. 304; for Robert Bloet, Henry of Huntingdon, *Epistola de Contemptu Mundi* (Appendix B to *Historia Anglorum*, R. S.), and Gerald of Wales, *Vita S. Remigii* in *Opera* (R. S.), vii. 31–2; for Flambard, Lawrence of Durham, *op. cit.*, p. 22; for Henry of Blois, Lena Voss, *Heinrich von Blois* (Historische Studien, Heft 210).

[2] See references given by F. M. Stenton, 'The Road System of Medieval England', *Economic History Review*, vii (1936).

[3] *Historia Monasterii de Abingdon*, ii. 150.

[4] Symeon of Durham, ii. 356–7.   [5] *Ibid.*, ii. 260.

[6] *Gesta Pontificum*, pp. 291–2.   [7] *Ibid.*, p. 308.   [8] *Ibid.*, p. 140.

nature of the economy of this period is reflected in some of
Henry I's measures and decrees. If Edward I's abolition of the
right of wreck is evidence that the activity of trade and commerce
'was becoming increasingly difficult to reconcile with the formal
feudal structure',[1] it is relevant to remember that Henry I also
issued an edict abolishing the right of wreck and giving the goods
of a wrecked ship to any survivors.[2] If the Assize of Measures of
1196 is connected with the growth of English industry, and
especially of the cloth industry,[3] it should be remembered that
Henry I also punished the use of false measures and prescribed
a standard width of cloth.[4] Just as the literary evidence shows that
there was no rigid feudal tradition which made the use of paid
troops unthinkable, so the evidence on economic organization
and resources shows that these did not make it necessary to confine military effort within the narrow limits of the *servitium
debitum* and the fyrd. The whole history of the development of
Anglo-Norman administration is intelligible only in terms of the
scale and the pressing needs of war finance: the expenditure on
the wages of troops, the construction and repair of castles, the
pensions to allies, the bribes which eased the course of campaigns
and diplomacy, and the upkeep of the bureaucracy itself.

Richard FitzNeal's statement on the financial cost of war was
indeed a platitude and a commonplace. But though platitudes are
by definition dull and commonplaces unoriginal, it is only by
recovering the commonplaces of a past age that the historian can
hope to understand the working of its institutions and the subtle-
ties of its politics. The truth and force of Richard FitzNeal's more
precise statement that the wars of the Anglo-Norman period were
financed from the *placita* and *conventiones* and from the urban
communities is amply borne out by the entries in the Pipe Roll
of 1130. For various fines and agreements the bishop of Ely was
charged over £1,500; Robert fitz Walter £1,000 for an agreement
with the king; Aubrey de Vere nearly £600; William de Pont de
l'Arche 1,000 marks for the office and daughter of Robert
Mauduit; the Jews of London were fined £2,000; and the chan-

[1] T. F. T. Plucknett, *Legislation of Edward I*, pp. 136–7.
[2] *Chronicon Monasterii de Bello*, p. 66.
[3] E. M. Carus-Wilson, 'The English Cloth Industry in the late Twelfth
and early Thirteenth Centuries', *Economic History Review*, xiv (1944), 43–4.
[4] William of Malmesbury, *Gesta Regum*, ii. 487.

cellor bought his office for £3,006 13s. 4d.[1] The magnitude of these sums can be measured by the fact that a Danegeld for the whole country was producing only about £3,500. In the past sheriffs had been running up considerable arrears of debt on the farms of their counties. In 1130 a former sheriff of Wiltshire accounted for the considerable sum of £1,023 0s. 2d. under this heading.[2] But Richard Bassett and Aubrey de Vere, who held eleven counties in custody for the year 1129–30, had not only to pay their farms in full but also to pay in a surcharge of 1,000 marks on these counties, and of this sum 600 marks went straight into the Norman war-chest.[3] It is not surprising that in this same year, 1130, Henry had bad dreams on the score of his exactions, dreams vividly illustrated in drawings by John of Worcester, who took his information from Henry's personal physician.[4]

But more than bad dreams were needed to relax the weight and alter the methods of war finance: it needed, we know, the feudal reaction which followed the death of Henry, the weakness and folly of Stephen, *fere ydiota*, expressed in his reckless concessions, the disputed succession and the long civil war in which, according to Richard FitzNeal, the vital expertise of the Exchequer itself was almost entirely wiped out. Yet the acceptance of these explanations of the civil war under Stephen depends more on the frequency with which they have been repeated than on any compelling evidence to enforce them. There would have been nothing unprecedented in a disputed succession; but the disputed successions of Rufus and Henry I had not resulted in prolonged civil war. And on this occasion it would be more accurate to hold that the civil war caused the disputed succession than that the disputed succession caused the civil war. For, as Henry of Winchester pointed out in 1141, the empress had not disputed the succession effectively at the outset.[5] If Stephen made wide formal concessions in his second charter, so too had Henry I; and Stephen was careful to make the reservation *salva regia et justa dignitate mea*.[6] If we accuse Stephen of weakly basing his claim to the throne on

---

[1] *Pipe Roll 31 Henry I*, pp. 44, 90, 53, 37, 149, 140.
[2] *Ibid.*, p. 16.   [3] *Ibid.*, p. 63.
[4] *The Chronicle of John of Worcester*, ed. Weaver, pp. 32–3 and frontispiece.
[5] William of Malmesbury, *Historia Novella* (R. S.), ii. 575. Cf. *Historia Pontificalis*, ed. R. L. Poole, Appendix VI.
[6] Stubbs, *Select Charters*, 9th ed., p. 144.

election—*Dei gratia assensu cleri et populus*[1]—we must bring the same charge against Henry I, who described himself in 1100 as *nutu Dei, a clero et a populo Angliae electus.*[2] That a reaction followed the death of Henry I is certain. Even one of Henry's porters put himself at the head of a band of mercenary knights and pillaged the neighbourhood of Winchester.[3] Many of the porter's betters had more substantial grievances and greater opportunities to assert their interests. There was Richard FitzGilbert, who had been in the hands of the Jews in 1130, and who now demanded great favours from Stephen[4]; Ranulf of Chester, heavily indebted to the crown in 1130 and also in the hands of the Jews[5]; and all those anxious to recover lands from the church, castles from the crown and honours from Henry's grantees. Further, there were the claims and menaces of the Welsh, the Scots and the men of Anjou, all now enjoying exceptionally able and determined leadership.

What is not clear is that from the outset Stephen showed weakness in yielding to these demands and folly in failing to deal with these menaces. He did not strip himself of power by keeping his general promises on Danegeld, disafforestation and the freedom of ecclesiastical elections.[6] He refused the demands of Richard FitzGilbert and Baldwin de Redvers.[7] He understood the vital importance of control of the castles and compelled the surrender of those of Norwich, Bampton, Exeter, Bedford and Bamborough.[8] Nor can Stephen be fairly accused of ignoring the dangers on the borders of Scotland, Wales and Normandy. In February 1136 he led a very large army north and obtained from King David the surrender of Wark, Alnwick, Norham and Newcastle.[9] In November of that year he refused the demand of the

[1] Jolliffe, *The Constitutional History of Medieval England*, p. 203.
[2] Stubbs, *Select Charters*, p. 120.
[3] *Gesta Stephani*, p. 6.
[4] *Pipe Roll 31 Henry I*, p. 53; *Gesta Stephani*, p. 12.
[5] *Pipe Roll 31 Henry I*, pp. 110, 149.
[6] Henry of Huntingdon, *Historia Anglorum*, p. 258. Stephen's promise to abolish Danegeld is not elsewhere recorded. For Stephen's breach of his promises on the forest, see Round, *Geoffrey de Mandeville*, p. 378.
[7] *Gesta Stephani*, p. 12; Richard of Hexham, *Historia*, in *Chronicles of the reign of Stephen*, etc., iii. 146–7.
[8] Henry of Huntingdon, p. 259; *Gesta Stephani*, pp. 19–32; John of Hexham, *Historia*, in Symeon of Durham, ii. 291.
[9] Richard of Hexham, p. 146. Cf. Henry of Huntingdon, pp. 258–9.

Scots that Northumberland be granted to Henry of Scotland.[1] In February 1138 he led a counter-attack against the Scots[2]; and later in the year his despatch of a contingent of knights contributed materially to the decision of the northerners to fight the battle of the Standard.[3] Stephen's decision to leave the Welsh marches to their fate was only taken after he had seen the marcher lords frittering away the troops and money which he had sent to them in considerable quantities.[4] Moreover, in March 1137 Stephen landed in Normandy and made vigorous attempts to destroy the forces of Geoffrey of Anjou.[5] Henry of Huntingdon, no partisan of Stephen, said of the king during this stay in Normandy, that 'he completed brilliantly everything that he began'[6]; and it is necessary to set this judgement, even if too favourable, against the same writer's later and more often quoted comment that it was the king's habit to begin many things vigorously and then to pursue them slothfully.[7]

Why then was Stephen able to act so firmly during the first two years of his reign? And why did his position weaken during the following eighteen months until in June 1139 he sanctioned the arrest of Roger of Salisbury and the other members of his family? For that action meant the abandonment of the personalities, the policies and the political interests on which the strength of the monarchy had so long rested. No simple answers can be given to these questions.[8] But contemporaries noticed and emphasized one factor which does much to explain both Stephen's early firmness and later weakness: finance. When William of Malmesbury had to explain why his patron, Robert of Gloucester, did homage to Stephen in April 1136, he pointed out that Stephen had acquired the great reserve of treasure built up by Henry I and had accordingly been able to recruit a large force of mercenaries drawn largely from Flanders and Brittany.[9] Henry of

[1] Richard of Hexham, p. 151. [2] *Ibid.*, p. 155.
[3] *Ibid.*, p. 161; John of Hexham, p. 292. [4] *Gesta Stephani*, pp. 11–14.
[5] Ordericus Vitalis, v. 81–91.
[6] Henry of Huntingdon, p. 260: 'omnia quae incepit luculente perfecit'.
[7] *Ibid.*, p. 283: 'mos regius erat, quod multa strenue inciperet, et segniter exsequeretur', referring to Stephen's conduct in 1151.
[8] For a recent discussion of the problem, see Isabel Megaw, 'The Ecclesiastical Policy of Stephen', *Essays in British and Irish History in honour of J. E. Todd*, ed. Cronne, Moody and Quinn.
[9] *Historia Novella*, p. 540.

Huntingdon gave precisely the same explanation for the fact that Geoffrey of Anjou concluded a truce with Stephen in 1137[1]; and from Orderic we learn that Geoffrey was then his wife's mercenary.[2] The strength of Robert and of Geoffrey was closely related to the size of Henry I's treasures in Normandy; the strength of Stephen to the much greater treasure left in England.[3] Other sources stress Stephen's military strength at this time. Richard of Hexham tells us that at the beginning of his reign Stephen 'collected very large bands of mercenary knights with which to carry out his policy in Normandy and England'.[4] The *Gesta Stephani* refers to his mobilization of a powerful force of knights who flocked to his support even before he seized the treasure at Winchester.[5] And Henry of Huntingdon described the army which Stephen led north in February 1136 as the largest within memory.[6] William of Ypres, Stephen's Flemish captain, had entered his service at least as early as 1137.[7] For the first two years of his reign Stephen was therefore able to follow the same policy as had his predecessor and to use the same instruments in poli..ics, administration and war.

But not even Henry I's treasure, supplemented by ordinary sources of revenue and by the windfall treasure of the archbishop of Canterbury, seized on his death in 1136,[8] could long support expenditure at the rate involved by the campaigns of the first three years of Stephen's reign. According to the *Gesta Stephani*, the siege of Exeter alone cost £10,000.[9] Apart from the sums transmitted to the Welsh marches and the direct cost of the campaigns against rebels, the Scots and Geoffrey of Anjou, Stephen had other expenses. The Easter court of 1136 was notable for its splendour and extravagance.[10] In 1137 Stephen bought off the

[1] Henry of Huntingdon, p. 260.

[2] Ordericus Vitalis, v. 81–2: 'stipendiarius conjugi suae factus'.

[3] For Robert of Gloucester's share of Henry I's treasure at Falaise, see Ordericus Vitalis, v. 50, and Robert of Torigni, p. 129; for the Empress Matilda's share, see *Gesta Stephani*, p. 30.

[4] *Historia*, p. 145.   [5] *Gesta Stephani*, p. 6.

[6] *Historia Anglorum*, pp. 258–9.

[7] Ordericus Vitalis, v. 82–4; *Historia Novella*, p. 543.

[8] *Gesta Stephani*, p. 7.

[9] *Ibid.*, p. 25. Cf. Henry of Huntingdon, p. 259: 'obsedit urbem Excestre . . . ibique diu morando, machinas multas construendo, multum thesauri sui absumpsit'.

[10] Henry of Huntingdon, p. 259.

claims of his brother Theobald for 2,000 marks and purchased the truce with Geoffrey of Anjou for an annual payment of 2,000 marks, the first instalment being paid at once.[1] Just as Stephen's possession of financial reserves helps to explain the nature of his actions during the first three years of his reign, so the running down and exhaustion of those reserves helps to explain both the mounting confidence of his opponents and the ability of a coalition of mercenaries and magnates to force the hand of the king in June 1139.

William of Newburgh tells us that in 1138 and 1139 the exhaustion of Henry I's treasures meant that Stephen could do less and had to act more gently, and that the evils then began.[2] Three other independent and contemporary sources emphasize Stephen's financial exhaustion and its consequences. William of Malmesbury says that in 1139 Stephen was making good his expenses by robbing others, and ascribes his attack on the church to the counsellors who persuaded the king that he need never lack money while the monasteries were full of treasure.[3] He adds that in 1140 Stephen ordered the currency to bë lightened because Henry's treasure was exhausted and he could not meet the expenditure on so many knights.[4] The *Gesta Stephani* similarly attributes Stephen's attack on the church to 'evil counsellors . . . and financial necessity, which admits no law or reason'.[5] And Henry of Huntingdon connects the evils of 1140 with the fact that the great royal treasure had disappeared.[6] The statement in the *Gesta* that Stephen's action against the bishops was instigated

---

[1] Robert of Torigni, p. 124.

[2] *Historia Rerum Anglicarum*, in *Chronicles of the reign of Stephen*, etc., i. 33.

[3] *Historia Novella*, pp. 547, 543.

[4] *Ibid.*, p. 562. This statement by a writer ordinarily careful on questions of coinage has sometimes been dismissed on the ground that it alleges debasement by Stephen, whereas the surviving coins are of a fine standard (Howlett in *Chronicles of the reign of Stephen*, etc., iii, pp. xxviii, lii; Corbett in *Cambridge Medieval History*, v. 553). But William of Malmesbury clearly refers to a reduction in the weight of the coins: 'pondus denariorum . . . alleviari'. There is, however, more evidence to support this charge against the coins issued by the Empress Matilda than against those of Stephen. See G. C. Brooke, *Catalogue of English Coins in the British Museum: The Norman Kings*, i, pp. lxxv, cxix.

[5] *Gesta Stephani*, pp. 18, 50. Cf. p. 74 for the depleted state of the treasury at Winchester after the battle of Lincoln.

[6] *Historia Anglorum*, p. 267: 'ingens thesauri copia jam deperierat'.

by evil advisers may perhaps be dismissed as the attempt of an apologist to exculpate the king. But William of Malmesbury, an Angevin partisan, also went out of his way to absolve Stephen and fix the responsibility on his advisers.[1] Contemporaries were then agreed in holding that financial need placed Stephen at the mercy of the dissident magnates and unpaid mercenary captains. What these men wanted is plain: crown lands, recognition of hereditary claims, control of castles and boroughs, freedom from the forest laws, patronage for their followers and spoliation of the church. And at the Council of Oxford in which the arrest of the bishops was ordered, a sweeping programme of despoiling the church in the interest of king and barons was formally adopted.[2]

It is impossible to explain the complicated events of these years solely in terms of finance. Nevertheless, the history of the first five years of Stephen's reign lends point to Richard FitzNeal's remark that it is the abundance or want of money which raises or depresses the power of princes.[3] That remark, like so much else in the Treasurer's preface, was a commonplace; and it is only worth while calling attention to the validity of these commonplaces on war and finance in the Anglo-Norman state because the nature of our evidence and of much of the work upon that evidence make it easy to miss their significance. The incidents of tenure by knight-service have left deep and enduring traces upon the records of English history, for those incidents were of permanent importance to the holders of land and to the crown. The shifting expedients of war finance—contracts for contingents of paid troops, pensions to allies, expenditure on fortifications and materials and manipulations of the currency—have left but few and faint traces in the records for the Anglo-Norman period, partly because they were shifting expedients and there was therefore the less need to preserve any written record of them. For that reason, the detailed history of the war finance of this period cannot be written. But it does not therefore follow that these expedients were insignificant at the time or that we must set the

[1] *Historia Novella*, p. 543.

[2] *Chronicle of John of Worcester*, p. 55: 'statutum est ut omnia per Angliam oppida, castella, munitiones quaeque in quibus secularia solent exerceri negotia, regis et baronum suorum iuri cedant'.

[3] *Dialogus de Scaccario*, p. 1.

political and social history of this period in a rigid framework of feudalism. We do not know how far those who owed knight-service performed it in person. Certainly the chroniclers and historians who are the primary sources for the political history of this period tell us of the presence of barons in sieges and cam-paigns; but they also tell us much about the paid service of mercenary troops, of other forms of war expenditure and of the relations between finance and policy. Moreover, they never use the term feudalism, that convenient but dangerous anachronism. 'Where would political history be', asked one great scholar, 'if it weꞇe not for the chronicles?' That was said by Tout.[1] It is difficult to argue that Orderic Vitalis and William of Malmesbury did not understand the society in which they lived; and fortunately just enough scraps of record evidence have survived to show that what they and other writers of the early twelfth century said on the general subject of war and finance deserves to be taken seriously.

[1] *Collected Papers of T. F. Tout*, iii. 18.

MERCENARIES AND THE *FAMILIA REGIS* UNDER HENRY I[1]

MARJORIE CHIBNALL

One of the most familiar allegories in the works of St. Anselm is his treatment of the service of God in terms of the service due to a secular prince.[2] Some men, he was fond of saying, fight in their lord's service to fulfil their duty; these already hold lands and are securely established and rooted. Others serve for wages; others still in the hope of winning back a lost patrimony. Comparisons between secular and spiritual service are common enough in the sermons and treatises of the time;[3] but Anselm's vivid allegory is so detailed and precise that it cannot be dismissed as a pious commonplace. It gives an inside glimpse of the household troops of the *familia regis*, both in the time of William Rufus and in the early years of Henry I, the truth of which is borne out by other sources.

That mercenaries played an important part in the armies of the Anglo-Norman kings, and that even at the beginning of the twelfth century money was one of the sinews of war are facts long familiar to historians;[4] but the rôle of the mercenaries varied according to military need. Both William the Conqueror and William II employed numerous mercenaries in their great enterprises;[5] it was not until the reign of Stephen and still more of Henry II that paid forces assumed the proportions of a professional army, composed chiefly of foot-soldiers, whose intervention often carried the day on the field of battle or decided the outcome of a siege.[6] Before this development took place, the reign of Henry I was still a time of 'old-style warfare, carried out by small feudal troops', and it was in the king's mounted household troops, the *familia regis*, that mercenaries were most effectively employed. The household troops were highly trained and mobile, and might be

---

[1] This article is based on a paper read during the 'Journées d'histoire du droit et des institutions des pays de l'Ouest de la France' at Angoulême in May, 1976.

[2] The allegory of the knights occurs in slightly different versions in the *Vita Anselmi* by Eadmer, ed. R. W. Southern, Nelson's Medieval Texts, 1962, pp. 94–5; *Dicta Anselmi*, c.10 (*Memorials of Saint Anselm*, ed. R. W. Southern and F. S. Schmitt, *Auctores Britannici Medii Aevi*, i, British Academy, 1969, pp. 150–1); and the anonymous *De Similitudinibus* (cf. ibid., pp. 12–13; Migne, *Patrologia latina*, clix, 651–2). Eadmer and Alexander have recorded different versions of the allegory.

[3] Cf. an anonymous treatise written c.1132–3, *Rescriptum cuiusdam pro monachis*, ed. R. Foreville and J. Leclercq, 'Un débat sur le sacerdoce des moines au xiie siècle', *Studia Anselmiana*, xli (1957), pp. 93–6.

[4] The question was clarified and focused by J. O. Prestwich in a fundamental article, 'War and finance in the Anglo-Norman state', *Transactions of the Royal Historical Society*, 5th ser. iv (1954), 19–43.

[5] C. Warren Hollister, *The Military Organisation of Norman England* (Oxford, 1965), pp. 168, 178–80.

[6] J. Boussard, 'Les mercenaires au xiie siècle; Henri II Plantagenet et les origines de l'armée de métier', *Bibliothèque de l'École des Chartes*, cvi (1945–6), 189–224.

used anywhere in the Anglo-Norman *regnum*;[7] this paper will, however, be concerned primarily with their activities in Normandy, which have not hitherto been studied in detail.[8] All Henry I's important campaigns after 1102, with the exception of his Welsh expeditions, were carried out in Normandy; it was there that the *familia regis* was normally on a war footing and castles with their garrisons had a particularly important part to play in the defence of the duchy. The names of some of the household captains and knights have been recorded by Norman historians, notably by Orderic Vitalis; it is even possible occasionally to trace their careers and to determine whether they served out of feudal duty, in return for wages, or in the hope of future gain.

The household knight whose career is most fully documented by Orderic is undoubtedly Ralph the Red of Pont-Échanfray. He came from a prominent and well-established local family of friends and benefactors of Saint-Evroult. A descendant, probably a grandson, of Heremberge Giroie and Walkelin of Pont-Échanfray, whose sons William and Ralph went to fight for Robert Guiscard in Apulia,[9] he and his brother Walkelin are mentioned for the first time in a charter of Saint-Evroult, *c.* 1100.[10] The two brothers came to the chapter-house of the abbey to ratify the gifts of their ancestors and Ralph, who had just been made a knight, received a palfrey as a gift from the abbot. The fief of Pont-Échanfray depended on the honour of Breteuil, and two or three years later Ralph fought in support of Eustace of Breteuil against Reginald of Grancey.[11] In 1106 he and his brother Walkelin left with Bohemond on his ill-fated expedition against Alexius Comnenus; after Bohemond's defeat at Durazzo Ralph was amongst those who went on to Constantinople, where his wife died, and thence to Jerusalem.[12] For the next twelve years his career is undocumented; in 1118 we hear of him again at Pont-Échanfray, and for two years he fought with distinction among Henry I's household troops before perishing in the wreck of the White Ship.[13] Even allowing for Orderic's bias in favour of a patron's family, the king seems to have valued his services, and quickly secured his release when he was captured. Yet the only reward known to have been given him was a grant out of the revenues of Glos, probably a money fief,

---

[7] The difficulty of finding an adequate single word to describe the territories where Henry I exercised authority is partly due to the ambiguous nature of his position in Normandy; for a detailed discussion of the whole question see C. Warren Hollister, 'Normandy, France and the Anglo-Norman *regnum*', *Speculum*, li (1976), 202–42; J. Le Patourel, 'The Norman succession, 996–1135', *English Historical Review*, lxxxvi (1971), 225–50.

[8] For the rôle of mercenaries in England see J. O. Prestwich, art. cit. supra n.4; Hollister, *The Military Organisatiion of Norman England*, pp. 167–90; John Beeler, *Warfare in England, 1066–1189* (Cornell University Press, Ithaca 1966), *passim*; and the important and suggestive account of household knights by R. Allen Brown, *The Normans and the Norman Conquest* (London, 1969), pp 230–2.

[9] *The Ecclesiastical History of Orderic ovitalis*, ed. M. Chibnall (Oxford Medieval Texts, 1969 ff.), ii. 30.

[10] *Orderici Vitalis Ecclesiasticae Historiae libri tredecim*, ed. A. Le Prévost (Société de l'histoire de France, Paris, 1838–55), v. 194.

[11] Orderic, ed. Le Prévost, iv. 186.

[12] Orderic, ed. Le Prévost, iv. 213, 239, 242–3.

[13] Orderic, ed. Le Prévost, iv. 326, 344–5, 35.–3, 367, 371, 417.

made by Ralph of Gael who had newly received the honour of Breteuil[14].

Ralph the Red's position was far from being a simple one. In the first place, Orderic never specifies whether he was an eldest son; the provision of a palfrey was sometimes a gift made to secure the means of livelihood for a younger son,[15] and his brother Walkelin may have inherited the patrimony. The importance of younger sons in troops of household knights has been amply illustrated in G. Duby's classic study of 'les jeunes'.[16] These men, as Duby had shown, came from good, often noble families and were fully trained and dubbed as knights; in Latin sources they are called *juvenes*, in romance literature *bacheliers*. Many were landless younger sons, owning only their war-horse, coat of mail and arms,[17] and out to establish themselves by winning the hand of an heiress from a grateful lord; the ransom of prisoners taken in battles and tournaments was an important source of wealth for them. Elder sons too, during their fathers' lifetime, might be prepared to sell their swords and gain practical experience of warfare. The trained knight would be regarded as 'young' until he was established in his own lands, usually until he was married and with children of his own; William the Marshall's 'youth' lasted for a quarter of a century. Ralph the Red may have been one of these 'juvenes', even though married, in his earlier wandering years. Later, possibly because the death of a father or an elder brother brought him the heritage of Pont-Échanfray, possibly because he was disappointed in his hopes of winning a patrimony in the East, he returned to Normandy. There is a further ambiguity in his relations with his lord, and it is not clear to whom he had sworn fealty. Orderic, by the use of the term 'baron' implies that he was a vassal of Eustace of Breteuil; but he never wavered in his loyalty to Henry I when Eustace rebelled. After the honour of Breteuil was given to Ralph of Gael he was sent to help capture the fortress of Breteuil with a troop of household knights led by Richard, the king's son, and his place remained in the *familia regis* even after Ralph of Gael had made him a grant that has every appearance of being a money-fief. Whether he ever took an oath of liege homage to Henry I is never made clear. He may have served in the household troops primarily in the hope of future reward.

Some of the other household knights named by Orderic can be identified as men of high birth and good prospects. Conspicuous among them is Henry de Pomeroy, heir to Joscelin, lord of Berry Pomeroy in Devon. His father was probably still alive when he began his service in the *familia regis*; later he inherited an honour that owed the service of thirty-two knights to the king, became one of the royal constables named in the *Constitutio domus regis*, and was given one of the king's natural daughters as his

[14] Orderic, ed. Le Prévost, iv. 372. According to Orderic the king would have rewarded him had he lived longer.

[15] Orderic, ed. Le Prévost, v. 184.

[16] G. Duby, 'Dans la France du Nord-Quest au XIIᵉ siècle: les 'jeunes' dans la société aristocratique', *Annales: Économies, Sociétés, Civilisations*, xix (1964), 835–46; cf. idem, 'La noblesse dans la France médiévale', *Revue historique*, ccxxvi (1961), 1–22.

[17] Anselm, in another allegory, specifies the essential possessions of a knight: his war-horse (his 'most trusty companion'), with bridle, saddle and spurs, and his arms, consisting of hauberk, helmet, shield, lance and sword; he could not be considered properly armed if even one of these was missing (*Memorials of St. Anselm* ed. Southern and Schmitt, pp. 97–8).

wife.[18] Two of the king's bastard sons, Robert, later earl of Gloucester, and Richard, who was drowned in the White Ship, constantly appear as leaders of the household troops.[19] Engenulf and Geoffrey of l'Aigle and Jordan of Auffay were among the young men of good family hoping to win or recover an inheritance;[20] William of Grandcourt, younger son of the count of Eu, may have been in the same category, but he sacrificed his position to help the king's enemy, Amaury of Montfort, to escape after Bourgthéroulde.[21] Some of the guardians of royal castles, such as Ranulf, vicomte of the Bessin, who had charge of the citadel of Évreux in 1123, and Robert de Chandos, lord of Caerleon, who was in command at Gisors in 1123, were undoubtedly important vassals, though they may have performed greater services than their feudal obligations required.[22] Rualon of Avranches, one of the Breton friends of Henry I's youth, won rewards for his service that raised him above his original status. He received the manor of Stanton Harcourt (Oxfordshire) shortly after Henry's accession; and later the king gave him as his wife Matilda, daughter and heir of Nigel of Monville, lord of Folkestone, together with the castle of Folkestone.[23]

Others, distinguished by nicknames such as Bertrand Rumex or Odo Borleng rather than family names, were probably men of more modest families, with just enough resources to provide themselves with the training and equipment of a knight. They served primarily as stipendiaries, but conspicuous skill and achievement might bring supplementary rewards. Hard as they are to identify in official records, it is at least possible that a charter of Henry I in favour of 'Odo, serviens meus' was granted for Odo Borleng. The charter was given at Rouen at an uncertain date in the reign, confirming the liberties of Odo and his heirs in his land in Bray (Berks.), held for 32d. annually.[24] The witnesses are named as Reginald de Pomeroy and William *armiger*. The editors of *Regesta* translate *serviens* as serjeant and suggest that this is a serjeanty connected with Philberds in Cresswell (Bray). But the common assumption that *serviens* is equivalent to serjeant has led to much misunderstanding and to an exaggeration of the importance of serjeanty tenure in the early twelfth century.[25] In this case the land may originally have been granted as a reward for services, and even if it was the same property which later supported a household serjeanty it was originally held for rent. The witnesses seem to connect the charter with the

[18] Orderic, ed. Le Prévost, iv. 453; I. J. Sanders, *English Baronies* (Oxford, 1963), pp. 106–7; G. H. White, 'The household of the Norman kings', *Transactions of the Royal Historical Society*, 4th ser. xxx (1948), 133–4, 151–2; *Complete Peerage* (revised edn. by G.E.C.), xi, App.D, p. 119.

[19] Orderic, ed. Le Prévost, iv. 341, 344, 350, 357, 367–8, 443.

[20] Orderic, ed. Le Prévost, iv, 324; Orderic, ed. Chibnall, iii. 258–60.

[21] Orderic, ed. Le Prévost, iv. 458–9.

[22] Orderic, ed. Le Prévost, iv. 450, 453, 456.

[23] Orderic, ed. Le Prévost, iv. 367; *Regesta regum Anglo-Normannorum*, ii. ed. C. Johnson and H. A. Cronne (Oxford, 1956), no. 528; T. Stapleton, 'The barony of William of Arques', *Archaeologia*, xxxi (1846), 216–36.

[24] *Calendar of Charter Rolls*, i. 408; *Regesta*, ii. no. 1956.

[25] Cf. Hollister, *Military Organisation of Norman England*, p. 130; E. G. Kimball, *Serjeanty Tenure in Medieval England* (Yale Historical Publications, Miscellany, xxx, 1936), pp. 7–9, 77 n.40. For Creswell in Bray see *Victoria County History of Berkshire*, iii. 100.

familia regis; Reginald (possibly a mistake for Robert) de Pomeroy may have served with his brother, Henry; and Odo Borleng's prowess and reputation at Bourgthéroulde suggest that he was a man likely to earn the king's rewards. The word *serviens* at this date was far from being a precise technical term; it could certainly be applied to mounted men more lightly armed than mailed knights as well as to those who owed other than military service, and in Normandy in particular it may also have been applied to the 'young' knights in the household troops. If Odo Borleng could be identified as the *Odo serviens* of Henry I's charter this would be of more than casual interest, for it would prove that occasionally at least the *servientes* of the charters may be equivalent to the *milites gregarii* of the chroniclers.

The battle of Bourgthéroulde, which put an end to the revolt of Waleran of Meulan and Amaury of Montfort in 1124, has a particular interest because of the composition of the royal forces. On this subject all sources are in agreement. John of Worcester calls them *milites regis*;[26] the Anglo-Saxon Chronicle 'the king's knights from all the castles round about'.[27] Robert of Torigny's account is fuller; the beginning is lost, but he refers to the captains as 'duces Henrici regis' and adds an important piece of information: that among their troops were 'equites sagitarii', or mounted archers.[28] Orderic's account is by far the most detailed: the troops consisted of three hundred *milites* commanded by Henry de Pomeroy and Odo Borleng, who were then in charge of the royal garrisons at Pont-Autou and Bernay, and possibly by William of Harcourt.[29] They were, in short, the king's household troops stationed in the neighbouring castles, probably a hundred to each castle.[30] Orderic's account of the engagement is enlivened by speeches which, though imaginary, are used to present a real situation. Like Robert of Torigny he refers to archers, who contributed to the success of the engagement by shooting down the rebels' horses before they could join battle with the royal troops. He makes it plain that the men were all mounted; Odo Borleng's troops dismounted to fight more resolutely. Most interesting as evidence of their standing are two speeches: the words he attributes to Odo in urging his men to battle, 'If we lack the courage to resist, how shall we ever dare to face the king again? We shall rightly forfeit our wages and our honour, and shall never again deserve to eat the king's bread'; and the scornful words attributed to Waleran when he saw Odo's men preparing to give battle, 'Far be it from us to fear these *gregarii et pagenses*'.

[26] *The Chronicle of John of Worcester 1118–1140,* ed. J. R. H. Weaver (Oxford, 1908), p. 18.

[27] *Anglo-Saxon Chronicle, s.a.* 1124.

[28] Interpolations in William of Jumièges, in *Gesta Normannorum Ducum,* ed. J. Marx (Société de l'histoire de Normandie, 1914), pp. 294–5.

[29] Orderic, ed. Le Prévost, iv. 453–8; William of Harcourt is described in the words 'regi adhaerens servabat' and it is not clear whether Orderic meant to imply that he too commanded a castle garrison. Possibly, since Henry of Huntingdon gives the credit for Waleran's capture to William of Tankarville, chamberlain of Normandy, (*Henrici archidiaconi Huntendunesis historia Anglorum*, ed. Thomas Arnold, Rolls Series, 1965 reprint, p. 245) he rather than William of Harcourt was a third commander.

[30] Cf. Robert of Torigny's interpolations in William of Jumièges (ed. J. Marx, p. 296), 'plurimas centurias militum in diversis locis hostibus propinquis apponebat'.

These, then, are soldiers of the king's household troops, earning his wages and eating his bread, like the household officers of the *Constitutio domus regis*;[31] highly-trained professionals, but not all of the same social standing or level of equipment. In charters and exchequer records these castle garrisons may appear as *milites et servientes*; some were archers, others fully armed knights, and it is certainly possible that some were vavassors or more lightly equipped mounted soldiers. The technical vocabulary of contemporary historians was apt to be loose and flexible, and *miles* could serve for almost any mounted soldier. Orderic hardly ever used the term *vavassor*, and then only with reference to peasant vavassors when he was copying a charter,[32] yet free vavassors frequently owed castle-guard in Normandy,[33] and must have been included in the castle garrisons whom he so frequently describes as *milites*. In the eyes of the haughty Waleran they could be dismissed as *gregarii et pagenses*, terms of contempt applied sometimes to mercenaries, sometimes to 'chevaliers de petite condition'.[34] Yet they played a vital part in the pacification and defence of the duchy, as the Anglo-Saxon Chronicle and Robert of Torigny no less than Orderic make plain. They provided the garrisons of the castles which Henry I was steadily drawing into his own hand, and on which the maintenance of his authority in Normandy depended.

The importance of the castles in Henry's defence of the duchy has been fully demonstrated by Professor Jean Yver.[35] The garrisons occupying them were more numerous and more permanent than would appear from the Pipe Roll of 1131 to have been the case in England. At Burton, for instance, one knight and 10 *servientes* with a janitor and watchman received wages of £21 5s. 10d.; at St. Briavel the numbers of the *servientes* are not stated, but together with a knight, a janitor and a watchman they received wages of only £14 5s. 7½d.[36] There is no comparison between these numbers and the troops up to a hundred strong which occur in Normandy. The use of household troops for prolonged garrison duty was not new; William I had placed troops of his *familia* under Alan the Red, lord of Richmond, in the siege castles blockading Sainte-Suzanne in 1084–6,[37] and William Rufus had left similar troops to hold the citadel of Le Mans under Clarembald of Lisores and Walter, son of Ansger.[38] Henry himself long before his accession had made sure of his hold on the castle of Domfront; troops of his *familia* were stationed there *c*.1092.[39] But his firm

---

[31] *Constitutio domus regis* in *Dialogus de Scaccario*, ed. Charles Johnson (Nelson's Medieval Texts, 1950), pp. 129–35.

[32] Orderic, ed. Chibnall, iii. 156.

[33] P. Guilhiermoz, *Essai sur l'origine de la noblesse en France* (Paris, 1902), pp. 183, 298–302; H. Navel, 'L'enquête de 1133 sur les fiefs de l'évêché de Bayeux', *Bulletin de la Société des Antiquaires de Normandie*, xlii (1934), 52–3.

[34] Cf. Guilhiermoz, *Essai*, p. 340; J. O. Prestwich in *English Historical Review*, lxxxi (1966), 107.

[35] J. Yver, 'Les châteaux-forts en Normandie', *Bulletin de la Société des Antiquaires de Normandie*, liii (1955–6), 28–115.

[36] *Pipe Roll, 31 Henry I*, ed. J. Hunter (Record Commission, 1833), pp. 76, 138.

[37] Orderic, ed. Chibnall, iv. 48.

[38] Orderic, ed. Chibnall, v. 256; cf. G. Gaimar, *L'Estoire des Engleis*, ed. A. Bell (Anglo-Norman Texts, xiv–xvi, Oxford, 1960), vv. 5781–3.

[39] Orderic, ed. Chibnall, iv. 292.

grip on the castles of the duchy and the size of the forces he maintained in them mark an advance, if not in policy, at least in effectiveness.[40]

Henry occasionally used mercenaries of another type, hired in large numbers for a limited period, during the major campaigns of the first half of his reign. William of Malmesbury writes of the Bretons from the regions near Domfront and Mont-Saint-Michel, whom Henry had known in his youth and later employed when he had special need of mercenaries.[41] These certainly included foot-soldiers and auxiliaries, and swelled the ranks of his army at Tinchebray in 1106.[42] He hired mercenaries occasionally later in his reign, for campaigns such as those in the Vexin in 1116–18, when the cause of his nephew, William Clito, was gaining strength and he could not always be sure of the loyalty of the Normans.[43] But the numbers engaged in the later pitched battles were small. At Brémule, where the kings of France and England met in 1119, the engagement was essentially between the forces of chivalry, reinforced on the English side by the archers and knights of the *familia regis*; it was almost as much a tournament as a battle.[44] Bourgthéroulde, as has already been shown, was an engagement between a small party of rebel knights and the *familia regis*. William of Malmesbury could write with some truth in his *Historia Novella* after the death of Henry I that the mercenaries, especially those from Flanders and Brittany, who flocked to serve under Stephen, had 'hated King Henry's peace because under it they had had but a scanty livelihood'. These casual mercenaries, often brutal and rapacious men with no respect for churches or the poor,[45] were certainly of a type which Henry employed only when he must. He had no wish to antagonize the Church, since he claimed to be the instrument of God sent to rescue Normandy from the misrule of Robert Curthose; besides this, the *corps d'élite* whom he

[40] Cf. Yver, 'Châteaux-forts', pp. 80–90; a striking example of his policy came when in 1119 he allowed William Talvas to recover his father's possessions in Alençon, Almenèches and elsewhere 'praeter dangiones, quos propriis excubitoriis assignavit' (Orderic, ed. Le Prévost, iv. 348). The paid royal garrisons in castles were so familiar that they passed as examples into moral treatises; cf. the simile of the castle in the treatise, *Rescriptum cuiusdam pro monachis* (*Studia Anselmiana*, xli (1957), p. 93): 'Sciendum quoque quia sicut maiora regum castella sive municipia specialius ad tuendam, ut dictum est, regiam dignitatem, numerosiore militum familia muniuntur, ita nichilominus et minores mansiuncule, ob deprimendam furum praedonumque rapacitatem, vel ad vicinorum, cum opus fuerit, inimicicias refellendas, minore quidam diligentia, sed tamen custodiuntur, singulis tamen, sicut maioribus, ita et minoribus, sua sibi competentia stipendia providentur'.

[41] William of Malmesbury, *De gestis regum Anglorum*, ed. W. Stubbs (Rolls Series, 1964 reprint), ii. 478.

[42] His army was large and included contingents of Bretons and Manceaux, though the figure of 40,000 given by the priest of Fécamp who witnessed the battle must be an exaggeration (*EHR* xxv (1910), 296; Robert of Torigny's interpolations in William of Jumièges, ed. J. Marx, p. 283; Orderic, ed. Le Prévost, iv. 229–30; Henry of Huntingdon, p. 235).

[43] Orderic, ed. Le Prévost, iv. 316, 'rex Buras munivit, ibique, quia plerosque Normannorum suspectos habuit, stipendiarios Britones et Anglos cum apparatu copioso constituit'.

[44] Orderic, ed. Le Prévost, iv. 355–61; *Chronica de Hida*, in *Liber monasterii de Hyda*, ed. E. Edwards, Rolls Series, 1886, pp. 316–8; Suger, *Vita Ludovici grossi regis*, ed. H. Waquet (Paris, 1929), c.xxvi, pp. 196–8; Henry of Huntingdon, pp. 241–2.

[45] William of Malmesbury, *Historia Novella*, ed. K. R. Potter (Nelson's Medieval Texts, 1955), p. 17. For the bad reputation of some mercenaries see also Orderic, ed. Le Prévost, iv. 366–7.

recruited and trained in his permanent household troops was far more effective.

Many of the knights in his *familia* were young men of good, even noble, families. It has been said of the knights who served for wages at this time that essentially they were of the same social class as those who served as vassals; and that any differences of rank that might exist certainly did not arise from the fact that they were paid.[46] Status was further confused by the close connexion between money-fiefs and the rewards given to household knights; though in law a clear distinction can be drawn between a knight receiving fixed wages and a feudal vassal, in practice the distinction was often blurred. Historians have hesitated between classifying the holders of money-fiefs as stipendiaries or vassals: most money-fiefs were lower in value than the rates of pay that became normal later, and some were granted as a reward for past service.[47] But whether feudal vassals, quasi-vassals or stipendiaries, the fully-equipped knights of the household troops, in common with the more lightly-armed archers and vavassors, took pride in loyal service to their lord. Their attitude is typified by that of the *milites stipendiarii* left to defend the castle of Bridgnorth in 1102 by Robert of Bellême; these men, when the castle was surrendered by the feudal captains without their consent, rode out bewailing their fate and calling the whole army to witness that they had been tricked into surrender, so that their capitulation might not bring contempt on other mercenaries.[48] One motive for this loyalty was certainly, in the case of the king's troops, hope of some reward over and above their wages. Henry I on his death-bed ordered his son Robert to make use of the treasure at Falaise to give wages and rewards to his household and his stipendiary knights;[49] that Robert probably did so is indicated by Robert of Torigny's statement that when Robert did homage to Stephen a little later he handed over Falaise, 'from which he had first removed a great part of king Henry's treasure, recently brought from England.' Henry ruled his Anglo-Norman *regnum* as a unity, using the money raised in England to support an army in Normandy.

If we return now to St. Anselm, it becomes clear that his allegory, though suggestive, must not be pushed too far. The three types of knight are not entirely distinct; the contractual element in much service was far from precisely defined. Feudal vassals might give service far beyond their strict duty for rewards in cash and kind; stipendiary knights might receive lands or money-5£efs for conspicuous service in addition to their wages. Some might be primarily motivated by the wish to regain a lost patrimony, but

[46] P. van Luyn, 'Les *milites* du xie siècle', *Le Moyen Age*, xxvi (1971), 31.

[47] They are called 'quasi-vassals' by Warren Hollister (*The Military Organisation of Norman England*, pp. 186–90). See also M. Sczaniecki, *Essai sur les fief-rentes* (Paris, 1946), pp. 22–30, 52 ff.

[48] Orderic, ed. Le Prévost, iv. 175.

[48] Orderic, ed. Le Prévost, v. 50. Literary references to paid service sometimes link wages with gifts; cf. Geffrei Gaimar, *L'Estoire des Engleis* (ed. A. Bell), v. 6258, where Walter Tirel is said to have come to serve William Rufus 'duns et soldeies recuillir'; *Studia Anselmiana*, xli (1957), p. 96, 'qui bene servierint quia merito percepturi sunt a dominis, et cotidiana stipendia, et postmodum pacta premia sive premissa'.

[49] Robert of Torigny, *Chronicle*, in *Chronicles of the Reigns of Stephen, Henry II and Richard I*, ed. R. Howlett, iv (Rolls Series 1889), p. 129. For the use of English money to pay troops in Normandy see Hollister, *The Military Organisation of Norman England*, p. 185.

there was an element of hope in the service of all. The best Christians, according to St. Anselm, were those who served God in the hope of regaining a lost paradise; and Henry I was well aware of the value of hope as a spur to loyalty and endeavour. In the later years of his reign the peace of Normandy was maintained by two things: his possession of strategically-placed castles where he could maintain his *familia*, and the *familia* itself — a loyal force, disciplined and well-trained, adequately paid thanks to the wealth of England, and motivated by the hope of future rewards.

The military household of the Norman kings

J. O. PRESTWICH

THE slight and scattered evidence for the military household of the Norman kings can be more easily assessed if it is compared with the much fuller evidence for the military household, *familia regis*, of Edward I. Tout was so impressed by the scale and comprehensiveness of this latter force that he described the developed armies of Edward I as 'the household in arms'. He put it more moderately, but still dramatically, when he attributed to Edward I's reign the expansion of the royal military household from 'a little company of peace-time guards' into 'the dimensions of a small army' consisting of bannerets and knights with their retinues, sergeants-at-arms, squires, infantry, crossbowmen, workmen and sailors, a force numbered in thousands, paid, equipped and supported by the household clerks of the wardrobe. Edward was thus provided with a steadily growing professional standing army at a time when the country 'was fast outgrowing the feudal conception of warfare in which the army was made up from the military tenants'.[1]

Tout paid proper tribute to the fundamental work of Morris on the Edwardian armies; but recent work has greatly enlarged our understanding of the role of the military household in war and government under Edward I. The standing core of this force consisted of cavalrymen. The bannerets and knights were retained by fees and grants for robes, those below the rank of knight drawing allowances for robes only. During a campaign all were paid wages and were also compensated for the value of any horses lost by themselves or any members of their retinues. Considered purely as a force of trained cavalry the household was of major importance in Edward's campaigns. It allowed him to strike quickly, as in the winter of 1276–7 when 110 horsemen of the household were pushed into Wales six months before the formal muster of the army. It could be expanded rapidly, as in the Flanders campaign of 1297 when its strength rose to 550 and formed the greater part of the cavalry throughout, 'the first to muster in something like its full strength and the only one which continued to grow throughout the period'.

1. T. F. Tout, *Chapters in the Administrative History of Mediaeval England* (Manchester, 1937), ii. 133, 138.

And for the largest single army raised by Edward I, in the Falkirk campaign of 1298, the household provided almost 800 men, over a quarter and perhaps a third of all the cavalry.[1]

But the importance of the military household in Edward's wars was much greater than these figures suggest. Knights of the household played a major role in mobilizing infantry for the first two Welsh campaigns. They were entrusted with separate commands, as in 1282 when Edward gave the army in South Wales to Robert Tiptoft, expressly placing the earls of Gloucester and Hereford under Tiptoft's orders. And although this arrangement had to be abandoned for political reasons, members of the household occupied dominant positions after the war in the conquered territories of North Wales. In 1284 the Savoyard Otto de Granson was made Justiciar of North Wales. He had entered Edward's service in 1258, had the Anglesey command in the first Welsh campaign and, after helping to reorganize Gascony, again in the second Welsh campaign. Another Savoyard was merely a sergeant of the household in 1284, though of all the members of Edward's military household his work has proved the most enduring; and he was fittingly given a grant of 3s. a day for life as a special reward for his 'good and laudable services'. This was James of St George, the architect of most of the great Edwardian castles and himself constable of Harlech castle in 1290. The constableships of Conway, Criccieth, Bere and later Beaumaris all went to household knights.[2]

Some leading members of the household were amphibious. William Leyburn was a highly experienced professional soldier who fought in all the Welsh campaigns from 1276 to 1287, was constable of Criccieth castle, served in Flanders in 1297 and at Falkirk in 1298, ending his career as a banneret of the household in the Caerlaverock campaign of 1300. Yet in 1294, when Edward ordered a major naval building programme, William Leyburn was appointed captain of all the seamen within Edward's territories, while another knight of the household, John Botetourt, served under him in command of a fleet of ninety-four ships. In 1297 Leyburn became the first English admiral, and in that capacity was sent to Bruges to arrange for naval co-operation with the Flemish.[3] It is reasonable to assume that it was not Leyburn's seamanship but his membership of the household, his long experience in commanding men, his administrative ability

1. J. E. Morris, The Welsh Wars of Edward I (Oxford, 1901); N. B. Lewis, 'The English Forces in Flanders, August–November 1297', in Studies in Medieval History presented to F. M. Powicke, ed. R. W. Hunt, W. A. Pantin, R. W. Southern (Oxford, 1948), p. 314. For much of what follows I am indebted to Michael Prestwich, War, Politics and Finance under Edward I (London, 1972), ch. ii.

2. C. L. Kingsford, 'Sir Otho de Grandison, 1238?–1328', Trans. Royal Hist. Soc., 3rd ser., iii (1909); A. J. Taylor, 'Master James of St. George', ante, lxv (1950).

3. Morris, Welsh Wars, pp. 121, 159, 210, 213, 278, 288; Parliamentary Writs, ed. Sir Francis Palgrave (London, 1827), i. 393–4; T. Rymer, Foedera (London, 1816), i. 861.

and his family tradition of service that led Edward to make this appointment.

Edward once wrote of Otto of Granson, who served him as soldier, administrator and diplomat from 1258 to 1307, that there was no one who could do his will better. It was this capacity of doing his will efficiently and loyally that Edward valued in the senior members of his military household, and he did not confine their responsibilities to military and naval commands. Edward drew on them largely for his provincial governors in Wales and Gascony. Some were temporarily detached for special tasks. William Latimer twice served on commissions appointed to investigate the malpractices of judges and forest officials, interrupting a long career as a professional soldier which extended from Edward's crusade to service in Scotland in 1300 as a banneret of the household. In the crisis of 1297 William Leyburn was one of the king's bannerets and knights associated with the sheriffs and given drastic powers to enforce the exaction of money from the clergy, to maintain order and to repress discontent. Robert Clifford, grandson of a household knight and himself prominent as a banneret in the campaigns in Scotland, was also justice of the forests north of the Trent and, from 1302, keeper of the bishopric of Durham. It was not only on campaigns that the bannerets of the household served together: of the eighty-nine lay magnates who were personally summoned to the parliament of Lincoln in 1301 nineteen were bannerets of the household who had been in receipt of the king's fees and robes in the previous year, together with an ex-steward and a future steward of the household. Many of the others had served in the Welsh wars as paid captains: Grey, Kyme, Basset, Huntercumbe, Pipard and Tateshall.[1]

If Edward 'preferred masterfulness to the arts of political management'[2] the military household was an essential instrument of his policies, though his mastery was never complete and was both challenged and weakened during the French and Scottish wars. If we measure the strength of the military household in terms of the numbers of bannerets and knights who were annually retained, we have a very rough but significant indication of the changes in Edward's political fortunes. In 1284–5, when Edward was at the height of his power after the conquest of Wales, there were 101 bannerets and knights; in 1301 only 54; and in 1306 the number fell to 45.[3] Edward's attempt to extend his right of purveyance, the acquisition

1. Michael Prestwich, *op .cit.*, p. 43 (Latimer); pp. 49, 146, 162, 235 (Clifford); *Parliamentary Writs*, i. 88–92 and *Liber Quotidianus Garderobae 28 Edward I* (Society of Antiquaries, 1787), pp. 188 ff. for the parliament of 1301 and the household bannerets of 1300. The ex-steward was Peter de Champvent, the future steward Robert la Warde.
2. K. B. McFarlane, 'Had Edward I a "Policy" towards the Earls?', in *The Nobility of Later Medieval England* (Oxford, 1973), p. 267.
3. Michael Prestwich, *op. cit.* pp. 46–47.

of supplies for the household by compulsory purchase, into a system of victualling the whole army was defeated in 1300, and in the following year a demand was made for the abolition of the right itself.

Nevertheless Edward's military household was an impressive creation. In recruiting it he drew on Gascony, Savoy, Wales and Scotland as well as on the English counties, on comital families as well as on those who rose from the ranks. The rewards for service were substantial but never sensational and almost always precarious. Fees were annual and wages were carefully calculated in relation to the exact number of days' service. Those fortunate enough to receive grants of land normally did so during the king's pleasure or for life. This helps to explain why so many members of Edward's military household int·oduced sons or relatives to their profession: Edward could count on family traditions of service. And the standards of loyalty were high. The treason of Thomas Turberville in 1295 was exceptional, and particularly scandalous to contemporaries since he was 'miles de familia regis', 'domesticus et praecipue domini regis Angliae familiaris', enjoying direct access to the king and knowledge of his plans.[1]

How new was the royal military household as an institution? Tout seems to have thought that as a significant military force it was virtually a creation of Edward I. When he estimated that the household contributed almost a third of the cavalry, or about 750 men-at-arms, for the Caerlaverock campaign of 1300, he commented that this was 'a far cry from the score of troopers whose wages were provided for in 1279'. He traced the origins of what he called 'an equally modest establishment of household infantry' all the way back to the mention of archers in the *Constitutio Domus Regis*, an account of the household probably compiled for King Stephen's benefit, shortly after his accession.[2] This view accorded well with the interpretation of Edward I's reign as decisive in replacing the feudal levy by paid forces as the basis of military organization.[3] The earls may have stood out against taking pay for fighting under Edward I, but, as McFarlane pointed out, they soon abandoned what he called 'this expensive self-denial'.[4] The future lay with the retaining fees and wages. When in June 1385 writs of summons to a general feudal levy were issued for the last time it was a deliberate archaism marking, as Dr Lewis held, 'the formal end of the system of military service

1. J. G. Edwards, 'The Treason of Thomas Turberville, 1295', in *Studies in Medieval History presented to F. M. Powicke*, p. 297, n. 2, where the reference to the Worcester Annals should be iv. 522.

2. *Chapters*, ii. 141, 136.

3. *E.g.* Sir Maurice Powicke, *The Thirteenth Century* (Oxford, 1953), p. 554: 'In broad terms, Henry III's armies until 1257 were based upon the feudal levy . . . whereas in Edward's time the feudal levy became subsidiary to the paid forces or was not summoned at all'.

4. McFarlane, *The Nobility of Later Medieval England*, p. 162.

which, for two and a half centuries following the Norman Conquest, had supplied the main strength of the national army'.[1]

Tout's great authority, the apparently decisive evidence of the Household Ordinance of 1279, and the generally held views of historians on the chronology of military organization long discouraged any search for evidence on the earlier history of the royal military household. Tout's own statement, made when explaining the scope of his great work on English medieval administrative history, that 'nearly the whole lay, and therefore most of the military, element in the household is foreign to my special purpose' was not given the weight it deserved.[2] But in the last quarter of a century the balance has begun to be redressed. In an unpublished thesis of 1953 Dr R. F. Walker established the importance of the military household in the Welsh wars of Henry III. It was maintained by fees, gifts and wages as under Edward I; its strength was expanded rapidly in the 1220s, reaching about seventy knights in 1228; and it supplied many of the commanders. Nicholas de Molis, a household knight and seneschal, much employed on military, administrative and diplomatic tasks, carried out the most striking feat of these campaigns when he led a small army from south Wales through Merioneth to Deganwy in the north in 1246.[3]

In 1955 Jolliffe, in his extraordinarily perceptive study of Angevin kingship, emphasized what he called the 'incalculable contribution' of the knights of the royal household to the regime of Henry II and his sons, stressing in particular their achievements when they were detached to serve in frontier shrievalties, as castellans, as keepers of escheats, and on diplomatic missions. Of the last decade of Henry II's reign Jolliffe observed that 'it was then the justice, the knight of the household and the chamber servant who, in quasi permanence, governed Normandy and England'. And in discussing the imperfect evidence for the *familia regis* in John's reign he ventured to doubt whether the *familia* of Edward I had been substantially larger in its standing membership. Jolliffe did not however suppose that the royal military household was created by Henry II: it was in the *Gesta Stephani* that he found 'a good description of the Knight of the Household, almost landless until endowed by his master, but strong in his influence and entrusted with vital military charges'.[4]

Tracing the identity and establishing the functions of the knights of the royal household before the reign of Edward I is not easy. Denholm–Young found them 'elusive people' in the thirteenth century.[5] Jolliffe showed what could be done from 'the drudgery of the rolls' and with a sensitive response to the vocabulary of familiar

1. *Ante*, lxxiii (1958), 1–26.   2. *Chapters*, i. 18.
3. R. F. Walker, 'The Anglo-Welsh Wars, 1216–67' (Oxford, D.Phil. thesis, 1953).
4. J. E. A. Jolliffe, *Angevin Kingship* (London, 1955), pp. 211, 63, 195, 143, n. 6.
5. N. Denholm-Young, *History and Heraldry, 1254 to 1310* (Oxford, 1965), p. 29.

administration; but he was forced to concede that little can be known of the corps of king's knights as an organized body in the Angevin period.[1] Similarly Professor Warren has stressed the difficulty of recognizing the importance of the knights in the service of Henry II, *familiares* such as Hugh de Cressy, an itinerant justice in 1176 and a recruiter of mercenaries in 1184, or Bertram de Verdun, sheriff and itinerant justice, sent on missions to Spain and Ireland and placed in charge of Acre during Richard I's crusade: only the frequency with which such men attested royal charters reveals how much Henry relied upon them.[2] For the Anglo-Norman period Professor Hollister was able to find a few references to the knights of the royal household, though noting that they were seldom mentioned in the narrative sources and adding the reservation that chroniclers 'might on occasion use the term *familia* loosely in such a way as to include enfeoffed knights who might be in the royal following on some particular campaign'. Nevertheless Hollister made the valid point that the warriors of the royal household represent a perennial element in English military organization, from the retinues of Alfred and the housecarles of Canute to King John's bachelors, and far beyond.[3]

It is however one thing to show that the Norman kings possessed a personal retinue or bodyguard and quite another matter to demonstrate, as was claimed in 1963, that the *familia regis* of the Anglo-Norman period, as in the reign of Edward I, 'supplied the standing professional element, capable of fighting independent actions and, for a major campaign, providing the framework into which other forces could be fitted'.[4] Working along some of the lines then suggested, though apparently in complete independence, Mrs Chibnall has recently made some valuable identifications of individual members of Henry I's *familia*, concluding that it was within this body that mercenaries were most effectively employed and that the *familia* gave Henry I a well-trained and adequately paid professional military force, ordinarily quartered out as castle garrisons but available for action in the field as a mounted *corps d'élite*. Nevertheless Mrs Chibnall held that it was not until the reign of Stephen and still more that of Henry II that paid forces assumed the proportions of a professional army; and she quoted with approval the description of Henry I's reign as a time of 'old-style warfare, carried out by small feudal troops'.[5]

1. *Angevin Kingship*, pp. 350, 279.
2. W. L. Warren, *Henry II* (London, 1973), pp. 309–10.
3. C. Warren Hollister, *The Military Organization of Norman England* (Oxford, 1965), pp. 174–5.
4. J. O. Prestwich, 'Anglo-Norman Feudalism and the Problem of Continuity', in *Past and Present*, no. 26 (1963), pp. 50–51.
5. Marjorie Chibnall, 'Mercenaries and the *familia regis* under Henry I', in *History*, lxii (1977), pp. 15–23.

Before considering the evidence of the chroniclers, who may not have understood the technical terms of military organization and whose figures for the strength of contingents cannot be accepted uncritically, it is worth looking again at the *Constitutio Domus Regis*, in which Tout found merely a handful of archers. These were members of the staff of the royal hunt, as were twenty sergeants, unnoticed by Tout.[1] If indeed the *Constitutio* 'includes all the members of the household', as one authority has declared,[2] it cannot be supposed that twenty sergeants and a few archers could have provided a useful nucleus, still less a general staff, for Henry I's field armies and castle garrisons. But the *Constitutio* also lists the constables, the master marshal and the four marshals who acted as his deputies. Of the master marshal it provides that he ought to have tallies of the gifts and wages, *dona et liberationes*, made from the king's treasure and chamber.[3] Who received these gifts and wages? The expression strongly suggests the *stipendia et donativa* by which Henry I's paid troops were maintained,[4] and anticipates the headings of *dona* and *vadia* recorded in the wardrobe accounts of Edward I as paid to members of the royal military household. Moreover the *Dialogue of the Exchequer* shows that under Henry II the constable and marshal were responsible for the wages of the royal troops.[5] Of the four deputy marshals the *Constitutio* lays it down that they served the *familia regis*, its clerks, knights and other officers.[6] It appears that the *familia regis* was treated as a body distinct from the *domus regis* which alone formed the subject-matter of the *Constitutio*, and that it required a substantial staff to administer it.

Household ordinances such as the *Constitutio* are no guide to the royal military household. It is now clear that the household ordinance of 1279 (of which the title is merely a French version of that of the *Constitutio*), with its twenty sergeants-at-arms, did not, as Tout supposed, record the full strength of Edward I's military household after the first Welsh war in which it had played so prominent a part.[7] Some confirmation of this reading of the *Constitutio* is provided by Walter Map. When praising the good order which had been maintained in the court of Henry I Map explains that Henry had himself drawn up written regulations for the *domus* and the *familia*, and in summarizing them he distinguished clearly between the two bodies.[8]

1. Ed. and trans. by C. Johnson in *Dialogus de Scaccario* (London, 1950), p. 135; Tout, *Chapters*, ii. 136.
2. G. H. White, 'The Household of the Norman Kings', in *Trans. Royal Hist. Soc.*, 4th ser. xxx (1948), p. 130.   3. Pp. 133-4.
4. Robert of Torigni's interpolation in William of Jumièges, *Gesta Normannorum Ducum*, ed. J. Marx (Paris, 1914), p. 296.
5. *Dialogus*, p. 20.   6. P. 134.   7. *Chapters*, ii. 141.
8. Walter Map, *De Nugis Curialium*, ed. M. R. James (Oxford, 1914), p. 219: 'Scriptas habebat domus et familie sue consuetudines, quas ipse statuerat; domus, ut semper esset omnibus habunda copiis . . .; familie, ne quis egeret, sed perciperet quisque certa donaria.'

Unluckily Map contented himself with saying that the regulations for the *familia* were framed so that no one should suffer want and each should receive his fixed rewards. But in another passage Map tells us that whenever Henry I heard of any young man on this side of the Alps who was anxious for a good start in life, he appointed him to the *familia*. To these recruits Henry paid a minimum of £5 a year and, when they were summoned for service, a shilling a day reckoned from the time of their leaving home.[1] Here we have what appears to be the fee and wages, the indenture of retainer so familiar in the fourteenth and fifteenth centuries. Map tells us that the influence of Henry's court extended throughout all Christendom, and there is independent evidence to show that in one instance at least it reached a very distant outpost. After the magnates of Antioch asked Fulk of Jerusalem to suggest a suitable candidate from the west who could marry the heiress to the principality of Antioch, and thus restore order and supply leadership, the choice finally fell on Raymond of Poitiers, the younger brother of the duke of Aquitaine. Raymond was then residing at the court of Henry I and it was on the advice of Henry, described as his benefactor, that he accepted the offer. Evidently Raymond's connection with the English court was of some standing, for he was then thirty-four and had been knighted by Henry.[2] It seems reasonable to infer that Raymond had been enrolled in Henry's *familia*, just as much later Amadeus of Savoy served in the military household of Edward I.

One piece of record evidence throws fuller light on the structure and capabilities of the military household of Henry I. By the treaty of March 1101 Count Robert of Flanders, in return for a fee or money fief of £500 a year, agreed to provide Henry I with 1,000 knights for service in England or Normandy, or with 500 knights for service in Maine. Henry undertook to maintain the Flemish knights and to compensate them for their losses, both in England and in Normandy, as it was his custom to do for his own military household – *sicut mos est reddere familie sue*. For campaigns in Maine it was provided that the Flemings should actually be in the military household, serving for a whole month if Henry wished to retain them for so long, and being maintained and compensated in the customary way.[3] The terms of this treaty are not easily reconciled with what is perhaps still the orthodox chronology of the development of military organization. Historians of the later Middle Ages have long been accustomed to stress the importance of the system of indentures, the replacement of the old feudal armies by the new contract armies. By the beginning of Edward III's reign 'it needed only the storm of a vast continental

1. Ibid. p. 235.
2. William of Tyre, *Historia Rerum in Partibus Transmarinis Gestarum*, xiv, ix, xx.
3. *Diplomatic Documents preserved in the Public Record Office*, ed. P. Chaplais (Oxford, 1964), i. 1101–1272, pp. 1–4.

war to prove the utter rottenness and decay of the rival system of service by feudal tenure'. A new system was needed, and this 'was found and widely applied in the Hundred Years' War in the form of indenture service'. These indentures specified 'the strength and composition of the contingents to be brought, the period and place of service, the rate of wages and bonus, compensation for lost horses, liability for . . . (the expenses) of transport and division of the "advantages of war", that is the ransom of prisoners and the tenure of captured castles'.[1] But the essentials of this 'new system' were already contained in the treaty of 1101: it specified the retaining fee, the strength of the contingents, the periods and places of service, compensation for losses and liability for the expenses of transport. It did not specify wage rates. But McFarlane noted that in most indentures of service during the Hundred Years' War the king's wages were so far stereotyped that it was enough to define them as 'usual'.[2] They were already 'usual' at the beginning of the twelfth century: Flemish knights were expected to be familiar with the customary terms of service in the military household of the kings of England. Nor does the treaty of 1101 stand alone as the product of an exceptional crisis: it was renewed, with some modifications, in 1110; and if William of Malmesbury is correct the first such treaty with Flanders had been concluded by Duke William on the eve of his conquest of England. Similar provisions may well have been included when Henry I granted a money fief to the count of Hainault in the late 1120s.[3]

If we combine the evidence of the treaty of 1101 with that of the *Constitutio*, remembering that the latter gives us the regulations for the *domus* only and not those for the *familia*, the structure and poten- tiality of Henry I's military household begin to appear impressive. Its officers included the constables, the master marshal and the deputy marshals: its members received bonus payments, regular wages and compensation for losses when on service; and it attracted men from outside Henry's dominions who were retained by annual fees. Moreover Henry envisaged that it could be expanded into a very large force, absorbing 500 or even 1,000 knights from Flanders alone.

Is it possible to assess the role of the military household in the campaigns of the Conqueror, Rufus and Henry I? Chroniclers had ordinarily little to say on the structure of military forces, though they make it plain that mercenaries were extensively employed. Orderic

---

1. A. E. Prince, 'The Army and Navy', in *The English Government at Work, 1327–1336*, ed. J. F. Willard and W. A. Morris (Cambridge, Mass., 1940), i. 354–5; N. B. Lewis, quoted by K. B. McFarlane in 'Bastard Feudalism', *Bulletin of the Institute of Historical Research*, xx (1945), pp. 163–4.

2. *The Nobility of Later Medieval England*, p. 23.

3. *Diplomatic Documents*, i. 5–8; William of Malmesbury, *Gesta Regum Anglorum*, ed. W. Stubbs (Rolls Series, 1889), ii. 478; B. D. Lyon, *From Fief to Indenture* (Cambridge, Mass., 1957), p. 35.

Vitalis, with his special interest in and knowledge of the Norman lay aristocracy, was exceptional in noting the presence and use of the *familia regis* in operations, and though his figures for its size cannot be taken literally, his general account deserves to be taken seriously. In Orderic's pages the military household makes its first significant appearance in the war of Sainte-Suzanne, which lasted for over two years, 1084-6. Faced with a resistance movement in Maine the Conqueror left the task of containing it to the *familia regis*. Orderic describes it as an expensive war. The royal troops were lavishly supplied with food and money, and the garrison of Sainte-Suzanne flourished on the ransoms of the many Norman prisoners they took. Orderic gives no figures, but it is clear from the standing of the commanders of the *familia* that a substantial force was involved.[1]

Under Rufus the military household appeared more prominently. It formed the spearhead of his penetration of Normandy in 1089 and 1090; it was active in the campaign for the Vexin which followed Rufus's acquisition of Normandy; and it supplied the garrisons of the castles in Maine. Although Count Helias was able to seize Le Mans itself in the summer of 1099, the grip which these garrisons kept on the rest of the county allowed Rufus to reassert his control and to recover the city.[2] Under Henry I members of the household were prominent in the campaigns of 1105 and 1106 which culminated in Henry I's decisive victory at Tinchebrai. Indeed it seems that the army which won that victory was controlled by the military household, for Orderic describes Henry as assembling its commanders and making his dispositions before the battle.[3] The household was similarly prominent in the campaigning of 1118 and 1119; and though Orderic does not mention it as taking part in the battle of Brémule, Henry of Huntingdon described it as then operating with Henry himself and forming one of the three divisions of the army.[4] Some support for this, at least as far as the cavalry forces were concerned, is provided by Orderic's figures. He credited Henry with 500 knights at Brémule; and a little later he described Henry as sending his son, Richard, with 200 knights of the household under the command of Ralph the Red and Rualon of Avranches to the relief of Breteuil.[5]

During the rebellion of Waleran of Meulan and Amaury of

1. *The Ecclesiastical History of Orderic Vitalis*, ed. and trans. by Marjorie Chibnall (Oxford, 1969-) (henceforth cited as Orderic), iv. 46-52. Orderic used the technical term, *regis familia*, though the consistency of his language is obscured in Mrs Chibnall's translation. In ii. 227, iv. 49 and 183 *regis familia* is rendered as 'the king's garrison' or 'garrison of king's men', while from v. 217 it is given as 'royal household troops'.

2. Orderic, iv. 182 (*regis familia*), 214 (*familiis eius*) v. 216 (*regis familia*), 254-6 (*regalis familia*). Henry of Huntingdon, *Historia Anglorum*, ed. T. Arnold (Rolls Series, 1879), p. 231, also reports Rufus's *familia* in Maine in 1099.

3. Orderic, vi. 88.

4. Orderic, vi. 220; Henry of Huntingdon, *Historia Anglorum*, p. 241.

5. Orderic, vi. 236, 246.

Montfort in 1123–4 Henry used his military household not in a coherent body, as at Brémule, but dispersed defensively as castle garrisons at Gisors, Évreux, Pont-Autou, Bernay and elsewhere. On the night of 24–25 March 1124 patrols detected a move by the rebel leaders; three detachments of the household, put by Orderic at 300 knights supported by horsed archers, were concentrated; and on 26 March they intercepted and defeated the rebel force at Bourg-théroulde. This battle, which brought the revolt to an end, was won by a force drawn exclusively from the royal military household. Orderic treated this engagement as of symbolic importance and composed revealing speeches for the rival leaders in which the household troops were urged to fight for their reputation and for their right to continue to draw the king's wages and eat his bread, while the rebels were reminded that they were the flower of the knighthood of all France and Normandy facing merely peasants and common soldiers.[1] In the case of one member of the household who took part in this engagement, Henry de Pomeroy, we know what his pay was and how much bread he was allowed, at least at the close of the reign. For he is listed in the *Constitutio* after the constables, and appears to have been one of the assistant constables.[2]

Orderic's figures of 200 and 300 knights for detachments of the military household in 1119 and 1124 seem insignificant when compared with his figure of 50,000 knights for the Conqueror's invasion army or that of 60,000 knights allegedly available to the Conqueror from England.[3] But later in his work Orderic's figures became more modest and more plausible. He ordinarily gave figures for the knights alone without attempting to assign numbers to the crossbowmen, archers, infantry, engineers and supply forces; and he was too fond of repeating the same figures for us to place full confidence in any one, such as the 300 knights of Bourgthéroulde. Nevertheless the proportions of his figures are interesting. He once credited Rufus with as many as 1,700 knights in the Maine campaign of 1098.[4] To Fulk of Anjou he assigned 500 knights in 1118, and to Henry I, after he had mobilized the full strength of Normandy in the same campaign, 1,000.[5] In the battle of Brémule he believed that 900 knights in all had been engaged, Henry I with 500 and the French with 400.[6] And in Stephen's reign he had Geoffrey of Anjou invading Normandy with 400 knights.[7] Hence when Orderic gave a strength of 200 knights to a detachment of Henry's household in 1119 and assessed the force which could be immediately concentrated from a small sector in 1124 at 300 knights, he was representing the *familia regis* of Henry I as a formidable force, contributing at least as high a

1. Orderic, vi. 346–50.
2. *Constitutio Domus Regis*, p. 134.
3. Orderic, ii. 168, 266.
4. Orderic, v. 246.
5. Orderic, vi. 194, 200.
6. Orderic, vi. 236.
7. Orderic, vi. 482.

proportion of the cavalry as did the household in the armies of Edward I.

From the reign of Henry II onwards the *familia regis* was more than a standing professional force of vital importance in the organ-ization of armies and the conduct of campaigns: it supplied kings with sheriffs, provincial governors, judges, councillors and diplo-mats; it was fortified by traditions of service in such families as the Cliffords and the Lestranges which provided recruits in generation after generation; and it came to attract the aristocracy, even members of comital families, into its ranks. When criticizing the notion of the higher nobility of later medieval England as 'growling and factious backwoodsmen', McFarlane instanced the striking record of the Montagus. Simon Montagu was a distinguished knight of the household under Edward I; his son rose to become steward of Edward II's household and seneschal of Gascony; his grandson, William, began as a yeoman of the household and was created Earl of Salisbury by Edward III. This advancement did not end the family connection with the household and royal service: a brother of the first earl was retained for life as a household knight, while a son became steward of the household under Richard II. And the second, third and fourth earls were active as captains and councillors for the greater part of the Hundred Years' War.[1]

These illustrations are taken from the period of 'bastard feudalism', and it is not to be expected that lay members of the household should have been of the same eminence or employed in administration and counsel as well as in war during the first century of true feudalism, when the feudal duties of knight service and counsel should have largely met the needs of the Norman kings. Household knights were then by definition, we have been taught, landless and unenfeoffed. There can be little doubt that the *familia regis* of the Conqueror and his sons was largely recruited from the professional knights whose low social status has been so effectively established by Dr Sally Harvey:[2] it was because these men formed the rank and file of the royal household at Bourgthéroulde that Waleran of Meulan rashly dismissed them as peasants and common soldiers. But other members of the military household were of higher status.

In her examination of the *familia regis* under Henry I Mrs Chibnall has identified twelve of its members mentioned by Orderic Vitalis. Some, such as Odo Borleng, appear to have been of modest families serving primarily for their wages. Others belonged to the Norman aristocracy. William de Grandcourt was a younger son of the count of Eu; Engenulf and Geoffrey de Laigle, though landless younger sons, came from a baronial family with major holdings in England

1. K. B. McFarlane, *The Nobility of Later Medieval England*, pp. 160–1.
2. Sally Harvey, 'The Knights and the Knight's Fee in England', in *Past and Present*, no. 49 (1970), pp. 3–43.

and Normandy; Ranulf, vicomte of the Bessin, and Robert de
Chandos were important vassals who 'may have performed greater
services than their feudal obligations required'. Mrs Chibnall sees
the *familia regis* as a composite body of feudal vassals, quasi-vassals
in receipt of money fiefs, and stipendiaries, all nerved by the hope of
future rewards in the form of cash bonuses, grants of land, or the
restoration of lost patrimonies.[1]

This analysis of the membership of the *familia regis* can be extended
and the conclusions modified. We may begin with Orderic's account
of the war of Sainte-Suzanne towards the close of the Conqueror's
reign. Among those mentioned by Orderic as taking part with the
familia regis were Alan the Red, count of Brittany and lord of Richmond, who commanded the household; William I de Warenne;
William count of Évreux; and Richer I de Laigle with his brother
Gilbert.[2] Were these men members of the household? They were
certainly not landless knights. Count Alan had probably led the
Breton contingent at Hastings, had been a frequent witness of the
Conqueror's charters, and by 1086 had accumulated the estates in
Yorkshire and ten other counties which made him the third richest
lay magnate in England, being immediately followed by William I
de Warenne.[3]

The history of the Laigle family is suggestive. Engenulf de Laigle
fought and was killed at Hastings. His two sons, Richer I and Gilbert,
were with the *familia regis* at Sainte-Suzanne, Richer being killed in
the campaign.[4] The career of Richer's son and heir, another Gilbert,
is rather better documented. He served with the *familia regis* and was
captured by the French when the household was raiding in the Vexin
in 1097–8. But he was soon ransomed, for in 1098 he and William
count of Évreux were placed in charge of Le Mans after its capture
by Rufus, and were given a strong detachment of household troops.[5]
He gave his loyalty to Henry I, who evidently valued his services in
the campaigns which culminated at Tinchebrai, for Gilbert was
rewarded with the honour of Pevensey, forfeited by William count
of Mortain.[6] Thereafter Gilbert's recorded services were as a
counsellor and judge. In 1108 he was at Norwich and, in the company of Roger of Salisbury and William II de Warenne, witnessed
the confirmation of an agreement made in the *curia regis*. In 1109 he
attended the council of Nottingham, and in 1110 he was one of the
witnesses on behalf of Henry I to the Treaty of Dover, renewing
with modifications the earlier Anglo-Flemish treaty of 1101. We last
encounter him as a judge in the royal *curia* in Normandy in 1111,

1. Marjorie Chibnall, *art. cit.*
2. Orderic, iv. 48–50.
3. J. F. A. Mason, 'The "Honour of Richmond" in 1806', *ante*, lxxviii (1963), 703–4.
4. Orderic, ii. 176 and n. 4, iv. 48–50.
5. Orderic, v. 216, 250.
6. I. J. Sanders, *English Baronies* (Oxford, 1960). p. 136.

serving with the archbishop of Rouen, the bishop of Lisieux, Robert of Beaumont, William II de Warenne, William of Tancarville, chamberlain, and William de Ferrers.[1]

By 1118 Gilbert was dead, and in that year his eldest son, Richer II, demanded his father's lands in England. Henry I refused, explaining that Richer's younger brothers, Engenulf and Geoffrey, were serving in the *familia regis* in the expectation of succeeding to the inheritance in England. This drove Richer into the arms of the French, and it was not until after Henry I's victory at Brémule in 1119 that Richer was finally reconciled with the king and received his father's lands in England as well as in Normandy.[2] He too, it seems, continued his family's connection with the royal military household, and it was through Richer II de Laigle that young Thomas Becket saw something of the court and was initiated into aristocratic pursuits.[3] Here we have four generations of a family in the service of the monarchy, three generations being connected with the military household.

The evidence for William I and William II de Warenne as members of the *familia regis* is similarly suggestive. William I de Warenne was a member of the new aristocracy formed in Normandy before the conquest of England, a relatively small but very powerful group deliberately created by Duke William, it has been suggested, 'to form a military élite attached to him personally and to provide a force which would enable him to control the lands he ruled, to beat down rivals at home and hold his own with neighbouring princes'.[4] The special trust which the Conqueror placed in William I de Warenne is attested by the special responsibilities assigned to him in England in 1067 and 1075, by his service with the *familia regis* at Sainte-Suzanne, and by the vast grants of land which made him the fourth richest lay magnate in England in 1086.[5] In 1088 Rufus rewarded or obtained his support by granting him four manors in Surrey, the great royal manor of Wakefield in Yorkshire and creating him earl of Surrey.[6] William II de Warenne temporarily deserted Henry I in 1101 but was reconciled in 1103. Thereafter he was consistently loyal. He commanded a division at Tinchebrai in 1106 and again at Brémule in 1119.[7] He was one of the sureties for Henry in the Anglo-Flemish

1. *Regesta Regum Anglo-Normannorum*, ii, ed. C. Johnson and H. A. Cronne (Oxford, 1956), nos. 875, 918–20, 941, 1002. Gilbert may also have served in Henry's Welsh campaign of 1114, *ibid*. nos. 1048–50.   2. Orderic, vi. 196–8, 250.

3. *Thómas Saga Erkibyskups*, ed. E. Magnússon (Rolls Series, 1875), i. 30.

4. J. Le Patourel, *The Norman Empire* (Oxford, 1976), p. 287, summarizing the findings of D. C. Douglas and L. Musset.

5. Orderic, ii. 196, 316, iv. 50. Orderic described William I de Warenne, together with Richard fitz Gilbert, as *praecipuus Angliae iusticiarius* and *vicarius regis* in 1075, and William's prominence in these operations is confirmed by Lanfranc, Ep. 35.

6. *Victoria History of the County of Surrey* (London, 1902), i. 340. See also the entries in *V.C.H. Surrey* ii under Shiere, Reigate, Dorking and Fetcham.

7. Orderic, v. 308, 314 (1101), vi. 14 (1103), 88 (1106), 234–6 and *Chronicon Monasterii de Hida*, ed. E. Edwards (Rolls Series, 1886), p. 317 (1119).

treaty of 1110 and a royal judge in Normandy in 1111. And he attended the great councils at Nottingham in 1109 and at Northampton in 1131.[1] Professor Le Patourel has worked out his itinerary and has established the highly significant fact that from 1111 to 1135 William II de Warenne was in Normandy during each of the seven separate stays of Henry I in the duchy, and in England during each of the six intervening periods which the king spent there.[2]

William I de Warenne's whole career strongly suggests that when he served with the *familia regis* at Sainte-Suzanne he did so, like the Laigle brothers, as a member of it. From 1103 William II de Warenne served Henry I as his father had served the Conqueror; and it is likely that he too did so as a member of the *familia*. Orderic's language suggests that those who, like Warenne, commanded divisions at Tinchebrai were drawn from the captains of the household with whom Henry made his dispositions for the battle.[3] Throughout the rest of his career William II de Warenne followed his master's movements on both sides of the Channel, serving him as a judge and councillor as well as in war and being frequently associated with known members of the household. Moreover the view that those listed by Orderic as fighting with the *familia regis* at Sainte-Suzanne did so as members of it is strengthened by the fact that a name which can be added to that list from a quite different source is also that of a member of the household. For Domesday Book records that the Conqueror gave land at Ludwell in Oxfordshire to Robert d'Oilli at the siege of Sainte-Suzanne; and Robert was a constable of the household.[4]

If William I de Warenne rose through the Conqueror's *familia* to become one of the greatest tenants-in-chief and an earl, and if William II de Warenne continued to serve and prosper in the same capacity, they were not the only great magnates to do so. A revealing incident is reported by Orderic in 1098. Count Helias of Maine was captured and handed over to Rufus as a prisoner. By the treaty which concluded Rufus's first campaign in Maine Le Mans and all that the Conqueror had held in Maine were acquired by Rufus. It was also agreed that the prisoners taken by both sides, including Count Helias, should be released. Helias then asked Rufus for two favours: that he should be allowed to keep his title of count and should be admitted to Rufus's military household, serving him as a *familiaris* until he should have earned the restoration of his lands and castles.[5]

---

1. *Regesta*, ii, nos. 941, 1002, 918–19, 1715.
2. J. Le Patourel, *The Norman Empire*, p. 295 and n. 3.
3. 'Magistratus familiae suae conuocauit, ad prelium omnes instruxit, breuiter commonuit.... Primam aciem rexit Rannulfus Baiocensis, secundam Rodbertus comes Melletensis, terciam uero Guillelmus de Guarenna' (Orderic, vi. 88).
4. D.B. i. 158b.
5. Orderic, v. 246–8: 'Obsecro igitur ut cum pristinae dignitatis uocabulo in tua me suscipias familia.'

Rufus, always ready to add good soldiers to his household, at first agreed. But Robert of Beaumont, count of Meulan, already described by Orderic as the leading man among the royal councillors and justices, dissuaded Rufus, his argument being that the offer was fraudulent but his real motive being fear that Helias would prove a dangerous rival in the royal household.[1]

Orderic's story shows that the military household was more than a fighting force: its leaders enjoyed the confidence of the king, shared in his counsels and judgments and stood at the centre of power, jealously guarding their privileges and opportunities. And the career of Robert of Beaumont is a striking illustration of the opportunities presented by service in the *familia regis*. Robert had a long military career: he was the only man to fight both in the battle of Hastings, which gave England to the Conqueror, and, as the commander of a division, in the battle of Tinchebrai, which gave Normandy to Henry I.[2] But it was as councillor and statesman that his chief work was done. In Eadmer's pages he appears as one of Rufus's chief councillors as early as 1093, prominent thereafter in the discussions and disputes between Anselm and Rufus, largely responsible for Henry I's obstinacy and prevarications over investiture and homage, being singled out for excommunication by Paschal II in 1105, and still giving his rulings on ecclesiastical issues in 1115. Nevertheless Eadmer praised him, after the settlement of the investiture dispute in 1107, as a lover of justice and gave him the credit, as the man most trusted by the king in public affairs, for Henry's abandonment of Rufus's evil ways.[3] Orderic gave particular emphasis to Robert of Beaumont's services to Henry in the critical early years of his reign. With his brother, Henry earl of Warwick, Robert took the lead in securing the throne for Henry. He gave astute advice on how to deal with disaffection in England on the eve of Robert Curthose's invasion in July 1101, and he profited largely from Henry's success, acquiring the midland estates of Ivo de Grand-mesnil.[4] In 1103 he was sent to Normandy on Henry's behalf and played a leading role in the campaigning which ended three years later with Henry's victory at Tinchebrai.[5] It was probably after Tinchebrai that his services were rewarded by the creation of the earldom of Leicester for him; and by 1107 or 1108 he was able to

1. Orderic, v. 248: 'in pretorio principali parem seu potiorem perpeti metuebat . . . uoluntas regis immutata est, et strenuus heros ne in familia regis computaretur repudiatus est'. Orderic's choice of *pretorium principale* as a synonym for *familia regis* is unusual and significant.

2. William of Poitiers, *Gesta Guillelmi ducis Normannorum et regis Anglorum*, ed. R. Foreville (Paris, 1952), p. 192; Orderic, vi. 88.

3. Eadmer, *Historia Novorum*, ed. M. Rule (Rolls Series, 1884), pp. 40, 62, 86, 163, 170-1, 191-2, 235.

4. Orderic, v. 314-16, vi. 18-20.

5. Orderic, vi. 44, 56.

review his extensive gains and to make careful provisions for the
succession of his twin sons to his lands on both sides of the Channel.[1]

To Henry of Huntingdon Robert of Beaumont, though un-
scrupulously acquisitive, was the wisest man in Christendom in
secular matters and the arbiter of peace and war between England
and France.[2] William of Malmesbury summed him up as *propugnator
justitiae, provisor victoriae*: a defender of justice in the courts and the
architect of victory in war.[3] A modern historian has described Robert
as one of Henry's dangerous friends, a 'malevolent force' in his
counsels.[4] Contemporaries were more charitable, and it is significant
that Eadmer should have agreed with William of Malmesbury in
praising him for his justice.

The third of Henry's commanders at Tinchebrai, alongside
William II de Warenne and Robert of Beaumont, was a man then
of lesser eminence, Ranulf le Meschin, *vicomte* of the Bessin. Seventeen years later, when Henry I correctly foresaw trouble in Normandy, Robert of Gloucester and Ranulf were sent to take charge of
the Norman defences. During the rebellion Ranulf commanded the
garrison at Évreux, while other members of the household were
detailed to Gisors, Pont-Autou and Bernay.[5] Mrs Chibnall accordingly classes Ranulf, as *vicomte* of the Bessin, among those members
of the household who were also important vassals.[6] But by 1123
Ranulf was not merely *vicomte* of the Bessin: he was earl of Chester
and had added the Avranchin to his Norman patrimony.[7] If Ranulf
had been a permanent member of the military household it would
help to explain the special trust which Henry placed in him, using
him as lord of the frontier settlement at Carlisle and as a long-serving
local justiciar of Lincolnshire, and recognizing his claim to Chester,
though he was no more than the cousin of the previous earl.[8]

Another magnate closely associated with the military household
for a limited period was Robert of Bellême. He was Rufus's *princeps
militiae* in the Vexin campaign of 1097, when the military household
played a prominent role. In the following year he was generously
subsidized for operations against Maine, being appointed *princeps
militiae* at Ballon and receiving from Rufus a force of over 300
knights. Orderic does not say that these knights belonged to the
royal military household, though this is probable; for in 1099, when

1. Orderic, vi. 20 and n. 1; *Regesta* ii, no. 843.
2. *Epistola de Contemptu Mundi*, printed in Appendix B to *Historia Anglorum*, p. 306.
3. *Gesta Regum*, ii. 483.
4. R. W. Southern, 'King Henry I', in *Medieval Humanism and Other Studies* (Oxford,
1970), p. 212.
5. Symeon of Durham, *Historia Regum*, ed. T. Arnold (Rolls Series, 1885), ii. 267-8;
Orderic, vi. 346.
6. *Art. cit.* p. 18.
7. *Complete Peerage*, iii. 166.
8. *Regesta*, ii, *passim*; J. C. Holt, 'Politics and Property in Early Medieval England',
in *Past and Present*, no. 57 (1972), pp. 51-52.

Le Mans fell, Robert of Bellême sent a message to Rufus asking for help, reporting that he himself was holding Ballon and that the *regalis familia* was successfully defending all the fortifications entrusted to it.[1] Robert was acting as a theatre commander supported by royal funds and troops of the royal military household; and it is significant that it was during these operations in Maine that he was allowed, for a price, to succeed to the earldom of Shrewsbury and to acquire the lands of Roger de Bully.[2]

Robert of Bellême's brother-in-law, Robert fitz Hamon, showed greater political judgment. He supported Rufus in the rebellion of 1088, was rewarded with the lands of Queen Matilda, conquered Glamorgan, founded Tewkesbury Abbey and was the benefactor of other religious houses, so that Orderic was able to class him among the greatest magnates in England in Rufus's reign.[3] He gave equally loyal service to Henry I from the outset of his reign, being prominent as a counsellor and soldier until in 1105 he received the disabling wound in Normandy from which he died in 1107.[4] A casual remark by Orderic reveals that when Robert fitz Hamon was captured by Duke Robert's supporters in 1105 he was serving as a member of the *familia regis*;[5] and it is probable that fitz Hamon, like Robert of Beaumont, had served continuously in the military households of both Rufus and Henry I.[6] According to Orderic it was the news of fitz Hamon's capture which prompted Henry I to cross to Normandy in the spring of 1105. Fitz Hamon's value to Henry I was independently emphasized by William of Malmesbury who singled him out, together with Roger of Gloucester, as among the followers dearest to Henry who were killed or fatally wounded in the campaigns for Normandy.[7]

Roger of Gloucester belonged to a family with strong official and household ties. Under the Conqueror Roger de Pitres was succeeded as sheriff of Gloucestershire by his brother Durand. It is probable

1. Orderic, v. 214, 242, 254–6; Henry of Huntingdon, *Historia Anglorum*, p. 231.
2. Orderic, v. 224–6.
3. Orderic, iv. 128, 182 and n. 1. For his activities in South Wales see Lynn H. Nelson, *The Normans in South Wales, 1070–1171* (Austin and London, 1961), pp. 94–108. *Regesta*, i, *passim*.
4. Orderic, vi. 56, 60; William of Malmesbury, *Gesta Regum*, ii, 474–5; *Regesta*, ii, *passim*.
5. Orderic, vi. 60: 'Rodbertum Haimonis filium aliosque nonnullos de familia regis ceperunt.'
6. According to William of Malmesbury it was Robert fitz Hamon who, on the day of Rufus's death, decided to report to the king the sinister dream of a foreign monk, and he did so because 'ei a secretis erat' (*Gesta Regum*, ii. 377–8). The story curiously anticipates the oath taken by members of the *familia regis* in John's reign: 'jurati quod, si illi aliquid audirent quod fuisset contra dominum regem, domino regi illud intimarent', quoted by Jolliffe, *Angevin Kingship*, p. 176, n. 1, from the Curia Regis Rolls. For *secretus* see Jolliffe, p. 183, on the greater and lesser men attached to the king as *aulici, privati, de consiliis, de secreto, familiares Regis*.
7. *Gesta Regum*, ii. 474–5. Orderic separately noted the death of Roger of Gloucester, *strenuus miles*, at the siege of Falaise (vi. 80 and n. 1).

that it was as a prominent member of the royal military household that Durand's son, Roger of Gloucester, was singled out by William of Malmesbury.[1] It is certain that the son of Roger de Pîtres, Walter of Gloucester, was a constable of the royal household from 1114.[2] Walter's son, Miles of Gloucester, was already a distinguished knight of the household in 1121, succeeded to his father's constableship in 1128 and served Henry I both as sheriff and justice and the Empress as a general, being rewarded with the earldom of Hereford in 1141.[3]

Round long ago pointed out that a number of families owed their rise under Henry I to the fact that Henry had drawn them into his service when he was merely a younger son and lord of the Cotentin; and these territorial links were extended by his practice when king, of recruiting paid troops from Brittany.[4] One distinguished member of the *familia regis* from this region was Brien fitz Count, an illegitimate son of Alan Fergant who commanded the Breton contingent at Tinchebrai. He was brought up, knighted and richly endowed with lands by Henry I.[5] By right of his wife he held Wallingford at farm from the crown and also controlled the lordship of Upper Gwent, centred on Abergavenny and adjoining Miles of Gloucester's lordship of Brecon. In the closing years of Henry I's reign he enjoyed the king's special trust and favour. He was one of only three men consulted on the major political issue of the marriage of the Empress to Geoffrey of Anjou, the others being Robert of Gloucester and the bishop of Lisieux, head of the Norman administration.[6] In 1129 he, again with Robert of Gloucester, audited the account of the royal treasure.[7] By 1130 his lands in ten English counties placed him among the greater territorial magnates.[8] And by 1131 he was a constable of the royal household through which he had risen.[9]

Two of the household knights prominent in the Brémule campaign of 1119 were or became men of substance in English society.

1. W. A. Morris, *The Medieval English Sheriff* (Manchester, 1927), p. 50, n. 62; *Regesta*, ii, p. xvi and no. 1041; Round, *Feudal England* (London, 1909), p. 313.

2. *Regesta*, ii, p. xvi and no. 1070. Walter was sheriff of Gloucestershire from 1097 to 1128 and enjoyed several grants from Henry I (Round, *Ancient Charters*, Pipe Roll Society, vol. 10 (1888), nos. 3 and 10; *Regesta*, ii. no, 1622).

3. *Complete Peerage*, vi. 451-2. Gerald of Wales described Miles as *juvenis de familia (regis) et miles insignis* at the time of his marriage to Sibyl, daughter of Bernard de Neufmarché (*Opera*, ed. J. F. Dimock (Rolls Series, 1868), vi. 29). For the date of this marriage see Round, *Ancient Charters*, no. 6.

4. J. H. Round, *Studies in Peerage and Family History* (London, 1901), pp. 124-5; William of Malmesbury, *Gesta Regum*, ii. 478. J. Le Patourel has taken this line of investigation much further (*The Norman Empire*, pp. 341-7).

5. H. W. C. Davis, 'Henry of Blois and Brian fitz Count', *ante*, xxv (1910), 302-3; Dom A. Morey and C. N. L. Brooke, *Gilbert Foliot and his Letters* (Cambridge, 1965), pp. 105-6.

6. William of Malmesbury, *Historia Novella*, ed. and trans. by K. R. Potter (London, 1955), p. 5.

7. *Pipe Roll 31 Henry I* (ed. J. Hunter, Record Commission, 1883), pp. 130-1.

8. *Ibid. passim.*

9. *Regesta*, ii, p. xvi; G. H. White, 'Constables under the Norman Kings', in *Genealogist*, n.s. xxxviii.

In that campaign Simon de Moulins, together with his colleagues Ralph the Red of Pont-Échanfray and Gilbert of Exmes, was given the command of Évreux after its capture by Henry I.[1] Simon's marriage to Adela de Montfort, a member of another and more eminent household family, brought him the honour of Haughley in Suffolk.[2] Later in the Brémule campaign Rualon of Avranches and Ralph the Red commanded 200 knights of the royal household under the leadership of Henry I's illegitimate son, Richard.[3] Rualon was provided for in England by being married to the heiress to the barony of Folkestone; and by 1129 he was sheriff of Kent.[4]

Other members of the military household were recruited from the families of unsuccessful rebels. The rebellion of earl Roger of Hereford in 1075 resulted in his imprisonment and the suppression of the earldom. Orderic, writing in about 1125, described his two sons, Reginald and Roger, as among the ablest soldiers in Henry I's retinue and seeking by arduous service to gain his favour. When Orderic wrote the brothers did not hold a foot of land in England; but by 1130 Reginald had obtained the hand and estates of a Wiltshire heiress.[5] It is probable that Henry treated the sons of Ivo de Grandmesnil similarly. In 1102 he inflicted a heavy fine on Ivo for his support of Robert Curthose in the previous year. Here Robert of Beaumont saw his opportunity. He agreed to intercede on Ivo's behalf with the king, advanced 500 marks to Ivo in order that he might go on crusade, and received in return Ivo's extensive midland estates for a period of fifteen years. Ivo's heir was then to marry Robert's niece and to recover his father's lands.[6] But at the end of the fifteen years Robert retained the lands and died unrepentant in the following year. According to Henry of Huntingdon the archbishop and other priests appeared at Robert's deathbed to urge him to restore the lands which he had acquired by force or trickery: otherwise his soul would go to hell. Unmoved by this forecast Robert replied, 'I shall give all to my sons: let them do what is proper for my salvation when I am dead'.[7] Robert's sons did nothing; but they were lucky. For two years later Henry I sent the two sons of Ivo de Grandmesnil back to England with orders that they were to receive their father's lands, and they were drowned in the wreck of the White Ship.[8]

It can be only a surmise that Ivo's sons had been serving in the *familia regis*. But such service was, as Anselm recognized, an established course for those who hoped to recover a lost patrimony.[9]

1. Orderic, vi. 230.   2. I. J. Sanders, *English Baronies*, p. 121.
3. Orderic, vi. 246.
4. I. J. Sanders, *English Baronies*, p. 45; *Pipe Roll 31 Henry I*, p. 63.
5. Orderic, ii. 318 and n. 5.   6. Orderic, vi. 18–20.
7. Henry of Huntingdon, *Epistola de Contemptu Mundi*, p. 307.
8. Orderic, vi. 304.
9. Eadmer, *Vita Anselmi*, ed. R. W. Southern (London, 1962), pp. 94–95.

Count Helias of Maine had proposed to serve Rufus in this way, and the hope of succeeding to the Laigle lands in England drew Engenulf and Gilbert de Laigle into Henry I's military household. Moreover Henry was less implacable to the families of those who had rebelled against his father and himself than is sometimes supposed. In 1119 he gave the honour of Breteuil to Ralph de Gael, son of the earl of East Anglia who had rebelled in 1075; in the same year he restored to William Talvas, son of Robert of Bellême, the Norman lands of his father (though without their castles); and for the greater part of his reign he employed as one of his chaplains John of Bayeux, son of Odo of Bayeux who had been arrested by the Conqueror and had rebelled against Rufus.[1] Many of those who sailed in the White Ship with the sons of Ivo de Grandmesnil had served in the *familia regis*: Ralph the Red, Gilbert d'Exmes, Engenulf and Geoffrey de Laigle. William Bigod was a steward of the household, while Hugh de Moulins is likely to have been serving with his elder brother, Simon. Edward of Salisbury, who had been Henry I's standard-bearer at the battle of Brémule, presumably as a member of the *familia*, had prudently disembarked before the White Ship sailed.[2]

Historians who have studied the household of the Norman kings have naturally taken the *Constitutio Domus Regis* as their guide and have been concerned to identify those who held the major offices and to define their functions. To most of these historians the greater lay office-holders have appeared generally unimpressive as military leaders or as administrators: they discharged primarily domestic functions or were converting their posts into titles of honour. The stewards were in charge of the hall and controlled the catering departments; the constables and marshals were primarily concerned with the king's horses and sport, discipline in the court, and billeting arrangements for a large establishment which was constantly on the move. Royal constables, as constables, were not entrusted with military commands: it was the feudal hierarchy which formed the chain of command in war.[3]

This domestic view of the lay side of the royal household is not easily brought into agreement with the careers of all those who held office as stewards or constables under the Norman kings. It was not as a catering officer that William fitz Osbern, steward to the Conqueror, took part in the planning, execution and consolidation of the Norman Conquest.[4] Eudo Dapifer, steward from the 1070s until his death in 1120 and prominent as a judge, administrator and counsellor for over three decades, also acted for all three Norman kings in

1. Orderic, vi. 214, 224, iv. 116 and n. 2.
2. Orderic, vi. 296–304; iv. 50 (for the Laigle brothers); vi. 236 (for Edward of Salisbury).
3. *E.g.* G. H. White, 'The Household of the Norman Kings', *ubi supra*.
4. William of Poitiers, *Gesta Guillelmi*, especially pp. 238–40: Orderic, ii, *passim* and p. 318: 'regis vicarius, Normannie dapifer et magister militum bellicosus.'

raising military forces and served on campaigns. He witnessed the
famous writ of summons to Aethelwig of Evesham, was with Rufus
at the siege of Newcastle in 1095, witnessed the military treaty with
Flanders in 1101, and accompanied Henry on the campaign against
Robert of Bellême in 1102.[1] Hamo Dapifer and Urse d'Abetôt were
sheriffs of Kent and Worcestershire respectively under Rufus: the
former inherited his office from his father, the latter was to hand it
on to his son. It is tempting to regard them as exemplifying the
powerful baronial sheriffs who, after the Conqueror's death, were
increasingly recognized as a menace to the state and it has been
suggested that Ranulf Flambard took the first steps in the long
process of reducing the power of such men.[2] Yet Hamo was a royal
steward as well as sheriff of Kent, while Urse d'Abetôt was a
constable of the household as well as sheriff of Worcestershire. And
in the latter part of Rufus's reign these two acted together with
Flambard, sometimes as witnesses of royal grants or orders, sometimes as an executive group entrusted with carrying out Rufus's
orders transmitted from Normandy.[3]

A revealing writ of 1099, issued by Rufus from Lillebonne and
witnessed by Robert of Beaumont, informed these three of a judgment in favour of the abbey of Fécamp and ordered them to send
Hugh of Buckland down to Sussex to enforce it.[4] For Hugh of
Buckland was picked out by Orderic as one of Henry I's new men,
raised up from the dust; and it is interesting to find the man entrusted with eight counties in the years after the battle of Tinchebrai
as already a trusted royal commissioner in the reign of Rufus.[5] Hamo
and Urse were not baronial sheriffs, survivals from an older order,
whose local interests and family aspirations set them in necessary
opposition to the centralizing policy of the monarchy and the 'new
men' who were its agents. They were officers of the royal household
who had also been entrusted with the custody of two counties of
great military importance; and knights of the household were to
continue to be employed as sheriffs throughout the twelfth and
thirteenth centuries. Under the Conqueror Urse's duties and interests
in Worcestershire seem to have claimed most of his energies: we
hear of him building the castle at Worcester, taking part in the
defence of the Severn valley against the rebels of 1075, and enlarging
his substantial estates at the expense of the churches of Worcester,
Evesham and Pershore.[6] But from the beginning of Rufus's reign

1. *Regesta*, i and ii *passim*; Round, *Feudal England*, p. 304; *Regesta*, i, no. 366 (1095), ii,
no. 515 (1101) and 592 (1102).
2. Morris, *The Medieval English Sheriff*, pp. 46 and n. 47, 72.
3. *Regesta*, i, nos. 416, 422–4.   4. *Regesta*, i, no. 416.
5. Orderic, vi. 16 and n. 4; *Chronicon Monasterii de Abingdon*, ed. J. Stevenson (Rolls
Series, 1858), ii. 117.
6. William of Malmesbury, *De gestis pontificum Anglorum*, ed. N. E. S. A. Hamilton
(Rolls Series, 1870), p. 253; Florence of Worcester, *Chronicon ex chronicis*, ed. B. Thorpe
(Eng. Hist. Soc., 1848), ii. 11; Morris, *Medieval Sheriff*, pp. 70–71.

Urse was increasingly active at court. He appeared as a royal officer at the trial of William of St Calais, bishop of Durham, in 1088,[1] and by the end of the reign he was one of the small group of ministers responsible for the government of England in the king's absence. Throughout the two reigns Urse was employed where he was most needed: as sheriff in the forward zone of Worcestershire and as a member of the central administration.

However it is only if we combine the evidence of the records with that of the chroniclers, above all of Orderic Vitalis, that the full significance of the *familia regis* emerges. In the royal records, dealing primarily with English affairs, the lay officers of the household appear as administrative agents of the Crown and have ordinarily been regarded as relatively insignificant by comparison with the greater churchmen: Lanfranc, Odo of Bayeux, William of St Calais, bishop of Durham, Walkelin, bishop of Winchester, Ranulf Flambard and Roger of Salisbury. William fitz Osbern was the only lay officer of the household to be created an earl in the three Norman reigns, whereas the number of royal chaplains rewarded with bishoprics was legion. But if we can trust Orderic Vitalis on the membership and military role of the *familia regis*, supplementing his evidence from a few other scattered statements and hints, it becomes impossible to regard the military household of the Norman kings as merely a 'modest establishment' by comparison with that of Edward I. The body of troops which was commanded by Robert of Bellême, which a count of Maine sought to enter and which the counts of Flanders joined as country members, which included Robert of Beaumont, *provisor victoriae* under Henry I, which supplied a prince of Antioch and those leaders of the Empress's cause in the civil war, Miles of Gloucester and Brien fitz Count, was a formidable force in war, prominent at Tinchebrai and Brémule, decisive at Bourgthéroulde, and controlling a network of castles from Carlisle to Le Mans and from Cardiff to Gisors.

Great lay magnates served in the military household and some rose to become earls. In addition to William fitz Osbern, created earl of Hereford in 1067, there were, if the suggestions made here can be accepted, William I de Warenne, created earl of Surrey in 1088, followed by William II de Warenne; Robert of Beaumont, created earl of Leicester early in Henry I's reign; and Ranulf le Meschin, earl of Chester from 1120. Robert of Gloucester, created an earl in 1122, should almost certainly be added. The core of Robert's earldom of Gloucester had been formed by his father-in-law, Robert fitz Hamon, a member of the military household; household troops often served under Robert of Gloucester, as Mrs Chibnall observed; and it was with another member of the military household that he carried out

1. *De injusta vexatione Willelmi*, in Symeon of Durham, i. 179.

the audit of the treasure in 1129. Here it is necessary to remember that Orderic's evidence on the membership of the *familia regis* is often precise, usually casual, sometimes allusive and necessarily incomplete. It is precise because he did not use the term *familia* loosely to describe those who happened to be with the king on a particular campaign, but knew that a detachment of the *familia* could be in Maine when the king was in England; and in the speech which he attributed to Odo Borleng before the engagement of Bourgthéroulde Orderic showed that he knew what the terms of membership of the *familia* were. Orderic's evidence is casual because he took the importance of the *familia* and the standing of its leading members for granted: only once, and then parenthetically, did he mention Robert fitz Hamon as a member. For the same reasons Orderic could be allusive. He never tells us explicitly that William II de Warenne was a member of the *familia*, though he seems to allude to this when describing William as serving Henry I for thirty-three years 'inter praecipuos ac familiares amicos';[1] and only other evidence makes William's membership highly probable. We happen to be well informed on the Laigle family and that of Ralph the Red since both were neighbours of and benefactors to Orderic's monastery of St Évroul. Hence Orderic's evidence on membership of the *familia regis* is necessarily incomplete, confined to certain families and to accounts of military operations in Normandy and Maine. In trying to form an estimate of the size and quality of the *familia regis* we must make a large allowance for those of its members whose activities were primarily in England and whose duties were administrative rather than military, thus ignored or little noticed by Orderic. Payn fitz John, for example, whose interests were advanced by Henry I at the expense of the Lacies in Herefordshire and who served with Miles of Gloucester as a justice in the western counties, looks very like a member of the *familia*, as does his brother, Eustace, similarly active in the north of England.[2]

Two other brothers who came from a modest family in the Cotentin had probably entered Henry I's service before his accession to the throne. The elder, William d'Aubigny, appears as Henry's butler in March 1101, and the younger, Nigel, was in Henry's service six months later.[3] According to tradition Nigel d'Aubigny began his career in the king's military household, with the duty of carrying the

1. Orderic, vi. 14.

2. W. E. Wightman, *The Lacy Family in England and Normandy, 1066–1194* (Oxford, 1966), pp. 175–80. Gerald of Wales linked Payn with Miles of Gloucester: 'qui duo tunc temporis inter regis secretarios et praecipuos consiliarios pro magnis habebantur' (*Opera*, vi. 34). For Eustace fitz John's activities in the north of England see *Pipe Roll 31 Henry I*, pp. 24, 26, 36, 131, 142, 143 and *Regesta*, ii, *passim*.

3. For Nigel's career and the formation of the honour of Mowbray see the valuable introduction by D. E. Greenway to her edition of the *Charters of the Honour of Mowbray, 1107–1191* (British Academy Records of Social and Economic History, n.s.i, 1972), pp. xvii–xxv.

king's bow (*juvenis de familia regis . . . portans arcum regis*) and distinguished himself at the battle of Tinchebrai.[1] Dr Greenway classes
Nigel as 'probably a superior kind of household knight' in this first
phase of his career; and until his death in 1129 Nigel enjoyed Henry's
special favour and trust. In 1107 Nigel was married to Matilda de
Laigle, sister of the household knight Gilbert de Laigle and formerly
the wife of Robert de Mowbray. To the Norman holdings Henry I
added the bulk of the Stuteville lands in the north of England and
these were enlarged both by Henry's generosity and Nigel's acquisi-
tiveness into one of the greatest English honours, owing a service of
sixty knights. Henry had now a new use for Nigel who until *c.* 1118
acted as provincial viceroy or local justiciar in Yorkshire and
Northumberland, with custody of York castle. But Nigel maintained
his personal connection with the court: he attended the council of
Nottingham in 1109, was with Henry during his stay in Normandy
from 1111 to 1113, and appeared again at the councils of Westminster
in 1115 and of Salisbury in 1116.[2]

It was at this last council that Nigel's high place in Henry's
counsels was emphatically demonstrated for he was then sent,
together with Robert de Beaumont, earl of Leicester, William II de
Warenne, earl of Surrey, and William de Tancarville, chamberlain,
to urge Thurstan, archbishop-elect of York, to make his profession
of obedience to Canterbury.[3] To Thurstan's followers it was im-
proper that Henry should have sent a delegation of two earls and
two nobles instead of ecclesiastics; but to us the significance lies in
the choice of four leading members of the household to convey the
king's will to Thurstan, himself a former king's clerk who, as the
delegation reminded him, owed so much to the favour of both Rufus
and Henry I. Shortly after this Nigel was recalled to Henry I's entourage. He divorced his first wife and at Henry's instance married
the sister of Hugh de Gournay in 1118. He fought in the battle of
Brémule and again in 1123, when together with Robert of Gloucester
he was in command at the siege of Montfort-sur-Risle.[4]

To Orderic Nigel d'Aubigny was merely a powerful man who
attracted attention because of his marriages into families in which
Orderic was interested and because of his role in Norman campaigns: it is only from other evidence that we can see the significance
of his rise through the military household and glimpse something
of the qualities which made him so loyal and versatile a servant of
Henry I. But though it is impossible to reconstruct in full the
membership of the *familia regis*, the fragmentary evidence which

1. Dugdale, *Monasticon Anglicanum*, ed. J. Caley, H. Ellis, B. Bandinel (London,
1817–30), vi, pt. 1, pp. 320–1.
2. *Regesta*, ii, nos. 918–19, 1003, 1015, 1015a, 1091.
3. Hugh the Chantor, *The History of the Church of York, 1066–1127*, ed. and trans. by
C. Johnson (London, 1961), p. 41.
4. Orderic, iv. 282–4, vi. 192, 236, 334.

survives is enough to demonstrate its importance in the political, administrative and military history of the Norman reigns. Its contribution to the continuity of royal policy is most strikingly exemplified in the career of Robert de Beaumont, while traditions of service were strong in such families as those of Warenne, Laigle and Gloucester. Its influence was perhaps most decisively exerted in the critical years following the death of Rufus. Those who had been the leading members of Rufus's *familia* then supported Henry I in his bid for the throne, in the rebellion by the Montgomeries and in the campaigns for Normandy; and their work was done not merely in the field but in the council chamber, in the shrievalties and in diplomacy. Nigel d'Aubigny's association with Robert of Beaumont in the delegation of 1116 illustrates Henry I's achievement in fusing together the older and the newer elements in his household: Nigel was then one of Henry's 'new men' and still childless, while it was fifty years since Robert of Beaumont had fought at Hastings.

The Norman *familia regis* was remarkably heterogeneous in its composition, both socially and geographically, and remarkably homogeneous in its loyalty. It included both great magnates and mercenaries serving on short-term contracts, and its members were drawn from Brittany, Flanders and France as well as from Normandy. Special ties of loyalty and even of friendship bound these men to the kings they served, and these cannot be explained merely by the royal wages and allowances of which Odo Borleng reminded his troops in 1124, or by the great territorial rewards of such men as William I de Warenne under the Conqueror, Robert fitz Hamon under Rufus, Nigel d'Aubigny and Brien fitz Count under Henry I.

Rufus's power to attract men to his service depended largely on his military reputation. He never fought a major battle and his gains owed more to his purse than to his sword. Yet to Anselm he was *prudens et strenuus*, to Orderic *militia clarus*, and to Suger *usui militie aptus*.[1] When writers attributed to Rufus the quality of *magnanimitas* and applied to him such epithets as *audax*, *protervus*, *strenuus*, *imperiosus*, *superbus*, *arrogans* and *turgidus*, together with numerous illustrative anecdotes, they sought to convey a sense of his self-confidence, boastfulness, ambition, a desire to shock, and a power of command which owed much to determination and something to calculated extravagance and ostentation. Although in action Rufus was usually cautious, often indecisive and sometimes unsuccessful, he contrived to give the impression that he was capable of great achievements, such as the conquest of Ireland and of France.[2] He was not the last general who has found it expedient to combine practical caution with personal panache.

---

1. Anselm, Ep. 192; Orderic, v. 200; Suger, *Vie de Louis VI le Gros*, ed. and trans. by H. Waquet (Paris, 1964), p. 6.
2. Gerald of Wales, *Opera*, vi. 109; Suger, p. 10. The Irish project had earlier been attributed to William the Conqueror (*The Anglo-Saxon Chronicle*, E version, s.a. 1087).

Rufus needed to hold out exciting prospects to those who served him. At a time when the Normans in the north were threatened by internal dissensions and external attacks those in the Mediterranean theatre maintained the impetus of conquest. They threatened Constantinople in 1083, sacked Rome in 1084 and, before Rufus's death, went on to complete the conquest of Sicily and to establish the principality of Antioch. There was an obvious danger that by comparison service in Normandy, Maine, England, Scotland and Wales would seem unrewarding. The Conqueror had recognized this danger when he arrested Odo of Bayeux in 1082, and again when he confiscated the lands of Baudry de Guitry, who had fought with the household at Sainte-Suzanne but then deserted for adventure in Spain.[1] Henry I feared the loss of his best knights in 1106 when, on the eve of the Tinchebrai campaign, he forbade Bohemond to enter England for a recruiting campaign backed by promises of the spoils of Constantinople.[2] It is significant that Ralph the Red, whose relatives had fought with Guiscard and who was later to serve with distinction in Henry's *familia*, should have joined Bohemond on this occasion.[3] Rotrou, count of Perche, was closely linked with Henry I and his court, being married to one of Henry's illegitimate daughters and being also the brother-in-law of Henry of Beaumont, earl of Warwick, and the uncle of Richer II de Laigle. But despite his loyalty to Henry Rotrou frequently succumbed to the temptations of Spain, and by 1125 had acquired the lordship of Tudela there.[4]

Nevertheless Walter Map, writing of the good discipline enforced on the young men of Henry I's military household, held that the reputation of Henry's court stood so high that men were drawn to it in preference to all others.[5] If the language of contemporaries can be trusted Henry I inspired friendship and affection in the members of his household. We read again and again of those such as David of Scotland, Hugh de Gournay, Brien fitz Count and the twin sons of Robert of Beaumont whom Henry brought up from boyhood, admitted to the friendship and fellowship of the household (*familiaris amicicia*; *familiaris conuiua et amicus*), knighted and rewarded.[6] Robert of Beaumont, in the speech attributed to him by Orderic in the crisis of 1101, repeatedly stressed the claims which Henry I had upon his friends.[7] William II de Warenne, after his reconciliation with Henry in 1103, was classed among Henry's closest friends for the rest of the reign; and Ralph the Red came to enjoy a similar intimacy after his rescue of the king's illegitimate son, Richard, during a campaign in the Vexin.[8] Sometimes the language is stronger. We are told of Henry's grief over the deaths of Robert fitz Hamon and Roger of

1. Orderic, iv. 50, 100 and n. 4.
2. Orderic, vi. 68: 'ne sibi electos milites de dicione sua subtraheret'.
3. Orderic, vi. 70.
4. Orderic, iv. 304 and n. 3, vi. 40 and n. 11, 196, 396 and n. 2.
5. *De Nugis Curialium*, p. 235.   6. Orderic, iv. 274, vi. 190, 328.
7. Orderic, v. 314–16.   8. Orderic, vi. 14, 220.

Gloucester, both very dear to him, and of his weeping for the loss of Ralph the Red and Gilbert of Exmes, drowned in the White Ship.[1] Nigel d'Aubigny, when he believed himself to be dying, addressed Henry as his very dear lord and reminded him of his love and very faithful service.[2] Orderic describes Robert of Beaumont as having been greatly loved by Henry I, while to Hugh the Chantor Thurstan of York had been similarly high in the affections of both Rufus and Henry.[3]

Some of these expressions may be discounted as the product of convention or flattery. The ties of loyalty and gratitude did not always hold, especially in the second generation. William II de Warenne deserted Henry I in 1101, though he was reconciled two years later.[4] Robert de Montfort, a constable who served Rufus as a commander in Maine and fought under Henry I at Tinchebrai, was exiled for treason in 1107.[5] Hugh de Gournay rebelled in 1118, though he was pardoned and restored to Henry's friendship in the following year.[6] And there are indications of wider disaffection and even treachery within the household in 1118 and 1119.[7] William de Grandcourt, a younger son of the count of Eu, fought as a knight of the household at Bourgthéroulde and captured the count of Evreux, but chose to desert rather than hand over his captive to Henry I.[8] Nevertheless Orderic was right to attribute Henry's successes to the superiority of his resources in friends as well as in wealth:[9] there can be no doubt of the strength of the loyalty and devotion of Robert of Beaumont in the first half of the reign and of Brien fitz Count in the second. We have been told that down to the mid-eleventh century the Norman knights remained bound to the duke by personal ties rather than by any method of land tenure, and that it was only in the second half of the eleventh century that they became primarily land-holders.[10] But in the military household of the Norman kings these highly personal ties retained all their old significance: those who carried the king's bow, like Nigel d'Aubigny, or who served him with wine at night, like Payn fitz John,[11] were able to win the king's trust and to be rewarded with wealth and power.

1. William of Malmesbury, *Gesta Regum*, ii. 474–5; Orderic, vi. 302.

2. *Charters of the Honour of Mowbray*, no. 2.

3. Orderic, vi. 328; Hugh the Chantor, p. 34. Thurstan was 'domesticus et carus' to Rufus, 'familiaris et acceptus et secretarius' to Henry I.

4. Orderic, v. 308, vi. 14.   5. Orderic, v. 246, 258, vi. 84, 100.

6. Orderic, vi. 188, 278.

7. Suger, p. 190: 'privata factione perterritus'; Orderic, vi. 194, 200: 'illi enim qui cum eo manducabant, nepoti suo aliisque inimicis eius fauebant'. See C. Warren Hollister, 'The Origins of the English Treasury', *ante*, xciii (1978), pp. 267–8, identifying Herbert the Chamberlain as the instigator of the plot to assassinate Henry I in 1118.

8. Orderic, vi. 350–2: 'de familia regis probus eques.'

9. Orderic, vi. 368: 'copiisque facultatum et amicorum.'

10. L. Musset, 'L'aristocratie normande au XIᵉ siècle', in *La Noblesse au Moyen Age*, ed. P. Contamine (Paris, 1976), p. 94.

11. The story of Payn fitz John and Henry I's wine is agreeably told by Walter Map, *De Nugis Curialium*, p. 220.

What were the financial and political costs of maintaining the military household? Rufus's generosity to his knights was notorious; but his household was not supported merely by pay. Wherever Rufus went his household is said to have plundered as if in enemy territory, and, according to Henry of Huntingdon, this was one of the abuses which led Anselm to go into exile.[1] Eadmer's account is more detailed. In 1108 Henry I, acting on the advice of Anselm and others, among whom Robert of Beaumont was the most influential, considered how the lot of the poor could be mitigated; and he began his reforms with the court. Under Rufus the court followers had looted indiscriminately: what they could not consume themselves they sold, and what they could not sell they destroyed. For any future offences of this kind Henry decreed severe penalties of mutilation.[2] Eadmer may have exaggerated both the evil and Anselm's part in the reform, but there is the independent testimony of Walter Map and William of Malmesbury on Henry's remedial measures. Map describes how Henry made public announcements of his future itinerary, giving precise dates and stopping places, so that all knew a month in advance where the court would be. Native and foreign merchants accompanied the court, which resembled a travelling fair, always well stocked with merchandise.[3] William of Malmesbury tells us that Henry laid down what members of the court could accept without payment, what they had to buy and at what prices: Henry, that is, issued regulations on purveyance.[4] It may also have been at this time that he is said to have dropped the three expensive annual feasts.[5] Robert of Beaumont introduced austerer standards of food and dress in the court, and though William of Malmesbury in defending Robert against the charge of meanness attributed these practices to views which Robert had picked up from Byzantine emissaries, it is likely that he was actuated by financial and political considerations.[6]

There was indeed a strain of puritanism at Henry's court, even if it was in part artificial and cultivated. The Easter sermon preached to Henry and his retinue by Serlo, bishop of Séez, directly after Henry had landed in Normandy to begin the campaigns which ended at Tinchebrai, curiously anticipates the seventeenth century. In the first part of his sermon the bishop dwelt on the sufferings of Normandy and on the injuries to the church; and after a suitable allusion to the psalmist he urged Henry to take up arms for the defence of his fatherland. Henry, seconded by Robert of Beaumont, promptly agreed. In the second part of his sermon the bishop took his text from St Paul and denounced as symbols of moral depravity the long hair and pointed shoes which had been fashionable at court since the Conqueror's time; and he invited Henry to set an appropriate

1. *Historia Anglorum*, p. 230.
2. *Historia Novorum*, pp. 192–3.
3. *De Nugis Curialium*, pp. 219, 235.
4. *Gesta Regum*, ii. 487.
5. *Ibid*. ii. 335.
6. *Ibid*. ii. 483.

example to his subjects. Again Henry agreed, and the bishop, conveniently ready with his shears, cut off the locks first of the king, then of Robert of Beaumont, and finally those of the whole *familia regis*.[1] Tinchebrai was a Roundhead victory, and the reforms which followed it included household reforms intended to produce a more sober and a better ordered court. It seems that the reform of the military household had some results. We hear no more of the licence enjoyed by Rufus's retinue. According to the tradition which came down to Walter Map Henry's court was so ordered that business was transacted in the mornings and the younger members of the military household only admitted to the king's presence in the afternoons, when the court became a school of companionship and respectable enjoyment.[2] Henry claimed to Pope Calixtus II that his court was one in which the virtues of justice and knightly discipline were taught.[3] In all this there was a considerable element of idealization and propaganda, but it was not propaganda in which Rufus could plausibly have indulged; and both Odo Borleng and Brien fitz Count took the ideals seriously.

If we combine the evidence of Eadmer, Orderic and William of Malmesbury it is tempting to think that Robert of Beaumont was largely influential in framing the policy of household reform after Tinchebrai. Robert was not only *provisor victoriae* but also *suasor concordiae*,[4] and if victory was to be followed by concord it was essential to impose on the military household the discipline which had been weakened or absent under Rufus, to control expenditure, and to lay down regulations on purveyance and billeting.[5] Robert's views on dress and diet may have been, as William of Malmesbury supposed, the product of personal conviction, but they were also politically expedient; and of all Henry's advisers Robert of Beaumont had the longest experience of the military household and the greatest political influence with the king. It is especially significant that Eadmer, naturally disposed to stress the beneficent influence of Anselm, should have made Robert of Beaumont responsible for bringing Henry to reject the practices of Rufus.[6]

There is one further piece of evidence which, though designed as a window giving on to a very different view, reflects from its surface

1. Orderic, vi. 60–66. 2. *De Nugis Curialium*, pp. 219–20, 235.
3. Orderic, vi. 288.
4. William of Malmesbury, *Gesta Regum*, ii. 483.
5. It seems that the citizens of London claimed, perhaps successfully, *c.* 1133–41, that the *familia regis* should not be billeted upon them compulsorily: 'infra muros ciuitatis nullus hospitetur, neque de mea familia neque de alia ui alicui hospitium liberetur' (F. Liebermann, *Die Gesetze der Angelsachsen* (Halle, 1903), i. 525). See the discussion by C. N. L. Brooke, G. Keir and S. Reynolds, 'Henry I's Charter for the City of London', in *Journal of the Society of Archivists*, vol. iv (1973), pp. 558–78. Similar provisions were made in Richard I's charters to Colchester and Lincoln (W. Stubbs, Select Charters, 9th ed. (Oxford, 1929), pp. 259–61).
6. *Historia Novorum*, pp. 191–2.

an image of the military household under the Norman kings. The great success of Geoffrey of Monmouth's *Historia Regum Britanniae* was in part due to its many anachronisms: its readers would have had little difficulty in recognizing the practices, institutions and even personalities of their own day recreated in Geoffrey's pages and transferred to a remote and romantic past. In his thorough study, *The Legendary History of Britain*, Dr Tatlock demonstrated in great detail the frequency of Geoffrey's allusions to recent events and practices.[1] Arthur's three annual crown-wearings parallel those of the Conqueror. Belinus was credited with a tower of marvellous size at London. Vortigern's first step towards gaining the crown was to acquire control of the treasure, and both Rufus and Henry I took the same prudent course. Sieges played a large part in warfare, and at Sparatinum Geoffrey introduced Greek fire, first made known to the west through the First Crusade. Hengist was seized in battle by the nosepiece of his helmet, just as the Conqueror is reported to have seized a man at Hastings. Geoffrey was so impressed by the accounts of the battle of Tinchebrai that he repeatedly made Aurelius and Arthur employ Henry I's tactic of a final and decisive cavalry charge from the flank by a force hitherto held in reserve.[2]

But faithfully as Geoffrey's work mirrored the society and warfare of his own day it contained, in Dr Tatlock's view, one surprising omission: political and social organization was pre-feudal or non-feudal, even where feudal assumptions and language should have been detected. Dr Tatlock found no suggestion of knights' fees, and armies were mostly composed of 'mere unmounted fighters or household guards rather than of feudal retainers with fiefs'.[3] Dr Tatlock offered various possible explanations for Geoffrey's remarkable silence on the feudal system. Perhaps feudalism was still inchoate in Geoffrey's day; or Geoffrey may have been vague or even ignorant; or on this one point he may have preferred 'a deliberate avoidance of usage known to be recent in the interests of verisimilitude for the well-informed'.[4] But feudalism should not have been inchoate in the middle of its first century; it seems unconvincing to attribute vagueness or ignorance to a writer who took trouble over crown-wearings, nosepieces, Greek fire and the tactics at Tinchebrai; and it is difficult to believe that Geoffrey both supposed his readers to have been so well-informed that they would at once detect the anachronism of placing Arthur in a feudal setting and so ignorant that they would accept the great antiquity of recent military innovations. The problem is unreal. If Geoffrey of Monmouth's work is compared not with the feudalism of historians but with the accounts which late eleventh

1. J. S. P. Tatlock, *The Legendary History of Britain* (Berkeley and Los Angeles, 1950).
2. *Ibid.* pp. 271, 326, 168, 322–3, 326–7, 343.
3. *Ibid.* pp. 299–301.
4. *Ibid.* pp. 300 ff.

and early twelfth-century writers gave of society and warfare in their own day, they will be found to correspond very closely. The feudal system is as inconspicuous in the pages of William of Poitiers, Orderic Vitalis and William of Malmesbury as in those of Geoffrey of Monmouth.

It is therefore significant that Geoffrey should have given such prominence to the place of the military household in war and politics throughout the *Historia*. The ingratitude of Goneril and Regan to Lear was shown by their cutting down of their father's *familia* until he was left with only one knight.[1] Similarly Orderic emphasized the poverty of the future Henry I after his expulsion from western Normandy in 1091 by describing him as accompanied by only one knight, one clerk and three squires.[2] Geoffrey was more inventive in his account of Vortigern's methods in procuring the murder of Constans and his own elevation to the throne. Vortigern first persuaded Constans to enlarge the military household for the better defence of the kingdom. A hundred Pictish knights were accordingly retained and lavishly maintained and rewarded by Vortigern. When Vortigern was confident of their complete attachment to him he alleged that he would have to leave Britain since he could not pay the wages of even fifty knights. Rather than lose their benefactor the Picts murdered Constans, and Vortigern executed the deluded Picts as traitors before seizing the throne.[3]

Arthur's heroic career and extensive conquests form the centre-piece of the *Historia*, and it is in this section that Geoffrey makes his most revealing remarks about the military household. When Arthur succeeded to a kingdom threatened with Saxon conquest his reputation for generosity attracted so many knights to his service that he was unable to pay them all; and it was in the hope of being able to pay his military household from the profits of war that he first attacked the Saxons.[4] Later in his reign Arthur recruited distinguished warriors from distant kingdoms and began to enlarge his *familia*. Nobles everywhere imitated the dress and military practices of Arthur's knights, and the king's own reputation for generosity reached the distant corners of the world and alarmed the rulers of Europe. It was indeed, Geoffrey explains, Arthur's purpose to conquer the whole of Europe; and it is significant that Geoffrey should have introduced these large ambitions with an account of Arthur's expansion of his *familia*.[5] Here Geoffrey of Monmouth was following very closely William of Malmesbury's account of Rufus, though the emphasis on the military household was his own. Rufus had initially

1. *Historia Regum Britanniae*, ed. E. Faral in *La Légende Arthurienne* (Paris, 1929), iii. 206, 208.
2. Orderic, iv. 252.
3. *Historia Regum Britanniae*, iii. 172–4.
4. *Ibid.* iii. 229.
5. *Ibid.* iii. 238–9.

recruited more knights than he could continue to pay; and Rufus's reputation for generosity had drawn the attention of the whole of the western world, reaching indeed as far as the east.[1] From other sources Geoffrey knew that Rufus had been credited with designs almost as large as those of Arthur. Later Gaimar was to include Rome in Rufus's dreams of conquest, deriving this claim from Brennius and Belinus, exactly as Geoffrey of Monmouth had derived Arthur's claim to Rome from these same mythical ancestors.[2] It is an interesting sidelight on the complex interplay between history and historical fiction in the twelfth century that Geoffrey should have modelled Arthur in part on Rufus and that Gaimar should then have improved his account of Rufus by borrowing touches from Geoffrey's Arthur.

The particular value of Geoffrey of Monmouth's evidence derives from his concern to make his narrative both convincing and absorbing by taking the practices with which his readers were familiar and projecting them back into a strange and exciting past. It would have been pointless to have expressed the pathos of Lear's humiliation by the whittling down of his household to a single knight unless Geoffrey's readers had known that the power and dignity of a king was reflected in the size of his *familia* and, perhaps, had remembered Prince Henry's humiliation in 1091. It would have been equally pointless to have shown Constans and Arthur preparing for defence and aggression by enlarging their military households if Geoffrey's readers had not recognized this from their own experience as an obvious move and been in consequence the more disposed to accept the stories of Vortigern's treachery and Arthur's victories. Arthur's practice of retaining knights from distant kingdoms for his household made his court appear the more brilliant because both Rufus and Henry I had increased their power and their reputations by the same means, though on a more modest scale.

The Anglo-Norman military forces were not then so different in structure from those of Edward I as historians have often represented them. In both, the king's military household supplied the standing professional element, capable of acting independently and, for major campaigns, of rapid expansion. The so-called indenture system was no innovation of Edward I's reign: its essential features were already established household custom, *mos familiae regis*, by the beginning of Henry I's reign. If Edward I recruited distinguished warriors from abroad for his household, so did Rufus and Henry I. If Robert Tiptoft rose by his military and administrative services in the household of Edward I, so did Brien fitz Count in that of Henry I. Purveyance for the household was stretched and distorted by

1. William of Malmesbury, *Gesta Regum*, ii. 368.
2. Geoffrey Gaimar, *Lestorie des Engles*, ed. T. D. Hardy and C. T. Martin (Rolls Series, 1888–9), i. 254.

Edward I so that it became a major political grievance; but Rufus had been guilty of similar malpractices. An investigation of the military household under the Norman kings indicates that there was a much higher degree of continuity in the military organization of medieval England than is commonly supposed.

Indeed the royal military household is a natural, though not an inevitable, product of energetic monarchical government largely preoccupied with internal security, defence and conquest. There are striking parallels between the *familia regis* of Henry I and, over five hundred years later, the *maison militaire* of Louis XIII of France. Professor Mousnier has shown that by the mid-seventeenth century the French royal military household was a *corps d'élite* consisting of between 6,000 and 7,000 troops. He has emphasized that its importance was not merely military but also social, political and administrative. It attracted both the greater and the lesser nobility to serve as members; its officers, like those of the much smaller civil household, were employed to transmit orders, to negotiate and to organize on behalf of the crown; its captains were detached to serve as governors of provinces and towns; and even ordinary members of the royal bodyguard were despatched to restore order in the towns during the popular revolts.[1] The earlier history of this force has been traced by M. Contamine, who found its modest beginnings under Charles V and showed that by the end of the fifteenth century it had a fighting strength of a thousand, 'une véritable petite armée', in which it was an honour for the French nobility to serve and which formed 'un des piliers de l'institution monarchique sous l'Ancien Régime'.[2]

The interest of an investigation of the military household of the Norman and Angevin kings is not confined to the sphere of formal military organization. It is also the history of the recruitment, management and use of men who served their kings not merely in war but also in the making of policy and in administration. Its subject-matter is extensive and varied: it includes adventurers such as Baudry de Guitry and the young Ralph the Red whose restlessness took them to Spain, Constantinople and Jerusalem; the predatory followers of Rufus whose approach was feared like that of an invading army; the professional soldiers with a strong sense of duty

1. R. Mousnier, *Paris, capitale au temps de Richelieu et de Mazarin* (Paris, 1978), pp. 103–5. Professor Mousnier gave an earlier and slightly fuller account in his Sorbonne lectures on *Paris au XVIIe siècle* (Les cours de Sorbonne, Paris, 1961), pp. 54–59, in which he stressed the need for further research. I am indebted to my wife, Menna Prestwich, for these references.

2. P. Contamine, *Guerre, État et Société à la Fin du Moyen Age, Études sur les armées des Rois de France, 1337–1494* (Paris and The Hague, 1972), pp. 294–7. M. Contamine recognized elsewhere that the royal military household in France had an earlier history, noting that in 1285 its knights formed the heart of Philip III's army (*ibid.* p. 104, n. 95). For the French *familia regis* in the early twelfth century see Suger, *Vie de Louis VI le Gros*, pp. 78, 156.

such as Walter fitz Ansger and Odo Borleng;[1] the conservative statesman, Robert of Beaumont; Miles of Gloucester and Brien fitz Count, ministers in the second half of Henry I's reign and commanders in his daughter's cause in the civil war; William of Ypres, the Flemish mercenary captain who with Faramus of Boulogne took control of Stephen's military household after the battle of Lincoln;[2] the murderers of Becket;[3] and Richard I and Richard II de Camville, the father dying in 1176 during a mission to Sicily after long service to both Stephen and Henry II, the son at Acre in 1191 after acting as a commander of the crusading fleet and co-governor of Cyprus.[4] Historians have made us familiar with the exchequer, chancery, chamber and wardrobe and with the king's clerks and chaplains so liberally rewarded for their service by the ecclesiastical patronage of the crown: justice has still to be done to the role of the *familia regis* and its lay members in the making and maintenance of the Norman and Angevin empires.

1. For Ralph the Red's adventures in the east see Orderic, vi. 104. Walter fitz Ansger served at Le Mans, 1098–1100, then joined Henry I in England and was with him in Normandy after Tinchebrai (Orderic, vi. 250; *Regesta*, ii, nos. 544, 912).

2. John of Hexham in Symeon of Durham, ii. 310.

3. *Materials for the History of Thomas Becket*, ed. J. C. Robertson (Rolls Series, 1875–85), ii. 429 ('de domestica regis familia'); iv. 70 ('quatuor milites de familia regis'). Other writers used less technical language of the four knights: 'quatuor domestici sui barones' (William fitz Stephen, *ibid*. iii. 128); 'de aulicis concubiculariis suis quatuor milites' (Herbert of Bosham, iii. 487); 'praeclari notissimique curiae regiae juvenes' (Anon II, iv. 128). But all sought to establish that the four knights were, or should have been, specially responsible agents of the king.

4. Jolliffe, misled by historians following Dugdale, conflated Richard I and Richard II de Camville to form a single figure whose life, from 1153 to 1191, 'was part of all the great enmities and enthusiasms of Henry II's forty years' (*Angevin Kingship*, p. 142, n. 4). Lady Stenton established the distinction between the two men in her introduction to *Pipe Rolls 3 and 4 Richard I* (Pipe Roll Society n.s. vol. ii, 1926), pp. xxv–xxvi, and the death of Richard I de Camville in 1176 is confirmed by Ralph de Diceto (*Opera Historica*, ed. W. Stubbs, Rolls Series, 1876), i. 417. Nevertheless Jolliffe was right to seize on the interest of the Camville family whose members successively served Stephen, Henry II, Richard I and John down to the death of Gerard de Camville in 1214.

THE STATUS OF THE NORMAN KNIGHT

R. Allen Brown

At a memorable dinner at The Queen's College, given for his former research pupils on the eve of his retirement, Mr J.O. Prestwich made, as the occasion demanded, an admirable speech. In this he first divided his guests into 'old' historians and 'new' historians, and then, deftly reshuffling and redealing the pack, showed that those who were 'old' were nevertheless sometimes 'new', and those who were 'new' were sometimes not as new as they thought. For myself, I was well pleased to be dealt first as an old historian, and I am quite sure that subsequent illustration of my occasional inadvertent lapses into newness were meant in the kindest fashion. Certainly as an historian I have always been as old as possible, and I become unrepentantly older as time passes and fashions change. Certainly, also, I have never felt older than of late in contemplating knights, and Norman knights especially, in the middle and second half of the eleventh century — a period of some consequence as that of the great Norman expansion into Maine, England and Britain, Italy, and Antioch on the First Crusade. One might, after all, in not too old-fashioned a spirit, call this the particular achievement of the Norman knights. We really ought to know what manner of men these were (not even the most avant-garde have yet made them women) and how they conducted themselves both on the field and off it, in peace as well as war. In fact, perhaps because élites are now out of fashion in the age of the Common Man (and Woman), these supermen have, amongst historians in our time, suffered 'a number of setbacks' and 'a loss of prestige', a severe social demotion, as, for example, Tony Hunt seeks to show in an heroic survey and summary of recent literature upon the subject.[1] The demotion, as it turns out, has been particularly severe in England and among English historians, ever suspicious, it would seem, of foreign (and right wing) things like feudalism, so that, while the good Old English thegn remains as illustrious as ever (five hides and all that), and not even elbowed out of the social scene by housecarls, the alien Norman knight has in some quarters been put firmly in his place as a man of peasant status or none. It seems to me it is high time that he was reasserted as the dominant figure in that society which in fact he did dominate after his resounding victory at Hastings, as he dominated also Normandy, southern Italy and Antioch. In saying this I do not at all wish to be controversial, but merely hope, in an old-fashioned way, that all right-thinking persons will agree with me when I say it.

I had intended to write this paper, on which I have been necessarily brooding for a number of years, without any preliminary reading for the

---

1 Tony Hunt, 'The Emergence of the Knight in France and England, 1000—1200' in *Knighthood in Medieval Literature*, ed. W.H. Jackson, Woodbridge 1981.

occasion, lest I might lose sight of the wood for all the innumerable trees and saplings — in Jolliffe-fashion, one might almost say, for that great man of one's youth always gave the impression of writing what he knew he had to say with very little reference to anybody else. In the event, my courage failed me, and I have tried to read or re-read everything relevant both old and new, upon which I could lay my hands. It has proved a mixed blessing. The best part has been to experience againt the excitement with which I first read Guilhiermoz[2] and Marc Bloch[3] many years ago (the fact that I once read Bloch by candle-light shows how old an historian I am), for the sheer erudition of the one and the continuous perception of the other beggar all description — which is not to say that neither had the other virtue. To begin by bowing the knee — better, doing homage — to both, seems to me appropriate when both are out of fashion, and Guilhiermoz almost vanished even from the footnotes of those who should know better.

Elsewhere, to my relief, things might be worse, at least upon the Continent. Germany, or the German-speaking lands of the German kingdom and Empire, it is agreed, were different and behind the times because of the survival of ancient Carolingian monarchy[4] (like England before 1066), but in France, which matters most as the cradle and very patrimony of feudalism, the knight is still — or, rather, has become again — a person of some consequence in the eleventh century. Though we are no longer allowed to believe with Guilhiermoz and Bloch (and Sir Richard Southern[5]) in the New Men taking over from a former Carolingian nobility in the disintegrating kingdom of the West Franks in the tenth century[6] (the absence of evidence for the lineage of the former being evidently a mere historical accident), the new military élite of knights has nevertheless socially arrived by the mid-eleventh century, when, in the Mâconais and elsewhere, the word *miles* has become a synonym for 'noble', and nobles, their lineage notwithstanding, are content to take it as a title.[7] There is nothing here, therefore, to persuade us to demote those Norman knights (with others from neighbouring lands) who fought and won at Hastings, or those who stayed (and those who came over to join them) to become the new secular ruling class and upper class in England and beyond. Indeed, since no-one on either side of the Channel or Atlantic has yet denied

2 P. Guilhiermoz, *Essai sur l'origine de la noblesse en France au moyen âge*, Paris 1902.

3 Marc Bloch, *La société féodale*, Paris 1939—40; *Feudal Society*, trans. L.A. Manyon, London 1961.

4 Thus the polite but firm rebuttal, as applicable to France, of Léopold Génicot's findings (in the second volume of his *L'économie namuroise au bas moyen age: Les hommes, la noblesse*, Louvain 1960) by Georges Duby, 'The nobility in medieval France' (1961), in his *Chivalrous Society*, 96—8. Duby, of course, has in recent years come to dominate this subject. Wherever possible reference will be given here to the collection and translation (by Cynthia Postan) of his more important essays published in this country as *The Chivalrous Society*, London 1977. That most useful volume provides a key to the original French publications (pp. 226—7) and the original date of the French publication will be noted here in parenthesis.

5 See especially the splendid passage in R.W. Southern, *The Making of the Middle Ages*, London 1953, 82 ff.

6 Duby, 98 ff: Jane Martindale, 'The French aristocracy in the early Middle Ages, a reappraisal', *Past and Present* No. 75, 1977.

7 Thus Duby, 'Lineage, nobility and knighthood' (1972); also e.g. 'The history and sociology of the medieval west' (1970), and 'The origins of knighthood' (1967); *Chivalrous Society*, 76—7, 85—6, 158 ff. For Normandy, however, cf. Musset and Bates, cited n. 8 below.

that all nobles or magnates in Normandy itself were New Men at least from 911 if not later,[8] we could almost, as Anglo-Normans, accept the whole Bloch thesis of a new military élite becoming a new social élite to form an aristocracy of knights, and all this before 1066. We can also be more relaxed than our French colleagues on the issue of nobility, since it is generally agreed that in post-Conquest England there was not one, *i.e.* in the strict sense of a closed and hereditary social class with privileges enshrined in law. For my part, all I want is for our knights to be Top People, upper class, real or potential, as I am sure they were, both in their own eyes and in those of others.

However, knights in England in and after 1066 have been far more savagely demoted by English historians than they have been on the Continent; which may at once suggest that something is wrong with us, since they are most unlikely to have lowered their status or diminished their military skills in crossing the Channel — quite the reverse, in fact. Thirty years ago Richard Glover[9] reduced the military potential of the Norman knights at Hastings to mere 'mounted javelineers' indulging in 'infantile' cavalry tactics and, as often as not, 'happily mixing it in on foot'. For all of this, though God may forgive him, I never shall; but meanwhile there are many who, evidently ignorant of the still neglected yet crucial subject of medieval warfare, are more than content to accept and repeat his misapprehensions. Twelve years ago Sally Harvey claimed that an analysis of Domesday Book 'reveals the normal landed basis of the eleventh-century knight to be about 1½ hides' which 'puts him only just above most well-to-do peasants',[10] and these views, too, now find much favour among the *avant-garde*. Very recently indeed John Gillingham found, once more again, little if any difference between the knight and thegn[11] — though perhaps that makes the former more socially respectable. There is no doubt that these are very serious matters, and we may well ask how these views have come about, clean contrary as they are not only to the opinions of past historians but also to those of most of our present Continental colleagues.

We will begin with status since that is very much the present concern of 'new' historians especially, and of their 'demography' (which seems to be the application of the dubious methods of sociology to the past) — though one would do well at the outset to insist with Guilhiermoz and Bloch that in the world of the mid-eleventh century status in secular society was intimately bound up with fighting. Oddly enough, F.M. Stenton, whom most would accept as an old historian, and whom I revere as is appropriate to one in a sense brought up by him and his lady wife, seems in this century to have begun the demotion of the knight in the England of 1066 and after. In 1932 in his

8 Cf. Lucien Musset who, while accepting a new aristocracy, keeps his knights humble at least until the mid-eleventh century; and David Bates who has his Norman knight even in 1066 'usually a simple soldier', and seeks to make his contemporary aristocracy a good deal less new than usual, all in accordance with the latest fashion. See Musset, 'L'aristocratie normande au xi[e] siècle' in *La Noblesse au Moyen Age xi[e]—xv[e]s: Essais à la mémoire de Robert Boutruche*, ed. Ph. Contamine, Paris 1976; Bates, *Normandy before 1066*, London and New York 1982 (e.g. 106—11, 125, 134—5). The latter work fortunately appeared too late for me to read before first writing this paper.

9 'English Warfare in 1066', *EHR* lxvii, 1952.

10 'The knight and the knight's fee in England', *Past and Present* No. 49, 1970, 15.

11 *Proceedings of the Battle Conference in Anglo-Norman Studies*, henceforth *Anglo-Norman Studies*, iv, 1981, 52.

First Century of English Feudalism he wrote that 'although knighthood in the eleventh century implied military proficiency, it carried no social distinction', and went on to call attention both to the rarity of the use of the word *miles* as a mark of distinction in twelfth-century charters, and to the *milites* in Domesday Book 'of a very inferior condition, whose holdings were small, and whose names were not thought worth the recording'.[12] In due course, in *Anglo-Saxon England*, first published in 1943 and which, one hopes, undergraduates still read, he wrote again that 'The ordinary knight of the eleventh century was a person of small means and insignificant condition'.[13] Since then matters have gone much further, as we have already seen, with Stenton's 'meagre knights' of the Domesday Survey, but let us consider first the matter of the use of *miles* as a title in charters, since Stenton's point of its rarity before the thirteenth century is also made by Sally Harvey.[14] The point is obviously of some consequence, for so long as *miles* retained its classical meaning of ordinary, common, soldier, no-one was likely to attach it to a personal name as a quasi-title or distinction.

Whatever may be the case in England (and Normandy?) in the twelfth century — and no-one knew his charters better than Sir Frank Stenton — there is no doubt whatever that in Norman charters of the eleventh century, and the tenth, and indeed from the beginning, the word *miles* is so used, attached to the names of witnesses and donors and others. The very first and earliest authentic charter in Marie Fauroux's splendid edition of the ducal *acta* of pre-Conquest Normandy[15] (dare one say still not appreciated in this country?), dating from 965 and the reign of Richard I, has Teofredus *miles* amongst its signatories, sandwiched between the count of Dreux and the duke of Normandy. Indeed this remarkable charter is almost sufficient evidence in itself for the conventional view of the elevated status of knighthood and vassalage alike, and of the feudalization of Norman society, even at this early date — which in the circumstances of Norman history, beginning in 911, is even earlier. The duke subscribes and thus confirms the deed whereby Walter count of Dreux himself approves the grant by his noble vassal Teodfredus (*nobilis vassallus Teodfredus*) of a church of the latter's benefice (*beneficii ipsius*) to St Peter at Chartres. And in the subscriptions, as we have seen, Teodfredus the noble vassal is Teodfredus, knight. From then on, *i.e.* for the whole of this period for which we have record, printed and well edited, knights, *milites*, as signatories or witnesses, and as donors, are common; and in the latter case, it is, of course, to be noted that they have lands (frequently allods) to give.[16] We may note in particular, perhaps, the two knight-signatories of a charter of Richard II, Osbern and Anfridus, who are in fact his brothers-in-law;[17] duke Robert subscribing *cum suis episcopis et militibus . . . atque aliis nobilibus*;[18] or duke William *cum omnibus suis militibus concedente* — which is evidently

12 First edn., Oxford 1932 (hereafter cited), 142—3.
13 Second edn., Oxford 1947, 628.
14 Harvey, 42.
15 Fauroux, no. 2. Charters subscribed by the duke as well as those issued in his name are included in her edition.
16 Fauroux, e.g. nos. 13, 16, 18, 24, 30, 43, 44, 69, 80, 86, 94, 107, 110 and, indeed, *passim*.
17 No. 44.
18 No. 43.

synonymous with the same duke William *et baronibus suis concedentibus,*[19] and also to be compared with the phraseology of the notification which informs us how William was brought to St.-Léger de Préaux, to make a confirmation of its property, *cum magno comitatu militum.*[20] There are knights of bishops and other magnates as well as of the duke.[21] Amongst them all we must certainly note the William, knight, who holds the castle of Moulins[22] (*Ego Willelmus miles, filius Walteri, qui castrum teneo de Molendinis . . .*), and we must also note that a man called *miles* in one document may not be so specified in another, for these documents are written by individual scribes, in no way writing for our benefit, and thus in no way amenable to a statistical approach. But, with the exception of one or two instances[23] — a clerk who appears in a list of knights (an error? a joke? a nick-name?) and five enigmatic *liberi milites* who raise more questions than they answer — the overwhelming impression one acquires from reading through the ducal charters of pre-Conquest Normandy is of an aristocracy of warrior knights, pre-eminently comprising men such as Richard [de Reviers], a knight of duke William and *vir quidam clarus genere seculari milicia deditus* who, campaigning with the duke against Henry I of France, was sent to take over the castle of Thimert near Chartres;[24] or John de Laval, a native of Maine, who when almost 30, *jam virilis esset et militari sub habitu, vir quippe ex illustri prosapia ortus degeret*, like Herluin wearied of the world of arms and gave himself as a monk with his land to Marmoutier[25] — which at this date is, one fears, a rather aristocratic thing to do.

What, then, are we to do with our Domesday *milites*, or, rather, those of Stenton and Sally Harvey? Not modes or medians or even histograms will convince me of the latter's contention that their alleged average holding of 1½ hides and prosperous peasant level of subsistence show any sort of norm for the knight in England in 1086.[26] One can, of course, emphasize the hazards of Domesday Book itself (to read the later Welldon-Finn is gloomily to conclude that no generalization at all may be made therefrom); the particular hazards of translating or interpreting Domesday nomenclature, in this case *miles*; and the especial hazards of a statistical approach to the Great Survey, or any other medieval record impatient of it. Duby cites with evident approval the propensity of the new historians and demographers to count 'everything capable of being counted in a continuous documentation', but he also remarks, as well he might, that such quantification influences the questions asked.[27] Of course Round was right to say that 'Much labour has been vainly spent on attempts to determine the true area of a knight's fee',[28] and Stenton was also right to point

19 Nos. 106, 107.
20 No. 149.
21 Fauroux, e.g. nos. 48, 130, 140, 202, 208, 227, 229.
22 No. 225.
23 Nos. 85, 199.
24 Fauroux, no. 147. The castle was under anathema and Richard, falling mortally ill, sent urgently to the bishop for his absolution and gave his land of Bourbesville (dép. Manche) to St. Peter at Chartres, to the subsequent irritation of his brothers.
25 No. 137.
26 Harvey, 15, and above.
27 'The history and sociology of the medieval west' (1970); *Chivalrous Society*, 82.
28 *Feudal England*, London 1909, 293. He also observed that 'Wonderful are the things that people look for in the pages of the great survey', 229. Cf. Harvey, 3.

out that the very concept of the knight's fee as the unit of land (or rather, land value) appropriate to a knight without vassals of his own was slow to form, as also such fees themselves were often the result of piecemeal accumulation.[29] Indeed, one might go further to suggest that it is an almost exclusive concentration upon the fee or fief, common to many historians, which has produced the curiosity of Sally Harvey's humble knight of prosperous peasant status. Our word 'feudal' (for 'feudalism' we have to wait until the nineteenth century) may have been coined from the Latin *feudum* meaning fief, but that was in the seventeenth century when the reality was largely gone. In the mid-eleventh century the reality was knights, and castles, rather than the fief which may or may not have supported both.

One might go even further yet and say that, if there was no real concept of the knight's fee in the England of 1086, so also, there or anywhere else, it was difficult to be just a knight, as a single isolated figure, *tout court* and by yourself. In reality you had to be the knight of someone else, to owe service to or take service with a lord, and serve with him and your peers in a group however small, to be of use and integrated in society. It is the absence of the household, the *familia* as one should say, recently set before us in all its fundamental importance by J.O. Prestwich,[30] that seems to me one worrying *lacuna* in Sally Harvey's highly intellectual exercise. To become a knight, to get on as a knight, and the way to the top if you were good and lucky and found favour, in that world was to take service with a lord. It might well not be easy to find a place if you or your family were undistinguished. At the age of 12 or 13 according to Suger,[31] a boy, *puer*, seeking a career in arms and the necessary military education which could be obtained nowhere else, would need to be placed by his father or other relative. Lords had standards, as duke Richard II of Normandy, we are told, liked to have gentlemen about him,[32] and the initiative of recruitment might be the other way about, as Henry I is said to have been on the look out for likely young men anywhere on this side of the Alps.[33] But of course there were other households than the king's or duke's, to which only the best connected or outstanding could aspire: you did the best you could or that could be done for you, rather like choosing schools some years ago. Once in and once a knight, a young man might feel, as a young man should, that the world was at his feet — and so it might be, for William Marshal rose from the household of Henry II's son to become earl of Pembroke and *rector regis et regni*. Worldly success through service was, of course, the acquisition of a fief or an heiress. Those Domesday *milites*, if they really only had 1½ hides of land, or, rather, rents therefrom, may well have just put a foot on the first rung of the ladder,[34] and it is certainly unwise to assume that they had no other means of livelihood or support.

We are approaching here the idea of the 'poor knight', which has, I believe,

---

29 *First Century*, 157 *et seq.*, and thus 'the twelfth century was far advanced before the clerks who wrote charters . . . allowed themselves the free use of the words *feudum militis*', 164.

30 'The military household of the Norman kings', *EHR* xcvi, 1981. See also Marjorie Chibnall, 'Mercenaries and the *Familia Regis* under Henry I', *History* lxii, 1977.

31 Guilhiermoz, 425.

32 D.C. Douglas, *EHR* lxi, 1946, 147.

33 Thus Walter Map, cited by Prestwich, 8.

34 Sally Harvey recognizes the possibility (p. 24), but for her they are poor knights none the less.

in our money-based and materialistic world, come to mean something very different among historians than it ever did among contemporaries. Before we leave the household, therefore, let us note that such glimpses of it as we have are aristocratic or gentlemanly at least. It is difficult in any case to suppose that erks and country bumpkins figured prominently among the household and the *familiares* of the king, or of any other lord, and when the young count Waleran of Meulan, before his defeat at Bourgthéroulde in 1124, hot-headed and 'anxious to prove his knighthood' (*militiae cupidus*), haughtily called the king's knights who opposed him *pagenses et gregarios* he did so as an insult and not a sociological observations.[35] The most precious and prolonged glimpse of the household of a great lord is that of count Gilbert of Brionne in the opening section of Gilbert Crispin's *Life of Herluin*. There we see for a while the household knights, clean-shaven and their hair cut like good Normans, all of them, I would suppose, 'noble' like Herluin himself, endlessly pursuing a round of gentlemanly activities, practising arms, riding on the count's business, acting on his behalf in law-suits, and dining in the hall.[36] The Bayeux Tapestry also, surely, shows us the household knights of count Guy of Ponthieu and of duke William similarly employed, armed, well-dressed and superbly mounted.[37] And the rewards of service could be great. Orderic tells us that Hugh, earl of Chester, in the Conqueror's England had a household more like an army, and was more prodigal than simply generous,[38] and William of Malmesbury says that William fitz Osbern, the Conqueror's closest friend, was so prodigal to his multitude of knights as to irritate the king.[39]

We approach the poor knight also via the wholly modern concept of the two levels of feudalism, spelt out specifically by Joseph R. Strayer in 1967[40] and widely prevalent. By this a yawning gap or gulf is fixed between those lords who had households of their own and the humble, simple and poor knights who served them. Though Strayer had his two levels becoming assimilated in the eleventh century, others have been slower,[41] and in Sally Harvey's work on her Domesday *milites* we find the concept of two levels given an altogether new dimension. Throughout we read not only of poor knights and lesser knights, but also of 'professional knights', 'active knights', 'serving knights' and 'fighting knights', all employed as synonymous terms and opposed to 'nominal knights' and even 'belted knights' *i.e.* their social superiors, the lords and substantial mesne tenants, who evidently seldom if ever fought at all.[42]

---

35 Orderic, vi, 350.
36 *Vita Herluini*, 87—91. For Herluin, see below, p. 26.
37 *BT*, Pls. 9—14.
38 Orderic, ii, 260.
39 *De Gestis Regum*, ii, 314.
40 'The Two Levels of Feudalism', in R.S. Hoyt (ed.), *Life and Thought in the early Middle Ages*, Minneapolis 1967, 51—65.
41 Cf Hunt, 'The Emergence of the Knight in France and England', 3.
42 Were I John Horace Round (who should be living at this hour) I would set out passages in my text in column and with much use of italics. But though some magnates do go on campaigns (p. 28), this seems the meaning or the implication of her text. Thus we read of 'two completely different social and tenurial classes, the influential knightly sub-tenants and the professional knights' (p. 5); and that, 'The important vassals did not themselves perform the military service due to the tenants-in-chief' (p. 12); or that, 'Disentangled from the nominal knights we are now free to follow up the position of the fighting professional' (p. 14). There seem to be three overlapping stages of the argument and its assumptions: (1) a study and analysis of the Domesday *milites*

One would rather suppose that in the secular society of the eleventh century (and earlier and later) with its wholly military ethos, the higher you stood socially the better you were expected to fight and the more martial you were supposed to be. The role of the king himself as war leader (to go no further down the social scale), before and after the feudal period as well as during it, is a fundamental in history. One must insist, I think, that the concept of the two levels of feudalism, and of knighthood, though it may have its uses, is simply misleading if it is forced into some kind of sociological pattern and imposed upon the protesting past. If one must measure status in crude materialistic terms of mere wealth and possessions, as contemporaries did not ('Rich in the abundance of poverty'[43] would make a fine contemporary concept on which to preach a sermon or give a lecture), than an infinite gradation of resources among the members of the knightly class, all of whom were a substantial cut above the peasants they despised, would be the way to do it. Of course not all knights were magnates and great lords, but all great lords and magnates, and kings and princes too, were knights, and that ensured as well as proves the social superiority of knighthood. Duke William himself was knighted in his youth according to William of Poitiers, who is not likely to be wrong in this though he characteristically adds that at the news a tremor ran through all France,[44] and the Bayeux Tapestry provides a superb illustration of the same duke's knighting of earl Harold.[45] It is clear from the pages of Orderic Vitalis and elsewhere that already by the mid-eleventh century knighthood was a distinction and a rank, given after long and sufficient training, both military and social, in the household, by the conferment of arms, and that it confirmed and established a protective and loyal relationship between the two parties.[46] The relationship between Herluin and his lord, count Gilbert, in Gilbert Crispin's *Life*, is not one between master and servant.[47] Duby writes perceptively of a common vocation of arms[48] which explains much, and vassalic commendation, we know, was an honourable bond between two men equally free. The notion of honourable service is another we have almost lost, together with the abundance of poverty. The young knights, if they had no place or fief, went off in companies of *juvenes*, 'bachelors',[49] in search of both, and of

---

(2) that there are no other *milites* in Domesday Book except those so specified (3) that all knights in England in 1086 conform to this alleged type, *i.e.* of the poor, 'professional' and 'fighting' knights *etc.*, as opposed to the occasionally mentioned 'nominal' knights and 'belted' knights, who are apparently the magnates and men of substance. Magnates and men of substance, indeed, are almost entirely absent from her consideration: hence the extraordinary statement that an analysis of Domesday Book reveals 'scarcely any instance of a knight holding the whole of a manor' (p. 21 — The king? All those tenants-in-chief?); or that cap. 11 of Henry I's Charter of Liberties (W. Stubbs, *Select Charters*, 9th edition, Oxford 1921, 119), which old historians like me, brought up on Stubb's *Charters*, had always been taught of considerable 'constitutional' importance, is 'explicitly confined to the serving knights', representatives evidently of 'professional classes of low birth', and thus of great annoyance to the magnates (p. 26).

43 Cf. Jonathan Sumption, *Pilgrimage: an image of medieval religion*, London 1975, 127.
44 *Gesta Guillelmi*, 13.
45 *BT*, Pl. 27.
46 See Brown, *The Normans and the Norman Conquest*, London 1969, 47; Duby, *Chivalrous Society*, index *sub* 'dubbing'; Guilhiermoz, especially 346—8, 393—421; Bloch, 312 ff.
47 *Vita Herluini*, 87—91.
48 *Chivalrous Society*, 79.
49 See especially Duby, 'Youth in aristocratic society' (1964); *Chivalrous Society*, 112 ff.

adventure and heiresses, 'happy and joyful on their horses' as Aimé of Monte Cassino described the Norman knights errant outside Venosa in Italy,[50] when all the world was young. *Per diversa loca militariter lucrum quaerentes* — 'seeking wealth as knights in many places' — is Geoffrey of Malaterra's description of the Hauteville brothers[51] amongst the Norman knights in southern Italy, and the mention of those dusty warriors reminds us again that the rewards of mere knighthood, without any extensive patrimony to start out from, could be huge. Of all the surplus Norman knights who sought their fortune in Italy in the course of the eleventh century, many lost their lives, but, of the rest, most gained fiefs, some principalities, and the son of one a kingdom. Of course not all knights made it to the top everywhere and anywhere, not even in Italy, or among the rich pickings of England, or in the hard-fought and harsh terrain of Antioch; any society, any class, any career-structure, has its failures as well as its successes; but to be a knight was to be potentially a lord or lordling, and the indispensable pre-condition of a worth-while career at arms and of social preferment. Beyond doubt, the ultimate degradation, and a fate worse than death, was to set one's hand to the plough. And if in this paragraph I have waxed a little romantic, that is necessary, for there is more to medieval history and knighthood than the statistical analysis of the returns of the Domesday commissioners compressed into Domesday book.

For myself, I have sometimes wondered of late if there ever was such a thing as a poor knight. Poverty is comparative, and subjective. I have no doubt there were many landless knights, and some enfeoffed, who thought themselves impoverished by the standard of their betters or their own ambition, but I doubt if Hod the peasant pitied them as they rode by (as they always did), any more than today's agricultural worker has much sympathy for the poverty-stricken student. None of those superbly armed and mounted knights on the Bayeux Tapestry look poor to me, and they seem unlikely to become poorer once the conquered provinces of England lie beneath the hooves of their horses. Did any knight, albeit landless and without a hide or acre to his name, really lead an impoverished life in the household of any lord, albeit not of the first rank? It must be remembered, too, that a lord's reputation will depend upon the turn-out and deportment of his men. The poor knight is certainly very elusive in the evidence which we have, and it is worth noting that the best known poor knight in Anglo-Norman history, Herluin the founder of Bec, grows considerably in status and in wealth if regarded at all closely. His biographer, Gilbert Crispin (scion of a knightly family and writing, of course, later, some time after 1093), in those invaluable early pages of his *Life*,[52] makes him as noble as he can, his mother related to the counts of Flanders. He is very well placed, in the household of count Gilbert of Brionne, who was himself the grandson of duke Richard I, and the count treats him with particular favour amongst those who are called the nobles (*primates*) of the household (*curia*). We are told that he was well connected with all the best families in Normandy, and it is made clear that a particular difficulty of

50 Amatus of Monte Cassino, *Storia de' Normanni*, ed. V. de Bartholomaeis, Rome 1935, 78—9.
51 Gaufridus Malaterra, *Historia Sicula*, I, v. ed. Migne, *Patrologia Latina*, t. 149, cols. 1103—4.
52 *Vita Herluini*, 87—91. See also C. Harper-Bill, 'Herluin, abbot of Bec, and his biographer', *Studies in Church History* xv, 1978.

Herluin in gaining his release from his lord's service to follow a life of religion is that he sought the release of his lands as well as himself. On one occasion, in breach with his lord and withdrawn from the household, he was nevertheless able to come to Gilbert's aid on campaign with twenty chosen knights (*delectos milites*). However humble Herluin's eventual foundation may have been in origin, it is clear that the poverty of the founder was very relative indeed. We may also, perhaps, turn to another well-known and contemporary poor or very moderate knight, though one this time land-holding. Tancred of Hauteville is almost invariably described as a petty (or the equivalent) baron in eleventh-century Normandy, although Geoffrey of Malaterra says that he served in the duke's household with ten knights under him (*in curia comitis decem milites sub se habens*) — which sounds very much like a *conroi* or Round's *constabularia*. He also tells us that, having twelve sons (by two wives) he had all of them trained and educated as knights from their adolescence, which may be thought almost the equivalent of sending them all to public schools. The Hauteville patrimony being obviously insufficient for such a brood once graduated, eight of them went off to Italy in turn, as from about 1035, *militariter lucrum quaerentes*.[53] And how, one may finally ask, did they and all those other poor knights from Normandy ever get there? I feel sure they did not walk, and they probably took a servant or two with them.

The time has come, indeed, to insert into this debate a measure of reality, the reality of war and tactics, horses and weapons, largely neglected by the *avant-garde*, even Duby, though not by Bloch or Guilhiermoz before them.[54] Whenever it was that the Franks developed heavy cavalry as the spearhead of their armies and the *corps d'élite*, remains as important a date in European history as ever it was in Brunner's classic thesis of the origins of feudalism[55] (so too does Lynn White's stirrup remain crucial, whenever it was exploited, for you cannot be a knight without it[56]). Such warfare and tactics, and more specifically those who practised them, were of necessity more expensive and more professional than infantry and foot-soldiers of whatever rank, and the central point of Brunner, Guilhiermoz and Bloch therefore remains, that the new military élite became inevitably in the circumstances of the age a social élite also. Like aerial warfare in 1940, more particularly that waged by Fighter Command and its German equivalent, this was a type of warfare in which only gentlemen could engage. One need have no doubt that it was first adopted by

53 Malaterra, I, iv, v. For Round's *constabularia*, see *Feudal England*, 259. For the *conroi*, see J.F. Verbruggan, 'La tactique militaire des armés de chevaliers', *Revue du Nord* xxix, 1947; Brown, 'Battle of Hastings', *Anglo-Norman Studies* iii, 1980, 16.
54 Cf. Colin Morris, '*Equestris Ordo*: chivalry as a vocation in the twelfth century', *Studies in Church History* xv, 89, 'We are dealing, not only or not primarily with the emergence of a new social class, but with a new style of fighting and above all of changing sensitivities'.
55 See B.S. Bachrach, 'Charles Martel, mounted shock combat, the stirrup and feudalism', *Studies in Medieval and Renaissance History* vii, 1970, and below, p. 30. The thesis is Heinrich Brunner, 'Der Reiterdienst und die Anfänge des Lehnswesens', in *Zeitschrift der Savigny-Stiftung für Rechtsgeschichte, Germanistische Abtheilung* viii, 1887, 1—38; reprinted in Brunner, *Forschungen zur Geschichte des deutschen und französischen Rechts*, Stuttgart 1894, 39—74.
56 Lynn T. White, *Medieval Technology and Social Change*, Oxford 1962, 1—38, 135—53. His chapter on 'The Stirrup' has also become something of a classic thesis, though Marc Bloch had pointed out the importance of the stirrup (and the horseshoe) long before him. For criticism, which does not at all affect the importance of the device, see R.H. Hilton and P.H. Sawyer in *Past and Present* xxiv, 1963.

rich nobles, as most good things in life descend from the top downwards. But nobles needed, as they always had needed, armed retainers of the best about them, and these now mounted warriors were obtained, trained and retained, not by central government raising cavalry regiments from public funds as in the modern period, but by lordship and vassalage and by the integrating and overlapping institutions of the household and the fief. Like J.O. Prestwich, I do not see my military household and *familia* as exclusively an early phase of feudalism giving way to enfiefment.[57] The alleged sociological pattern of the landless household knight being replaced by the enfiefed knight is as false, I would suggest, as exaggerated versions of the 'two levels of feudalism'. Each generation needs the household, and each generation has its sons and younger sons to fill it.

As Marc Bloch observed in a sentence whose simplicity is profound, 'in order to possess a warhorse and to equip oneself from head to foot, it was necessary to be fairly well-off or else to be assisted by someone richer than oneself'.[58] The arms and armour necessary for knighthood were or came to be lance and sword, shield, helmet and the hauberk, the long coat of mail which, as the distinguishing feature of the armed knight, comes to have almost mystical properties in an age of symbolism. The cost of it all, but more especially the sword and hauberk, was very heavy. Marc Bloch cites a land-owner in Suabia in 761 exchanging his ancestral fields and a slave for a horse and sword and a Norman charter of 1043—8 refers to a hauberk worth seven *livres*.[59] Beyond doubt much more work is required on these vital matters, but meanwhile a friend of mine, learned in arms and armour and who practises what he teaches,[60] tells me that it may take him some 140 hours to make a hauberk (and even so not one of the finest quality but with rings merely butted as opposed to rivetted) and up to 200 hours to make a sword of eleventh-century pattern (though even so without any inscription, inlay or any other decoration). And then there were the horses. Not any horse will do for the battlefield, and more particularly for the shock-combat of the knights, as Sally Harvey and John Gillingham seem to think.[61] The warhorse, specially bred and trained for what it had to do, the prince of horses in the field, was enormously expensive. I do not know what significance Sally Harvey wishes us to attach to her £1 Domesday sumpter horses (*i.e.* pack horses) which she mentions in con-nection with her Domesday *milites*[62], but no one I know would wish to ride one at Hastings, and in the mid-eleventh century Gilbert Crispin obtained from the abbot of Jumièges a horse worth 20 *livres* and Roger of Montgomery one worth 30.[63] Nor is this necessarily all. Knights engaged at Hastings would presumably need more than one war-horse to be effective (as they were) in a battle which began at 9 a.m. and went on until after dusk. (One nowadays

57 Cf. therefore Duby where the notion is explicit and implicit, e.g. *Chivalrous Society*, 83, 86—7.
58 *Feudal Society*, 152.
59 *Feudal Society*, 152; Fauroux, no. 113.
60 Mr Ian Peirce of Battle, Sussex.
61 Harvey, 20; Gillingham, *Anglo-Norman Studies* iv, 53. Those who will have no difference between Norman knights and Old English thegns are bound to close their eyes to this difference too.
62 Harvey, 40.
63 Fauroux, nos. 113, 188.

needs a string of polo ponies for an afternoon's engagement on Smiths Lawn). Nor would a war-horse ridden the seven miles from the new Hastings castle to the battlefield be in the best condition on arrival. It is thought that the war-horse — *destrier, dextrarius* — gets its name from being led by the right-hand (*O.E.D.*) and one should envisage the eleventh-century equivalent of race-horses in horse-boxes on the road to Newmarket. In such a case, one will need another horse to ride (the palfrey?) for one does not walk (perish the thought!). Therefore one soon needs a boy, esquire, or servant, to look after these horses, and he must ride also to keep up, and to keep up one's own status (the rouncey or common hack will do for him, no doubt).[64] The upkeep of all these horses by the household in which the knights served must have been a problem, and has even been suggested as one motivation for enfiefment. Occasionally we may hear an echo of this particular reality, as when, in a charter of c. 1066 to the abbey of Beaumont-lès-Tours,[65] Roger de Malfillastre carefully reserves the pasture of his horses and of the horses of his knights (*equitum*), or when, soon after the Conquest, Robert de Curzon, with the leave of the Norman sheriff Roger Bigod, invaded the demesne manor of the monks of St Edmund at Southwold in Suffolk to obtain pasture for his horses.[66].

The expense of knighthood, however, is not confined to the sheer cost of horses, armour and weapons and the maintenance of all three. (The aethling Athelstan's sword-polisher in Ethelred II's will (c. 1014)[67] held no sinecure, for blades then corroded very easily, while the thought of a hauberk in the rain would make any batman blanch.) Far greater was the cost of professionalism. By this I mean that mounted warfare required a life-time's dedication from an early age, in order especially to acquire the horsemanship necessary to manage those great stallion warhorses in the heat and noise of battle, to deliver from the brute's heaving back all those accurate sword strokes which the *chansons* endlessly admire, above all to take part effectively in the shock-tactic of the charge. If, as I never cease to say in lectures, it demands a life-time's dedication to produce the equestrian skills of Harvey Smith, or, a better analogy perhaps, H.R.H. the Princess Anne, by how much more would this be necessary when life itself, and honour, were at stake? Hence the Carolingian maxim later echoed by the poet, and duly quoted by Marc Bloch: 'You can make a horseman of a lad at puberty; after that, never'; and again, 'He who has stayed at school till the age of twelve, and never ridden a horse, is fit only to be a priest'.[68] For all this it was necessary to be released from, and elevated above, the sordid necessity of earning a livelihood by any other means; and the

---

64 See Guilhiermoz, 466 *et seq.* In their rule, admittedly compiled in the thirteenth century, the Knights of the Temple were limited to three horses each and one esquire, because of their poverty. For Templar practice and information about contemporary horses I am much indebted to my pupil Mr Matthew Bennett.

65 Fauroux, no. 227.

66 *Memorials of St. Edmund's Abbey*, ed. Thomas Arnold, RS, i (1890), 79. I owe this reference to Antonia Gransden; cf. her paper on 'Baldwin, abbot of Bury St. Edmunds', *Anglo-Norman Studies* iv, 68.

67 *Anglo-Norman Wills*, ed. Dorothy Whitelock, Cambridge 1930, no. 20, p. 61. For another sword polisher see Alfred's laws, cap. 19. 3 (F.L. Attenborough, *Laws of the Earliest English Kings, Cambridge 1922*, 74; Whitelock, *EHD* i, first edn., London 1955, 376). I owe these references to Dr A.R. Rumble.

68 *Feudal Society*, 152, 293—4.

answer was the household and the fief. The result was not only the knight, and the superb fighting machine of trained and disciplined man and horse, but also the pride of professionalism, the happy warrior, and the élan of an élite. Georges Duby has called for a social history of the horse[69] (does the innate social superiority of the man on the horse start here?), but there are not many horsy figures among academics, any more than the sheer love of war — 'fresh and joyful war'[70] — and physical achievement finds much sympathy in academe.

I am very well aware that inherent in all I am saying is the vital question of date. I seek to establish the status of knights, and Norman knights in particular, as a secular upper class, real or potential, in the second half of the eleventh century, and to do it I have tried to confine myself to contemporary evidence. This is necessary because it is very generally held that the knight became (yet) more socially elevated, exclusive and aristocratic in the course of the twelfth century. Be that as it may, the larger question is surely that of origins. For me the central and fundamental element in feudalism is the knight, and the mystery of feudal history is when, and also why, the Franks began to develop cavalry, more particularly heavy cavalry, as their main military arm. The conventional reason given, that the idea came to Charles Martel at or after the battle of Poitiers in 732 against the Muslims, is anything but convincing, nor does an alleged military revolution at that time seem to fit the facts of Carolingian military history in so far as they are known or studied.[71] Clearly there must have been a beginning, when things were neither so developed nor so sophisticated as they became. But it is certain that by the mid-eleventh century Norman knights at least (and let us therefore add those allied knights from neighbouring regions whom the Conqueror took into his service in 1066) were a military élite, and therefore a social élite, and that in particular they were already developing, or had developed, their most devastating tactic of the couched lance and the charge.[72] This alone may explain much. This is what Anna Comnena had in mind when she wrote of the Frankish chivalry at the time of the First Crusade that the charging knight would pierce the walls of Babylon.[73] This, too, made knightly warfare even more exclusive, and did wonders for morale. Those endless Norman victories in the eleventh century across the breadth of the known world gave them that headiest of all feelings, that God is on our side. By the twelfth century they could believe that they held victory as a fief from God.[74] One needs some better explanation for all those feats of arms than that the Normans were good fighters, or even were a new Chosen People blessed by God in Holy War. It was the Norman heavy cavalry of knights, of course combined with infantry in set engagements, and their charge, of course controlled by discipline and

69 *Chivalrous Society*, 163.

70 Bloch, 293.

71 Bachrach, *Studies in Medieval and Renaissance History* vii, 49ff. Cf. David Bullough, *The Age of Charlemagne*, London 1965, 36.

72 See D.J.A. Ross, 'L'originalité de "Turoldus": le maniement de lance', *Cahiers de civilisation médiévale* vi, 1963; Brown, 'Battle of Hastings', *Anglo-Norman Studies* iii, 12—13. Do not see Glover, 'English Warfare in 1066', *EHR* lxvii, 1952.

73 *Alexiad of Anna Comnena*, ed. and trans. E.R.A. Sewter, Harmondsworth 1969, 416.

74 See J. Le Patourel, *The Norman Empire*, Oxford 1976, 353—4. Cf. Ailred of Rievaulx in *Chronicles of the Reigns of Stephen, Henry II and Richard I*, ed. R. Howlett, RS iii, 1896, 185—6.

training to be delivered at the right moment (clean contrary to the idiot myth of feudal warfare propagated by Oman), that carried all before it in this age. Nothing is more impressive as one reads, for example, of the amazing exploits of the Normans in southern Italy, making all due allowance for the proud exaggerations of the chroniclers, than the way in which comparatively small numbers of invariably outnumbered knights, rode through their enemies, Greek or Lombard, like a knife through butter. With his initial 200 knights obtained as the marriage portion of his first wife Aubrey, Robert Guiscard, one candidate for the most outstanding of the Hautevilles, became from his first castle of San Marco Argentano the lord of all Calabria. So on to Sicily, to which they shipped their horses with them, and where on a May morning in 1061, Roger of Hauteville took the city of Messina with an advance party of less than 500 knights, before his elder brother Robert had crossed with the main army.

If in the course of the twelfth century, knights in the Anglo-Norman and Angevin dominions as elsewhere became more aristocratic, more exclusive, fewer, as it seems generally to be agreed, we need to know the reasons for it. Perhaps some are to be found in inflation, though Duby eschews it,[75] and I as an 'old historian' cannot be expected to understand it. In England some may also lie in constant overseas campaigning, though that did not deter duke William's knights in 1066. Perhaps the last remark provides a clue, pointing to an explanation of an almost demographic kind. In the great days of Norman expansion as many knights as possible were needed and there were opportunities on every hand. In the twelfth century demand diminished, and the endless source of fiefs to reward and breed knights dried up, as earlier generations became established in England and Wales and southern Scotland and Ireland, in Italy and Sicily and Antioch. What I do know is that there was no soaring cost, save via inflation, of a knight's equipment in the twelfth century to explain it, and therein no basic change. On seals and in sculpture and illumination the familiar representation of the knight remains the same in all essentials until the surcoat and the pot-helm of Richard I's day. Neither of those can be thought to cause much increase in expense, and if plate armour did, we have to wait until the fourteenth century for its full adoption.[76] In any case if knights a century after Hastings, for whatever cause, were becoming even more exclusive, that does not make their predecessors lower-class. The élitism was already there when duke William sailed for England in 1066. The ideas and ideals, it is agreed, of the Peace and Truce of God,[77] of the Three Orders ordained by God, clergy, knights and peasants,[78] and of Holy War,[79] all developed in the course of the eleventh century and all of them elevated

---

75 *Chivalrous Society*, 183.
76 Cf. therefore Harvey, 39, 40; Tony Hunt, 'The emergence of the knight in France and England', 11'; Duby, *Chivalrous Society*, 184.
77 Bloch, 412ff; Morris, '*Equestris Ordo*'; Duby, 'Laity and the peace of God' (1966); *Chivalrous Society*, 123ff.
78 Guilhiermoz, 357—8; Bloch, 291—2; Morris, '*Equestris Ordo*'; Duby, 'The origins of a system of social classification' (1972), *Chivalrous Society*, 88ff, and his book, *The Three Orders*, trans. A. Goldhammer, Chicago and London 1980 (original French Edition, 1978)
79 See especially D.C. Douglas (not least for the Norman contribution), *The Norman Achievement*, London 1969, 89ff. See also J.M. Wallace-Hadrill, 'War and peace in the earlier Middle Ages', *TRHS* (5) xxv, 1975.

knighthood in society. One does not have to wait for St. Bernard for knights to be respectable. We might obtain a new dimension to our studies by investigating contemporary art, especially sculpture, which affords not only invaluable technical information about arms and armour but also a measure of the prestige of knighthood, and the appeal of chivalry to the imagination of men and women second only to such favourite Biblical scenes as the Annunciation or the Nativity, the Flight into Egypt or Doubting Thomas. I speak very much as an amateur, but a celebration of knighthood relevant to this paper seems to run from, let us say, the jousting knights of St.-Georges-de-Boscherville in Normandy (thought to be reset from an earlier building) to the knights representing Virtues overcoming Vices at Aulnay.[80] In the real world room must be found, no doubt, for failures and drop-outs, and even for enigmatic Norman *vavassores*,[81] survivors, it seems, from earlier generations; but if we wish to know about the Norman knight, his prowess and his status, in England in the second half of the eleventh century, we do not, *pace* Sally Harvey, 'abandon our hindsight view of the splendidly equipped figure . . . afforded by the late medieval knight'[82] but look at the splendidly equipped and mounted figures on the contemporary Bayeux Tapestry.

80 If the great typanum of comparable date (c. 1130?) on the west front at Conques shows amongst many other scenes a knight being dragged down to Hell, that emphasizes scarcely less a knightly dominance of society.
81 See H. Navel, 'L'enquête de 1133 sur les fiefs de l'Evéché de Bayeux', *Bulletin de la Soc. des Antiquaires de Normandie* xlii, 1934, 51—2, 60, 70 ff. Cf. Bloch, 177.
82 Harvey, 4.

WILLIAM THE BASTARD AT WAR

John Gillingham

As Allen Brown observed at the end of his paper on his battle at his conference, almost the only thing about the Norman Conquest that isn't controversial is the fact that the Normans won the Battle of Hastings. How and why they won remain matters of opinion. In Allen's view – and, characteristically, he described himself as being 'at least as unbiassed as William of Poitiers' – they owed their victory to their 'superior military techniques' and to William's 'superior general-ship'.[1] Now much has been written about military techniques and organisation, both Norman and Anglo-Saxon, but almost nothing has been written about William's generalship. Although what he did – and what Harold did – in 1066 itself has been endlessly discussed, no real attempt has been made to put that decisive campaign into the context of William's whole career as a war leader. Even William's military experience in the years prior to 1066 – the experience on which he presumably drew as he contemplated the greatest enterprise of his life – has been often mentioned but hardly analysed.[2] This omission is all the more curious in view of the fact that the materials for such a study are ready to hand. One of the conqueror's own chaplains wrote an account of his master's life in which he consciously chose to portray him as a model of generalship. Time and again William of Poitiers compares William with the great generals of antiquity, and time and again he concludes that William was the greater soldier. His account of the campaign of 1066 culminates in a sustained comparison between the Norman invasion of England and the Roman invasion of Britain, demon-strating – at least to the author's own satisfaction – that William had faced greater difficulties than Julius Caesar and yet had achieved a much more impressive degree of success.[3] Since the chaplain was writing in the 1070s, and writing a work clearly destined for his master's ears, this was presumably a demonstration very much to William's taste. Throughout his work indeed it is evident that WP was saying what he felt his lord would like to hear. He was producing a justification of William the Conqueror and, at times, a nauseatingly sycophantic one. One of his earliest known readers, Orderic Vitalis, son of an English mother and a Norman father, was clearly shocked by WP's account of the harrying of the North and was moved to comment: 'When I think of the helpless children, the young people in the prime of life, and those whose hair was

---

[1] R. Allen Brown, 'The Battle of Hastings', *Battle* iii, 21.
[2] Except in the excellent but brief chapter entitled 'Military Society and the Art of War' in F. Barlow, *William I and the Norman Conquest*, 1965.
[3] *Gesta Guillelmi*, 68, 156, 162, 168, 232–4, 246–54; probably also Orderic ii, 234.

now grey with age, all alike condemned to die of hunger, then I am so stirred to pity that I would simply lament what was done, rather than vainly attempt, with empty adulation, to flatter the perpetrator of such infamy'.[4] It is also evident that WP was, as R. H. C. Davis has put it, 'intent on producing a work of great literature', a self-conscious stylist, insistently parading his easy mastery of a wide range of classical Latin literature, 'flattering himself' as well as the Conqueror.[5] Reading him indeed I am irresistibly reminded of the opening words of Geoffrey Parker's chapter on warfare in the thematic companion volume to the *New Cambridge Modern History*: 'Part of the charm of Renaissance writers is their firm conviction that . . . the heroes of antiquity would have been miserable failures as Renaissance men, even as Renaissance soldiers'.[6] By these criteria William of Poitiers was a Renaissance writer and William the Bastard a Renaissance soldier. And so indeed they were.

But there is no need to dismiss the work on this account.[7] On the contrary. These features are so obvious that they are relatively easy to make allowances for. Moreover from the point of view of the student of war, the history of WP has two great advantages. First, it was written by someone close to the court, a member, as it were, of the duke's headquarters staff. Second, it was written by an author who had himself been a soldier. In Orderic's words, 'before he entered the church he had himself been keenly involved in the business of war. He had borne arms in the service of his prince and, having himself lived through the dire perils of war, was all the better placed to give an accurate description of the conflicts he had seen'.[8] His account of William's career may be a biassed one, but it is the bias of a man who, on the subject of war at least, knew exactly what he was talking about. Since I have had the good fortune never to have been more than an armchair soldier, I shall follow very closely in the footsteps of William of Poitiers.

My intention then is twofold. Firstly to take Duke William's military career as a model of eleventh-century generalship.[9] Secondly to put the 1066 campaign into the context of mid-eleventh century warfare. This means that in this paper I shall have relatively little to say about the last period of William's career, the years after 1075 when he no longer enjoyed the fortunate constellation of political circumstances which had characterised the 1060s and early 1070s and

[4] Orderic ii, 232.

[5] R. H. C. Davis, 'William of Poitiers and his History of William the Conqueror' in R. H. C. Davis and J. M. Wallace-Hadrill, eds., *The Writing of History in the Middle Ages. Essays presented to R. W. Southern*, Oxford 1981, 71–100, esp. 72.

[6] G. Parker, 'Warfare' in *The New Cambridge Modern History* xiii, Companion Volume, ed. P. Burke, Cambridge 1979, 201.

[7] Any more than it would be right, on similar grounds, to dismiss Richer of Rheims as a source for late tenth-century warfare. See the comments, valuable on this and on all aspects of war in this period, of John France, 'La Guerre dans la France féodale à la fin du IXe et au Xe siècle', *Revue Belge d'Histoire Militaire* xxiii, 1979, 177–198, esp. 179, 192–3.

[8] Orderic ii, 258.

[9] In this respect an exercise very similar to J. Gillingham, 'Richard I and the science of war in the Middle Ages', J. Gillingham and J. C. Holt, eds., *War and Government in the Middle Ages. Essays in honour of J. O. Prestwich*, Woodbridge 1984, 78–91.

when, in consequence, his generalship faltered.[10] In Orderic's words, 'In the last thirteen years of his life he never once succeeded in putting an army to flight or capturing by military skill any fortress to which he laid siege.'[11] WP's task as panegyrist was made distinctly easier by the fact that he happened to be writing at a time when William's military reputation was at its peak.[12] Bearing in mind the defeats and setbacks of William's later career it is doubtless easier for me to be a little more detached.

I begin with an example of the panegyrist at work: WP's treatment of the battle of Val-ès-Dunes (1047), the first military incident to be reported in the surviving portion of his text. Here WP gives the impression that Duke William was in overall command of the 'loyalist' troops, with King Henry I of France merely lending useful assistance.[13] But since in 1047 the king was the greater man in rank, in age and in experience of war, common sense alone suggests that WP was being misleading, probably deliberately so.[14] And in this case common sense is confirmed by the language of William of Jumièges' account of the battle, written half a dozen years earlier than WP's.[15]

If, in fact, it was King Henry who was the army commander at Val-ès-Dunes, then it becomes possible to draw a rather striking conclusion. In 1066, as Frank Barlow pointed out, William had no previous experience of command in a set battle.[16] Whether or not it is quite right to go on to say, as Barlow does, that until he faced Harold, William had never deployed his own army in the face of a large

[10] The high drama of 1066 rather obscures the fact William's military career falls quite naturally into three parts: the period up to 1060 when he was generally on the defensive against both internal and external enemies; the years of expansion between 1060 and 1075; and finally the period between 1076 and 1087 when he was once again on the defensive.

[11] Orderic ii, 350. In view of the defeats and setbacks which William suffered at Dol in 1076, Gerberoi in 1079, La Flèche in 1081 and St Suzanne in 1084–5, Orderic's judgement seems better grounded than Barlow's 'once he had caught the wind he never got becalmed', Barlow, xvi.

[12] Some idea of his reputation in the mid-1070s can be gathered from the rumour that he was planning to attack Aachen and seize the empire reported by Lampert of Hersfeld under the year 1074. Lampert of Hersfeld, *Annales* ed. O. Holder-Egger, Scriptores Rerum Germanicarum in usum scholarum, Hanover 1894, 195.

[13] *Gesta Guillelmi*, 16–18.

[14] The king, in WP's words, was *vir strenuus et nominatus in rebus bellicis*, a competent and cautious advisor to the young soldier, *Gesta Guillelmi*, 24, 82.

[15] 'rex cum duce', Jumièges, 123. Despite this most historians, e.g. Michel de Boüard, *Guillaume le Conquérant*, Paris 1984, 205, or R. Allen Brown, *The Normans*, Woodbridge 1984, 44–5, or David Bates, *Normandy before 1066*, 1982, 73, continue to follow WP in implying that William was in charge at Val-ès-Dunes. More in line with WJ's emphasis is D. C. Douglas, *William the Conqueror*, London 1964, 49. I would like to emphasise that impressed as I am by WP's qualities as a historian of war, I am almost equally impressed by WJ, monk though he may have been. Perhaps indeed in a society where no monastery was immune from the consequences of war – usually destructive, but sometimes in the more acceptable form of gifts from the contrite warrior – it was natural for observant monks to be well informed about war. On WJ see E. M. C. Van Houts, *Gesta Normannorum Ducum*, Groningen 1983, and on the relationship between WJ and WP, Davis, 'William of Poitiers' 76–80.

[16] Barlow, 33. One implication of this is that the engagement in 1057 which is conventionally referred to as the 'battle of Varaville' was in fact not a battle. Here I entirely agree with Barlow, 33 and de Boüard, 205, that it was not. See below p. 153. Of course if we eliminate Val-ès-Dunes and Varaville from the roll of William's battle honours then it becomes a little harder to see him as the general who, when he rode into the field of Hastings 'had never fought a battle which he had not won', Brown, *The Normans*, 45. Cf. R. Allen Brown, *The Normans and the Norman Conquest*, 1969, 49.

enemy force, probably depends on what is meant by 'in the face of', but it is undoubtedly true that although there were earlier occasions when William offered battle, and may have done so seriously, in fact no battle actually took place.[17] In passing it should also be noted that, so far as we can tell, in the summer of 1066 Harold too was without experience of command in a set battle.[18] What makes this point all the more striking is the observation that at Hastings 'the core of the army was a force of fighting men seasoned in the many wars Duke William had fought'.[19] It follows that there were many wars but very few battles.[20] In that case three questions at once arise. The first, why were battles so rare? The second, just what was William's normal style of warfare? The third, why in 1066 did he depart from his familiar methods and try something of which he had no experience?

   To start with the first question. Hastings, as every schoolgirl knows, was a decisive victory. And this is how it was understood in the eleventh century.[21] Moreover the battle of Val-ès-Dunes also seems to have been regarded as being decisive. It is true that the defeated Guy of Brionne was able to remain in revolt for a long time afterwards – for three years according to Orderic – nonetheless it does look as though as a result of the battle the military initiative passed into William's hands.[22] But if one of the more dramatic events in William's early career had indeed been his participation in a decisive victory in battle, then this only sharpens the question.[23] Why, if he had learned that battles could bring important advantages to the victor, did he subsequently and for so long avoid

[17] On William offering battle see below pp. 150–1.
[18] Though it should be noted that we know a great deal less about Harold's military career than we do about William's. It might, however, be argued that it generally was the case that when battles occurred it was between commanders who had little or no experience of battle. On the battle of Lewes, for example, David Carpenter has observed that 'not a single person on either side in 1264 had ever been in one', D. Carpenter, *The Battles of Lewes and Evesham 1264/5*, Keele 1987, 17.
[19] M. Chibnall, *Anglo-Norman England 1066–1166*, Oxford 1986, 9–10.
[20] Exactly how many wars it is hard to know, but a likely minimum is that he went to war in at least thirteen of the years between 1047 and 1065. Very probably he went to war more often than this but given the gaps in the sources, – none of them by authors who were setting out to compile detailed annals – and given the well-known chronological problems which they present, (see Davis, 'William of Poitiers' 75–77 and Bates, Appendix A) we are unlikely to get much further than this minimum estimate. But we must always bear Chibnall's warning in mind. 'In dealing with a period where the evidence is so exiguous and warfare was almost continuous, it is important not to imagine that the few engagements of which we have some knowledge, even if accurately reported, were the only things that happened', Orderic ii, 365.
[21] *Gesta Guillelmi*, 208, 248.
[22] Jumièges, 123; *Gesta Guillelmi*, 18–20; Orderic vi, 210.
[23] Since the first section of WP's History is missing, we have to rely upon WJ for William's earliest military experiences. Whether or not the undated recapture of Falaise (Jumièges, 118) actually was his first experience of war – WJ could well have discreetly passed over less happy experiences, particularly in the previous months when King Henry had invaded Normandy, burned down the ducal town of Argentan, and returned home laden with plunder (Jumièges, 117–8) – the episode nicely illustrates the generalisation, important as it is well-known, that 'the military strategy of the period was based almost entirely on the castle or town', Barlow, 30. See also the chapter on 'The castle in war' in R. A. Brown, *English Castles*, 2nd edn., 1976.

battle?[24] For there can, I think, be no doubt that he did avoid battle, i.e. the absence of battles in the years 1048 to 1065 is not simply because other generals were afraid of William and ran away whenever he approached. This is undeniably one of the impressions which WP tries to create.[25] Unfortunately he significantly weakens his case in a passage in which he comments generally on William's defence of Normandy from the time of his youth up until his forty-fifth year. He remarks that whenever King Henry attacked, William went out of his way to avoid battle.[26]

Why then did William avoid battle when it could be decisive? The answer surely is, precisely because it could be decisive. Decisive for the loser as well as for the victor and no general could ever be absolutely certain of victory. So far as we can see Hastings was a very close run thing, and Val-ès-Dunes may have been as well.[27] Indeed it is unlikely that any given battle would take place unless both commanders felt they had a reasonable chance of victory. In a fairly evenly balanced situation a few minutes of confusion or panic and the patient work of months or even years might be undone. Moreover although battle might tip the strategic balance one way or the other, it does not follow that all battles did. The advantage won by William's victory over the northern rebels at York in 1069 was to be very short-lived. Later that same year the North was up in arms again, the Danes landed, Edgar Atheling returned to the fray and an army 'marching in high spirits' re-captured York.[28] More directly relevant to the subject of William's generalship prior to 1066 is the battle of Mortemer in 1054. Here Count Robert of Eu won the victory which effectively put an end to King Henry's invasion in that year, but it neither altered the balance of power in northern France nor led to the break-up of the Capetian-Angevin alliance against William. Thus in 1057 the allies were to invade Normandy again, and it is just possible that they did so

---

[24] In De Boüard's view William disliked battle so intensely that he fought only two (Val-ès-Dunes and Hastings) in his whole career, and even these two were forced upon him by his adversaries, De Boüard, 205. By my reckoning William the general fought two or three battles, Hastings, probably York 1069 (in both of these it was William who took the initiative) and Gerberoi 1079; and William the soldier fought in a fourth (Val-ès-Dunes).

[25] E.g. *Gesta Guillelmi*, 40, 78, 110.

[26] *Gesta Guillelmi*, 28. True he ascribes this to William's laudable concern for the royal dignity and to his memory of their former friendship, but royal dignity may have meant more to William after 1066 (when WP was writing) than it had before. Moreover, as WP himself notes, other Normans were less troubled by such scruples.

[27] WP emphasises the strength of the opposition at Val-ès-Dunes – 'the greater part of Normandy' (*Gesta Guillelmi*, 16) and this, together with WJ's statement that 'the king and the duke were undaunted by their enemies' fierce attacks' (*Jumièges*, 123), might be thought to imply that they had been dangerous attacks. The stories told by Wace in the *Roman de Rou*, composed in the 1160s and 1170s, might be taken to reinforce the impression that the issue hung long in the balance, but it is surely rash to attempt to reconstruct the course of the battle – as do De Boüard, 127–31 and Douglas, 50–1, – from tales told and songs sung for a hundred years before they reached the ears of the man who wrote them down. We only have to listen to a modern guide at a historical monument to realise that topographical precision is not the slightest guarantee of historical accuracy. See also Matthew Bennett, 'Poetry as history? The "Roman de Rou" of Wace as a source for the Norman Conquest', *Battle* v, 21–39. All we really know about Val-ès-Dunes is that Henry and William won it.

[28] ASC 'D' *ad annum* 1069.

in 1058 as well.[29] What was really decisive was neither Mortemer nor William's own victory in the engagement at Varaville in 1057, but the fact that both Henry I and Geoffrey Martel happened to die in 1060.[30] Even victory in battle might, in other words, bring only limited rewards, whereas there was always the possibility that defeat might be disastrous. Seeking battle was a high-risk strategy.

Moreover if the imminent prospect of battle brought to all men the terrible fear of injury, or death, or shame, then to none more so than the commander himself.[31] This is because it was always clear that the surest way to win a battle was to kill or capture the opposing commander. Thus the critical importance of the moment at Hastings when William calmed the fears of his men by showing them that he was still alive and well.[32] It was not only that Harold – and his brothers – died at Hastings. Harold Hardrada and Tostig were killed at Stamford Bridge. Conan of Brittany had been killed at the Battle of Conquereuil in 992. William fitzOsbern was to be killed at Cassel in 1070.[33] Since we know that, as things turned out, William managed to survive his battles, it is easy to forget the very great risks he was taking. At Gerberoi his horse was killed under him, and 'he who brought up another for him, Toki of Wallingford, was immediately killed by a bolt from a crossbow'.[34] William escaped with an injury to his hand. It sounds minor but just such an injury was to cost William Clito his life in 1128.[35] Hastings was clearly no exception. If WP is right in saying that William had three horses killed under him then it may have been merely a matter of luck as to whether it was he or Harold who was killed first.[36] Even if he escaped death or injury a prince had reason to worry about the political

---

[29] O. Guillot, *Le comte d'Anjou et son entourage au XIe siècle*, Paris 1972, 81, citing the *Cart. de Notre Dame du Ronceray*, no. 80, 'Anno . . . MLVIII quando profectus est comes in Normanniam cum exercitu cum rege Francie Henrico super comitem Guillelmum'.

[30] As WP implicitly recognised when, immediately after reporting their deaths, he announced his intention of turning to the subject of William's conquests, *Gesta Guillelmi*, 84–6.

[31] See, e.g., Orderic's account of a confrontation between William and Fulk le Réchin, probably in 1081: 'Dum utraeque acies ad ambiguum certamen pararentur, horribilesque pro morte et miseriis quae mortem reproborum sequuntur, timores mentibus multorum ingererentur' (Orderic ii, 308–10).

[32] *Gesta Guillelmi*, 190; *BT* ed. D. M. Wilson, pl. 68. By the early twelfth century it was believed that King Henry had had a close shave at Val-ès-Dunes, *De gestis regum* ii, 287.

[33] Orderic ii, 282.

[34] *ASC* 'D' *ad annum* 1079.

[35] Symeon ii, 282–3. This Durham author was exceptionally well-informed, perhaps reflecting the diplomatic interests of Bishop Flambard.

[36] *Gesta Guillelmi*, 198. I am not convinced that WJ ever really said that Harold was killed at the beginning of the battle, *in primo militum congressu* (Jumièges, 135). The train of thought indicated by the sentences before and after the sentence containing this phrase, in particular the words at the beginning of the next sentence, 'Comperientes itaque Angli regem suum mortem oppetiisse . . . iam nocte imminente' suggests to me that what WJ actually wrote was *in postremo militum congressu*; *postremo* then being misread by a copyist who overlooked the *post* abbreviation. WJ's autograph does not survive, so all extant MSS may derive from an early copy already containing this scribal error. See the stemma in Van Houts, 67.

consequences of being taken prisoner.[37] To judge from WP's account of the capture of William of Aquitaine in 1033 and of Theobald of Blois in 1058, it looks as though William's advisers were well aware of this danger.[38]

In the light of all these considerations it would be reasonable to imagine that an eleventh-century prince might be a little nervous about battle. Thanks to the remarkable *Fragmentum Historiae Andegavensis* written by Count Fulk le Réchin, we can show that at least one such prince certainly was. The climax of Fulk's brief history of the counts of Anjou (written in 1096) comes when he describes the war of succession between him and his brother Geoffrey (1060–68):

> 'Time and again we made war (*guerram*) one upon the other. With interludes for truces this tribulation went on for eight years altogether. Then, on the instructions of Pope Alexander, I released my brother from the chains in which I held him, but still he attacked me yet again, laying siege to my fortress (*castrum*) of Brissac. There I rode against him with those princes whom God, in his clemency, permitted to join me, and I fought with him a pitched battle in which, by God's grace, I overcame him; and he was captured and handed over to me, and a thousand of his men with him.'[39]

Only on one other occasion does Fulk refer to God's grace, and that is in his reference to Fulk Nerra's victory, *Dei gratia*, over Count Odo of Blois in the battle of Pontlevoy.[40] Battle was a desperate business; the risks terrible; the outcome uncertain. As Fulk Rechin's language shows, it was at this perilous moment that events were felt to move out of human control and into the hands of God. Since then the rewards might be limited while the risks were always terrible, it is not surprising that prudent commanders should prefer to look for other methods, methods which 'did relatively little harm if things turned out badly, and yet brought great gains when they turned out well'.[41] This, after all, would be the professional approach to war and, as Allen Brown has so often emphasised, these were men whose approach was professional through and through.[42] This, moreover, was the advice they received from Vegetius, author of that late Roman handbook on war which, throughout the middle ages and beyond, was to

---

[37] William of Malmesbury was to have some sympathetic words for the plight of politically valuable prisoners, *De gestis regum* ii, 288.

[38] *Gesta Guillelmi*, 32–4. Slightly later examples that come readily to mind are Robert Curthose at Tinchebrai and King Stephen at Lincoln.

[39] L. Halphen and R. Poupardin, ed., *Chroniques des comtes d'Anjou et des seigneurs d'Amboise*, Paris 1913, 237. This time Geoffrey stayed in prison. Fulk Rechin was one of the enemies who were to give William such a hard time in the later years of his life. I entirely agree with Jim Bradbury's re-assessment of this prince elsewhere in this volume.

[40] Halphen and Poupardin, 234.

[41] 'Quae si male cesserint, minus noceant, si bene, plurimum prosint', Vegetius, *Epitoma rei militaris*, ed. C. Lang, Leipzig 1885, 91–2.

[42] Here the appropriate footnote is surely Brown, *passim*.

remain 'the soldier's Bible'.[43] For Vegetius was emphatic. Battle should be the last resort. Everything else should be tried first.[44]

What then were these other methods? What was William's normal style of warfare in the years between 1047 and 1066? I begin with an analysis of William on the attack.[45] By far his greatest success before 1066 was his conquest of Maine and WP is very clear as to how this was achieved. His principal target was Le Mans itself, *validissima urbs, caput atque munimentum terrae*. But rather than an immediate and direct assault on the city itself, William preferred a different way. 'This then was his chosen method of conquest. He sowed terror in the land by his frequent and lengthy invasions; he devastated vineyards, fields and estates; he seized neighbouring strongpoints and where advisable put garrisons in them; in short he incessantly inflicted innumerable calamities upon the land.'[46] In these succinct phrases we have an excellent outline of the basic strategy of attack: the intention is to seize fortresses and the standard preliminary is to ravage the surrounding countryside.[47] In 1073, when William had to recover Maine, he adopted the same methods. In the words of the ASC, 'In this year king William led an English and French host oversea and conquered the province of Maine, and the English laid it completely waste; they destroyed the vineyards, burnt down the towns, and completely devastated the countryside, and brought it all into subjection to William.'[48] Similarly William's enemies were expected to operate in the same way. When Henry I invaded Normandy in 1054, he came, according to William of Poitiers, with the intention of 'destroying *oppida*, burning villages, here putting to the sword, there seizing plunder, and so in the end reducing the whole land to a miserable desert'.[49] Since no system of magazines and supply lines was capable of sustaining an army embarked on operations in enemy territory it followed that armies were forced to forage to stay alive.[50] Of course foraging and ravaging are not quite identical activities, but the fact

[43] On Vegetius see W. Goffart, 'The date and purpose of Vegetius' *De Re Militari*', *Traditio* xxxiii, 1977. I have not seen B. S. Bachrach, 'The practical use of Vegetius' *De Re Militari* during the early middle ages', *The Historian* xlvii, 1985. But wide of the mark is D. J. A. Ross's notion (in 'The Prince Answers Back: "Les Enseignemens de Theodore Paliologue"', C. Harper-Bill and R. Harvey eds., *The Ideals and Practice of Medieval Knighthood*, Woodbridge 1986, 165) that even when he wrote Vegetius was 'hopelessly out of date'. Eternal common-sense principles – R. C. Smail's apt description of Vegetius' strategic maxims – do not date.

[44] 'Ideo omnia ante cogitanda sunt, ante temptanda, ante facienda sunt, quam ad ultimum veniatur abruptum.' Vegetius, 86.

[45] A narrative of William's wars would take up more space than I have here and would, in any case, be superfluous. For a recent excellent chronological summary of his campaigns in their political and military context see Bates, 73–83.

[46] *Gesta Guillelmi*, 90. Characteristically WP explains that this was because William wished to avoid unnecessary bloodshed.

[47] As, in the next century, Jordan Fantosme was to put it: 'Let him . . . lay waste their country . . . then besiege their castles' (R. C. Johnston, ed., *Jordan Fantosme's Chronicle*, Oxford 1981, 11.439–50). See Gillingham, 83–4.

[48] *ASC* 'E' *ad annum* 1073.

[49] *Gesta Guillelmi*, 70; cf. 'ad Calcivum subvertendum territorium . . . ad demoliendum comitatum Embroicensem' (Jumièges, 129).

[50] M. Van Creveld, *Supplying War. Logistics from Wallenstein to Patton*. Cambridge 1977, 7–10. Van Creveld's analysis, based on seventeenth century conditions, applies *a fortiori* to the eleventh.

remains that in most circumstances one man's foraging is another man's ravaging. Thus 'the usual method, indeed the very aim of warfare was to live at the enemy's expense' and by doing so compel him to give in to your demands.[51] Ravaging, and foraging while ravaging, was the principal strategy of attack. All this was strictly the Gospel according to Vegetius. 'The main and principal point in war is to secure plenty of provisions for oneself and to destroy the enemy by famine.'[52] The point about ravaging, and foraging while ravaging, was that it was directed simultaneously to both these ends. At one and the same time moreover it suited both the overall campaign strategy of the commander and the individual interest of the ordinary soldier who was fighting for private profit, for plunder. A method which worked on all these levels at once was clearly a supremely efficient one.

WP's account of the 1063 conquest of Maine is, of course, phrased in very general terms. None the less it is precisely these strategic generalisations which enable us to make sense of his much more detailed account of the earliest episodes in the history of Norman military pressure on the county of Maine, pressure which dated back to the early 1050s. It all began with a counter-attack, William's reaction to a threatening advance made by the most formidable warrior of the day, Count Geoffrey Martel of Anjou.[53] At an unknown date, but probably *c.* 1051 when he acquired a firm grip on Maine, Geoffrey Martel took control of Alençon and Domfront, 'the former within, the latter adjoining the borders of Normandy'.[54] According to WJ, having placed troops in the fortress of Domfront, Geoffrey began to ravage Normandy. Indeed according to WP, it was precisely the licence to plunder which Geoffrey gave them which made his lordship so attractive to the men of Domfront and Alençon.[55] William responded by launching an attack on Domfront. The strength of this fortress's site meant that it could not be taken by assault so, after an initial attempt to take it by surprise had failed owing to treachery within his own ranks, William settled down to build four siege castles in an attempt to starve it into submission.[56] He adopted, in other words, a strategy of blockade and attrition. But a phrase like 'settling down' to besiege should not be taken to mean that William had adopted an inactive 'wait and see' style of warfare. On the contrary. In WP's words, 'he went out riding by day and night, or lay hidden under cover, to see whether attacks could be launched against those who were attempting to bring in

[51] Van Creveld, 23, 27, 32.
[52] 'In omni expeditione unum est et maximum telum, ut tibi sufficiat victus, hostes frangat inopia' (Vegetius, 69). Thus, as Matthew Bennett has pointed out in 'The Status of the Squire: the Northern Evidence', *Ideals and Practice* (as n. 43), 4, even in the *chansons de geste* ravaging is portrayed as an entirely commonplace activity.
[53] For his great reputation as a soldier see *Gesta Guillelmi*, 32, 42; Orderic ii, 104; Halphen and Poupardin, 235.
[54] *Gesta Guillelmi*, 42. On the date see Bates, 255–7.
[55] Jumièges, 124; *Gesta Guillelmi*, 38.
[56] *Gesta Guillelmi*, 36. That William initially hoped to take Domfront by surprise seems a very plausible interpretation of WP's words. See De Boüard, 199.

supplies, or carrying messages, or trying to ambush his foragers'.[57] The struggle for Domfront very quickly resolved into a struggle for supplies, a typical example of Vegetian warfare. Precisely this, in the seventeenth and eighteenth centuries, was still the cardinal problem in war: how to capture a town before the resources of the surrounding country gave out.[58]

When he heard that Geoffrey was bringing an army to the relief of Domfront, William, leaving troops behind to maintain the siege, rapidly advanced to meet him. But no battle occurred. Geoffrey, according to WP, was suddenly overcome by fear and fled before he even caught sight of the Norman army.[59] To historians who assumed that most medieval generals were keen to fight battles, this apparently timid behaviour on the part of so formidable a warrior cried out for explanation. Thus Halphen believed that it must have taken a diversionary attack on Anjou to make him turn back, and so he dated these events to 1049 when there is evidence for a campaign waged by Henry I in the Loire valley.[60] It is likely, however, that Geoffrey's withdrawal was both sensible and normal, calling for no special explanation. According to WP, after his adversary's ignominious retreat, William was free to lay waste his rich lands, but, under-standing the wisdom of restraint in victory, he decided not to do so.[61] What this most probably means is that Geoffrey's army, though it presumably retreated, had none the less remained close enough to inhibit William's ravaging.[62] In that case William was now in a fix. With his army stationary before Domfront he faced very great logistical problems.[63] It may be that at this stage of the campaign Geoffrey Martel had reason to believe that he had obtained the upper hand. But William, acting with startling speed and ferocity, turned the tables. He turned suddenly against Alençon and took it with scarcely a blow being struck.[64] The additional information provided by WJ allows us to glimpse the reality behind WP's vague and bland words. A fort across the river from Alençon was seized, fired and some of the defenders brutally punished. William's ferocity persuaded the citizens of Alençon that, if they wished to retain their feet and hands, they had better surrender at once. Equally impressed the garrison of Domfront also decided to yield.[65] The notoriety of the atrocity at Alençon – as Barlow pointed out, WP's silence is good evidence that it was regarded as barbarous – has, quite naturally, tended to overshadow the other details in WJ's

---

[57] *Gesta Guillelmi*, 38.

[58] Van Creveld, 28.

[59] *Gesta Guillelmi*, 38–40.

[60] L. Halphen, *Le comtè d'Anjou au XIe siècle*, Paris 1906, 72–4; followed by Guillot, 72 n.320. De Boüard (200–1), while dating the Domfront campaign to 1051, none the less retained Halphen's explanation; so also Barlow, 19. At least Douglas (59–60) inserted the word 'perhaps' when writing that Geoffrey left Maine 'owing to a threat to Anjou by King Henry'.

[61] *Gesta Guillelmi*, 40–2.

[62] This, it may be, is the manoeuvre that Harold had failed to carry out when he was taken by surprise by William's rapid advance.

[63] Van Creveld, 25. And for William's insistence on keeping moving in 1066 see below, p. 157.

[64] *Gesta Guillelmi*, 42.

[65] Jumièges, 126–7.

account.[66] But these too are very valuable. We are told that William turned on Alençon because his scouts had informed him that the town was in a poor state of readiness; that he then rode through the night and attacked at dawn; finally, having taken and garrisoned Alençon, he returned to Domfront 'in great haste'.[67] Unquestionably the Domfront campaign is an extremely illuminating one. It illustrates some very characteristic features of William the Bastard at war. Within a closely-supervised strategy of attrition he succeeded because he ensured that he was kept well-informed – frequently riding out on patrol himself – because he moved rapidly and because he was prepared to be brutal.

The next stage in the Norman Conquest of Maine came in 1055. William ordered the construction of a *castrum* at Ambrières (in the lordship of Geoffrey of Mayenne, a vassal of Martel), and, reports William of Poitiers, the lord of Mayenne knew only too well what this portended: once they had completed Ambrières the Normans would have a free hand to raid, ravage and lay waste his lands.[68] Geoffrey Martel swore to protect his vassal and approached Ambrières, where William, with his army, eagerly awaited his arrival. Geoffrey, however, proved a disappointment, preferring to keep his distance. Despite this apparent timidity on Geoffrey's part, it is evident that his strategy did in fact achieve a degree of success. William withdrew from Ambrières. According to WP he did so because both princes and ordinary soldiers were complaining about food shortages.[69] In other words Geoffrey had successfully undermined William's capacity to supply his troops, presumably by making it unsafe for them to go out foraging. Geoffrey was now in a position to launch an assault on the Norman garrison of Ambrières unimpeded by the presence of William's army. As it turned out, however, his assault failed and William was sufficiently determined to muster fresh troops and return to the scene of the action. Now it would have been Geoffrey's turn, as commander of the army laying siege to Ambrières, to suffer the logistical consequences of immobility and so it is hardly surprising to find him retreating in the face of the Norman advance. Thus William was able to consolidate his hold on Ambrières. Soon afterwards Geoffrey de Mayenne drew the appropriate conclusion and submitted.[70]

Two years earlier the revolt of William of Arques had precipitated a series of

---

[66] Barlow, 20. For the nature of the insult see E. M. C. Van Houts, 'The origins of Herleva, mother of William the Conqueror' *EHR* ci, 1986, 399–404. For additional evidence that William came to have the reputation of being an unusually ruthless soldier see J. F. Benton, ed., *Self and Society in Medieval France. The Memoirs of Abbot Guibert of Nogent*, New York 1970, 69.

[67] In WJ's account of William's earliest known campaign we find a similar emphasis on the speed of the young duke's movements (Jumièges, 118, 126–7). Once again one of Vegetius' maxims is to the point: 'courage is worth more than numbers, and speed is worth more than courage', cited by P. Contamine, *War in the Middle Ages*, (trans. M. Jones), 1984, 252.

[68] Thus if ravaging was a preliminary to seizing fortresses, so also seizing fortresses was a preliminary to ravaging. In 1074, for example, 'Philip the king of France sent a letter to him (Edgar Atheling), . . . he would give him the castle of Montreuil so that thereafter he could daily work mischief upon his enemies' (*ASC* D).

[69] *Gesta Guillelmi*, 76. If William's decision to offer battle before Ambrières meant that his army remained immobile for a while then this would have materially added to his logistical problems.

[70] *Gesta Guillelmi*, 76–80.

events which were more characteristic of the defensive warfare of the first period of the duke's military career and which, at any rate as described by WP, were dominated throughout by the question of supplies. First on the scene were the duke's *principes militiae* based at Rouen. They at once did their best to prevent foodstuffs and other supplies being carried to Arques in preparation for the expected siege. But the waggons were too well guarded. By the time William arrived – so great, we are told, was the haste with which he had ridden from the Cotentin that all his horses but six had fallen exhausted by the wayside – there was nothing for it but to build a siege-castle and lay a blockade. Some time later while William, who could not afford to be immobilised for long by the siege of a single castle, was away on other business, King Henry I marched to the relief of Arques. Not all went as he would have wished. He suffered heavy casualties when a section of his army was ambushed by the blockading force, and he was unable to dislodge them from their siege-castle. None the less before returning to France he managed to get both supplies and reinforcements into Arques. In the end, however, hunger forced the garrison of Arques to surrender, and the image of starving men gave WP the opportunity for a few literary flourishes, including, of course, an allusion to Vegetius: *famis acrimonia saevius et arctius quam armis.*[71]

In this period what strategy did William employ when he was confronted by an invading army, as in 1053, 1054 and 1057? As we know already, thanks to WP, he preferred to avoid battle (see above p. 145). But just what did this involve? Did it, for example, mean that he decided to take refuge in his castles and hope for the best?[72] The clearest statement of the defensive strategy he in fact adopted comes in William of Malmesbury's description of how the duke handled the great invasion of 1054. In this year King Henry launched a two-pronged attack on Normandy, one army under his brother's command, entering northeast Normandy, and the other, which he commanded, invading the Evreçin. Faced by this threat William, according to William of Malmesbury, manoeuvred 'so that he neither came to a close engagement nor yet allowed his land to be devastated'.[73] This of course is a twelfth century, not an eleventh-century version, but the point is that WM had read what both WJ and WP wrote about 1054 and, in the light of his understanding of the practice of his own day, he was drawing out and laying bare the strategic principles, principles which are, in any event, implicit in their accounts. Thus WJ wrote that 'with some of his men he shadowed the king and inflicted punishment on any member of the royal army whom he was able to catch'.[74] As this passage makes plain the point of having a force in the field and bringing it fairly close to – 'shadowing' – the invading army was to deter the invaders from detaching small units from their main force, in other words, as WM realised, to prevent them ravaging and foraging. Obviously any defender who could catch an invader while some of his

[71] *Gesta Guillelmi*, 54–62. cf. Vegetius, 69.

[72] The method suggested by J. Beeler, *Warfare in Feudal Europe*, 1971, 57.

[73] 'ut nec cominus pugnandi copiam faceret, nec provinciam coram se vastari sineret' (*De gestis regum* ii, 290).

[74] Jumièges, 129–30.

troops were dispersed ravaging was in a strong position. Thus Orderic describes how, in 1069, the Danes landed a great army at Ipswich but were then, *in praedam diffusi*, caught by local levies and defeated, losing thirty men. A little later the same invaders met a similar fate when they landed at Norwich and once again went plundering.[75]

In the great invasion of 1054 it was an incident of this sort which was to prove decisive. In the words of William of Jumièges, the duke 'forthwith picked a force of soldiers and sent them with all speed to check the pillagers of the Pays de Caux . . . they came up with the French at Mortemer, finding them engaged in arson and the shameful sports of women. They attacked immediately at daybreak'.[76] Commenting on this passage, Beeler noted, evidently with some surprise, that Robert of Eu (the victorious commander) 'seems to have been aware of the value of surprise'.[77] The tone here is very characteristic of some modern historians' approach to medieval warfare – though not, needless to say, of RAB's. The defeat of his brother's army at Mortemer persuaded Henry to call off his invasion. It is clear that William's commanders adopted the same defensive strategy in both 1053 (see below p. 154) and 1057. In 1057 Henry and Geoffrey were defeated at the crossing of the River Dives when the tide came in at Varaville cutting off the rear of their army and exposing it to attack. William came up rapidly and cut it to pieces.[78] William of Poitiers offers the additional information that William attacked *cum exigua manu virorum* and this reinforces the impression that he was once again shadowing the invader, not looking for a pitched battle but ready to exploit any opportunity that presented itself.[79]

Of course it would be different if the invader chose to seek battle, called in his incendiaries and foraging parties, and advanced with a concentrated force. Assuming the defender wished to avoid battle then there was probably little he could do except retreat – or as WP might say 'flee' – taking care to stay just out of reach of the invading force. On the other hand the invader could not advance far in this fashion. Sooner or later, and probably sooner, he would be forced to send out foraging parties and then the defender's opportunities would come.[80]

In fact, of course, since systematic ravaging was the principal strategy of attack, it followed that a defensive strategy based on shadowing and harrassing was an extremely effective one. From the point of view of the invading troops, once they could no longer go plundering then soldiering lost its appeal and they just wanted to go home. Paid troops could still, of course, expect their wages, but

---

[75] Orderic ii, 226.

[76] Jumièges, 129–30. In this brief passage note the number of words denoting speed and timing: *protinus, celerrime, illico mane*.

[77] Beeler, 45. But the attempt to surprise one's opponent was, of course, normal in medieval warfare, even indeed in so-called chivalrous warfare. For a discussion of this see J. Gillingham, 'War and Chivalry in the History of William the Marshal' in P. R. Coss and S. D. Lloyd, eds. *Thirteenth Century England: ii*, Woodbridge, 1988. For the importance of surprise in both the northern and southern campaigns of 1066 see Brown, 'Hastings', 7–9.

[78] 'alacriter superveniens', Jumièges, 131.

[79] *Gesta Guillelmi*, 80–82.

[80] Presumably it was being able to foresee this that made William decide not to advance into Maine in 1051 (above p. 150).

even they would presumably regret the loss of the anticipated bonus of loot; and, as for unpaid troops, their enthusiasm for war presumably sank even lower. According to William of Malmesbury, after Stamford Bridge Harold made the mistake of not sharing out the plunder and as a result he was to have few with him at Hastings except *stipendiarios et mercenarios milites*.[81]

A strategy of shadowing and harrassing involved rapid movement, often with fairly small forces; it involved sudden attacks and equally swift retreats. It is hard to conceive of a type of warfare more dependent upon good group discipline.[82] Equally it is hard to envisage a type of warfare in which tricks like feigned flights would be more natural and more frequently practised. Thus, for example, the feigned flight by which a section of King Henry's army was trapped and ambushed in 1053.[83] So there would be nothing in the least remarkable about the employment of such tricks in the Battle of Hastings.[84]

Clearly in this sort of warfare reconnaissance was vital; and being vital, was standard practice.[85] Significantly William of Poitiers mentions the normal only in order to contrast it with what was not normal. For William, in his biographer's words, was more solicitous of the army's safety than he was of his own life. Therefore, dissatisfied with the customary practice of relying on other men's reconnaissance, he was in the habit of going out on patrol himself. Immediately after landing in England he went on patrol with an escort of just twenty-five men, including one of his key military advisers, William fitz Osbern.[86] Similarly on his 1068 Exeter campaign he rode ahead of the main army 'to reconnoitre the ground and walls and to discover what preparations the enemy were making'.[87] And the implication of William of Poitiers' account of the Domfront campaign (see above p. 149) is that this was a habit which William had developed early. Naturally advance information was particularly valuable; it was therefore normal practice to employ spies.[88] At the same time, of course, spies only become news when they are caught. Thus we hear about one sent across the Channel by Harold because he happened to be detected and was then employed by William as part of his propaganda war against the 'usurper'.[89]

Equally, of course, enemies tried to keep their intentions and movements

---

[81] *De gestis regum* i, 281–2.
[82] This point is nicely made in Brown, *The Norman Conquest*, 51, though to call this a 'wait and see' method is perhaps to give an unduly passive label to what was an extremely active form of defence.
[83] Jumièges, 120.
[84] *Gesta Guillelmi*, 194. Yet this is a matter on which despite the entirely justified comments of Brown, 'Hastings', 16, doubts continue to be raised. See J. M. Carter, 'The Feigned Flight at Hastings Re-considered', *The Anglo-Norman Anonymous* vi (January 1988).
[85] The early thirteenth-century History of William the Marshal contains several object lessons on how to organise effective reconnaissance. See Gillingham, 'War and Chivalry'.
[86] *Gesta Guillelmi*, 168. This, in WP's opinion, was another of the ways in which William was a greater man than the generals of antiquity. For another medieval commander who liked to involve himself in reconnaissance work, see J. Gillingham, *Richard the Lionheart*. 1978, 193–4, 272, 284–6.
[87] Orderic ii, 212.
[88] Presumably this is one of the reasons for the common practice of sending envoys into the enemy camp. See, e.g., *Gesta Guillelmi*, 38–40, and, in 1066, 172–9. If the good general went out on patrol himself, then the ideal king acted as his own spy, *De gestis regum* i, 126.
[89] *Gesta Guillelmi*, 154–6.

secret. There is an interesting contrast between the invasion of 1054 when, says William of Poitiers, the duke knew the disposition of the French forces in advance, and the invasion of 1057 when, says William, for fear of the duke they tried to keep their plans secret.[90] Since in 1057, unlike 1054, they were able to penetrate deep into Normandy and 'burn and ravage the duchy all the way to the sea', it seems that this is a panegyrist's way of saying that they had actually succeeded in keeping William in the dark.[91]

In general, of course, William succeeded and he succeeded because his information was good – as in the capture of Alençon (above p. 151). Above all his information was good in 1066. It is possible that the timing of the Norman fleet's move to St Valéry from the mouth of the Dives just four days after the dispersal of Harold's war-fleet was no coincidence but the result of information supplied by William's 'frigates'.[92] What is certain is that William owed his chance of victory at Hastings to the fact that he learned of Harold's movements in time. In time, but if we can trust WP's account of the nervous mood in the Norman camp when they learned that Harold was advancing rapidly and that his fleet had cut off their retreat to Normandy, then only just in time. Fearing a surprise attack, possibly at night, William hurriedly called to arms the men left behind in the camp – for the greater part of the army was out foraging. In his anxiety William even put his hauberk on the wrong way round. According to William of Jumièges, the Normans stood to arms throughout the night, fearing an attack.[93] In fact, of course, the attack never came. Perhaps, as RAB suggests, Harold halted at or near the ridge at Battle in order to rest his troops, and this respite enabled William to seize the initiative.[94]

If this is so then it is ironic that Harold's fatal miscalculation may, in part, have been the consequence of information he had obtained himself while on his own involuntary 'reconnaissance patrol' in Normandy in 1064. As an eyewitness of the Breton campaign of that year he had enjoyed a rare opportunity to observe William's military style at close quarters, and what he saw, if we may trust WP, was a cautiously conducted war of attrition. The approach of William's relieving army forced Conan of Brittany to abandon his siege of Dol (a strongpoint whose lord, Ruallon, was at the time William's ally). Aware, however, of the problems of taking a large army into unknown and unproductive territory, *per regiones vastas, famelicas, ignotas*, William decided not to pursue Conan. Indeed soon afterwards supply problems compelled him to return to Normandy. Then, learning that Conan had joined forces with Count Geoffrey of Anjou (Fulk Rechin's brother), he re-entered Brittany but ordered his men to refrain from

[90] 'hostem distributum praenovit' (1054) (*Gesta Guillelmi*, 70); 'Famam tamen sui motus, quantum potuere, occultantes', (1057) (*ibid.* 80).
[91] *Gesta Guillelmi*, 80. Similarly the fact that William had to withdraw in haste from Dol in 1076 makes it plain that on that occasion too his information gathering system had broken down (Orderic ii, 352; *ASC* D and E *ad annum* 1076).
[92] As suggested by C. M. Gillmor, 'Naval Logistics of the Cross-Channel Operation, 1066', *Battle* vii, 124.
[93] *Gesta Guillelmi*, 180–2; Jumièges, 135.
[94] Brown, 'Hastings', 9.

ravaging, presumably because the enemy army was in the vicinity – though according to WP the order was given purely out of consideration for the interests of the lord of Dol on whose territory he was encamped. In the event there was no battle and once again both sides withdrew, though it is characteristic of WP that he should say that William returned home while his enemies fled.[95]

Perhaps if Harold had witnessed William's sudden strike against Alençon in 1051 he might have been more on his guard in 1066. As it was, however, what he saw was a very typical example of William at war – a campaign in which the duke seems to have been prudently content with a small gain: the preservation of the allegiance of the lord of Dol, just as in 1055 he had been content with the establishment of an outpost at Ambrières. In 1064 there was no sign of an aggressive, battle-seeking, risk-taking strategy. On the contrary it was a struggle of attrition in which, more than anything else, questions of supply seemed to dominate the course of events, a campaign very much in the style of all the other campaigns of the last fifteen years – a good guide, Harold might have thought in the summer of 1066, to the kind of war he was facing now.

Certainly it is clear that throughout the summer of 1066 the organisation of supplies was crucial. Given the fact that armies normally followed the call of their stomachs and kept on the move in order to stay alive, the month when the Norman troops were based at Dives-sur-Mer obviously caused enormous logistical problems. B. S. Bachrach's calculation of what was involved when an army of 14,000 men, including non-combatants, and 2–3,000 horses, remained immobile for a month makes fascinating reading: the 9,000 cartloads of grain, straw, wine and firewood, the river of 700,000 gallons of urine which the horses would have produced, the mountain of five million pounds of horse-shit which it would have taken 5,000 cartloads to remove (presumably, on sanitary grounds, not the same carts as those that brought in the food and drink).[96] We do not need to accept a single detail of Bachrach's calculation to know that, on the general point, he must be absolutely right. The logistical problems which William faced must have been massive ones; and, as Allen Brown observed, he 'triumphantly overcame' them. By contrast, Brown argues, Harold did not.[97] Throughout the summer the English forces were stationed along the south coast but 'when the festival of the Nativity of St Mary (8 September) came, the men's provisions had run out, and no one could keep them there any longer'.[98] In Allen Brown's words, Harold's failure to solve 'logistical problems which were, if anything on a lesser scale than those which Duke William triumphantly overcame' was 'potentially disastrous' and 'must throw light on the Old English military organization and its efficacy'.[99] But this implied criticism underestimates the additional problems which Harold, as defender, had to face. He had to wait,

[95] *Gesta Guillelmi*, 110–12.
[96] B. S. Bachrach, 'Some observations on the military administration of the Norman Conquest' *Battle* viii, esp. 11–15, developing the point made by Gillmor. 'Naval Logistics', 124.
[97] Brown, 'Hastings', 6–7.
[98] *ASC* C.
[99] Brown, 'Hastings', 6–7.

probably not knowing just when and where the attack would come. Yet he had to be prepared. Moreover as defender he suffered a second significant disadvantage, and one of which William of Poitiers was well aware, as he shows in a speech he put into the duke's mouth. 'He (i.e. Harold) does not have the courage to promise his men the least part of that which belongs to me. I, on the other hand, shall promise and give away not only my own possessions but also those which, at the moment, are said to belong to him. Victory will go to the man who is prepared to be generous not only with his own property but also with that of his enemy'.[100] In fact, of course, despite these disadvantages, Harold actually held his forces together from May until early September, i.e. for longer than William did. Moreover the fact that Harold was eventually forced to disband his army made no difference in the end – since William did not attack in early or mid-September. Perhaps indeed at this time the winds were against him.[101]

Even after the crushing victory at Hastings the question of supplies continued to matter. William's triumphal progress faltered in Kent when, as a result of eating meat and drinking water – presumably the wine had run out – many died of dysentery and even more, according to William of Poitiers, nearly did so. Luckily for William the political disarray of the English after Hastings meant that there was no one to challenge the Normans at this critical juncture. A little later the duke himself fell seriously ill. Nonetheless, in a striking illustration of the problems faced by an immobile army, he permitted no delay for fear they would run out of supplies.[102] If William's speech to the magnates at Dives-sur-Mer accurately reflects the kind of thinking in the Norman HQ, then it may well be that, aware of the attacker's advantage, they deliberately decided to postpone the invasion, to use delay, in other words, as a calculated manoeuvre in a war of attrition, as well, of course, as a means of avoiding battle in unfavourable circumstances, at sea or when disembarking. This suggestion, first made by Marjorie Chibnall, would fit very well with everything we know about William's military career up to that date.[103]

The gospel according to Vegetius said that only in the most exceptional circumstances should a general risk battle.[104] By the night of 13–14 October 1066 we are clearly in such exceptional circumstances. Harold had brought his army close enough to William's to prevent it ravaging; he had also, according to WP, sent a fleet round to cut off William's retreat.[105] In this situation it was obvious that William had no real choice but to risk battle. But it was also so

[100] *Gesta Guillelmi*, 158.
[101] Although WP insists that William was waiting for a favourable wind throughout the time he was at Dives, it is only after he had arrived at St Valéry that we hear of prayers for a south wind (*Gesta Guillelmi*, 150, 158–60). It is also worth noting that neither WJ nor the *Carmen de Hastingae Proelio* mention Dives as a port of embarkation. For them prayers and/or favourable winds relate only to St Valéry, Jumièges, 134; *Carmen*, 4–6.
[102] *Gesta Guillelmi*, 212.
[103] 'The delay may have been a deliberate tactic of William' (Chibnall, ll); cf. Brown, 'Hastings' n. 20.
[104] Vegetius, 86–91.
[105] *Gesta Guillelmi*, 180–4.

obvious that William might find himself in this situation that it must surely have been anticipated. Indeed it is hard to see how William could have derived an advantage in any way commensurate with the scale of preparations for this war unless he brought Harold to battle. In that case it may well be that for the first time in his life he adopted a battle-seeking strategy, and that the ravaging of East Sussex was intended partly as a provocation to draw Harold into striking range.[106] William may have offered battle before, but that is one thing; beginning a campaign with the intention of bringing the enemy to battle quite another.[107] In that case the delay and attrition of the summer of 1066 might have been employed as a tactical device within a battle-seeking strategy.

But 1066 was exceptional. Just how exceptional is shown by the style of warfare in England during the next five years. There was probably a battle at York in 1069, and once again it was one in which William was able to take his opponents by surprise.[108] In essence, however, it was to take another long drawn-out war of attrition before William could feel confident that England was a conquered country. The guerilla warfare waged by the English was the normal medieval defence strategy of shadowing and harassing adapted to local conditions, i.e. in a land of few castles the resistance leaders tended to make their bases not in castles but in the wild country.[109] In this grim struggle the castles built by the Normans played a vital role.[110] They enabled the occupying power to control the main towns and to keep at least a watching brief over the main roads. They also functioned as prisons for hostages meant to guarantee the loyalty of local society.[111] But above all else resistance was overcome by ravaging. Thus the Norman Conquest ended, not with a battle, but with a ravaging, the Harrying of the North, the supreme example of the soldier's brutal art. And this, in Orderic's words, 'I do not dare to praise': *laudare non audeo*.[112]

---

[106] *Gesta Guillelmi*, 180. I.e. whichever strategy you adopted, ravaging remained an important component.

[107] Of course it takes two to make a battle. It may be that, as I have suggested elsewhere (Gillingham, 'Richard I', 85), Harold was adopting the standard defensive strategy. Or it may be that, encouraged by his success in the Battle of Stamford Bridge, Harold himself wanted to repeat this new and intoxicating experience. Cf. Commynes's comment on the effect of the battle of Montlhéry on the mind of Charles of Burgundy (Philippe de Commynes, *Memoirs*, trans. M. Jones, Harmondsworth 1972, 79). Either way, during the night and early morning of 13–14 October, Harold was tactically outmanoeuvred.

[108] 'King William came unexpectedly upon them from the south with an overwhelming host, and routed them'. *ASC* D.

[109] S. Reynolds, 'Eadric Silvaticus and the English Resistance' *BIHR* liv, 1981, 102–5.

[110] 'For in the lands of the English there were very few of those fortifications which the French call castles; in consequence the English, for all their martial qualities and valour, were at a disadvantage when it came to resisting their enemies' (Orderic ii, 218). This famous judgement is one which Orderic may well have taken over from the old soldier himself; at this point Orderic is still using the lost part of WP's text.

[111] Turgot, later of Durham and St Andrews, 'unus erat inter alios qui, nuper subjugata Normannis Anglia, obsides pro tota Lindesia in Lindicolino castro custodiebatur' (Symeon ii, 202).

[112] Orderic ii, 232 (above pp. 141–2).

The Battle of Hastings

R. ALLEN BROWN

I had thought of beginning with an explanation of my temerity in presenting to this assembly a paper in which there is little new beyond what I wrote in my book some years ago,[1] but, finding myself, like the Normans in the generally accepted version of the battle, in grave difficulties in the Malfosse at the end thereof, I now know there is no time for any lengthy *apologia*. Suffice it to say, therefore, that I thought we should have an account of Hastings on our agenda and in our *Proceedings*, for others to alter later if they wish or can, and that I was selfish enough to want to write it myself.[2]

There must be, however, an introduction which places the Battle of Hastings in a treble context. The broadest is the context of medieval military history, more specifically its neglect and, worse than neglect, the travesty which is generally made of it. Of course there are honourable exceptions,[3] but, neglected for the most part by serious historians, the subject tends to fall into the hands of antiquarians, amateurs and, not least, retired military gentlemen with whom an admittedly valuable military experience is no substitute for historical knowledge and scholarship. Such neglect is amazing, for war is one of the fundamentals of history and as such is far too important to be left to military historians as I have unhappily defined them. Michael Howard, on the first page of his *Franco–Prussian War*,[4] observed of the French defeat at Sedan in 1870 that it was 'the result not simply of a faulty command but of a faulty military system; and the military system of a nation is not an independent section of the social system but an aspect of it in its totality'. Yet while we are told often enough that feudal society is society organized for war, there is no Michael Howard for the so-called Middle Ages. In his absence, what we know in London as the myth of medieval warfare, or more specifically of the feudal period, has become established and appears ineradicable. It is represented in English historical literature by Sir Charles Oman's *A History of the Art of War in the Middle Ages*,[5] which was first written as an undergraduate prize essay in 1884 and thereafter, expanded but only slightly ameliorated, went on to become the standard work which it has ever since remained. Moreover, the first, and worst, edition was quite recently reissued by the Cornell University Press,[6] without a word of warning (quite the reverse) to the student for whom it is intended. In that edition the young Oman wrote, amongst many other

161

outrageous travesties of the truth, that while 'arrogance and stupidity combined to give a certain definite colour to the proceedings of the average feudal host', nevertheless 'a feudal force presented an assemblage of unsoldierlike qualities such as have seldom been known to coexist'.[7] I will not go on, but here is the myth of feudal warfare as disorganized and amateur chaos in all its unbelievable absurdity. Further it is not, of course, confined either to this country or to Oman, for the erudite works of Spatz[8] and Delbrück,[9] invariably cited in footnotes as authorities for Hastings, are little or no better in their conviction that contemporary warfare was, above all, lacking in discipline—a point to which we shall assuredly return.

The second context, with some apology, is feudalism and the origin of feudalism in this country. It is a sharp indication of the fundamental importance of military history properly understood and properly studied, that the 'military' question of whether Old English armies in the eleventh century used cavalry or not—which even Maitland thought only a matter of tactics as opposed to anything fundamental[10]—is basic to the larger question of the presence or absence of feudalism in England on the eve of the Norman Conquest. No cavalry, no knights, we may say; and no knights, no feudalism. Yet in the virtual absence of any serious study of military matters by serious historians, the old arguments seem never to be ended, and it is well-known that one of the few recent studies of 'English Warfare in 1066', by Mr Richard Glover,[11] argues for the use of cavalry by Old English armies, though not at Hastings itself—and without, unless I am mistaken, ever seeing the profound social implications of what he was saying. To this we shall obviously have to return, albeit as briefly as possible. And, lastly, all this brings me to my third context of this or any study of the Battle of Hastings, for which I do not so much apologise as express my profound regret. I refer, of course, to that controversy, leading to or even based on prejudice, which still does vitiate the study of almost every aspect of the Norman Conquest of England, and not least, of course, any study of that most famous of victories on Saturday, 14 October 1066. Pots call kettles black and the disinterested pursuit of truth is lost in the fog of war and forgotten in the heat of battle. Freeman himself, for whom the defeat of clean-limbed Liberal Englishmen on that occasion was an agony to be explained away only by the foreign use of Dirty Tricks like horses and archery, would have stood in admiration at that latest study of the battle which comes as close as it is possible to get to making Hastings an English victory and attributes what little credit there is for the real victors to participants called the French and not the Normans.[12]

The contexts thus delineated, let us approach our actual subject with the observation that we probably have more information and potential knowledge about Hastings than any other medieval battle—appropriately, and fortunately, enough, since it is also one of the most decisive battles in Western history. This observation remains true, I hasten to add (lest I be thought out of date), even if R. H. C. Davis has successfully dismissed the *Song of the Battle of Hastings* from the canon of early or contemporary and acceptable texts for the study of the Norman Conquest[13]—as I am inclined to think that he has, though we shall in some respects miss it—and even if Eleanor Searle has dismissed the Conqueror's vow before the battle, to found an abbey on the site of his victory if God granted it, to the realm of monastic myth—as, again, I am much afraid she has.[14] For we are left with the long and detailed account of William of Poitiers, who had every qualification to write it save that of an eye-witness, including that of having first been a knight in the service of the duke before he became his chaplain. We have also the near-miraculous survival of the Bayeux Tapestry, more than one quarter of whose length is explicitly devoted to the battle and whose patron, it is now generally agreed, was Odo bishop of Bayeux, the Conqueror's half-brother and certainly present on the field.[15] To these two outstanding sources we add, of course, the briefer testimony of other con-temporary and near-contemporary accounts in William of Jumièges, the Anglo-Saxon Chronicle and Florence of Worcester; and to these we add in turn, though with increasing scholarly caution, the accounts and traditions recorded in such later sources as William of Malmesbury, Henry of Hunting-don and even Wace (who may give us the correct number of ships in the Norman fleet[16])—and here I would add also those local traditions which survive to be enshrined, for example, in the *Chronicle of Battle Abbey*, and indeed survive, alive and well, even today. Further, the mention of local tradition brings me to that other type of evidence, topographical, even archaeological, which we are so fortunate as to possess for the Battle of Hastings. We know the site of the engagement (Fig. 1): we know with an unusual degree of precision where it was fought, and thus, with the aid of the generous literary and artistic evidence, we have a good chance of knowing *how* it was fought also. The Normans like others in this period were adept at putting great buildings on difficult sites, as witness Mont St Michel, but such dramatic undertakings require a good reason, usually religious or military. If the Conqueror's vow before the battle to found his penitential abbey on the battlefield is now discredited, there remains no reason at all to disbelieve the tradition preserved at Battle of his eventual determination to build his church with its high altar on the spot where Harold fell, and only this can satisfactorily explain its awkward architectural position, on a hill requiring artificial levelling, and without water. The first monks from Marmoutier and the lush valleys of the Loire were appalled when they initially surveyed the site, and promptly chose a better one, north-west of the present abbey, which was still marked in the 1180's. The king when he heard of this was exceeding wrath, and sweeping aside all difficulties 'ordered them to lay the foundations of the church speedily and on the very spot where his enemy had fallen and the victory been won . . . And so at length, the foundations were laid of what was in those days thought an outstanding building, and they prudently erected the high altar as the king had commanded, on the very place where Harold's emblem, which they call a "standard" [*sic*], was seen to have fallen'.[17] (Which spot, incidentally, according to the chron-icle, had been carefully marked at the end of the battle.[18])

All save the very narrowest military historian of the old school would accept

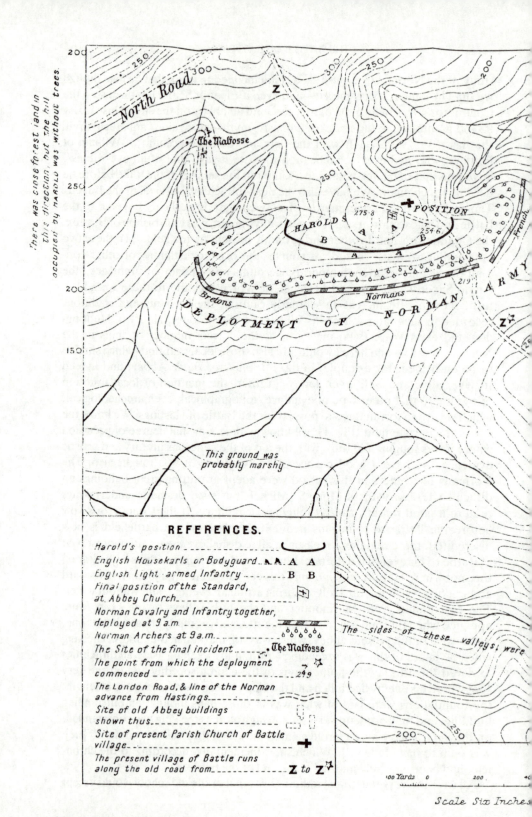

Map 1. *Map of the Battle of Hastings by General E. Renouard James, from F. H. Baring, Domes...*

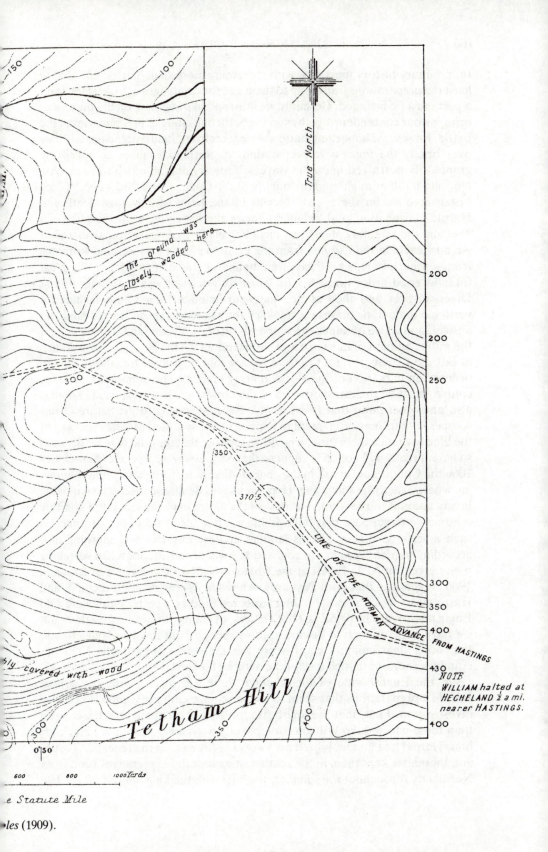

The ground was closely wooded here

True North

150

100

200

200

250

300

350

310.5

LINE OF THE NORMAN ADVANCE

FROM HASTINGS

300

350

400

430

400

NOTE
WILLIAM halted at
HECHELAND ½ a mi.
nearer HASTINGS.

...bly covered with wood

Tetham Hill

300

350

400

0 30'

600   800   1000 Yards

...e Statute Mile

...les (1909).

that military history must deal with something more than battles, and that at least the preparations leading up to them and the campaigns of which they form a part must be included. Certainly we must spend some time on the process of bringing our contenders together on the battlefield and the preliminaries of the battle, for several important matters arise therefrom. I must unfortunately pass over briefly the impressive preparations in Normandy, many of which are graphically portrayed upon the Bayeux Tapestry and all of which illuminate Norman military might and the quality of the Conqueror's leadership.[19] They began at once on the speedy receipt of the news of Edward's death and Harold's coronation, and included a series of great councils, the building of a fleet and the assembly of an army including many volunteers from overseas (if we now exclude the *Carmen* from the canon we must also exclude Normans from southern Italy, who always were unlikely), the maintenance of that great force in good order through more than six weeks of weary waiting, first at Dives-sur-Mer and then at St Valery-sur-Somme.[20] They also included a veritable diplomatic offensive, to which for whatever reason Harold made no answer, and which obtained the support both of the Papacy and, so to speak, of the public opinion of most of Latin Christendom for the Norman cause. When at last the Conqueror got the wind we are told he prayed for, the rapid and ordered embarkation of the Norman army must also be admired, and so, of course, must be the transportation of the horses across the Channel. There is also one other point that I would add. Because, owing to the nature of our sources, events may often seem to happen in the so-called Middle Ages out of the blue without explanation, it is silly to suppose that they did so in reality; and so here it really will not do to suppose that on the evening tide of 27 September 1066 the Conqueror set sail in the general direction of England without knowing where exactly he was going. Hypothesis is as dangerous as it is unavoidable in any account of the whole business of the Norman Conquest, but it is surely reasonable to suppose that duke William, after such careful preparations on such a scale as this, made his landfall at Pevensey the next morning also according to plan. And in this connection I would call attention to a searching paper given by A. J. Taylor at the Château-Gaillard Conference at Battle in 1966, suggesting that both Pevensey, which the Normans first occupied, and Hastings, to which they soon afterwards repaired as a better base, were Old English boroughs in 1066.[21] At both places, of course, they raised castles—but we have quite enough to discuss in this paper without involving ourselves in that other quasi-military controversy, *viz* the origin of castles in England, equally significant though it is for the nature of society.

On the English side of the Channel there are three points concerning Harold's preparations that seem to me to require emphasis, and also further investigation. First, that the logistical problems, if anything on a lesser scale than those which duke William triumphantly overcame, proved too much for him. Harold had first mobilized his forces in May against the renegade Tostig, and thereafter kept them in the south-east against the expected invasion from Normandy throughout the summer, the fleet with the king himself off the Isle of Wight and the fyrd 'everywhere along by the sea'. But, says the 'C' version of the Chronicle, 'in the end it was no use. When it was the Feast of the Nativity of St Mary (8 Sept.), the provisions of the people were gone, and nobody could keep them there any longer'.[22] In short, the army had to be dismissed and the ships sent back to London (with losses on the way). The potentially disastrous incident calls out for explanation from Anglo-Saxon military historians, and must throw light on the Old English military organization and its efficacy in the situation it had to face in 1066. My second point to call for emphasis and investigation is the striking ease with which Old English leaders, not only the king, are able to raise fleets in this period, whether it be, for example, Tostig in 1066 or the Godwinsons in 1052. On the broadest interpretation, I should like to think this reflects the essentially Anglo-Scandinavian nature of our Old English society, but, if so, it throws into sharper contrast the situation in Normandy, the land after all of the Norsemen, where a fleet—or at least a suitable fleet—had to be constructed for the invasion. Perhaps in feudal society, with its emphasis upon horses, knight service and chivalry, navies were taken less seriously. Third and last, it has always seemed to me amazing that Harold should have had no foreknowledge or expectation of Harold Hardrada's impending invasion from Norway; yet all military preparations of his own that we hear of are in the south-east against Normandy, and the 'C' version says specifically that 'Harold, king of Norway, came *by surprise* north into the Tyne', the English king being informed at the very moment of disembarking at London from his fleet returned from the Isle of Wight.[23]

Harold's dramatic reaction to the news of the Norwegian landing, compounded as it soon was by the defeat of the northern earls Edwin and Morcar at Gate Fulford on 20 September, is well known—his assembly of an army, his great and impressively rapid march north, his muster of his forces at Tadcaster on 24 September. Then on the morning of the 25th he 'went right on through York' to take Harold Hardrada, now with his ally Tostig, 'by surprise' at Stamford Bridge and win a great victory.[24] One would dearly like to know how these things were done precisely, in terms of the raising of troops, and of what kind, and of their movement; but again there are three points for us of particular relevance to the subsequent engagement at Hastings. The first is Richard Glover's recent resurrection of the credibility of Snorri Sturluson, whose *Heimskringla* contains the only detailed account of the battle, as evidence for the Old English use of cavalry at it.[25] Glover, of course, does not seek to argue for the use of cavalry by Harold at Hastings, which in the light of the abundant evidence to the contrary would be impossible; but in a somewhat unnecessary defence of Old English armies against their detractors who are nowadays few if any, he seeks to show that they could use cavalry when they wished but did not so wish at Hastings because it was for them a defensive action. The latter proposition is merely a misguided hypothesis, and the former, dependent exclusively upon Snorri Sturluson's thirteenth-century account of Stamford Bridge of demonstrable unreliability, is simply unacceptable. There is more than sufficient contemporary evidence to show that Old

English armies habitually fought on foot, and so did their time-honoured opponents, the Danes and the Norse.[26] In this at least Freeman was right, and Stamford Bridge was the last major battle fought on English soil in the ancient manner, hand to hand and axe to axe.[27] Our next point must be that of course the engagements of Gate Fulford and Stamford Bridge, fought within a week of each other (20 and 25 September) must have seriously affected Harold's strength at Hastings three weeks later. And the third point is that Harold's brilliant success at Stamford Bridge and the manner of it—the rapidity of movement, the thundering march north (190 miles from London to York) and the taking of the Norwegians by surprise—surely determined his conduct of his next and immediate campaign against the Normans. Of that I wrote in my book of 'reckless and impulsive haste'[28] and I think I still stand by it, though the qualification should be added that the ravaging by duke William of Sussex, the very patrimony of the house of Godwin,[29] would, according to contemporary notions of honour, demand immediate retaliation to demonstrate and defend one's lordship. Nevertheless, in terms of military appreciation, we are also surely right to see in Harold's movements before Hastings the intention to repeat the strategy and tactics which had given him such success at Stamford Bridge. Within two weeks or thirteen days at most from his receipt of the news of William's landing (on or soon after 1 October and traditionally at York) he had repeated his great march, this time in the reverse direction from York to London, delayed in the latter city for what was clearly the minimum time to make his final preparations and raise more troops, and made another forced march over the fifty-seven miles from London to Battle to engage his enemy.[30] William of Jumièges and William of Poitiers followed by Orderic Vitalis all state that Harold's intention was to take William by surprise, the last two adding even the possibility of a night attack.[31]

In the event it was not to be, but before we proceed to duke William's counter measures it may surely be urged that all this precipitate speed was as unwise as it was unsuccessful. For time, like the homeland, was on Harold's side and ran against the Norman duke, at the end of a long and hazardous line of communications across the Channel (Poitiers followed by Orderic—and the *Carmen* for what it is worth—say that Harold sent a fleet to cut off the Normans[32]), in an alien country, and not even knowing at first who his opponent would be, Harold or Harold Hardrada. And certainly Harold's haste brought material disadvantages: fatigue must have been amongst them, though I know of no contemporary source to say so, and lack of numbers on the scale he might have had is another. For that, the 'E' version of the Chronicle explicitly states that the king fought with William 'before all the army had come',[33] and Florence of Worcester is both more emphatic and more detailed. Commenting on Harold's haste, he writes 'and although he knew very well that some of the bravest men in all England had fallen in the two battles [*i.e.* Fulford and Stamford Bridge], and that half his army was not yet assembled, yet he did not hesitate to meet his enemy in Sussex as quickly as he could, and nine miles from Hastings he gave them battle, before a third of his army was drawn up'.[34]

On the second of those two seemingly cumulative statements by Florence we shall have occasion to comment again in a moment, but meanwhile there seems a case here for bad generalship for anyone who wants to take it up.

Although according to the Oman myth of medieval warfare reconnaissance was seldom if ever practiced by commanders in the feudal period, it is clear that duke William at Hastings, unlike Harold Hardrada at Stamford Bridge, learnt of Harold's approach in ample time to prepare his counter measures and put them into practice. Further, while the night before the battle is not explicitly mentioned by William of Poitiers, it is quite clear from his account supplemented by William of Jumièges that the news was received the day before the battle, *i.e.* on Friday, 13 October. In Poitiers the mounted patrols return to report Harold's rapid advance while the greater part of the Norman army is out foraging,[35] while in Jumièges the duke orders his army to stand to arms from dusk to dawn in case of a night attack, and at day-break moves off in the known direction of the enemy.[36] From Hedgland on Telham Hill, according to the local tradition in the Battle Chronicle,[37] the scouts of the advancing Norman army first saw the English on the Battle ridge two miles away, and the battle itself began at 'the third hour' or 9 a.m. according to Poitiers, Jumièges and Florence of Worcester.[38] From Hastings to Battle there are some seven miles to be covered by foot as well as horse. The decisive speed of all this is impressive enough as it is: clearly we cannot envisage the report of the English approach being received that morning as well, as has sometimes been maintained,[39] and to the accumulated evidence and argument we may cautiously add the later traditions (most memorably written up, of course, by Wace) of how the two armies passed the night before the battle, the Normans in prayer and the English in whooping it up.[40] No contemporary source in fact gives us any details of how Harold spent the night before his last engagement, but though William of Jumièges has him marching through the night to appear on the battlefield in the morning,[41] he must surely have rested his troops, presumably not far from the modern Battle and its ridge, from which he evidently first saw the Norman host advancing[42] and upon which he then arrayed his troops. If this reconstruction of events be accepted, two points follow. The first is that far from succumbing to a surprise attack, William (by good reconnaissance) turned the tables upon Harold, seized the initiative, and took his opponent by surprise; and the second is that Harold cannot possibly have selected the place of battle well in advance, as Freeman insisted and others have since suggested.[43] The one version of the Anglo-Saxon Chronicle which is contemporary explicitly states that 'William came against him [Harold] by surprise before his army was drawn up in battle array',[44] and Florence, as we have seen, has Harold engage the Normans 'before a third of his army was drawn up'.[45] If, as thus seems certain, Harold lost the initiative and was constrained to fight at that place and time by William's advance from Hastings, then all the more credit to him for selecting on the spur of the moment a site so admirably suited to the defensive tactics which alone he could offer—but yet it was not perfect. There was no way of withdrawal save the narrow isthmus which is now Battle High Street and along which he had come, while the space on the ridge was so confined that according to Florence many deserted before the action began.[46] Finally, in view of what has been written one should at least suggest that, far from 'supine loitering' on the Sussex coast (the phrase is Richard Glover's[47]) the Norman duke, since his landing at Pevensey, had achieved one of the most difficult strategic intentions, of drawing his opponent to give him the decisive action which he wanted, and that as soon as possible and without leaving his beach-head and his fleet. In this the ravaging of the countryside about Pevensey and Hastings, which William of Poitiers cites as one reason for Harold's haste,[48] may well have been a deliberate and calculated provocation—as may indeed have been the landing in Sussex in the first place.[49]

If the *Carmen de Hastingae Proelio* is to be dismissed, then we are confined for detailed contemporary information about the Battle of Hastings itself to William of Poitiers and the Bayeux Tapestry. Generous as both sources are, hypothesis is inevitable, but it must be informed by a knowledge of the warfare of the period. Later sources must be used with discretion since tradition and even myth soon gather about so famous and even elegiac an occasion. Something of a modern consensus puts the numbers of each army at some 7000 men.[50] On the English side one assumes this number to have been made up of the quasi-professional housecarls[51] of the king and of the households of his brothers and other great lords, well-armed thegns (if the distinction be allowed) who had ridden with Harold from London or even from York or come in since, together with less well-armed levies from neighbouring shires. The élite of housecarls is not mentioned specifically, *eo nomine*, in any contemporary source, though the two-handed battle-axe, their weapon *par excellence*, is much in evidence in the account (it is *hache norresche* in Wace and *haches danesches* in Benoit de Sainte-More[52]). William of Malmesbury seems to vouch for their predominance when he states[53] that Harold had with him mostly stipendiary troops *(stipendiarios et mercenarios milites)* and comparatively few from the provinces *(ex provincialibus)* i.e. the local levies, *vulgariter dicitur* 'fyrd', and it seems to me that in this connection more attention than is usual should be paid to William of Poitiers' unique remark that abundant help *(copiosa auxilia)* had been sent to the English from their kith and kin in Denmark.[54] The king planted his standard and took up his own position thereby on the highest point of the ridge, where the high altar of the abbey church was later to be placed.[55] According to William of Malmesbury his two brothers were with him there,[56] but since Gyrth and Leofwine were killed early in the battle[57] and long before Harold they were presumably in a different part of the line, and presumably with their own contingents—which in turn may be further reason to suppose that the housecarls were disposed along the entire English front and not massed in the centre as some commentators have argued.[58] The English position comprised the whole crest of the ridge facing south towards the Normans and extending for some 6-800 yards, *i.e.* 400 yards to the west or right of the king and standard, where the ground falls steeply away, and 2-400 yards to the east or left, where it ended roughly opposite the present 'Chequers' inn or somewhere between the junction of the Hastings and Sedlescombe roads and the school on the latter.[59] (Fig. 1) The entire English host, from the king downward, were dismounted to fight on foot. Of this there is not a shadow of doubt and all sources, contemporary and later, are agreed[60]—though one may and should add that this fact only makes it extremely improbable that Old English armies ever fought in any other manner. To a complete absence of cavalry, it seems there has to be added a more surprising deficiency of archers[61]—because, one can only surmise, Harold's rapidity of movement eliminated most of those who had to march on foot. We do not know how many ranks composed the line, but we do know that they stood in very close order, so close, wrote William of Poitiers, that the dead could scarcely fall and the wounded could not remove themselves from the action.[62] This, then, was the famous formation of the 'shield-wall', the 'war-hedge' of the Song of Maldon,[63] though an element of poetic licence must be allowed it, for clearly the shields must part for the weapons to be wielded and the great two-handed battle-axe especially required space on either side (it also, as Wace pointed out, left the warrior raising it dangerously off his guard.[64] Doubtless we must assume experience, training and team-work, all of which are as necessary for the effective use of ancient hand weapons as they are for modern military technology).

Against this seemingly impregnable position, at the foot of the steep slope of the ridge, the Norman duke deployed his forces in three lines, archers and, less certainly, crossbow-men in front,[65] heavy infantry, some at least with mail coats, next, and the heavy cavalry of knights and esquires not, as is sometimes said, in reserve but in the rear, to deliver the hoped for *coup de grâce* of their irresistable shock charge.[66] Such are the dispositions listed by William of Poitiers.[67] In the absence of the *Carmen* we have to be less confident than heretofore on the three lateral divisions (*i.e.* each in the above formation) of Bretons on the left (west), Normans in the centre and French on the right (east), though Poitiers later refers to the Bretons being on the left, and has duke William in the centre of the knights—and thus we may assume with Norman contingents—where he could direct operations by voice and gesture.[68] The presence of large numbers of well-armed infantry, who were given an important rôle to play, in the Norman army should remind us that Hastings was a battle of cavalry against infantry only in the sense that the English had no cavalry, not that the Normans had no infantry. It should also dispel another lingering Oman myth that infantry was despised by the commanders of the feudal period.[69] Nevertheless, the tactics of their enemy at Hastings were a source of some wonder to the hard-riding Norman and Frankish cavalry and their writers. 'It was,' wrote William of Poitiers, 'a strange kind of battle, one side attacking with all mobility, the other withstanding, as though rooted to the soil.'[70]

At Hastings, however, the battle having opened with a terrible sound of trumpets on both sides, the Norman infantry went in first until, having achieved no marked success, they were followed by the knights, spurring their horses up the hill. And thus, writes William of Poitiers, the last became first. Again, there was no success, which failure Poitiers carefully explains by the superiority of the English position on the hill-top, their dense ranks and close order, and the effectiveness of their arms (presumably their axes), which could easily cleave both shield and armour (presumably hauberk).[71] At this point in his narrative Poitiers proceeds to the first and real retreat of the Norman forces and the first climax of the battle.

But at this point we must pause to consider the true use and tactics of the Norman heavy cavalry of knights at Hastings—or indeed of Frankish chivalry anywhere else in this age—in the light of Richard Glover's tendentious remarks.[72] Seeking, as we have noted, to upgrade the Old English military capacity, and thus seeking to show that they could use cavalry when they wished, he turns, in the most unforgivable section of his monograph, to denigrate the Norman, so to achieve, by levelling up on the one hand and levelling down on the other, a kind of double equality. In any case, runs his argument, there was nothing to the Norman use of cavalry in this period, anyone could do it; and he goes on to speak of 'infantile' Norman cavalry tactics, and of Norman knights at Hastings as mere 'mounted javelineers' while citing yet others without horses as 'happily mixing it in on foot'. All this is said to be based on the evidence of the Bayeux Tapestry, but, to dismiss the last allegation first, I can find only one or two [sic] candidates for dismounted knights on the Tapestry[73] and they and any others there may have been in a similar predicament are likely to have had their horses killed under them (and to have been thus anything but happy)—as duke William had three horses killed under him that day according to William of Poitiers.[74] As for the infantile cavalry tactics, one must read above all D. J. A. Ross on these matters.[75] While we have the unimpeachable testimony of Ordericus Vitalis for the throwing of spears from the saddle as a knightly skill to be practiced,[76] it was obviously not very effective in battle and it is accordingly very difficult indeed to find certain instances of it in the Bayeux Tapestry's depiction of Hastings.[77] Those many knights on the Tapestry apparently brandishing their lances above their heads, and whom Mr Glover assumes to be about to throw them, are in fact about to strike over-arm in the manner most likely against infantry,[78] the two methods of using the lance on horseback inherited from antiquity being the overarm and underarm[79] thrust (Pl. 1, 2). Already at this date, however, what is to be the classic medieval usage of the couched lance was being developed, whereby with a heavier lance, no longer a spear, locked under the rider's arm, the whole momentum of horse and armoured horseman is concentrated in the point, to make possible the shock tactic of the charge. This is what Anna Comnena had in mind when she wrote of the Frankish chivalry of the time of the First Crusade that the charging knight would pierce the walls of Babylon.[80] Some of the Norman knights depicted on th Tapestry are quite clearly couching their lances,[81] (Pl. 3) and the fact is all the more remarkable in that the new tactic was developed on the Continent for the unhorsing of horsed opponents of whom there were none at Hastings. All the relevant evidence of the Tapestry,

the Norman side appears top right (B.T. Pl. 62)

Plate 2   Norman knights at Hastings: the lance used overarm (B.T. Pl. 63)

properly understood, points in the same direction, *viz* of the Norman chivalry in the van of the new developments: the hevier lances in some cases clearly shown,[81] the gonfanons on lances which are obviously not meant therefore to be thrown away,[83] the built-up saddle-bows to hold the rider in his seat at the shock of contact, and the very long stirrup leathers to afford the same security.[84] In the literary sources, including William of Poitiers, it is true that the *arme blanche* of the sword is more prominent than the lance, but this is presumably because the latter was liable to break at the first contact (thereafter to be renewed), and it is significant that in Poitiers' account of Hastings William the Conqueror is found at the end of the battle with the stump of a broken lance in his hand.[85]

To revert to the progress of the battle as recounted in the narrative of William of Poitiers,[86] after the failure of the initial hard-pressed assaults to make any significant impression on the English line, the Bretons and other auxiliaries on the Norman left, both horse and foot, began to fall back. The movement spread as such movements will, fanned by an ugly rumour that the duke was dead—though this alone, Poitiers assures us, could have caused the Normans themselves to yield. Some of the English forces, with or without orders,[87] began to advance down the hill in pursuit—and we reach one of the two best known incidents in the battle, dramatically depicted on the Tapestry,[88] as the duke himself stops the rot. Galloping in front of his retreating troops, 'shouting and brandishing his lance', he lifted his helmet to reveal himself and harangued the faint-hearted. 'Look at me. I am alive, and, by God's help, I shall win. What madness puts you to flight . . .' etc. On the Tapestry count Eustace of Boulogne on the right points to the living, gesticulating duke (who in this scene bears a mace) while on the left bishop Odo, also with a mace *'comfortat pueros', i.e.* turns back the young men, the *tirones*, the esquires, who are about to ride off the field.[89] The duke himself, sword in hand, then led a counter attack and the Normans, enflamed, surrounded and cut down those who had pursued them down the hill.

After this crisis the general assault upon the English position was renewed by the knights especially, any breaches made being followed up by the men of Maine and Aquitaine, the French and the Bretons, 'but above all by the Normans with a courage beyond compare'. Thus William of Poitiers,[90] who goes on to praise the exploits in particular of the young lordling or *tiro*, Robert, the son of Roger de Beaumont, who in this his first battle particularly distinguished himself at the head of his contingent over on the right wing. But, Poitiers continues, 'the Normans and their allies, realizing that they could not overcome an enemy so numerous and standing so firm without great loss to themselves, retreated, deliberately feigning flight'—*terga dederunt, fugam ex industria simulantes*—remembering what success had attended their counter-attack upon the pursuing English after the recent real retreat.[91] And so we reach the second of the best-known incidents of the battle, the feigned flight, according to William of Poitiers twice repeated, and very well attested by all the principal sources for Hastings, contemporary and later, save only, perhaps,

Plate 3 Norman knights at Hastings: the lance couched and the overarm thrust (B.T. Pl. 65)

Plate 4 Pl. 67 from the Bayeux Tapestry, *with the caption 'Hic ceciderunt simul Angli et Franci in prelio'*

the Bayeux Tapestry, whose medium scarcely lent itself to its depiction.[92] Further, the attested manoeuvre was triumphantly successful, so much so that William of Malmesbury, the historian, in his *Gesta Regum* (*c.*1125) presented it in his account as the turning point of the battle and the chief reason for the eventual Norman victory.[93] Each time numbers of English were tempted to break ranks and drawn down from the ridge in pursuit, to be cut down as the knights wheeled their horses (*regiratis equis*[94]). Yet most modern commentators and *soi-disant* military historians have doubted the feigned flight to the point of its rejection.[95] For this they have no reason whatever save the persistent and persisting myth of Oman and others to which I have so often, and necessarily, referred. The feigned flight, so the argument runs, cannot have happened because it could not have happened; and it could not have happened because it would have required to a high degree discipline and training which feudal armies, and most especially the exhibitionist knights who formed them, notoriously did not possess. The truth is, of course, that our Frankish knights and Norman knights were as professional as the age could make them, born and bred to war and trained from early youth, in the household which is the contingent of a lord, in the art and science of horsemanship and arms. Not only do we have entirely acceptable, one might almost say overwhelming, evidence for the tactic of the feigned flight employed at Hastings, but we also have further evidence of its practice on other occasions by other knights of this generation—by the Normans at St Aubin-le-Cauf near Arques in 1052-3 and near Messina in 1060, and by Robert le Frison of Flanders at Cassel in 1071.[96] If this is not enough, then we can find much earlier references to the manoeuvre, which was thus evidently a well-known *ruse de guerre*, in *e.g.* Nithard under the year 842, over two-hundred years before Hastings, and in Dudo of St Quentin writing in the first decades of the eleventh century.[97] Clearly of all the arguments which surround the Norman Conquest and Hastings, this one at least must stop. If some military writers, blind in the arrogance of their ignorance, still demur, the key to understanding the feigned flight in practice is the *conroi*,[98] the comparatively small unit of the feudal host, presumably to be identified with the contingents and military households of individual lords, each marked out by the *gonfanon* of its leader. Such units, trained together over long, arduous years, and bound by the companionship of expertise, had ample discipline and the capacity not only to work and fight together but also to combine with other similar units. One need not, if one does not wish to, envisage the entire Norman cavalry at Hastings, or even very large sections of it, executing the feigned flight *en masse*—though personally I would not put it past them.

Still those many of the English who were left stood firm, 'still a formidable force and extremely difficult to surround'. Thus William of Poitiers,[99] and the last words are significant as presumably indicating that no part of the ridge had yet been taken. There follows, as the English at last seem to begin to weaken, what in the event becomes the final Norman all-out assault with horse and foot. Poitiers' prose rises to the occasion as in his poetic onomatopoeia one can almost hear the shock and thud of battle—*sagittant, feriunt, perfodiunt Normanni*. *Sagittant* is perhaps important here as a possible source for the later tradition of arrows shot on a high trajectory at this stage in the battle. It is not otherwise mentioned by Poitiers and appears first in Henry of Huntingdon to be worked up by Wace, which means its credentials are not very good.[100] And so we approach the final scenes of the battle, admittedly blurred, as the fog of war descends and the autumnal daylight wanes, as king Harold is slain and the English at length give way. It seems appropriate to quote William of Poitiers,[101] in the absence of the *Carmen* the nearest of our sources to the events he describes. Again he achieves a poetic and this time elegiac note in a paragraph admirably beginning *Jam inclinato die* . . . 'Now as the day declined the English army realized beyond doubt that they could no longer stand against the Normans. They knew that they were reduced by heavy losses; that the king himself, with his brothers and many magnates of the realm had fallen; that those who still stood were almost drained of strength; that they could expect no help. They saw the Normans not much diminished by casualties, threatening them more keenly than in the beginning, as if they had found new strength in the fight; they saw that fury of the duke who spared no one who resisted him; they saw that courage which could only find rest in victory. They therefore turned to flight . . . some on looted horses, many on foot; some along the roads, many across country.'

For the victorious Normans only the matter of the Malfosse remained, but for us there are two matters and the first is the death of the king. It is notable that no details at all of the manner of Harold's death are given by William of Poitiers, and the same is true of William of Jumièges who makes, indeed, a rare mistake in having him slain by lethal wounds at the beginning instead of the end of the battle—in which he was to be followed by Ordericus Vitalis.[102] It is perhaps strange, too, that there is no tradition of the matter in the Chronicle of Battle Abbey (where Harold is slain by a chance blow[103]), though it was certainly not the business of the monks there to contribute to any cult of the dead king and usurper. The Bayeux Tapestry, however, as our second detailed and contemporary source after William of Poitiers, has its famous scene, labelled '*Hic Harold rex interfectus est*', where *Harold* is written above the figure with an arrow in the eye and *interfectus est* above the falling figure being cut down by a mounted knight whose sword is against its thigh.[104] In recent years it has been fashionable to say that contemporary artistic convention prevents both figures from being Harold, that only the second one is (*interfectus est*) but the first is not, and that therefore the tradition of Harold's being slain by an arrow in the eye is false, derived probably from a misunderstanding of the Tapestry. In 1978, however, Dr N. P. Brooks in a paper given at the first Battle Conference and entitled 'The authority and interpretation of the Bayeux Tapestry'[105] re-examined the whole question and showed beyond reasonable doubt that the Tapestry *did* intend both figures to represent the stricken king. The tradition therefore—perhaps one of the best known facts in all English history after the date 1066 itself—is thus restored to something more than respectability as derived from no less an authority than the Tapestry, before taking off via Baudri de Bourgueil, William of Malmesbury, Henry of Huntingdon and, inevitably, Wace.[106] Perhaps matters should be left there, but the lack of detail in William of Poitiers especially remains curious and may prompt two further comments. The first is that William of Malmesbury's account, though close to the Tapestry, may yet provide some explanation. There, Harold is first lethally struck by a chance arrow which pierced his brain and then slashed on the thigh by the sword of a knight as he lay prostrate—for which cowardly and shameful act the unfortunate knight was subsequently stripped of his knighthood by William *(militia pulsus est)*. Here then are no feats of arms to be celebrated by the victorious duke's biographer. But what cannot be accepted is the version of the death of Harold given by the *Carmen* and its interpretation by its recent editors, wherein there is no arrow but the king is slain by four knights led by duke William himself.[107] Had William, duke of the Normans, with only three companions, attacked the heavily defended headquarters of the English army—which is what the alleged exploit amounts to—to kill the king and thereby take the crown, far from being hushed up as Morton and Munz will have it, the feat of arms would have been bruited abroad in every court and *chanson* in Latin Christendom and beyond. Meanwhile, as it seems to me, the whole improbable incident recorded by the *Carmen* goes far to condemn that source itself.

And so we come finally to the Malfosse incident, by which of course I mean what we all think we mean, the well-known incident at the end of the battle— more precisely, *after* the end of the battle—in which the Norman knights, hotly pursuing the fleeing English, ride pell-mell in the gathering gloom and broken countryside into a deep fosse or ravine with heavy and tragic losses. The dilemma is, however, that for this incident there is very little if any contemporary evidence; most modern commentators, with no excuse at all after Marx's edition of 1914, having confused Ordericus Vitalis' interpolations in William of Jumièges with William of Jumièges himself.[108] The story (and perhaps we must use such a word) clearly has its origins in William of Poitiers, yet in his version there is no Malfosse in the generally accepted sense of the Normans riding into it.[109] Some of the fleeing English are encouraged to make a stand by 'a broken rampart or entrenchment [the word used is *vallum* with its suggestion of a man-made obstacle] and a labyrinth of ditches'. Duke William comes galloping up, armed only with the stump of a broken lance, intent on attacking even though he assumes they are English reinforcements. He meets, already there, count Eustace of Boulogne with a contingent of fifty knights, all of whom are withdrawing. Eustace advises the duke also to withdraw, and even as he speaks is severely wounded between the shoulder blades by a missile and has to be helped away. The duke, nothing daunted, equating caution with defeat, presses on and tramples his enemies underfoot *[sic]*. We are given no military details of the brief action save the statement that a number of Normans lost their lives because their prowess was inhibited by the difficult country. For anything else and more familiar we have to wait until Ordericus Vitalis'

Interpolations in William of Jumièges, dating from before 1109 to after 1113.[110] There[111] we are told that 'when the Normans saw the English fleeing from the battlefield they pursued them relentlessly through the whole night until Sunday [evidently one may detect elements of exaggeration in this] but to their own harm. For by chance long grasses concealed an ancient rampart *(antiquuum aggerem)* and as the Normans came galloping up they fell, one on top of the other, in a struggling mass of horses and arms'. There then follow some sentences on casualties (15000) and God's judgement on both sides, which must surely relate to the whole battle. Here, then, is a recognizable Malfosse incident, but we do not get, so to speak, the full version until Ordericus Vitalis' *Ecclesiastical History* where, in his Book III finished in the early 1120's,[112] in his account of the battle which in general follows William of Poitiers very closely, he awkwardly combines William's passage on the post-battle affair with his own seemingly independent version from the Interpolations.[113] Both are given more or less verbatim but cut into each other, to produce a combined version which seems to me to have given Orderic much trouble. The result of all this is that pursuing Normans ride into an *antiquuum aggerem*, as in the Interpolations. The English, encouraged by this, and also by the *praeruptum uallum* and labyrinth of ditches as in William of Poitiers, make a stand and inflict severe losses. Next we have the passage from the Interpolations on casualties on both sides, wherein Engenulf castellan of Laigle is named amongst the Normans[114] and which is now much more ambiguous than before as to whether it relates to the Malfosse incident or the whole battle. Finally we have the advent of duke William, his meeting with count Eustace and his dealing with the situation, as in William of Poitiers.

After Orderic there is nothing, so far as I can see, until the Battle Abbey Chronicle of the late twelfth century, where, at the end of the battle, 'a final disaster was revealed to the eyes of all'.[115] A little ambiguously we are told that 'just where the fighting was going on, and stretching for a considerable distance, an immense ditch yawned'. Hidden by brambles and thistles it engulfed great numbers, especially of pursuing Normans—'For, when, all unknowing, they came galloping on, their terrific impetus carried them headlong down into it, and they died tragically, pounded to pieces'. The author goes on to say that the place of the disaster (which now becomes a 'deep pit') is known in his day as the *Malfosse*. He does not, unfortunately, identify it on the ground—and nor am I going to try to do so, partly because, as I think you will have anticipated, in my essentially literary approach there is more, and worse, to come. Meanwhile it is rather alarmingly clear that the literary credentials of the well-known *Malfosse* incident *after* the Battle of Hastings—which henceforward we had best call Version A—are not very good. This Version A may well begin in William of Poitiers, *i.e.* one of our two best and contemporary sources; but he says nothing of its best-known feature of knights riding into a ditch—he says nothing, in short, of the *Malfosse*. For that we have to wait until Ordericus Vitalis (who may have had his own source, which may have been the family of Engenulf castellan of Laigle[116]), and after him there is nothing until the local

Battle Chronicle of *c*.1180—where and when, incidentally, we meet for the first time the word, the name, *Malfosse*. The situation is equally alarming in negative terms; that is to say, these are the only sources to relate Version A, which does not appear in any others. The negative side of the dilemma is best emphasized by stressing that Version A does not even appear in Wace who, though not in my view a source altogether to be despised for the Norman Conquest, is certainly not a man ever knowingly to omit a good story.

Let us therefore turn to what I will call Version B, wherein a Malfosse incident occurs not at the end but in the middle of the Battle of Hastings. For this, too, it appears we can begin with one of our two best, contemporary sources, this time the Bayeux Tapestry, and I refer back again to that enigmatic scene—artistically magnificent—labelled *Hic ceciderunt simul Angli et Franci in prelio*[117] (Pl. 4). It occurs in the middle of the battle, and, more specifically, immediately between the scene representing the death of Harold's brothers Gyrth and Leofwine and that representing the real retreat of the Norman forces, *i.e.* the scene of bishop Odo's turning back the retreating young men or esquires and of duke William's bearing of his head to show he is alive. I have previously suggested that this possibly may be the Tapestry's representation of the feigned flight[118] (which, in that case, would precede and not follow the real retreat), but what matters to us now is what is actually shown, namely a group of Stenton's 'half-armed peasants'[119] making a stand upon a hillock, at the foot of which, and in a marsh or bog,[120] Norman cavalry are in grave difficulties. If one has studied all the sources for the Battle of Hastings one cannot but be reminded by this scene of the Malfosse incident and, more important, William of Malmesbury in his *Gesta Regum* of *c*.1125 thus interpreted it. Evidently knowing his Tapestry, and following it closely here as he does for the death of Harold,[121] having told us how, unable to force an issue any other way, duke William ordered the feigned flight with devastating effect, he goes on to say that the English nevertheless took their toll by frequently making stands. Thus for example, 'getting possession of a hillock *(occupato tumulo)*, they drove down the Normans . . . into the valley beneath where, easily hurling their javelins and rolling down stones upon them, they destroyed them to a man'. Then he adds, 'Besides, by a short passage, with which they were acquainted, avoiding a deep ditch *(fossatum quoddam praeruptum*, wherein we may have an echo of William of Poitiers, whose account of the battle William of Malmesbury also uses), they trod under foot such a multitude of their enemies in that place that they made the hollow level with the plain by the heaps of carcasses'. Here, then, is certainly a Malfosse incident in the middle of the battle. Henry of Huntingdon, writing at much the same date (*c*.1125-30?), also has a Malfosse incident in the midst of the battle, and as part of the feigned flight,[122] in which the Normans ride into a great but concealed ditch *(quandam foveam magnam dolose protectam)*. So also does the ebullient Wace, though in his account the disaster occurs in the course of the real retreat of the Norman forces (which, as in the *Carmen* and perhaps the Bayeux Tapestry, follows the feigned flight) and the fosse *(sic)* is that which Harold had caused to be dug before the battle began.[123] Wace's rival, Benoit de Ste-Maure[124] has no Malfosse incident of any kind, either during or after the battle, and nor do the *Carmen*, Gaimar,[125] the *Brevis Relatio*[126] or Baudri de Bourgueil whose early date would have made his testimony especially valuable.[127]

And there, I am afraid, we must leave it. There are thus two versions of the Malfosse incident, A and B, both, it must be confessed, making a somewhat shaky start in one or other of the two most detailed and certainly early accounts of the Battle of Hastings, and I can find no way of choosing between them.[128] Two maddening points remain. One is (and the feeling of frustration will be familiar to many of you) that, as it turns out, J. H. Round said all that I have said, and more, in his diatribes against E. A. Freeman some eighty years ago.[129] The other is that the Malfosse incident, whether or not it took place, whenever it took place, and wherever it took place, quite simply does not matter—that is to say, that as a disaster which overtook the Normans it demonstrably did not effect the issue of the battle. And that, I think, gives me my cue to end this paper, and to do so by returning to the safe ground of what is known and certain. It may conceivably surprise our very welcome French participants at this Conference that almost everything about the Norman Conquest is controversial amongst English-speaking historians, but one thing I do insist upon, which is that the Normans won at Hastings. They won, this paper would suggest, amongst other means by superior military techniques and by superior generalship—and they also gained, I would further suggest, one of the most decisive victories of Western history. But because, though I thus perceive the truth and cling to it, I am at least as unbiassed as William of Poitiers, let me finally end by quoting that splendid epitaph of William of Malmesbury upon the English—'they were few in number but brave in the extreme'.[130]

BATTLES IN ENGLAND AND NORMANDY, 1066-1154

Jim Bradbury

There has been a tendency in recent years to neglect the study of battles, as a somewhat outmoded approach to history. An example would be the excellent volume on the Hundred Years War, edited by Fowler, in which virtually every possible aspect of the war is considered, with the exception of the battles.[1] It is true that such an approach has in the past been used at the expense of studies of campaigns, or political and social sides of warfare. Views on battle have certainly been modified by a study within the broader context, but this should encourage cross-fertilisation between the various fields, and not neglect of any one. A study of battles can indeed stimulate ideas in other areas of history. For example, if dismounted knights are significant in twelfth-century battles, can one find a social explanation of that significance? Perhaps Anglo-Norman historians are less narrow than some of their colleagues, and the example given is of course one provided by Dr Chibnall.[2]

The intention of this paper is to ask some questions of the battles in the century following the Norman Conquest, without necessarily anticipating clear answers. A question raised by those with even a passing interest in the period is, why there were so few battles. Professor Hollister, in his important work on 'The Military Organization of Norman England', discusses five battles which he suggests were 'the only ones of any significance in the Anglo-Norman age'.[3] Some would see this as a sign that battles were not especially important in the warfare of this period: sieges were common, and therefore more significant. But significance surely does not rest only in quantity. In any case, one of the most obvious features of Norman warfare is the close, almost inseparable, relationship between sieges and battles. Two responses to the question come to mind. Professor Hollister was concerned with those battles which had been described in sufficient detail to allow some discussion of tactics. There were certainly more battles, many of which were at least as large in scale as Bourgthéroulde, but are given little space by the chroniclers. There were at least fifteen lesser battles in the period.[4] A second consideration is the frequency with which battles were avoided. Sometimes this was achieved by a form of truce or treaty, sometimes simply by backing down from a challenge.

[1] K. Fowler, *The Hundred Years War*, London 1971.
[2] Dr Chibnall presented a paper on this subject to the conference at St Mary's, Strawberry Hill, on 'Knighthood and Chivalry'. The paper will not be published, but the material will appear in Dr Chibnall's forthcoming book on *Orderic Vitalis and His World*. Professor Hollister's work, including his paper in these proceedings, is another honourable exception.
[3] C. W. Hollister, *The Military Organization of Norman England*, Oxford 1965, 128.
[4] Other battles include: Fagaduna 1075, Gerberoi 1079, Chaumont 1098 where seven hundred horses were killed, Exmes 1102, Alençon 1118, Vaudreuil 1136 where five hundred knights fought on one side, Caen 1138, Clitheroe 1138, Barnstaple 1139, Winchester 1141, Wilton 1143, Montfort 1154, and in Wales in 1088, 1095, 1097 with two battles in 1136.

Negotiation before battle was a common occurrence, and should not be treated as an empty formality, since there were occasions when it succeeded in preventing a fight. Presumably this occurred when neither side was confident of ultimate victory. An obvious reason for avoiding battle was the knowledge that one's opponents had greater numerical strength. The more cautious commander often took note, and abandoned the field, as for example, Robert of Gloucester at Faringdon, or Louis of France at Cosne, when he was 'brought to his senses by sound counsel', and moved off. Matilda intended to leave Winchester when the arrival of the Londoners gave the edge to her opponents, but in that instance the decision could not be executed in time.[5] The older and wiser were generally those to advise that discretion was the better part of valour. Louis VI at Brémule, Waleran at Bourgthéroulde, David of Scots at the Standard, and Stephen at Lincoln, were all advised to avoid battle because of their opponents' strength.[6] In all these cases the advice was ignored, and the commanders lived to rue their decisions. Age seems commonly to have engendered caution, and is expressed nicely in the words of the mother of Sulpice of Amboise, when her son decided on war without consulting her: I am not an imbecile yet. My advanced age still leaves me some sense. Look at the forces against you. 'It is uncertain who will be favoured by the chance of arms, but I fear it will not be you.'[7] She was right.

Numerical inferiority was not the only consideration; lack of morale, unreliable troops, poorly trained, armed or disciplined men had also to be taken into account before risking battle. Stephen in Normandy was clearly worried about the loyalty of his forces, and in the end their quarrels caused him to abandon the campaign. In the year of the Standard, Stephen led an expedition north, but called it off when it was feared his own men were in league with the Scots. Other reasons given were the onset of Lent, and the failure of supplies, both perfectly valid reasons for backing out of a campaign, but perhaps in this instance excuses. In the case of the Scots at the Standard, it was the quality of the troops that led to Robert Bruce advising David against fighting. He asked the king if he wanted his future to depend upon the hotheaded but poorly armed and disciplined Galwegians.[8]

Nor should we exaggerate the Norman eagerness for blood. No doubt religious scruples were useful as excuses, and could be ignored on occasion, but they must also have played a real part in the decision-making of commanders. The avoidance of bloodshed, the observance of truces, the necessity to have a just cause, were important for propaganda purposes, but perhaps in practice too. There was a twelfth-century code of war, as well as that so brilliantly examined by Keen in the later medieval period.[9] Orderic speaks of a 'brotherhood of arms'. This may have been a kind of class solidarity, and certainly common soldiers were not treated in the same manner as knights, but it contains at least the germs of a more humane attitude to war. No doubt Orderic was being idealistic when he wrote that at Brémule: 'as Christian soldiers they did not thirst for the blood of their brothers'. But Geoffrey

---

5 Faringdon: ed. R. Howlett, *Chronicles of the Reigns of Stephen, Henry II and Richard I*, RS 1889, iv, 150; Cosne: L. Halphen and R. Poupardin, *Chroniques des Comtes d'Anjou et des Seigneurs d'Amboise*, Paris 1913, 200; Winchester: Huntingdon, 275.

6 Brémule: Orderic, vi, 234; Bourgthéroulde: Orderic, vi, 350; Standard: Ailred in Howlett, iii, 192; Lincoln: K. R. Potter, *Gesta Stephani*, Oxford 1976, 112.

7 Halphen and Poupardin, 126-7.

8 Normandy: Orderic, vi, 482-6; Scotland: T. Arnold, *Symeon of Durham*, RS 1882-5, ii, 284; Standard: Howlett, iii, 192.

9 M. H. Keen, *The Laws of War in the Late Middle Ages*, London 1965.

of Anjou expresses a similar sentiment in the 'Historia Gaufredi Ducis': 'If we are knights, we should have compassion on fellow knights, especially those at our mercy'.[10] There was a growing concern in the Church about the circumstances in which war could be approved, and especially about the fighting of Christian against Christian. It is unlikely that men were eager for battle on every possible occasion. One tag quoted in the Angevin chronicle is: 'Nothing is more shameful than to wage war on one with whom you have lived in friendship'; and Robert son of Lisiard expresses the desire to avoid battle with his own previous household comrades.[11] Clearly also there were anxieties in confronting one's feudal lord, except in approved circumstances.

Common sense, religious scruples, practical difficulties, the realistic weighing of consequences, could all be important pressures against battle, but undoubtedly the most potent deterrent was fear of defeat. Consider the consequences of defeat for some of those involved in our Norman battles. Harold Godwinson lost his throne, his kingdom, his estates, his family, as well as his life. For Robert Curthose, defeat meant the loss of his duchy and life imprisonment. For Louis, Brémule meant a loss of face, sighs and sniggers in every corner of Europe north of the Alps. For Waleran, Bourgthéroulde meant the blighting of his ambitions and imprisonment. For three of his leading tenants is meant blinding: two for breaking liege homage to the king, one at least in part for composing satirical verses against Henry.[12] Through Lincoln, Stephen lost his throne temporarily and the duchy of Normandy for good. He was imprisoned at Bristol, in chains after he had shown a tendency to wander.[13] He was indeed fortunate not to suffer the same fate as Robert Curthose, saved only by the victory his supporters won in the Rout of Winchester. Such could be the consequences of defeat, and they were not to be contemplated lightly.

Wise commanders therefore avoided battle whenever possible. The outstanding success in this respect must be Geoffrey le Bel. In his invasion of Normandy between 1135 and 1145, he undertook a series of sieges, and used diplomatic pressure. He was prepared to retreat when discretion dictated and in the event won the duchy without having to fight a single pitched battle. Other commanders were not so fortunate as Geoffrey, but some at least shared the same attitude. Battle was a last resort, to be avoided unless victory seemed assured, in the knowledge that chance would always be a factor in what Orderic called 'the uncertain verdict of battle'.[14]

One begins to wonder why battles occurred at all. The answer must be, when either both commanders were confident of victory, in which case one of them had probably miscalculated, or when one expected victory and the other was physically or mentally trapped in a situation from which he could not or would not back down. The point in fighting a battle was to make sure of victory, and equally therefore to make certain one would not be defeated. Let us see how far this attitude is reflected in the battle tactics of Norman warfare in the west.

In order to examine tactics fruitfully we need to clear the ground in two respects. Firstly it is important to value the evidence we use, chiefly chronicle evidence, to

[10] Orderic, vi, 240; Halphen and Poupardin, 196.
[11] Halphen and Poupardin, 206.
[12] Orderic, vi, 242, 352. I am grateful to David Crouch for allowing me to read the draft of his thesis (Cardiff 1983) on the Beaumonts, particularly with regard to their tenants and Bourg- théroulde.
[13] *Historia Novella*, 50.
[14] Orderic, ii, 309: 'ambiguum certamen'; compare Ailred in Howlett, iii, 185: 'incertos de victoria, fluctuare animo'.

employ the best and earliest accounts. This may seem an unnecessary point, until one uses some modern accounts and realises that the normal process is to take every piece of evidence from all quality of sources and construct a jigsaw account of battles. What is needed is chiefly an exercise in pruning. As a part of this process it is also necessary to review the practice of evaluating medieval tactics by consideration of the ground over which the battles were fought. In ninety-nine cases out of a hundred, precise location of a battle is guesswork, often very broad guesswork indeed. It may be fun to try and identify a site, but to give a proper account we should rely on historical evidence, and not historical fiction.

Our starting point is the Battle of Hastings, the details of which need not detain us long, since Professor Brown has so recently reviewed the battle for this conference. 'If he could blunder here he could blunder anywhere', refers of course to Freeman and Hastings, and is not a comment that we require.[15] Harold seems to have miscalculated in choosing to fight at this time, apparently in order to achieve surprise. Hastings is the exception in our battles, as being the only one where a positive location can be asserted with some assurance. Traditionally the high altar of the Abbey was sited on the spot where Harold set his standard and was killed. But even Hastings may require some caution in this respect. The earliest detailed account, in William of Poitiers, gives only an approximate location, telling us little more than that the battle was fought on a hill near the edge of the woodlands. The Anglo-Saxon Chronicle, though giving few details of the conflict, mentions that the English assembled by the hoary apple tree.[16] This has normally been identified as on Caldbec Hill, and most accounts then take the Saxon army forward, but the Chronicle gives the impression that this is where the battle was fought. The Malfosse provides another difficulty. Professor Searle has made the interesting suggestion that the local place-name might relate not to an incident in the battle, but to a burial ditch.[17] If this were so, its siting to the north is also odd, since one would expect a burial ditch to be near the centre of action. On the evidence quoted so far, one might be inclined to locate the battle on Caldbec Hill. The identification with the present site depends of course on the Battle Abbey Chronicle, which is not an absolutely reliable witness. Its account of William's vow has been questioned by Professor Searle.[18] It is true that the words put into William's mouth, forecasting that the supply of wine in the Abbey would be more abundant than water, seem to have been confirmed by the recent sherry reception, but it remains true that the tale of the hill has no greater antiquity than that of the vow. Nevertheless, common sense would agree that the tradition of placing the Abbey named after the battle on the actual site seems likely and remains acceptable. The point here is not to move the battlefield, but to demonstrate the problems of locating battles even when one has apparently sound evidence. Our other battles are far more difficult to locate with precision than Hastings.

There are a few points in the tactics of Hastings that we need to linger over. It must be asserted that the English fought on foot. Glover's view that Snorre is 'an important and dependable' witness for this eleventh-century battle is not acceptable,

---

15 R. A. Brown, 'The Battle of Hastings', *ante*, iii, 1980. J. H. Round, *Feudal England*, London 1895, 332.
16 *Gesta Guillelmi*, 186; *ASC*, 143: C. Plummer, *Two of the Saxon Chronicles Parallel*, 2v, Oxford 1892, i, 199.
17 *Battle Chronicle*, 16.
18 *Battle Chronicle*, 16, 20, 23, 38, 40, 44, 46; 36-44.

and on it depends the argument for Anglo-Saxon cavalry.[19] The comment in Florence of Worcester on the Welsh border incident of 1055 is decisive: that Earl Ralph 'ordered the English to fight on horseback against their custom'.[20] Equally convincing is the fact that, although Hastings is well covered for a medieval battle, there is no mention of English cavalry. If the Anglo-Saxons had normally used cavalry, they would surely have employed it at Hastings.

On the Norman side we need to consider the two main elements in their attack. There is no question that the Normans used cavalry, but there is a problem over how they used it. Ross has suggested that the couched lance was only now in the process of development, and the evidence of the Tapestry on this is certainly ambiguous: some lances are used couched, and some over-arm.[21] One thing is clear, the English line was not broken by one massive cavalry charge, though there seems no reason against believing that feigned flights were used and with effect. The other main factor in the Norman victory was archery. Its significance at Hastings has sometimes been overlooked. The dispute over the arrow in the eye seems now to have been settled.[22] Archery was used at two points in the battle: to open hostilities, apparently without great effect; and in the final assault, during which Harold was killed. In the Tapestry the archers are using ordinary wooden bows, not short-bows which are composite and have a distinctive shape.[23] Ordinary wooden bows are technically the same as longbows, but of a lesser length, to judge by the Tapestry. The bows at Hastings were effective, however, and could not have been much shorter than five feet or they would have lacked sufficient range and impact. Despite the suggestion by Morton and Muntz, the editors of the 'Carmen', that one archer on the Tapestry is a crossbowman, it must be asserted that all the archers shown are using ordinary bows, there are no crossbowmen. The 'Carmen' mentions the use of crossbows in the battle, but its value as an early source is now open to doubt.[24] There is, however, no need to discard this idea, since William of Poitiers also refers to 'balistae' in a context where crossbowmen must be meant.[25] References to crossbows in the eleventh and twelfth centuries are common enough, and clearly were used in the Norman armies of the period. One of the more interesting mentions of the weapon is in Orderic's account of the quarrel between Henry I and his natural daughter, Juliana. Henry besieged his daughter, and was not prepared for her reaction when invited to see her. 'She had a crossbow ready drawn for the purpose and shot a bolt at her father, but failed to injure him since God protected him.' She had to surrender, and her father, more lenient than was his wont, allowed her to escape by leaping down from the walls 'to fall shamefully with bare buttocks into the depths of the moat' and the freezing February waters.[26] We may then summarise that the

19 R. Glover, 'English Warfare in 1066', *EHR* xvii, 1952, 1-18.
20 Worcester, i, 213: 'Anglos contra morem in equis pugnare jussit'.
21 D. J. A. Ross, 'L'originalité de "Turoldus": le maniement de la lance', *Cahiers de Civilisation Médiévale* vi, 1963, 127-38.
22 D. Bernstein, 'The Blinding of Harold and the Meaning of the Bayeux Tapestry', *ante*, v, 1982. Although I do not accept all the author's conclusions, the discovery of evidence for an arrow in the falling figure removes any doubt that the Tapestry's version showed Harold to have been hit by an arrow.
23 Twenty-nine archers are depicted on the Tapestry, all have ordinary wooden bows. These are analysed in more detail in J. Bradbury, *The Medieval Archer*, to be published shortly.
24 *Carmen*, 115. *BT*, pl. 61, pl. X. R. H. C. Davis, 'The *Carmen de Hastingae Proelio*', *EHR* xciii, 1978, 241-61; and the discussion on the Carmen in *ante*, ii, 1979.
25 *Gesta Guillelmi*, 185: 'Pedites in fronte locavit, sagittis armatos et balistis'.
26 Orderic, vi, 212-14.

Norman tactics that won Hastings involved a combination of cavalry and archers, using both ordinary bows and crossbows.

The first major battle in either England or Normandy after Hastings was at Tinchebrai in 1106, exactly forty years after the great victory, as William of Malmesbury noted.[27] It brought to a climax the struggle between the sons of the Conqueror for control of kingdom and duchy. Like so many other battles in the period, Tinchebrai arose from a siege, both sieges and battles being essentially tests of lordship. Henry I had besieged the castle of Tinchebrai during the course of his invasion of Normandy. The castle belonged to William, Count of Mortain, who appealed to Robert Curthose for aid. In such a situation, the overlord either admitted the loss, or had to contest the siege in the field. In this case Curthose chose to accept the challenge, and brought an army to the relief of Tinchebrai. Often, especially if outnumbered, the challenger would then, his bluff called, abandon the siege, but Henry chose to make a stand.

Henry I himself, in a letter, tells us that the battle was fought 'before Tinchebrai'.[28] During the siege Henry had constructed a siege castle, but we do not know its position. The ruins of the castle now sit on the hill of Tinchebrai, and clearly the battle was fought on the level ground below the castle, closer than that we cannot get. Similarly, we know that Henry placed a force of cavalry under Helias of Maine at a distance, out of sight of Curthose, but we do not even know in which direction.

For many years historians disputed the extent of Henry I's use of dismounted knights in the battle, according to whether they favoured the account by Orderic or that by Henry of Huntingdon. The matter was settled through the use of the letter from a priest of Fécamp. This document has had an extraordinary history. It was first printed in 1872 by Delisle in his edition of Robert of Torigny, but ignored until its 're-discovery' by H. W. C. Davis in 1909. It afterwards emerged that Davis had not himself seen the original, only a copy made for him. This copy made exactly the same error as the version by Delisle, omitting an important line. Only in 1910 was this corrected. Even then, oddly enough, the missing line was printed with a minor mistake, the addition of a word that does not appear in the manuscript. The line refers to the dismounting of Henry's second division. This letter was written immediately after Tinchebrai, and gives a detailed account of Henry's army.[29] According to the priest Henry's first line consisted of men from Bayeux, Avranches and Coutances, all on foot. In the second line were the king and his barons, all similarly on foot. Seven hundred cavalry were ranged with each line. In addition there was the flanking cavalry force under Helias of Maine. According to Henry of Huntingdon and the sources that followed him, Curthose also dismounted men, but with no indication of the numbers. Curthose charged against his brother's army, and with some effect 'since the duke and his troops had been well trained in the wars of Jerusalem'. The meaning of this can only be conjectured, but following Smail's analysis of crusading methods, it probably should be taken as indicating a

---

27 *De gestis regum*, ii, 475.

28 Eadmer, 184: 'ante Tenerchebraicum'.

29 L. Delisle, *Chronique de Robert de Torigni*, Rouen 1872, i, 129; H. W. C. Davis, 'A Contemporary Account of the Battle of Tinchebrai', *EHR* xxiv, 1909, 728–32; 'The Battle of Tinchebrai: A Correction', *EHR* xxv, 1910, 295–6. The letter is in Bodleian, Jesus College MS li, f.104, where the actual line reads: 'omnes pedites. In secunda rex cum innumeris baronibus suis omnes similiter/pedites'.

concerted cavalry charge using couched lances.[30] The charge made an impact, but it was held. To the sound of shouts, presumably as a signal, the hidden cavalry force now attacked from the side. The ducal army was shattered and Curthose himself captured.

The second of our main battles was fought at Alençon in 1118. It does not appear in most military discussions of the period. One reason for this may be that it does not figure in the Anglo-Norman chronicles, except briefly in Orderic, no doubt because Henry I suffered a defeat which most chroniclers in England and Normandy thought it best to pass over in silence. There is, however, an account of the battle in the Angevin chronicles.[31] There is not time here to discuss in detail the difficulties of the Angevin sources, but some brief explanation must be made, since we are now dealing with a source that cannot compare in authority with the letter of the priest of Fécamp.

The earliest manuscripts of the 'Gesta Consulum Andegavorum' are mid twelfth-century, and already show signs of numerous alterations to lost originals. The best known of these chroniclers is John of Marmoutier, who revised the 'Gesta', and added a life of Geoffrey le Bel. John names a series of earlier writers on whom he depended. The historians of the chronicles have played subtle games attempting to ascribe particular versions and additions to the authors named by John.[32] It is a somewhat unprofitable game, since there are too many unknown factors, and it seems better to refer to manuscripts than to conjectural authors. In the form we possess them, the 'Gesta' are mid twelfth-century revisions and additions to earlier versions, in the form of deeds ascribed in chronological order to the Counts of Anjou. From internal evidence it is clear that sources from Loches and Tours played an important part in this compilation.

It has been generally agreed that BN. 6218 is the earliest version, and this was used for Halphen and Poupardin's edition. BN. 6006, however, comes from about the same period, and was preferred for the earlier Marchegay and Salmon edition. The latter manuscript includes the account of Alençon, which would therefore seem to be an addition of the mid twelfth-century. The account demonstrates an interest in Maine, particularly in emphasising the role of Lisiard of Sablé in the battle. As a battle account it is detailed and interesting, but also has inaccuracies and seems already to contain elements of legend.[33] At the same time, the basic outline of the account is confirmed by Orderic. Clearly it is not an account on which to rely too heavily, but it is a narrative of an important battle, and at the very least reflects the ideas of battle in the mind of its writer.

[30] On Curthose dismounting, see Huntingdon, 235, and the 'Draco' in Howlett, ii, 649. On 'wars of Jerusalem' see Huntingdon, 235: 'assuetusque bellis Jerosolimitanis'. R. C. Smail, *Crusading Warfare, 1097-1193*, Cambridge 1956, 199, 203; and compare F. Gabrieli, *Arab Historians of the Crusades*, London 1969, 58.
[31] The Angevin account appears in P. Marchegay and A. Salmon, *Chroniques des Comtes d'Anjou*, 2nd edn, 1871, 144-51; and in Halphen and Poupardin, 155-61. Briefer references are in Orderic, vi, 206-8; and H. Waquet, *Suger: Vie de Louis VI le Gros*, Paris 1929, 192.
[32] For commentary on the authorship of the Angevin chronicles, see the introduction by E. Mabille to Marchegay and Salmon, 1871; L. Halphen, *Étude sur les Chroniques des Comtes d'Anjou et des Seigneurs d'Amboise*, Paris 1906; and the introduction to Halphen and Poupardin.
[33] P. J. Odolant-Desnos, *Mémoires Historiques sur la Ville d'Alençon et sur ses Seigneurs*, 2nd edn, Paris 1858, i, 371, discussed the problem of people mentioned in the Angevin Chronicle in connection with Alençon who could not have been present, though possible solutions can be offered. For a comment on the legendary aspect, see K. Norgate, *England under the Angevin Kings*, 2 v, London 1887, i, 236.

Alençon had long been a bone of contention, just on the Norman side of the Maine boundary. Its citizens had no great reason to recall the past with any fondness for the Normans. Robert I had made its lord sue for mercy with a saddle on his shoulders, and, according to William of Jumièges, poison in his heart.[34] On another famous occasion the Conqueror had taken bitter revenge on the citizens for taunting him with skins over the walls. In 1118 Alençon was held for Henry I by his nephew Stephen. The latter had created resentment by his treatment of the citizens and their wives, and they, probably needing little encouragement, had invited in Fulk of Anjou. The latter came to besiege the castle, setting himself up in a defended 'park'.[35] Yet again, the challenge of a siege was accepted. Henry, coming to the relief of Alençon, faced battle if he wished to succeed. Fulk's forces remained within the park, and in the early stages there was a series of sorties rather than a pitched battle. Fulk sent out three groups, each consisting of knights and archers, and each in turn forced to return to the park. In the meantime a second Angevin force, under Lisiard of Sablé, was approaching the scene. At a distance of four miles they could hear the clamour and wails from the conflict. They speeded up in order to join the fight. They dismounted in a wooded valley, mustered and, when dressed for war in leg armour, mail coats and helmets, drew up their lines. The first consisted of Lisiard of Sablé with knights, archers and foot. As they approached, they shouted and at a signal rushed upon the enemy. The horses, knights and foot of Henry I suffered severely at the hands of the Angevin archers, and Theobald of Blois was wounded by a light blow on the forehead. Fulk then issued from the park with his main army, calling, 'Look knights, knights, here comes your count. I am your brother, lord and master, and whatever you see me doing, you do the same.' The final assault was a cavalry charge, reinforced by archers and crossbowmen. After the victory, Alençon surrendered to Fulk. The Latin does not make it clear if Lisiard's force remained dismounted and fought on foot, or whether they were also cavalry, but the Angevin tactics involved a combination of archers and cavalry, and perhaps dismounted men as well.[36]

The Battle of Brémule in 1119 is a deservedly famous occasion, though the size of the armies involved does not seem to have been great. It was the 'battle of the two kings', the supreme test of lordship after Louis' invasion of Normandy.[37] Again the sources require some discussion. It is useful to have accounts from both sides, and the assistance of such chroniclers as Suger, Orderic and Henry of Huntingdon. One important source, although not unknown, has been rather neglected by military historians, and that is the Hyde Chronicle.[38] The reason for the neglect is not clear, since it has long been in print, is a full account, and possibly the earliest, being in a manuscript that breaks off in 1121 and was probably written soon after that. Like many works it displays partisanship, in this case for the Warenne family. There are some difficulties in that the Hyde Chronicle differs in some details from other

---

34 Jumièges, 139, 193; 171. *Gesta Guillelmi*, 43.
35 Halphen and Poupardin, 156. There is a modern park in Alençon in an ideal position for besieging the castle.
36 Halphen and Poupardin, 158: 'descenderuntque in quadam valle amena et nemorosa, disellatis equis et recenciatis, induti etiam toracibus, loricis et galeis, ordinaverunt acies suas'.
37 Orderic, vi, 240: 'In duorum certamine regum'; Suger, 196; Huntingdon, 241-2; Orderic, vi, 234-42.
38 E. Edwards, *Liber Monasterii de Hyda*, RS, 1866, 316-18. The Manuscript is BL, Cotton MS, Domitian xiv.

accounts, but not to any greater extent than the other sources differ from each other. In the overall picture there is general agreement.

The precise site cannot be identified, beyond noting that Henry's scouts were posted on the hill of Verclives, and according to Orderic 'near the hill is an open field and a wide plain called Brémule', and here the battle was fought.[39] Verclives is only a small height, and again the battle was fought on level ground suitable for cavalry. This is significant when one recalls that Henry I chose the point of contact and, although using dismounted men, seems also to have taken into consideration his intended use of cavalry. Louis did not have a large force, but ignored advice not to fight, being himself impatient and angry. It is not clear if Henry's sons were mounted or not, but Henry stationed himself with the dismounted men. Louis ordered a charge, which all the chroniclers agree lacked discipline, and we might suggest was not properly concerted. Although archers are not specifically mentioned, it is likely, as Dr Chibnall suggests, that Orderic's mention of William Crispin's horses being 'quickly killed' means by archery.[40] Despite lack of order, the French charge had some impact, but was held by the line of dismounted men. In the fighting Henry I was wounded by blows on the head, but was saved by the mail hood of his hauberk. The French were broken, and Louis, after further adventures, returned to Andely.

Bourgthéroulde in 1124 was a relatively minor affair with no kings, one side even lacking a magnate to command. It remains an interesting conflict for us, because of Orderic's detailed narrative.[41] It is quite impossible to provide a location for this battle. Most of the brief notices of the battle refer to it as being at or near Bourg-théroulde, Robert of Torigny referring to it as 'near to the town which they call Bourgthéroulde', and a chronicle of Rouen places it between Bourgthéroulde and Boissy-le-Chatel. Orderic seems to support this in his main account, but on a second occasion mentions apparently the same battle as being at Rougemoutiers, several miles away to the north.[42] The whole area in any case is pretty level, and we can only note that the battle occurred when Waleran of Meulan, in revolt against Henry I, was returning from a relief expedition to his besieged and isolated castle at Vatteville in the direction of Beaumont. He found his return blocked by a force of Henry's household troops collected from nearby castle garrisons. The young Waleran insisted on fighting against advice. After discussion, the royal household troops, being set an example by Odo Borleng, decided to dismount. Odo outlined the plan 'for one section of our men to dismount for battle and fight on foot, while the rest remain mounted ready for the fray. Let us also place a force of archers in the first line and compel the enemy troop to slow down by wounding their horses.'[43] It would be difficult to give a clearer analysis of the general tactics of the period. Robert of Torigny says that mounted archers were sent forward against the enemy right.[44] Probably they fought on foot, but certainly these household archers decided the issue. The charging horses were brought down, including that of Waleran himself who was captured.

The battlefield of the Standard fought in 1138 is marked by a monument beside the A167 road north out of Northallerton, but like most such markers seems to have

[39] Orderic, vi, 236: 'latissima planicies quae ab incolis Brenmula vocitatur'.
[40] Orderic, vi, 238; Orderic, vi, xxi.
[41] Orderic, vi, 346-56.
[42] Jumièges, 295: 'haud procul a villa, quam vocant Burgum Turoldi'. *RHF*, xii, 784: 'prope Burgum-Turoldi et Buxeium'. Orderic, vi, 348: 'prope Burgum Turoldi', but Orderic, vi, 356: 'in territorio Rubri Monasterii'.
[43] Orderic, vi, 348.
[44] Jumièges, 294-5.

been positioned rather arbitrarily. Some historians have placed the battle eastwards of the town, but this northern spot is the most likely. The English battle speech was made from a hill, but this has been given more significance than it deserves. There are several low rises in the vicinity, any one of which would answer, but the main feature of the area is its general flatness. Ailred, who should have been familiar with the geography, says it was fought 'in a broad plain' near Northallerton.[45] There is a tradition of burials at Scotpits Lane.[46] This is the most promising indication of the site, and would place it some way south of that traditionally accepted. The move would fit better with Richard of Hexham's two miles from Northallerton. There are several full accounts of the battle, including that by Richard of Hexham, but most of the others seem to stem from Henry of Huntingdon.[47]

The composition of the armies was less unusual than is often suggested. There were undisciplined Galwegians in the Scottish armies, whose presence proved disastrous to King David, and parish levies on the English side, but both sides were controlled by Norman knights. The importance of Stephen's household knights under Bernard of Balliol has certainly been underestimated. It was only after their arrival that the English felt numerically strong enough to engage in battle.[48] The pattern of the English army fits closely to that found in the battles we have already covered: archers, dismounted knights, and a reserve force of cavalry. David of Scots also dismounted part of his force. David, like Harold Godwinson at Hastings, pinned his hopes on a surprise attack, in this case through the fog, and like Harold he failed to achieve it. The battle hinged on his decision to allow the Galwegians to disrupt his plan so they could take what they saw as their rightful place in the van. They made an aggressive but ill-disciplined advance and were shot down by the English archers. One of the Lothian chiefs was felled by an arrow, and the Galwegians fled. According to Ailred, 'as a hedgehog is covered with spines, so were the Galwegians with arrows'.[49] The king's son, Henry, led a gallant charge, which had initial success, but was held off, apparently by the English cavalry.

Finally, we come to Lincoln in 1141, the last major battle of the Norman period. Some historians have located this battle to the north of the city, but a position to the west is more likely, though the chronicles are not specific. They do tell us of the rebel forces crossing marshy ground, after changing their line of approach, and this probably indicates the Foss Dyke. But again, the main point is that, apart from the rise of Lincoln itself, the whole area is flat and the battle was fought over level ground.

Once more the battle arose from a siege. Ranulf of Chester had seized Lincoln castle by a trick and Stephen had responded to an appeal from the bishop and the citizens to attempt recovery by a siege. An army was collected in the west by Ranulf and Robert of Gloucester, and came to the relief. Their army seems to have been larger, and Stephen again was faced with problems over the loyalty of his own force. Against advice, he chose to fight, primarily it would seem for psychological reasons, not wishing to emulate the cowardice of his father. He refused 'to stain his reputation by the disgrace of flight'.[50] Baldwin FitzGilbert made Stephen's battle speech for

45 Howlett, iii, 182: 'in campo latissimo'. See also VCH, *Yorkshire*, i, 160.
46 A. H. Burne, *More Battlefields of England*, London 1952, 96-9.
47 Huntingdon, 262-5; Howlett, iii, 162; Orderic, vi, 522.
48 Howlett, iii, 160-1.
49 Howlett, iii, 196.
50 *Gesta Stephani*, 112; Huntingdon, 271-3.

him. Henry of Huntingdon indulges himself with the battle speeches, in which most of the commanders are insulted for reasons ranging from cowardice to unutterable filthiness in behaviour. Again both sides dismounted some knights but retained some cavalry. The first clash destroyed the poorly armed Welsh on the rebel side, but the earls retaliated and dealt the decisive blow by breaking the royal cavalry. Stephen was left with infantry forces, and surrounded. He fought with his sword till it broke, and then with an axe given him by a citizen of Lincoln. He resisted 'like a lion, grinding his teeth and foaming at the mouth like a boar' until hit on the head by a rock.[51]

Let us then summarise the battle tactics employed in this century after Hastings. There are three common elements: knights who are dismounted to fight with the foot; archers usually placed in a forward position; and cavalry normally reserved for a decisive charge. Our final problem is to try and explain why these tactics were used.

Were they novel or unique tactics, something confined to England and Normandy? It seems not. Leo the Wise had said of the Franks: 'when their soldiers are hard pressed in a cavalry fight, they will turn their horses loose, dismount, and stand back to back against superior numbers, rather than flee'. At the Battle of the Dyle in 891, knights were dismounted by Arnulf against the Vikings. According to Morice, the Bretons dismounted against the Angevins in the second Battle of Conquereux in 992, and it is possible that knights dismounted at Pontlevoy in 1016. In a later period, during the Second Crusade, Conrad III dismounted knights at Damascus in 1148, and William of Tyre makes the interesting comment that this was the 'custom of the Teutons when they were faced with a crisis in battle'. The famous Byzantine remark that the Franks were ungainly when they fought on foot, nevertheless suggests that this did occur.[52]

It seems likely then that this was not a new practice in 1106, nor one confined to England and Normandy. The view of Professor Hollister, and of Lachauvelaye before him, that this was a result of Anglo-Saxon influence, does not therefore seem to be supported.[53] No doubt the experience of Hastings reinforced the view that good infantry could be effective against cavalry, but twelfth-century tactics were far from being a reproduction of English tactics, and there is little evidence that the knights who dismounted were of Old English extraction. Only one Englishman is mentioned in any situation where dismounting occurred, and that is the somewhat unusual case of Edgar the Atheling with Curthose. When 'English' knights are mentioned, it is never certain that they were Anglo-Saxons, and generally more likely that they were Normans who had settled in England. Of the many named examples of men who dismounted, all were of Norman or French extraction. The interesting incident in 1101, when Henry I 'went among the ranks (of the English assembled to face the anticipated invasion of Curthose) instructing them how to elude the ferocity of the cavalry by opposing their shields, and how to return their strokes', does not

[51] Howlett, iv, 140-1.
[52] C. Oman, *A History of the Art of Warfare in the Middle Ages*, 2v, 2nd edn, 1924, i, 204, 357; F. C. Liskenne and J. B. B. Sauvan, 'L'Empereur Leon: Institutions Militaires', *Bibliothèque Historique et Militaire*, iii, Paris 1850, 524-5. On the Dyle, *MGH*, l, 1826. On Conquereux and Pontlevoy, P-H. Morice, *Histoire Ecclésiastique et Civile de Brétagne*, 2v, Paris 1750, i, 65. On Damascus, E. A. Babcock and A. C. Krey, *William Archbishop of Tyre, A History of Deeds done Beyond the Sea*, New York 1943, i, 189. On the Franks, E. R. A. Sewter, *The Alexiad of Anna Comnena*, Harmondsworth 1969, 416.
[53] J. Lachauvelaye, *Guerres des Français et des Anglais du XIe au XVe siècle*, Paris 1875, i, 13, 34. Hollister, 127-9. Compare Norgate, i, 13.

suggest that the expertise and influence in developing the tactics against cavalry was of English origin.[54] It is nonetheless interesting in showing Henry I's familiarity with such tactics several years before Tinchebrai. The fact that both sides dismounted in that battle also argues against it as the result of English influence, and in favour of a development in continental warfare by that time.

It remains interesting that dismounting knights in the Norman period became almost invariable in battle. There was no hint of the practice at Hastings, where the Conqueror's knights were 'astonished to see him on foot', when he was unhorsed.[55] The chronicles give some explanation of dismounting, which may be analysed as 'lest they take to flight', 'to remove the hope of flight', and in order that 'they might fight with more determination', usually in conjunction with an oath 'to conquer or to die'.[56] Can we interpret this in tactical terms? The greatest fear of any commander was defeat. Cavalry offered the best hope of a sudden blow and victory, but how could one insure against an opponent's cavalry charge? On the defensive, cavalry was likely to break, horses were vulnerable. Good infantry had a better chance of withstanding a charge. Both the Normans and the English at Hastings possessed heavy infantry, but in this period there was a limit to how many well armed infantry could be provided. A simple solution to the problem of strengthening infantry, particularly in a crisis, was to take some of your best armed and trained men, even if trained as cavalry, and use them to reinforce the infantry. Stephen at Lincoln, in the view of Henry of Huntingdon, dismounted knights and disposed his lines for 'maximum safety'.[57] As Geoffrey of Monmouth put it: the side that stands firm in the first assault, achieves victory in the end.[58]

A related explanation is to be found in the use of archers. Western armies were not the only ones that had to find an answer to the growing power of the concerted charge. On crusade, several responses were attempted to what the Byzantines called the 'irresistible' charge of the Franks: wagons pushed forward at the moment of the charge, iron caltrops, or especially missile weapons that could hit the vulnerable horses before the charge was delivered.[59] This last answer was also employed in the West. Archers were effective, but they were also vulnerable. In the East the archers were mounted, and could shoot and move away from danger. In the West they were normally on foot, and on their own would be vulnerable against cavalry, hence the use of dismounted men and spearmen to protect them, hence at the Standard the dismounted men were 'mixed in' with the archers in the front line.[60] It was a tactic that would re-emerge in the Hundred Years War.

In short, the tactics of this period were probably not of English origin, though they might have received some influence from that quarter. They were tactics that developed out of ordinary Frankish methods of war, and were distinguished by the combination of archers, heavy infantry and cavalry, in a period when the greatest threat was the concerted cavalry charge, and the greatest concern of military commanders was to find an answer to that charge.

---

54 *De gestis regum*, ii, 472.
55 *Gesta Guillelmi*, 198: 'Mirantes eum peditem sui milites'.
56 Huntingdon, 235, 269, 271. Suger, 196. Howlett, iii, 189.
57 Huntingdon, 271: 'cum summo securitate'.
58 A. Griscom, *The Historia Regum Britanniae of Geoffrey of Monmouth*, London 1929, 486. Geoffrey is of considerable interest for the warfare of his own age.
59 Alexiad, 163, 416, 165, 416.
60 Huntingdon, 263: 'sagittarii equitibus inmixti'.

RICHARD I AND THE SCIENCE OF WAR
IN THE MIDDLE AGES[1]

John Gillingham

So far as most historians are concerned there was no such thing as a science of war in the Middle Ages.[2] This is a profoundly mistaken view, but for the purposes of this paper I propose to concentrate on one aspect of war only — strategy, the planning and conduct of campaigns, and in particular in the 12th and 13th centuries, though I shall try to draw out some of the wider implications for other periods.[3] My chief reason for this choice is the fact that strategy still remains the most neglected area of medieval military history. It is true that the days when a book on the history of war turned out to be little more than a history of battles are almost gone. Modern scholars have tended to investigate subjects like military obligation, organization, recruitment, pay, armament and the ethos of war — all of them important subjects. As a result most recent historians have been so busy getting their armies into the field that they have left themselves little room in which to consider what they did once they were there. Thus in a recent admirable survey of the whole subject Philippe Contamine devotes only nine out of four hundred pages of printed text to strategy — rather less, for example, than he gives to the subject of courage. Even so Contamine's conclusion is worth emphasising — that medieval generals were 'capables de concevoir et d'exécuter une "grande stratégie"'[4] — and much of what follows will be an elaboration of some of the points which

1 I am grateful to John Prestwich for his kindness in reading a draft of this essay. Needless to say he did not at the time know where I intended to publish it. Had he done so he might have been less helpful than usual. I first gave some shape to these ideas in a lecture delivered to an audience at the Tower of London in March 1980, so for the invitation and the original stimulus I owe a debt of thanks to Peter Hammond and his colleagues at the Tower.
2 See, for example, the powerfully expressed conclusion to Ferdinand Lot, *L'art militaire et les armées au Moyen Age*, Paris 1946, ii, 449. My choice of the term 'the science of war' is, of course, intended to provoke scepticism. But notice Jean de Bueil's opinion: 'Car je puis dire . . . que la conduite de la guerre est artifficieuse et subtille; par quoy s'i convient gouverner par art et par science' and his description of La Hire as 'ung bon docteur en ceste science', Jean de Bueil, *Le Jouvencel* ed. C. Favre and L. Lecestre, Paris 1887—9, i 15, ii 246. Also the phrase *in scientia et virtute bellandi* in the early 13th century *Genealogia comitum Flandrensium* MGH ix 333.
3 I shall deal with the purely military conduct of campaigns, not with 'grand strategy' in the sense of political and diplomatic alliance-building, nor with information-gathering (spying) — though both of these were, of course, parts of the normal preliminaries of war.
4 Philippe Contamine, *La Guerre au Moyen Age*, Paris 1980, 365—78, 406—18. Most of Contamine's examples are drawn from the 14th and 15th centuries whereas I shall be chiefly concerned with an earlier period. The chapter on strategy in J.F. Verbruggen, *The Art of Warfare in Western Europe during the Middle Ages*, Amsterdam 1977, 249—300, consists largely of a summary of a dozen or so late 13th and early 14th century projects, most of them schemes for a new crusade. Thus he deals mainly with 'grand designs' while I shall restrict myself to a discussion of the practice of war — though see Verbruggen 283—4, 288.

he makes.

As will become apparent it could equally well be said that I am doing no more than transferring to a wider stage many of the insights contained in R.C. Smail's *Crusading Warfare*.[5] Yet although this book was published as long ago as 1956 few historians, not even military historians, can be said to have come to terms with his findings. For example, in one recent, and rightly much praised book, John Keegan doubts whether 'generalship' and 'planning' are concepts which can usefully be applied to medieval warfare.[6] In the opinion of the Chichele Professor of the History of War it was in the sixteenth century that 'cautious professional competence took the place of the quest for glory in the planning and conduct of campaigns.'[7] Thus it is hardly surprising that if we turn to current encyclopaedias we find the view that 'strategy was notably absent' from medieval warfare and it was in 1453 (!) that 'a new military age dawned'.[8] If such opinions still hold the field then the fault is undoubtedly ours; as medieval historians we have clearly failed to puncture some of the more widely held misconceptions about the Middle Ages.

My own strategy will be twofold. First, to take Richard I's military career as a model of medieval generalship.[9] Second, to use vernacular sources wherever possible, in the belief that the vernacular brings us closer than Latin to the thoughts and actions of soldiers. In particular I have relied heavily on three chronicles: *L'Estoire de la Guerre Sainte* by Ambroise; Joinville's *Life of St Louis*; and Jordan Fantosme's *Chronicle*. Two of the three deal primarily with warfare in the Middle East and this is no accident. We know much more about crusading warfare than we do about contemporary warfare in the West and where we have more evidence it is easier to work out the logic behind military operations. Thus Richard's reputation as a general rests very largely on his conduct of the war against Saladin but in fact, of course, he fought many more campaigns than this. When he went on crusade he had eighteen years of warfare behind him. So far as we know his earliest firsthand experience of war came in 1173 when he was fifteen years old. In the summer of that year he joined in the great revolt against his father Henry II, and took part in an attack on eastern Normandy — an attack which was launched by Count Philip of Flanders.[10] Since Count Philip was well-known as one of the shrewdest soldiers of the day, it seems likely that Richard began his apprenticeship under a good master.[11] After 1173 Richard went to war in 1174, 1175, 1176, 1177, etc. etc. In

5 R.C. Smail, *Crusading Warfare 1097—1193*, Cambridge 1956.

6 John Keegan, *The Face of Battle*, Harmondsworth 1978, 336.

7 Michael Howard, *War in European History*, Oxford 1977, p. 27. In part these views rest on the assumption that medieval armies were 'mere crowds', Keegan 175—6 and compare Howard, 56: 'Feudal men-at-arms were totally, gloriously indisciplined.' But on the importance of discipline in the face of the enemy see Smail 124—30 and Verbruggen 76—94.

8 *The New Encyclopaedia Britannica*, 15th edn., Chicago 1974, vol. 19, 558—9, 576—7; *Encyclopaedia Americana*, New York 1977, vol. 25, 772—3. A remarkably similar view was expressed by Geoffrey Parker in his chapter 'Warfare' in *The New Cambridge Modern History*, Vol. XIII, *Companion Volume* ed. P. Burke, Cambridge 1979.

9 Richard's reputation for political negligence has never prevented military historians from recognising his competence in their field, e.g. Smail 203, Verbruggen 210—12. For a fine recent assessment of Richard's grasp of strategy see J.O. Prestwich, 'Richard Coeur de Lion: *Rex Bellicosus*', Accademia Nazionale dei Lincei. *Problemi attuali di scienza e di cultura* 253, 1981, 3—15.

10 Roger of Howden, *Gesta Regis Henrici Secundi* ed. W. Stubbs, RS 1867, i 49.

11 'Felipe de Flandres, li proz/Qui par son sens sormontot toz/Cels qui estoient a son tens'

the year 1180 we know nothing of Richard's movements, so we simply cannot say whether he went to war or not, but apart from this one gap, we know that he was on campaign in every year between 1173 and his crusade. He then missed a year when he was sitting in prison in Germany, but as soon as he was released he threw himself into the compelling military task of throwing Philip Augustus out of those lands which he had grabbed while Richard was in prison. So between 1173 and his death in 1199 Richard had something like 25 years at war and in these circumstances it is obviously misleading to concentrate on just one small part of his military career to the exclusion of the rest. Indeed if we can believe Ambroise one reason for Richard's successes in the Mediterranean, in Sicily, in Cyprus and in Palestine, was that his followers were full of confidence, conscious that they were men of 'tried renown' who knew more of the art of war than did many of their enemies.[12]

How then should we analyse these 25 years of campaigning? Much of it, of course, consists of laying siege to one or more strongpoints.[13] To this subject I shall return, but for the moment I want to look at warfare in the field. In his chapter on 'The Latin Field Army in Action' R.C. Smail divided armies' activities into three categories. (1) Campaigns without battle. (2) Fighting on the march. (3) Pitched battles.[14] If we accept these categories, as I think we should, and ask how many pitched battles Richard fought, then the answer is only two or three. It is arguable whether or not the famous action at Arsuf on 7 September 1191 should be counted as a battle. It was, in Smail's terms, simply a particularly heavy attack on an army on the march. The charge of the crusader knights forced Saladin to break off the engagement, but two days later he was once again harassing the march just as he had done throughout the fortnight since the army left Acre.[15] However since it seems that the bulk of the forces on both sides became involved in the fighting at Arsuf, I am prepared to count it as a battle. It is equally arguable whether or not the action outside Jaffa on 5 August 1192 should be termed a pitched battle. Richard drew up his troops in so solid a defensive formation that the Muslims never closed with them. Spearmen and crossbowmen, working together like the pikemen and musketeers of a later age, presented so formidable an array that Saladin's cavalry always veered away at the last moment. Eventually Richard himself went over to the attack but it looks as though Saladin's troops were thoroughly demoralized and in no mood to fight — so much so that the day was famous chiefly for Richard's individual prowess and a chivalrous gesture on the part

Histoire de Guillaume la Maréchal, 3 vols., ed. P. Meyer (Paris, 1891—1901) i, 11. 2715—7, cf. 11 3065—6. See also the description of him as 'Felipe le Pugnaire' and 'le noble guerreur' in ed. R.C. Johnston, *Jordan Fantosme's Chronicle*, Oxford 1981, 11. 28, 438 ff.

12 'Mais nos savions plus de guere' Ambroise, *L'Estoire de la Guerre Sainte* ed. G. Paris, Paris 1897, 1. 1512. I shall usually quote from the splendidly doggerel translation of M.J. Hubert and J. La Monte, *The Crusade of Richard Lionheart*, New York 1941,

13 As did both Richard's first campaign — the siege of Drincourt 1173, Howden, *Gesta*, i 49 — and his last. The campaign of 1199 involved the siege not just of Chalus-Chabrol but also of Nontron, Montagut and probably eleven other places in the Limousin, including Limoges itself. See John Gillingham, 'The Unromantic Death of Richard I' *Speculum* liv, 1979, 18—41, especially 29—31. Richard's first known independent action was an attempt on La Rochelle in 1174; see John Gillingham, *Richard the Lionheart*, London 1978, 67—8. His troops on crusade were characterised by Ambroise as men 'Qui mainte vile aveient prise' Ambroise 1. 742.

14 Smail 138—203.

15 Ambroise 11. 6915—6922; Smail 162-5.

of Saladin.[16] Obviously the line of demarcation between a pitched battle and other forms of combat is not always a clear one, but for the purposes of this paper, in order not to make things too easy for myself, I am also prepared to count Jaffa as a battle.

Yet although there may be some degree of uncertainty about the number of Richard's battles on crusade, what is certain is that he did not adopt a battle-seeking strategy. Not once did he go after Saladin's army and try to destroy it. This is not because the 'hot-headed Westerner' once out East became infected by the ultra-cautious strategy of the Franks of Outremer.[17] In all the wars which Richard fought in the West, he fought only one battle and this came fairly early in his military career in May 1176, when he defeated a force of Brabançons employed by a coalition of rebels from the Angoumois and Limousin.[18] Moreover if we compare Richard with his contemporaries then it is clear that there was nothing unusual about this apparent reluctance to fight battles. Henry II, for example, in his whole life never fought a single battle — though Jordan Fantosme described him as 'the greatest conqueror since Charlemagne'.[19] Philip Augustus fought only one — Bouvines in 1214 — and although that battle brought the victory which crowned his career, we should note that he had been trying to avoid battle and fought only when it became unavoidable.[20] These kings were successful rulers who regularly mustered troops and led them to war — but they did not fight battles. It was not just timid commanders like Philip Augustus who avoided battle. Even a man like Richard I who at times in skirmishes and on reconnaissance patrols seems to have been recklessly brave, did not seek battle. In this sense Richard's military career was an unremarkable one but it is surely worth noting that the most famous soldier of the day shared to the full the reluctance of less distinguished commanders.[21]

Battles then were rare events. This is an observation which has become a commonplace.[22] Yet historians seem to have been content to stop there. Very rarely have they gone on to ask what it was that armies were doing when they were not fighting battles. Thus books on the art of war in the middle ages still tend to focus on battles, and not on the army's typical activities; they concentrate on the exceptional rather than the routine, indeed they fail to make clear just what the routine was.[23] And it is with this neglected side of warfare, the

---

16 Ambroise 11. 11455—11652. The most recent account of these events from Saladin's point of view certainly makes it appear that no battle took place, M.C. Lyons and D.E.P. Jackson, *Saladin: The Politics of the Holy War*, Cambridge 1982, 358.

17 So lucidly demonstrated by Smail, 138—40.

18 Howden, *Gesta* i 120. And see below n. 25. His famous encounters with Philip Augustus, at Fréteval 4 July 1194 and near Gisors 28 September 1198, were pursuits not battles, since on both occasions Philip ran for cover and made no effort to fight.

19 Fantosme 11. 111—13.

20 Georges Duby, *Le Dimanche de Bouvines*, Paris 1973, 156.

21 Compare Fulk Rechin's summary account of the military career of his turbulent grandfather Fulk Nerra. In over fifty years as count of Anjou (987—1040) Fulk, described as a man of *probitas magna et admirabilis* fought just two pitched battles: *Chroniques des comtes d'Anjou et des seigneurs d'Amboise* ed. L. Halphen and R. Poupardin, Paris 1913, 233—4.

22 See, for example, Duby, 142 f; Verbruggen, 288; J.H. Beeler, *Warfare in Feudal Europe 780—1200*, Ithaca 1971, 45, 57, 116. H. Delbrück, *Geschichte der Kriegskunst im Rahmen der politischen Geschichte* Part 3, 2nd edn. Berlin 1923, 344—5.

23 One of the few authors to devote much attention to an army's 'typical activities' is H.J.

planning of a routine campaign, that I shall be concerned.

Most campaigns did not end in battle largely because both commanders were reluctant to risk battle. This was in accord with the advice given in what is perhaps the best book ever written on medieval warfare — and one read by many medieval commanders: the *De Re Militari* by Vegetius. This late Roman handbook on war remained popular thoughout the middle ages and was frequently translated into the vernacular.[24] Vegetius' advice on giving battle was quite simple: Don't. Well, you might occasionally, if you heavily outnumbered your enemy, if their morale was poor, their supplies short, if they were tired and poorly led, then in these circumstances you might, but otherwise, no. Normally battle was the last resort. 'Every plan therefore is to be considered, every expedient tried and every method taken before matters are brought to this last extremity'.[25] Some rulers indeed took this advice so much to heart that they actually issued formal prohibitions, ordering their commanders not to engage in battle: Charles V after Poitiers, Louis XI after Montlhéry, Charles VII during the greater part of his reign.[26] Why this hostility to battle both in the commonplace theory of Vegetius and in the normal practice of medieval generals? What were the potential advantages and disadvantages of battle?

If the aim of war was either to win or hold territory and this meant taking or keeping strongpoints — castles and fortified towns — then victory in battle might, in some circumstances, bring a decisive advantage.[27] It did, for example for Saladin in 1187 and probably would have done even if he had not captured Guy of Lusignan at the Battle of Hattin. Crucial here was the kingdom of Jerusalem's desperate shortage of garrison troops. In these circumstances a battle-seeking strategy made sense — and in these circumstances ravaging could be used in order to provoke or tempt the defender to battle.[28] It made sense, for example, for William of Normandy in 1066 since, given both the

Hewitt, *The Black Prince's expedition of 1355—1357*, Manchester 1958, 46—75; H.J. Hewitt, *The Organization of War under Edward III*, Manchester 1966, 99—118. See also Eric Christiansen, *The Northern Crusades: The Baltic and the Catholic Frontier 1100—1525*, London 1980, 160—69.
24 Walter Goffart, 'The date and purpose of Vegetius' *De Re Militari*, *Traditio* 33, 1977, 65—100; Alexander Murray, *Reason and Society in the Middle Ages*, Oxford 1978, 127—30; Diane Bornstein, 'Military Strategy in Malory and Vegetius' *De Re Militari*, *Comparative Literature Studies 9*, 1972, 123—129.
25 Vegetius, *Epitoma rei militaris*, ed. C. Lang, Leipzig 1885, 86—9 and, in particular p. 86 'Ideo omnia ante cogitanda sunt, ante temptanda, ante facienda sunt, quam ad ultimum veniatur abruptum.' It seems likely that Richard indeed held all the advantages when he fought his 1176 battle against the Brabançons. According to Howden 'magnum exercitum congrevagit de Pictavia, et magna militum multitudo de circumjacentibus regionibus ad eum confluebat, propter ipsius stipendia quae illis dabantur. Et cum omnes essent congregati, promovit exercitum suum . . ,' Howden, *Gesta* i 120. The contrast between medieval and modern attitudes to battle can be overdrawn. As Delbrück noted — though with some reluctance — 'Auch ein moderner Feldherr schlägt in der Regel nicht, ohne dass er auf den Sieg rechnet,' Delbrück, vol. 3, 345. It may well be the case that much of Vegetius' strategic advice consisted of no more than 'eternal common-sense principles' (Smail, 15 n.l.); but platitudes have their uses.
26 Contamine 379.
27 As was pointed out by the author of the *Chronica de gestis consulum Andegavorum*, a work closely linked with the Angevin court of the mid 12th century, Halphen and Poupardin 55—6.
28 R.C. Smail, 'The Predicaments of Guy of Lusignan 1183—1187', in *Outremer — Studies in the History of the Crusading Kingdom of Jerusalem. Presented to Joshua Prawer*, Jerusalem 1982, 159—176. cf. Guillaume de Poitiers, *Histoire de Guillaume le Conquérant* ed. Raymond Foreville, Paris 1952, 180.

volatile nature of Northern French politics and the massive preparations which the 1066 expedition had required, it was highly improbable that he would ever again have so large an army at his disposal.[29] Guy of Lusignan, of course, was also faced by the dangerous temptation of having an exceptionally large army under his command and, in the end, he chose a battle-risking strategy.[30] (On the other hand it seems unlikely that this was Harold Godwineson's predicament in October 1066).

But the fact that some victories in battle brought decisive gains — and these, of course, are the famous battles — should not lead us into assuming that most victories did. If we take the example of Richard's three victories in battle then one was decisive but two were not. His defeat of the *routiers* in 1176 facilitated the rapid capture of all the major rebel strongholds, including both Limoges and Angoulême.[31] On the other hand neither Arsuf (1191) nor Jaffa (1192) resulted in a signficant shift of the strategic balance in his favour. From the attacker's point of view if the defender's strongpoints were still able to offer prolonged resistance, allowing the defender time to re-organise and raise fresh troops, then victory in battle would have achieved little. From the defender's point of view if he could force the enemy to withdraw without battle then he would have achieved his aim with relatively little risk. Battle was a desperately chancy business. A few minutes of confusion or panic and the patient work of months or years might be undone. Moreover although comparatively few knights were actually killed in battle, the king or prince who committed his cause to battle was also putting himself in jeopardy since it was always clear that the surest way to win a battle was to kill or capture the opposing commander.[32] As Smail pointed out in the course of a superb analysis of the defensive strategy of the Franks of Outremer, in a well-managed campaign 'the rewards of victory could be won by other means which did not involve the penalties of defeat.'[33]

What then were these 'other means'? What, in other words, were Richard's twenty five years of campaigning all about? I begin with some advice on how to make war, advice attributed to Count Philip of Flanders, and recorded in Jordan Fantosme's metrical *Chronicle*. In the course of a 'reasoned speech' the count envisages William, King of the Scots invading Northumbria as an ally of Louis VII of France.

> Let him aid you in war, swiftly and without delay
> Destroy your foes and lay waste their country
> By fire and burning let all be set alight
> That nothing be left for them, either in wood or meadow
> Of which in the morning they could have a meal.

29 R. Allen Brown, *The Normans and the Norman Conquest*, London 1969, 145—52.
30 On Guy's motives see Smail, 'The Predicaments' and Hans Eberhard Mayer, 'Henry II of England and the Holy Land' *EHR* xcvii, 1982, 721—39.
31 Howden, *Gesta* i 120—1.
32 On the eve of Agincourt 'eighteen esquires of the French army . . . bound themselves by oath that . . . they would with their united strength force themselves sufficiently near to the king of England to strike the crown from off his head, or that they would all die, which they did', Harris Nicholas, *The History of the Battle of Agincourt*, London 1833, 250.
33 Smail, *Crusading Warfare* 139. Cf. Vegetius, 91—2: 'Illa enim ante temptanda sunt, quae si male cesserint, minus noceant, si bene, plurimum prosint.'

Then with his *united* force let him besiege their castles.

....

Thus should war be begun: such is my advice.
First lay waste the land.[34]

The aim, in other words, is to capture your opponents' strongpoints, but the first stage is to ravage the countryside in order to deprive them of supplies — 'so that nothing is left for them . . . of which they could have a meal'. *Then* besiege their castles. This was in fact the strategy adopted by King William during his invasion of the north in 1173. Eventually an English army moved up to confront him; William made a brave speech about standing and fighting, about never yielding a single foot of the land which rightfully belonged to him — all the proper sentiments — but in fact he withdrew. He left Northumbria, however, in ruin, devastated in extreme famine. As the poet said —

King William knows well how to fight his foe
How to grieve and damage them.[35]

If one looks at Richard's campaigns in Europe, whether against rebels in Aquitaine or against King Philip of France, this, it is soon clear, is the pattern to which they conform — a pattern of ravaging and besieging.[36]

In 12th and 13th century sources ravaging is frequently referred to but infrequently described. One source, however, the *Chanson des Lorrains* contains an unusually detailed description of an army advancing through enemy territory which is well worth quoting.

The march begins. Out in front are the scouts and incendiaries. After them come the foragers whose job it is to collect the spoils and carry them in the great baggage train. Soon all is in tumult. The peasants, having just come out to the fields, turn back, uttering loud cries. The shepherds gather their flocks and drive them towards the neighbouring woods in the hope of saving them. The incendiaries set the villages on fire and the foragers visit and sack them. The terrified inhabitants are either burned or led away with their hands tied to be held for ransom. Everywhere bells ring the alarm; a surge of fear sweeps over the countryside. Wherever you look you can see helmets glinting in the sun, pennons waving in the breeze, the whole plain covered with horsemen. Money, cattle, mules and sheep are all seized. The smoke billows and spreads, flames crackle. Peasants and shepherds scatter in all directions.[37]

34 Fantosme 11. 439—50 (my italics). With minor alterations I preferred to retain the familiar lines of Howlett's translation, *Chronicles of the Reigns of Stephen, Henry II and Richard I*, ed. R. Howlett, vol. 3, RS 1886, 241—3. The sequence of first ravaging then besieging is well brought out in the 'Plantagenet' account (see n. 27) of Geoffrey Martel's attack on Tours, Halphen and Poupardin 55—6.
35 Fantosme 11. 657—8.
36 See, for example, the importance of devastation as a preliminary to the most famous of Richard's early deeds, the capture of Taillebourg in 1179, Ralph Diceto, *Opera Historica* ed. W. Stubbs, RS 1876, i 431—2. Time and again Geoffrey of Vigeois, a chronicler who had the misfortune to live in a war zone, emphasises the ravaging of the Limousin carried out by Richard, his subordinates and his enemies, especially in the years 1182—84, *Recueil des historiens des Gaules et de la France* 18, Paris 1879, 212—23.
37 Quoted in Achille Luchaire, *Social France at the time of Philip Augustus* trans. E.B. Krehbiel, London 1912, 261.

It is clear that there was nothing unusual about this. This is how Charlemagne operated: we might think of Einhard's description of Avar territory turned into desert by Charlemagne's armies and of the huge waggon loads of plunder.[38] This is how Edward III, the Black Prince, and Henry V operated: remember Henry V's dictum: war without fire is like sausages without mustard.[39] This indeed is the essence of war as perceived by Vegetius: 'the main and principal point in war is to secure plenty of provisions for oneself and to destroy the enemy by famine. Famine is more terrible than the sword.'[40] The point about ravaging was that it simultaneously achieved both these ends. Moreover as an efficient method of waging war it made sense not only from the point of view of the overall campaign strategy of the army commander; it made sense also from the point of view of the individual soldier who was fighting for private profit, for plunder.

In the face of this threat to his territory what strategy could the defender adopt? His main object would be to deprive the attacker of supplies either by preventing him from ravaging (or 'foraging' as it is frequently and euphemistically termed) or — in cases where the attacker was chiefly relying on his supply lines — by cutting those supply lines. In the first instance the defender's usual strategy was to assemble an army and move it up to confront the invader. If he approached too close then he might find himself compelled to fight a battle in unfavourable circumstances — as happened to Harold in October 1066 — but it was not necessary to come as close as this in order to achieve his aim. The mere presence of an opposing army somewhere in the vicinity was normally enough to force the invader to keep his own army together and thus prevent him from ravaging and plundering — since these were operations which involved the dispersal of troops over a wide area. As Count Philip advised, after the devastation 'Then with his *united* force let him besiege their castles.' The ravaging, in other words, was done by scattered forces.

Obviously any defender who could catch an invader while his troops were dispersed had won a great advantage.[41] Reconnaissance was vital for both sides. In 1173 King William was informed of the English advance and withdrew; in 1174 he was attacked at Alnwick while his troops were scattered and he himself was captured. Jordan Fantosme reports a discussion between the English commanders as they advanced towards Alnwick.

> Said Ranulf de Glanville: Let us act wisely.
> Let us send a scout to estimate their numbers.[42]

---

38 Éginhard, *Vie de Charlemagne* ed. and trans. L. Halphen, 3rd edn. Paris 1947, pp. 38—40.
39 The culinary opinion attributed to Henry V by Juvenal des Ursins, *Histoire de Charles VI* in ed. J.A. Buchon, *Choix des Chroniques*, Paris 1875, p. 565. 'il respondit que ce n'estoit que usance de guerre, et que guerre sans feu ne valoit rien, non plus que andouilles sans moustarde.'
40 'Saepius enim penuria quam pugna consumit exercitum et ferro saevior fames est . . . In omni expeditione unum est et maximum telum, ut tibi sufficiat victus, hostes frangat inopia.' Vegetius, 69.
41 See, for example, *Gesta Henrici Quinti* ed. and trans. F. Taylor and J.S. Roskell, Oxford 1975, 22. Vegetius pointed out that in these circumstances an able commander had an ideal opportunity to 'blood' his less experienced troops, Vegetius, 91.
42 Fantosme 11. 1738—9

They do this and on learning that most of the Scots were away plundering the countryside, they rode through the night and took William by surprise while he was guarded only by a small force. Normally, of course, commanders were not as careless as William had been, but it is clear from this example that the defender only had to keep his own army in being in order to achieve his objective of stopping the enemy from ravaging. From the point of view of the invading troops once they could no longer go out plundering, soldiering lost its appeal and they just wanted to go home. Unquestionably there were men who enjoyed going to war, but there were very few, if any, who enjoyed the imminent prospect of a pitched battle.

In the case where an invader was relying more on supply lines than ravaging then the defender's obvious course was to try to cut those lines. The most dramatic example of the successful use of this strategy is undoubtedly the Egyptian campaign of 1249—50. After the crusaders had captured Damietta (summer 1249) Louis IX held a council meeting:

> The king summoned all the barons of the army to decide in what direction he should go, whether to Alexandria or to Cairo. The good Comte Pierre Bretagne, as well as the majority of the barons, agreed in advising him to go and besiege Alexandria, because that city had a good harbour, where the ships bringing food for the army could land their supplies. But the Comte d'Artois was of a contrary opinion, maintaining that he would never agree to their going anywhere except to Cairo, because it was the chief city in the kingdom of Egypt, and if you wished to kill the serpent, you must first of all crush its head. The king rejected the barons' advice in favour of his brother's.[43]

So the crusaders advanced up the Nile. In February 1250 they won a battle at Mansourah. Joinville's setpiece description contains a splendid account of the chaos and confusion of the battle and, incidentally, makes clear the crucial role of the king's contingent of crossbowmen. But the victory brought no real advantage to the crusaders. Egyptian re-inforcements came up and both sides settled down — once again — to the round of trench warfare and mutual artillery bombardment that is so typical of medieval war.

> A fortnight later the Turks did something that came as a great shock to our people. In order to starve us they took several of their galleys lying upstream above our camp, and after dragging them overland put them back into the river, a good league below the place where our tents were pitched. These galleys caused a famine among us; for because they were there no one dared to come up the river from Damietta to bring us fresh supplies of food.[44]

The sickness in the crusader camp then reached such devastating proportions that total surrender became unavoidable. The whole army, king and nobles all included, either died or were made prisoner. Not even the battles of Hattin and Hastings had been as decisive as this. Vegetius, of course, had made the point

---

43 Joinville, *The Life of Saint Louis* in trans. M.R.B. Shaw, *Chronicles of the Crusades*, Harmondsworth 1963, 210.
44 Joinville 237.

explicit: 'Time and opportunity may help to retrieve other misfortunes, but where forage and provisions have not been carefully provided for, the evil is utterly without remedy.'[45] The Egyptian campaign of 1250 is certainly exceptional in the scale of its consequences but it serves to highlight the crucial — and perennial — problem of the relationship between supply and disease. In this context it is worth noting the Third Crusade casualty list preserved by Roger of Howden.[46] Of the 98 people on the list fourteen are picked out as being either drowned, captured or killed. Presumably at least most of the other eighty-four died of other causes of which the diseases of the army camp are by far the most likely.[47] Ambroise made the point:

> I dare say too with certainty,
> By famine and by malady
> More than 3,000 were struck down
> At the siege of Acre and in the town.

Though it should be said that in Ambroise's eyes an even bigger killer was self-imposed chastity.

> In pilgrims' hearing I declare
> A hundred thousand men died there
> Because from women they abstained.
> 'Twas for love they restrained
> Themselves. They had not perished thus
> Had they not been abstemious.[48]

The principal duty of a general then was to ensure that his troops were kept reasonably fit and well-fed and usually, of course, there were plenty of women with the army.[49] The point is an obvious one, but its implications are rarely brought out. What, for example, did an army camp look like? Ambroise describes one for us:

> As if it were a market town
> Oxen and cows and goats and swine
> Most vigorous and fair and fine
> And rams and sheep and lambs were there
> And many a goodly colt and mare
> And cock and hen and fat capon
> And full-fleshed mules —.[50]

45 'Deinde reliquis casibus potest in tempore subveniri, pabulatio et annona in necessitate remedium non habent, nisi ante condantur.' Vegetius, 69. See, for example, the fate of the German army in Asia Minor in 1190, Lyons and Jackson 315.
46 Howden, *Gesta* ii 147—50.
47 During the American-Mexican war of 1846—8, for example, 1100 U.S. soldiers died of disease and only 150 as a result of enemy action. See the table in Parker, *Warfare*, 216.
48 Ambroise 11. 12, 237 ff.
49 So many essential services did female camp followers perform that an army without women is hard to imagine; see, for example, the reference to their work of washing, cleaning and de-lousing the troops, — *E d'espucer valeient singes* Ambroise 11. 5696—99. In crusader armies, of course, women were always felt to be a problem and indeed in Muslim eyes their activities, whether military or sexual, sometimes took on legendary proportions. See the passage from Imad ad-Din quoted in F. Gabrieli, *Arab Historians of the Crusades*, London 1969, 204—7.
50 Ambroise 11. 1676—84. See Joinville, 233 for a reference to 'the butchers and . . . the women

Problems of disease and supply were doubtless more prominent in the Middle East but they were obviously in no sense confined to that theatre of war. No sooner had Henry II taken the cross than he wrote to Frederick Barbarossa, Bela of Hungary and Isaac Angelus to ensure that his army had an adequate market — *victualium copiosum mercatum* — as it passed through their territories.[51] When Richard I returned to Normandy in 1194 to find Philip Augustus laying siege to Verneuil his response was to send a force round to the east of Verneuil to cut the French king's supply lines. This compelled Philip to abandon the siege — in such haste indeed that he left behind rich pickings for the garrison of Verneuil.[52] In 1197 Philip invaded Flanders and Count Baldwin, instead of bringing the French to battle, concentrated on blocking roads and breaking down bridges. No supply wagons could get through and so the French troops were forced to try to live off the land i.e. they were forced to ravage when it was dangerous for them to do so. Dispersed in this manner they became hopelessly vulnerable to Count Baldwin's well-timed counter-attacks. According to the Coggeshall chronicler they even suffered the indignity of being beaten by bands of Flemish women. As a result Philip had to sue for peace and accept humiliating terms.[53]

What about the strategy of attack?

Richard, of course, is famous as an aggressive commander — leading the attempt to capture Jerusalem, and then, later in the 1190s, recovering the territory lost while he was in prison. A close look at these campaigns makes it clear that supply problems were decisive in the shaping of strategy. Turning first to the crusade, we find that, having captured Cyprus, Richard used it as a supply base. On his arrival at Acre he was given a rapturous welcome — and Ambroise explains why.

> The king, by taking Cyprus, had
> Made all the army to be glad
> For therefrom would they food derive
> To keep the mighty host alive.[54]

After the capture of Acre Richard then led the army south along the coast road to Jaffa, the nearest port to Jerusalem. The army was accompanied by supply ships and the waggon train, of course; even so Muslim observers noted there were not enough transport animals and so Richard ordered that each man

---

who sold provisions'. According to al-Maqrizi there were no less than 7,000 shops in Saladin's army market outside Acre. The opposing Frankish market may well have been smaller; on the other hand it seems to have outstripped the Muslim camp in terms of wine-shops and brothels, Lyons and Jackson 308, 329.

51 Diceto, ii 51—54.

52 'Tant fist li reis qui molt fu sages/Que trestoz toli les passages/Par unt la viande veneit/A rei qui le siege teneit/E par icest mesestance/S'en departi le reis de France.' *Histoire de Guillaume* 11. 10491—96. Rigord, *Gesta Philippi Augusti* ed. H.F. Delaborde, *Oeuvres de Rigord et de Guillaume le Breton*, Paris 1882—85, i 127.

53 Roger of Howden, *Chronica*, ed. W. Stubbs, RS 1868—71, iv 20; Ralph of Coggeshall, *Chronicon Anglicanum* ed. J. Stevenson, RS 1875, 77—8; William of Newburgh, *Historia Rerum Anglicarum* ed. R. Howlett in *Chronicles*, ii 495—6.

54 Ambroise 11. 2366—70; Cf. 11. 1896—1902; 2102—6. John Prestwich has adduced plausible grounds for believing that the conquest of Cyprus, far from being accidental, may have been in Richard's mind from the outside of his crusade, Prestwich, 8—9, 12.

should carry ten days supply of food. This meant that they advanced very slowly — covering the 81 miles to Jaffa in 19 days — but they got there in a classic demonstration of fighting on the march. It was a dogged march which won the admiration of Saladin's secretary, who was well aware that the slow pace was conditioned by the needs of the heavily burdened foot soldiers.[55] But even so this rate of four miles a day was lightning fast when compared with the speed of the advance from Jaffa towards Jerusalem.

The army began to leave Jaffa on 31 October 1191. On 22 November it camped at Ramleh, approximately ten miles inland. Why was the advance so slow? Because if they had simply marched inland Saladin would cut off their supplies. Therefore the road behind them had to be protected by castles and since Saladin had systematically been destroying all strongpoints (except Jerusalem itself), this meant that they had to be, equally methodically, rebuilt.[56] At Ramleh Richard waited six weeks, stockpiling supplies, while the winter weather got worse and worse.[57] What was Richard doing? Why the delay? Because essentially this was a war of skirmishing and attrition. The question was, who could hold their army together the longer, Richard or Saladin? Winter was traditionally the season when supplies ran out and armies were disbanded. Saladin's men were tired and hungry and wanted to go home. Eventually Saladin had to bow to this pressure; he himself withdrew behind the walls of Jerusalem while the bulk of his army dispersed. Now at last Richard could advance again. By early January he was at Beit Nuba, another ten miles inland and about twelve miles from Jerusalem. He had brought with him enough supplies to be able to lay siege to the city and then, having captured it, to stand siege himself.[58] But, as is well known, he never advanced those last twelve miles. On a second occasion, six months later in June 1192, he again advanced to Beit Nuba — and this time, having fortified the roads, was able to do so more quickly. This time the journey from the coast took only five days. But again at Beit Nuba he gave the order to withdraw. On both occasions it is clear that the question of supplies was uppermost in the mind of the army council. Despite all their efforts, that supply line to the coast just looked too vulnerable — and even if they did take Jerusalem and hold it while the crusaders were there, what would happen when they returned to Europe? The answer to this question was clear and there can be no doubt that, in terms of military strategy, Richard and his advisers took the right decision — though they were of course bitterly unpopular ones.[59] In purely military terms Jerusalem was not a sensible objective — and Richard indeed had been reluctant to go for it in the first place. His own strategy had been to march down the coast, capture Ascalon and Daran, cutting the caravan route between Egypt and Syria, and then go for an attack on Egypt itself — the standard 13th

55 Ambroise 11. 5549 ff. Verbruggen 212—15.
56 Ambroise 11. 7029 ff; 7181—3; 7209—14; 7447—60; 7614—5; Lyons and Jackson 341. More drastic than Saladin was Theobald IV of Champagne in 1229 when 'he set fire to all his towns himself before his enemies could reach them so that they would not find them full of supplies', Joinville, 184.
57 Ambroise 11. 7471—78, cf. 7635—42.
58 Ambroise 11. 7610—53.
59 Ambroise 11. 7,700—16; 10,161—70. Lyons and Jackson 345—6.

century strategy, and a sensible one.[60]

About Richard's campaigns in the West we possess much less detailed information than we do about the crusade, but I would like to call attention to one matter — the building of Château-Gaillard. We know that in the space of two years up to September 1198 he spent about £11,500 on this. This is a fantastically large sum. In the whole of his reign he spent £7,000 on *all* English castles. The nearest approach to the expenditure on Château-Gaillard is the sum of nearly £7,000 spent on Dover between 1180 and 1190.[61] So £11,500 in two years is phenomenal. What was it for? The conventional answer is that it was meant to defend Rouen, to plug a gap in the Norman defences. But in the years of its building Richard was not on the defensive. He was recovering those castles which had been lost while he was in prison in Germany, so a place has to be found for Château-Gaillard within a strategy of aggression. Château-Gaillard and the new town Andeli, associated with it, was to be the forward base from which the Vexin was conquered. Men and supplies could be sent up the Seine from the main arsenal at Rouen. Richard built river boats — long ships — for this purpose. Or they could travel by road, taking a more direct route which crossed the Seine twice — at Pont de l'Arche and Portjoie. Richard we know built bridges, residences and castles along this royal and military road between Rouen and Andeli. The pattern of Richard's advance into the Vexin is, in other words, a very similar one to the pattern of Richard's advance from Jaffa.[62]

By way of conclusion I would like to make two points, one particular and one general. First, that as an army commander Richard was very far from being the impetuous leader of romantic legend.[63] Rather, his usual approach was methodical and carefully prepared. His strategy was based on the systematic use of magazines, supply lines and ravaging, the 'strategy of manoeuvre' which is usually associated with a later period, but the strategy which was in fact adopted by all good medieval generals. This kind of war is largely a matter of effective administration and one of the most comic of modern misunderstandings of Richard I is the widely accepted view that he was a poor administrator.[64]

Secondly, developing further this view of medieval warfare, I would argue that victory in battle normally offered rewards sufficient to offset the risks involved only in those societies where the science of fortification was relatively poorly developed. But, as is well known, throughout most of the European

---

60 Gillingham, *Richard* 194, 300—1.

61 R.A. Brown, *English Castles* (2nd edn.) 1976, 160—61.

62 Gillingham, *Richard* 262—265. Delaborde, i 207—209. Undoubtedly Richard's intention was 'to recover territory not to gain it' (Prestwich 11), but within the Vexin, as elsewhere along the Angevin—Capetian frontier, this meant adopting an aggressive campaign strategy.

63 It remains true of course, that his prowess and recklessness made him a legend in his own lifetime. This was an image of the king which he himself took pains to cultivate — not surprisingly since it was politically valuable and helped to maintain the morale of his troops, Prestwich 4—5, 14; Gillingham, *Richard*, 284—5.

64 On the importance of administrative preparation, Keegan 296. According to the *Encyclopaedia Americana* 773, Montgomery's successes in World War II induced British military experts to add two 'new' ideas to their list of strategic maxims; thorough administrative preparation and careful provision for the maintenance of troop morale!

Middle Ages this science was a higly developed one. Fortification consumed a significant proportion of men's financial resources and, on the whole, the technology of defence was more than equal to the challenging technology of artillery. In these circumstances a Napoleonic or Clausewitzian *Niederwerfungsstrategie* made little sense.[65] It may well be that for much of its history England has been a special case in that relatively little was spent on fortification. This seems to have been so before 1066 and was certainly so from the 15th century onwards, when English patrons and their architects — unlike their continental counterparts — felt no compulsion to develop defence systems capable of resisting the revolutionary siege artillery of the late 14th century. In consequence warfare in England has been fairly battle-orientated, both in the Wars of the Roses and in civil wars of the 17th century.[66] But in this respect the military history of England has been a peculiar one. In European medieval history as a whole battles are rare and making war did not normally involve seeking battle.

The dominance of the fortified strongpoint meant that wars were mostly wars of attrition and that, in consequence, there was a demand for soldiers who were experts in this kind of war: garrison troops, artillerymen (engineers) and bowmen, incendiaries and foragers. The infantry arm, in other words, was vitally important. Cavalry, of course, was also important, particularly when out on reconnaissance patrol or escorting and guarding foraging parties. But it would be difficult to think of generalisations more misleading than such statements as in the Middle Ages 'the principal arm in any military force was the heavy cavalry' or that as a result of 'deeply significant' Renaissance innovations 'defence became superior to offence' and infantry 'more decisive'.[67] All such statements are based upon a view of medieval warfare which sees it as being largely composed of battles dominated by the charge of heavily armoured knights. But against this view, distorted by its reliance on evidence concerning exceptional and therefore news-worthy occasions we must bear in mind the routine reality of medieval warfare, and the army commander's constant effort 'to secure plenty of provisions for himself and to destroy the enemy by famine'. For the medieval reality of war was very like the medieval theory of war as outlined by Vegetius and it was in his cautious mastery of the logistics of Vegetian warfare that even a 'romantic hero' like Richard I showed his real competence as a general.

65 It is for this reason that some historians have concluded that in the Middle Ages strategy 'im höheren Sinne des Wortes' could not really have existed, Delbrück 3, 344.
66 There is the further point that in civil wars both sides, in order not to alienate the people whose support they are seeking, are usually under great pressure to avoid ravaging and to bring the war to a swift conclusion. They are thus more willing to seek and to risk battle — to act, as Defoe put it in commenting on the English Civil Wars 'as if they had been in haste to have their Brains knock'd out'. John Gillingham, *The Wars of the Roses*, London 1981, 15—50; John Gillingham, *Cromwell: Portrait of a Soldier*, London 1976, 23—28.
67 Parker, 201—3.

SECURING THE NORTH:
INVASION AND THE STRATEGY OF DEFENCE IN TWELFTH-CENTURY ANGLO-SCOTTISH WARFARE

Matthew Strickland

The northern border of the Anglo-Norman kingdom presented the Norman and Angevin kings with one of the most significant problems of defence outside Normandy and the Vexin. Unlike Wales, whose fragmented polity of petty warring kingdoms restricted the nature of aggression largely to guerilla warfare within its own boundaries, sporadic revolt and the harrying of marcher lordships, Scotland confronted the rulers of England with a kingdom increasingly unified, and increasingly adopting Norman social, political and military institutions.[1] The Scots were consistently able to field large armies and carry war far beyond the frontier into England. Though much weaker than her southern neighbour in wealth, manpower and military technology, Scotland exploited the political and strategic embarrassments of the English kings to the full. It is far from accidental that the two principal periods of Scottish aggression in the twelfth century should correspond to the civil war of Stephen's reign and the great revolt of 1173–4 against Henry II. It was the war of 1173–4 which first revealed the full strategic potential of the 'Auld Alliance' with France, of such fundamental importance to future Anglo-Scottish affairs.[2]

Anglo-Scottish relations were not, of course, on a constant war footing. Indeed, the twelfth century saw sustained periods of peaceful and even harmonious co-existence.[3] Yet to emphasize the disparity between such lengthy periods of *de facto* peace that existed between 1093 and 1136, 1154–1173, and 1174–1209 and the comparatively brief periods of war is to run the risk of distortion by hindsight. For to contemporaries, the political *status quo* was always potentially volatile, and the Scottish kings' claim to Cumbria and Northumbria provided a constant *casus*

---

[1] For general discussions of these developments see R. L. G. Ritchie, *The Normans in Scotland* (Edinburgh, 1954); A. A. M. Duncan, *Scotland: The Making of the Kingdom* (Edinburgh, 1975); G. W. S. Barrow, *The Anglo-Norman Era in Scottish History* (Oxford, 1980); G. W. S. Barrow, *Kingship and Unity: Scotland 1000–1306* (London, 1981).

[2] William the Lion's alliance with France in 1173–4 formed part of a wider coalition centred on the Young King, to whom William had sworn homage and fealty. It was the culmination, however, of several years of shared Franco-Scottish antipathy against Henry II (Duncan, 227–9). The fullest contemporary description of the alliance and its diplomatic background is furnished by Jordan Fantosme (*Jordan Fantosme's Chronicle*, ed. and trans. R. C. Johnston (Oxford, 1981), hereafter Fantosme), ll. 242–458. Fantosme clearly regarded Louis VII as the prime mover in enlisting the support of the Scots king for the allied cause.

[3] For general surveys of Anglo-Scottish relations in this period see Ritchie, *passim*; Duncan, 216–55; W. L. Warren, *Henry II* (London, 1973), 169–87; A. O. Anderson, 'Anglo-Scottish Relations from Constantine II to William', *Scottish Historical Review* xli (1963), 1–20.

belli.[4] The threat of invasion was never too distant, the problems of defence remained ever present.

I propose to approach the subject of Anglo-Norman defence of the northern border principally through a study of the campaigns of 1138 and 1173–4, which represented the most serious incursions by a Scottish army into England during the twelfth century, and in particular to examine two closely connected themes. The first is the role of the castle in defence and its relationship to the operations of the English field army. The second is the circumstances in which pitched battle was offered, denied or joined. A major trend in recent medieval military historiography has been to stress – and rightly so – the caution and reluctance of commanders to engage in full-scale battle unless circumstances weighed heavily in their favour.[5] The majority of this work, however, has concerned either warfare between the rulers of the principalities of north-west France, where opposing forces were of a similar nature, or warfare in the Latin East, where armies might enjoy at least the potential for being evenly matched. By contrast, Anglo-Scottish warfare presents us with a theatre of war in which there was a permanent and decisive military imbalance in favour of the southern kingdom. A sophisticated and professional Anglo-Norman military elite confronted the hybrid forces of a tribal amalgam bolstered by a small core of newly planted feudal settlers, mercenaries and Franco-Norman adventurers.[6] The composition of the Scottish armies, the paucity of defensive equipment among the native infantry and in particular their lack of a powerful cavalry arm profoundly affected the strategy of the respective armies. On the one hand, Anglo-Norman commanders consistently sought to exploit this disparity, and in so doing displayed considerably less reluctance about offering battle than their counterparts in other theatres of war. On the other, the Scots sought to avoid full-scale engagements wherever possible. For them, the caution in committing troops to battle displayed by many contemporary commanders was not a choice, but a necessity. The disastrous outcome of the one major engagement where the Scots had assumed the offensive, that of the Standard in 1138, only served to highlight these dictates and emphasize the wisdom of non-engagement.

Any discussion of border defence must, of course, begin with the castle. It was one of Allen Brown's central contentions that we must view the castle as a multi-functional unit; as an administrative centre, as a base for offensive as much as defensive operations, and above all as a seigneurial residence.[7] The following observations will, I hope, only serve to reinforce these views, but given that the needs of defence were integral to the conception of the castle, it is worth using the

---

4 On the nature of these claims see Duncan, 216–55. Cf. also M. O. Anderson, 'Lothian and the Early Scottish Kings', *Scottish Historical Review* xxxix (1960), 98–112.

5 See in particular R. C. Smail, *Crusading Warfare, 1097–1193* (Cambridge, 1956), especially 138–204; J. Bradbury, 'Battles in England and Normandy, 1066–1154', *ante* vi, 1984, 1–12; J. Gillingham, 'Richard I and the Science of War in the Middle Ages', *War and Government in the Middle Ages*, ed. J. Gillingham and J. C. Holt (Woodbridge, 1984), 78–91; J. Gillingham, 'War and Chivalry in the History of William the Marshal', *Thirteenth-Century England II. Proceedings of the Newcastle upon Tyne Conference, 1987*, ed. P. R. Cross and S. D. Lloyd (1988), 1–13; J. Gillingham, 'William the Bastard at War', *Studies in Medieval History Presented to R. Allen Brown*, ed. C. Harper-Bill, C. J. Holdsworth and J. L. Nelson (Woodbridge, 1989), 141–158.

6 Below, 190–4.

7 R. A. Brown, *English Castles* (London, 3rd edn, 1976), particularly 172–213.

Anglo-Scottish evidence as a case study to examine the function of the castle in frontier defence.

Scottish attacks on England were invariably heralded by assaults on castles such as Wark, Carlisle or Norham, and the narrative sources give the firm impression that these frontier fortresses, supported by others further behind the border, formed the primary element of defence.[8] Jordan Fantosme, for example, devotes much of his poem to the heroic defence of Wark, Carlisle, Alnwick, Prudhoe and Newcastle by Henry II's castellans.[9] Looking, moreover, at a map plotting the location and density of castles in Cumbria, Northumberland and Yorkshire it is tempting to suppose the existence of a castle 'network' and to speak in terms of 'defence in depth'. Professor John Beeler, indeed, took such a notion to its extremes by suggesting that the majority of early Norman castles in England, both royal and baronial, had been sited according to some coherent strategic masterplan, designed principally by William I, in order to meet the needs of national defence.[10] It is not my intention here to discuss Beeler's thesis in detail. Professor Hollister has already provided a balanced critique, which accepts elements of a planned defence, such as the rapes of Sussex or the three great earldoms of the Welsh marches, yet rejects 'the idea of a national – an *English* – system of defensive strongholds against some foreign invader'.[11]

For the Northern march, Beeler is surely right to point to the significance of the fact, first observed by Hunter-Blair, that of the fifteen Northumbrian baronies eight had castles prior to 1189, but seven did not.[12] This suggests that castle distribution, far from being the result of indiscriminate building, might be profoundly affected by royal policy on the licensing of castles.[13] But one must not

[8] Hence in 1136, David had seized the fortresses of Carlisle, Wark, Alnwick, Norham and Newcastle (Richard of Hexham, *De gestis regis Stephani et de bello Standardi* (hereafter Richard of Hexham), ed. J. Raine, *The Priory of Hexham, its Chroniclers, Endowments and Annals*, 2 vols (Surtees Society, xliv, 1868) (I, 63–10), 72; John of Hexham, *Historia Johannis, prioris Haugustadensis ecclesiae* (hereafter John of Hexham), ed. J. Raine, *The Priory of Hexham, its Chroniclers, Endowments and Annals*, 2 vols (Surtees Society, xliv, 1868) (I, 107–72), 114; Huntingdon, 258). The Scots retained Carlisle throughout Stephen's reign until Henry forced its restoration by Malcolm IV. Its recapture was one of William the Lion's chief goals, and he laid siege to it in both 1173 and 1174 (Fantosme ll. 609–24, 645–68; *Gesta regis Henrici secundi Benedicti abbatis*, ed. W. Stubbs, 2 vols (RS, 1867), 65. Because of its location, Wark frequently bore the brunt of initial Scottish assaults. In January 1138, William fitzDuncan led an unsuccessful dawn attack on Wark, which was followed shortly by an investment by David's main army (Richard of Hexham, 77; John of Hexham, 115). Wark was William's first target in 1173, and he besieged it again in 1174 (Fantosme ll. 477–81). Jordan Fantosme considered attacks on Wark as so synonymous with the declaration of war that on William the Lion's decision to invade England in 1173, he notes that among the Scots, 'You could hear many shouts of: "Let us go and capture the castle of Wark in England!" – no need to go far to hear them' (Fantosme ll. 461–2).
[9] Fantosme ll. 477–688, 1143–1446, 1475–1708.
[10] J. H. Beeler, 'Castles and Strategy in Norman and Early Angevin England', *Speculum* xxxi (1956), 581–601.
[11] C. W. Hollister, *The Military Organization of Norman England* (Oxford, 1965), 161–6.
[12] Beeler, 'Castles and Strategy', 592; C. H. Hunter-Blair, 'The Early Castles of Northumberland', *Archaeologia Aeliana*, fourth series, xxii (1944), 119.
[13] On royal castle policy see R. A. Brown, 'Royal Castle Building in England, 1154–1216', *EHR* lxx (1955), 353–98; R. A. Brown, 'A List of Castles, 1154–1216', *EHR* lxxiv (1959), 249–89. On the closely related subject of rendability see C. L. H. Coulson, 'Rendability and Castellation in Medieval France', *Château Gaillard* vi (1972), 59–67; C. L. H. Coulson, 'Fortress Policy in Capetian Tradition and Angevin Practice: Aspects of the Conquest of Normandy by Philip II', *ante* vi, 1984, 13–38; C. L. H. Coulson, 'The Impact of Bouvines upon the Fortress Policy of Philip Augustus', *Studies . . . Presented to R. Allen Brown*, 71–80.

confuse such a royal policy of castle-building, licensing or appropriation of baronial castles with the existence of a co-ordinated network of castles operating in war as a defensive entity. For it is highly questionable whether the majority of northern border castles were ever conceived of as a coherent grouping, with each forming an integral link in a carefully planned chain. Not only did the border itself fluctuate significantly during this period, particularly in the north-western marches,[14] but also the castles themselves were constructed piecemeal over an extended period of time. Thus, for example, Newcastle was begun in 1080, Carlisle in 1092, but Norham as late as 1121.[15]

Whether designed as a coherent system or not, moreover, the vagaries of political allegiance would have severely disrupted any such inter-dependence. For in both 1138 and 1173–4, the collusion of baronial elements with the Scots ensured the neutrality or even the active support of the garrisons of strategically important castles. Hence in 1138, Eustace fitz John, who held the castles of Alnwick and Malton, sided with David I.[16] His defection would have also brought the great fortress of Bamburgh into the Scottish ambit had not King Stephen earlier removed it from his custody.[17] As it was, Eustace's garrison of Malton sallied out and burned several villages in the vicinity while the English forces were engaged with the Scots at the battle of the Standard.[18] In 1173–4, treachery weakened the northern defences still further. The position of the bishop of Durham, Hugh du Puiset, was at best ambivalent in 1173, and his *de facto* neutrality ensured that the episcopal castles of Norham and Durham, two of the most important defences of north-east Northumbria, offered the Scots no resistance.[19] By 1174, he was regarded as being openly in league with William the Lion.[20] His castle of

---

[14] For the changes in the border see G. W. S. Barrow, 'The Anglo-Scottish Border', *The Kingdom of the Scots. Government, Church and Society from the Eleventh to the Fourteenth Century* (London, 1973), 139–61.

[15] *Symeonis monachi opera omnia* (hereafter Simeon), ed. T. Arnold, 2 vols (RS, 1882–5), II, 211; *ASC* 'E' 1092; Simeon, II, 260.

[16] Richard of Hexham, 84, who notes how he 'had long secretly favoured the king of Scotland'; John of Hexham, 118. Eustace had been an intimate of Henry I (*Gesta Stephani*, ed. and trans. K. Potter, with an introduction by R. H. C. Davis (Oxford, 1973), 54–5, xxviii–xxix; *Relatio venerabilis Aelredi, abbatis Rievallensis, de Standardo* (hereafter *Relatio*, ed. R. Howlett, *Chronicles and Memorials of the Reigns of Stephen, Henry II and Richard* I, III (RS, 1886), 191.

[17] John of Hexham, 118. Ailred, *Relatio*, 191, says that it was in retaliation for the seizure of Bamburgh that Eustace sided with Stephen, but it seems more likely that Stephen's move had been prompted by suspicions of treason well before.

[18] Richard of Hexham, 93–4. Eustace himself fought with David at the Standard against the English (*Relatio*, 191).

[19] Ralph of Diceto noted that William the Lion invaded in 1173, '*per fines itaque episcopi Dunolmensis securum transitum habens*' (*Radulfi de Diceto decani Lundoniensis opera historica* (hereafter Diceto), ed. W. Stubbs, 2 vols (RS, 1876), I, 376). In the same campaign, Jordan Fantosme has William say: 'There is none to stand in my path – who is there to fear? The bishop of Durham – behold his messenger – writes to me that he has no stomach for war, and that I shall have nought to complain of in the way of interference from him or his forces' (Fantosme ll. 532–6). It was du Puiset, however, who was responsible for purchasing a truce with William from 13 January until the end of March, 1174 (*Gesta Henrici* I, 64). For a detailed discussion of the bishop's role in the war of 1173–4 see G. V. Scammell, *Hugh du Puiset, Bishop of Durham* (Cambridge, 1956), 35–43.

[20] Fantosme ll. 1597–8, where Jordan has the bishop of Winchester tell Henry II that ' "he is hand in glove with King William" '. Du Puiset had summoned 500 Flemings and forty French knights under the command of his nephew, Hugh, count of Bar, but their arrival in Northumbria coincided with William's capture at Alnwick. The bishop thus dismissed his Flemings but placed the French knights in Northallerton (*Gesta Henrici* I, 67).

Northallerton formed part of a rebel enclave in Yorkshire in conjunction with Roger de Mowbray's castles of Thirsk, Malzeard and Kinard Ferry in Axholme.[21] Equally dangerous was the possession of the castle and honour of Huntingdon by William the Lion's younger brother David, who in 1174 conducted successful forays against the royalist garrisons of the south midlands.[22] It is impossible to see how an effective castle 'system' could have operated under such conditions.

Indeed, an analysis of the campaigns of 1138 and 1173–4 strongly suggests that far from acting as a cohesive network, castles in times of war operated largely as independent, self-contained units. Hence in 1138, David I had been able to isolate first Norham then Wark, taking both castles without interference from other northern garrisons.[23] Similarly, Brough, Appleby, Liddell and Harbottle fell to William the Lion in 1174 without any recorded attempts at relief by neighbouring castellans.[24] The previous year, William had been able to advance in turn on Wark, Alnwick, Warkworth, Newcastle, Prudhoe and Carlisle without encountering any co-ordinated resistance.[25] Rather, each garrison came to individual terms with William, and where castellans were granted conditional respite, they seem to have sent for aid not to adjacent fortresses but much further south to the justiciar, Richard de Lucy.[26] It was only when William was withdrawing north in both 1173 and 1174 that some of the Northumbrian castellans swelled the ranks of the English field army in giving pursuit.[27] In short, there is little evidence for sustained tactical co-ordination or even extensive communication between the garrisons of the Cumbrian or Northumbrian castles.

Still more striking, however, is the impression that several castles in the marches were unprepared for war when it came. In 1138, the bishop of Durham earned censure for not having fortified Norham as the times required, despite its having fallen to the Scots only two years previously.[28] In 1173, the garrisons of both

---

[21] *Gesta Henrici* I, 48, 64; Diceto, I, 379, 384–5.

[22] *Gesta Henrici* I, 48; Fantosme ll. 1107–31. For the role of Earl David in the war of 1173–4 see K. J. Stringer, *Earl David of Huntingdon, 1152–1219. A Study in Anglo-Scottish History* (Edinburgh 1985), 19–29.

[23] Richard of Hexham, 82–3, 84, 94–5, 99–100; John of Hexham, 117–8.

[24] *Gesta Henrici* I, 65; Fantosme ll. 1457–1506.

[25] Fantosme ll. 477–668.

[26] Fantosme ll. 500–15, 538–43. The castellan of Wark, Roger de Stuteville, is made to say that he will either 'send missives sealed with wax' to the king or 'cross the sea' to Normandy to seek aid from Henry II in person (Fantosme ll. 501, 511–12). It is probable, however, that this is more of a literary device to highlight the personal and immediate nature of de Stuteville's loyalty to the king, and that in reality he would have dealt directly with the justiciar. Jordan subsequently implies that Roger went south but did not leave England ('*alad en Englettere*', l. 526), a view supported by the fact that he succeeded in levying a relief force and returning to Wark within forty days (Fantosme ll. 525–9). Whatever the source of de Stuteville's relieving army, it was clearly not raised from the Northumbrian garrisons. In 1174, it was to Richard de Lucy that Robert de Vaux first appealed for aid when granted respite by William the Lion (Fantosme ll. 1507–13).

[27] Fantosme ll. 759–62, 1710–15.

[28] Richard of Hexham, 83, '*quia non pro sua opportunitate et temporis necessitate castrum suum muniverat*'. It seems certain, however, that unlike his later successor Hugh du Puiset, Bishop Geoffrey was not in collusion with the Scots. For when Norham had fallen, David offered to return it to the bishop and make reparation for any damage inflicted if he would abandon Stephen and swear fealty to David. Geoffrey refused and Norham was consequently demolished. Such lack of foresight seems to have been surprisingly common. Cf. below n. 33. Similarly, the author of the *Gesta Stephani* attempted to explain Henry of Blois' lack of support for his brother following Stephen's capture at Lincoln in 1141 in terms of inadequate logistical planning. Describing the dilemma in which Blois found himself, the *Gesta* noted

Wark and Alnwick did not feel themselves strong enough to resist William the Lion without petitioning him for respite to seek reinforcements.[29] In the same year, the defences of Warkworth were felt to be so inadequate that its custodian, Roger fitzRichard, abandoned it and fell back on Newcastle.[30] In 1174, the castle of Appleby was found virtually undefended when attacked by William the Lion, that of Brough inadequately garrisoned despite the precedent of the previous year's hostilities.[31] In certain cases, such negligence might smack of treachery – the castellan of Appleby, Gospatric fitzHorm, and the few who comprised his garrison were amerced by Henry II after the war[32] – but more significantly, such evidence suggests that not all castles were deemed to be defensible in a full-scale war.[33] Warkworth doubtless had continued to act as a fortified seigneurial residence and to be employed for the administrative functions of lordship, yet in 1173 was considered indefensible against a major Scottish invasion.[34] By contrast, other

that 'it was most difficult to support the king's cause and restore it to its former flourishing condition, above all because he had not provisioned or garrisoned his castles sufficiently enough' (*Gesta Stephani*, 118–9).

[29] Fantosme ll. 500–1, 510–15; 541–4, 555–8. Jordan noted of Roger de Stuteville, the castellan of Wark, that 'he realized that the force at his command was not going to help him at all against the army of the Scots that presses hard on them' (Fantosme ll. 484–5). By contrast, once Roger succeeded in using his respite to bring back a larger force, 'he was able to tell the king of Scotland that he was free to attack him with his Flemings and that he will confidently await them' (*ibid.* ll. 527–9).

[30] Fantosme ll. 561–4, where Jordan notes 'for the castle, its wall and embankment are feeble; Roger fitzRichard, a valiant knight, had had it in ward, but he could not defend it'. That Warkworth was deemed indefensible despite having a stone curtain by 1173 further suggests that only the strongest of the border castles were adjudged capable of resisting a major attack. Given this, the construction of the stone *enceinte* would seem to have as much to do with seigneurial status and the display of wealth as purely defensive concerns. These defences, and a stone hall, may have been erected by Earl Henry after his possession of Northumberland from 1139 (Hunter-Blair, 'Early Castles', 129–31; C. H. Hunter-Blair and H. L. Honeyman, *Warkworth Castle* (Department of the Environment Official Handbook, twelfth impression, 1977), 5–6.

[31] Fantosme ll. 1457–62, 1475–1506. See also below, n.32.

[32] *PR 22 Henry II*, 119–20. It is perhaps no coincidence that the entry concerning the amercement of the garrison of Appleby is followed by the recording of a debt of thirty marks owed by one William fitzWilliam, '*ut habeat duellum versus Gospatric filius Orm*' (*PR 22 Henry II*, 121). Nevertheless, the entry for Appleby supports Jordan's insistence that the castle was surrendered merely through cowardice and inadequate manning rather than treachery (Fantosme ll. 1458–62). Gospatric was amerced 500 marks '*quia reddidit castellum regis de Appelbi regi Scottorum*', but that many others were fined for being '*ad consilium reddendi castri*' suggests that the decision to capitulate was taken by the garrison as a whole. Only one man in the entry for the county, a Udard de Brougham, was unequivocally amerced '*quia fuit cum inimicis regis*' and there is no reason to assume his connection with the garrison of Appleby. The Pipe Roll entry also clearly shows that Gospatric's 'garrison' consisted only of domestic officers or civilians; among those fined for their counsel of despair were William *dispensator*, William *clericus* of Appleby, Robert the steward of Hugh de Moreville, two cooks, a miller, a tailor, an embroiderer (*plumarius*) and a mercerer.

[33] This conclusion is supported by several other examples of the same phenomenon in other theatres of war. Hence the *Gesta Stephani* notes how in 1136 Alured, son of Judhael of Totnes, became one of the sworn allies of Baldwin de Redvers against Stephen. 'But as he had a castle that was ruinous and weak, and inadequately fortified for the protection of his followers, he left it completely empty and ungarrisoned'. The castle was probably Barnstable (*Gesta Stephani*, 36–7, 36 n. 1). In 1142, the Empress's forces had fortified Cirencester, but on his arrival there, Stephen was able to raze it to the ground 'finding the castle empty because the garrison had stolen away' (*Gesta Stephani*, 92). In 1173, Henry II was able to take Breteuil, since Robert of Leicester had fled to Louis VII, leaving his fortress '*sine custodia*' (*Gesta Henrici* I, 51).

[34] For a complementary discussion in an Irish context of certain castles appearing primarily as fortified residences rather than major fortresses, see T. E. McNeill, 'Great Towers in Irish Castles, c.1175–1225', above pp. 99–118.

major fortresses such as Newcastle, Wark and Norham had had considerable amounts of money expended on them in the years prior to 1173.[35] In this context, it may be significant that we hear nothing from the chroniclers of the smaller baronial castles of the area such as Bothal, Bolam, Wooler, Bellingham, Gunnerton or Haltwhistle. Clearly, the modest scale of their defences was not designed to resist large-scale Scottish incursions, being capable of defence only against the smallest of raiding parties.[36] By the same token, whether they were abandoned or defended in times of invasion, such fortified residences offered the Scots little strategic gain. Rather, both David and William the Lion concentrated their main efforts against a smaller number of key strongholds.

Added to such considerations was the fundamental fact that castles, no matter how densely sited or how individually strong, could not in themselves halt the incursions of an invading army. Indeed, one of the most striking features of Anglo-Scottish warfare in the late eleventh and twelfth centuries was the ease with which the Scots could repeatedly harry the northern counties and even penetrate significant distances into England. In 1070, Malcolm Canmore had laid waste the whole of Teesdale and Cleveland, and in 1079 he ravaged up to the Tyne.[37] Though in 1091 he only reached Durham before being repulsed, he had still managed to inflict considerable damage in Northumbria.[38] Malcolm's invasions came, of course, at a period when Norman control of the north, with its concomitant castle-building, was only in its first stages of consolidation, but the inability to prevent widespread harrying holds equally true of the major Anglo-Saxon defences such as Durham and Bamburgh.[39] Scottish kings, moreover, could achieve similar degrees of penetration even after the proliferation of castles north of the Humber. Hence on failing to take Wark in January 1138, David marched south and devastated as far as the Tyne without opposition.[40] He invaded again

---

[35] Thus in the financial year 1167-8, Henry II spent £120 19s 6d on Newcastle and £30 on Bamburgh. Between 1171-3 a further £439 6s 8d was expended on Newcastle. Expenditure of £425 between 1170-3, followed by a further £44 16s 6d in 1173-4, saw the construction of the great tower at Bowes. Just over £382 was spent on Wark between 1157-1161, reflecting a period of particularly strained Anglo-Scottish relations. Further behind the border, Scarborough seems to have been high on Henry's priorities, with £589 15s 8d being spent on it between 1158-1164, and a further £57 1s 3d in 1167-8. These sums are all calculated from the tables of royal expenditure on castles compiled by Brown, 'Royal Castle Building', particularly 379-80. Exact sums are unavailable for Norham, but on Henry II's orders Hugh du Puiset rebuilt the castle constructed by Rannulf Flambard and destroyed by the Scots in 1138, adding a great keep and a stone curtain in the years prior to 1173 (Simeon, I, 168; Hunter-Blair, 'Early Castles', 138-141; C. H. Hunter-Blair and H. L. Honeyman, *Norham Castle* (Department of the Environment Official Handbook, sixth impression 1978), 5-6).

[36] Hunter-Blair, 'Early Castles', 121-2, 146-8, 160-4.

[37] Simeon, II, 190-1; *ASC* 'E', 1097. In 1061, Malcolm had harried Tostig's earldom of Northumbria and had laid waste Lindisfarne (Simeon, II, 174-5).

[38] *ASC* 'E', 1091; Huntingdon, 216; Worcester, II, 28; *De miraculis et translationibus sancti Cuthberti* in Simeon, II, 338-40.

[39] Thus when Malcolm II invaded Northumbria, probably c.1006, the ageing Earl Waltheof shut himself up in Bamburgh while the Scots blockaded Durham. The Scots were defeated only when Waltheof's son, Uhtred, led a combined force of Northumbrians and the men of York against them in battle (*De obsessione Dunelmi* in Simeon, I, 215-6). In 1039, by contrast, the defenders of Durham sallied out and routed the Scottish besiegers under King Duncan (Simeon, I, 90-1).

[40] Richard of Hexham, 77-9. One section of the army crossed the Tyne and 'slew innumerable folk in the desert places, and ravaged in the same manner the most part of the land of St Cuthbert toward the west' (Richard of Hexham, 79). John of Hexham, 115-17, noted that a massacre of civilians occurred at Tanfield, south of the Tyne.

after Easter, and was able to ravage the eastern seaboard as far as Durham.[41] He invaded a third time that year in September, and was only halted at Northallerton in Yorkshire where the English army had stood its ground.[42] Prior to this engagement, his Galwegians had devastated Cumbria and penetrated as far as Clitheroe in Lancashire.[43] Similarly, in both 1173 and 1174, William the Lion was able to circumvent the major Northumbrian and Cumbrian fortresses and ravage at will until compelled to retire by the arrival of the Anglo-Norman field army.[44] Like the Germans with the Maginot line, the Scots could simply go round the main English castles if they so chose.

It is often remarked that an invading commander was loath to leave pockets of enemy resistance in his rear. Castle garrisons might sally out and either engage the enemy force or disrupt lines of communication. Thus in 1138, knights had sallied out from Wark, attacked David's supply train and engaged the retinue of Earl Henry, killing some and taking others for ransom.[45] Yet in practice – at least in this theatre of war – such forays were rare occurrences. No similar sallies by any other garrison against the Scots are recorded either in 1138 or 1173–4.[46] Robert de Vaux, the castellan of Carlisle, joined in chasing William the Lion back across the border in 1173, but this was only on the arrival of a large relief force under Richard de Lucy.[47] And yet one of the principal mechanisms of the castle was to act as a fortified base from which knights could control the countryside.[48]

Two principal reasons account for the lack of such offensive action by castle garrisons. First, a wise invading commander might detach a section of his army to invest a potentially disruptive garrison while his main army plundered and burnt. Hence in 1138, the majority of David's army laid siege to Norham while his nephew, William fitzDuncan, led the Galwegians and other units on a great harrying raid into Yorkshire and Lancashire.[49] Shortly afterwards, having failed to take Wark by storm a second time, David entrusted its blockade to two of his leading men while he led his army past Bamburgh and Mitford to the Tyne, laying waste all in his path.[50] The inability of Wark's garrison to replenish its supplies by foraging led to its eventual surrender through starvation.[51] In 1174, having

---

41 Richard of Hexham, 81–2; John of Hexham, 117.

42 Richard of Hexham, 84–90.

43 John of Hexham, 117; Richard of Hexham, 82.

44 Fantosme ll. 477–758, 1139–1507, 1634–1826; *Gesta Henrici* I, 64–7; William of Newburgh, *Historia rerum anglicarum* (hereafter Newburgh), ed. R. Howlett, *Chronicles and Memorials of the Reigns of Stephen, Henry II and Richard I* (RS, 1884) (I, 1–408, II, 409–53), 177, 181–5.

45 Richard of Hexham, 84; John of Hexham, 117–18.

46 I have discounted the rash foray of the *'juvenes'* of Hexham against a Scottish thegn and his band in 1138, when a group of young men rushed out and slew the leader of a foraging party which they believed intended to despoil Hexham abbey. The Scots army nearly destroyed the town in reprisal, but were prevented from so doing by William fitzDuncan, David's nephew and leader of the advance guard (John of Hexham, 115–16). This incident was clearly not an effective sally executed by knights from a fortified base.

47 Fantosme ll. 759–62.

48 Brown, *English Castles*, 172–3, 198–9.

49 Richard of Hexham, 82–3; John of Hexham, 117.

50 Richard of Hexham, 84–5.

51 Richard of Hexham, 100; John of Hexham, 118. The need to re-victual themselves may have been one of the principal reasons for their sally against David's supply train. Certainly, David seems not to have expected such offensive action and was incensed at the attack, which prompted him to renew the siege of Wark (Richard of Hexham, 84).

spread out his main army to ravage the vicinity, William the Lion blockaded Alnwick with his *familia* 'lest perchance a group of knights should break out from it and so disturb the robbers who were pillaging all around them'.[52]

The second explanation lies in the very small size of the northern castles' garrisons. In 1138, the garrison of Norham consisted of only nine knights with an unspecified number of retainers, while that of Wark seems not to have exceeded twenty-four horsemen.[53] In 1174, ten knights and forty sergeants held Wark against sustained assault by William the Lion.[54] In a purely defensive role, such small numbers were considered perfectly adequate. Richard of Hexham records how even though some of Norham's nine knights were wounded, they incurred great ignominy for surrendering to David too easily, since they had plenty of provisions and the ditches and keep were very strong.[55] It is eloquent testimony to the supremacy of the art of defence over that of assault that strongholds such as Wark, Prudhoe or Carlisle could successfully hold off the assaults of entire Scottish armies numbering in thousands.[56] Neither David or William ever attempted to take Bamburgh.[57]

Yet no matter how effective in defence, such limited garrison numbers did not permit the formation of a mobile field force or direct engagement with enemy forces of any size outside the protection of their walls.[58] Without the ability of the

---

[52] Newburgh, 183. Earlier that year William had blockaded Carlisle with part of his army while he led the main force first on a raid through Northumbria then back to Cumbria to assault Appleby, Brough and other fortresses (*Gesta Henrici* I, 65).

[53] Richard of Hexham, 83. Both Richard and John of Hexham note that when Wark finally surrendered to David late in 1138, the starving garrison had eaten all their horses save one still alive and one in salt. As a recognition of their gallant defence, David gave them free egress with their arms and supplied them with twenty-four horses (Richard of Hexham, 100; John of Hexham, 118). This suggests that the garrison comprised this number of horsemen, but whether all were knights or whether some were mounted sergeants is unknown.

[54] *PR 20 Henry II*, 105. This figure provides a useful check on Fantosme, who gives a not unrealistic estimate of the garrison strength of Wark in 1174 as 'more than twenty knights' and 'the best sergeants that ever baron had in his service' (Fantosme ll. 1193–4). Compare this modest garrison to that of thirty knights and sixty archers with armour that defended Mowbray's rebel stronghold of Malzeard in 1174 (Gerald of Wales, *De vita Galfridi archiepiscopi Eboracensis* (hereafter *Vita Galfridi*), *Opera* IV, ed. J. S. Brewer (RS, 1873), 367).

[55] Richard of Hexham, 83.

[56] See, for example, the first siege of Wark in 1138 (Richard of Hexham, 77–8); Carlisle, 1173 (Fantosme ll. 645–68); Wark, 1174 (Fantosme ll. 1185–1269); Prudhoe, 1174 (Fantosme ll. 1643–85).

[57] In 1138, the '*juvenes*' of Bamburgh taunted the Scots as their army passed by the fortress, '*temere praesumentes de munitione valli quod extruerant ante castrum*' (John of Hexham, 118). Some of the enraged Scots stormed this outwork and slew about one hundred people (John of Hexham, 118; Richard of Hexham, 84–5). This was not an attempt to take the castle itself, which the Scots were clearly intending to bypass. Similarly, when in 1136 David succeeded in taking Alnwick, Carlisle, Wark, Newcastle and Norham, he failed to gain Bamburgh, but the circumstances suggest that this was a failure of guile or diplomacy, and that he had not actually invested this impregnable site.

[58] Henry I's campaign of 1124 furnishes a fine example of the effective operation of this process. The army that defeated Amaury de Montfort and Waleran de Meulan at Bourgthéroulde was composed of elements of the *familia regis*, which had been stationed, seemingly in units of one hundred strong, in neighbouring castles then drawn together to form a small but formidable field force of around 300 knights supported by mounted archers (Orderic VI, 348–51; *ASC* 'E' 1124; Robert of Torigni's interpolations in Jumièges, 296). See especially M. Chibnall, 'Mercenaries and the *Familia Regis* under Henry I', *History* lxii, 19–21, where the comparison is rightly stressed between the small sizes of garrisons in English castles revealed by the Pipe Roll of 1131 and those of castles in Normandy. Operations in Normandy were always on a radically different scale to those on the Scottish march. In

garrison to make effective sallies, the castle was thus unable to protect the surrounding countryside from ravaging, the most immediate and fundamental expression of enemy hostilities. With a powerful invading force operating in the vicinity, the castle could only provide a static defence, sheltering the persons, property and livestock of those fortunate enough to have gained the safety of its walls. Castles might hold up an attacking commander if he laid siege to them, or tie down elements of his army in blockade, but such decisions were largely at the discretion of the invader. Here at last, however, we find the essential defensive value of the castle. For the conquest of a disputed region could only be achieved by the occupation or the destruction of its castles. The mechanism of ravaging, though vital for the victualling of an army living off the land and for the provision of booty could not in itself effect long-term strategic gains.[59] It was only in exceptional circumstances arising from Stephen's political and military embarrassments that David's series of forays in 1138 succeeded in gaining the cession of Northumbria the following year, despite his defeat at the Standard.[60] In 1173 by contrast, Henry II's summary rejection of William the Lion's claims left the Scots king in no doubt that he could only gain Northumberland by conquest.[61] The principal objective in war therefore was not simply the despoliation of these disputed areas through ravaging but their physical occupation.

Hence for all their ability to inflict widespread economic damage, the capture of key fortresses lay at the heart of Scottish strategy. David's first act of intervention in 1136 had been the seizure, achieved less by force than by the exploitation of the uncertainties of succession and allegiance following the death of Henry I, of the chief border castles of Carlisle, Wark, Norham and Newcastle.[62] In 1138, he conducted the sieges of Norham and Wark with singular determination, and succeeded in destroying both before finally retreating north.[63] A study of Jordan

1216, John drew forces from at least twelve garrisons to form a force under the direction of Fawkes de Bréauté, whose task was to draw Prince Louis' forces away from the sieges of Windsor and Dover (*Rogeri de Wendover flores historiarum*, ed. H. O. Coxe, 5 vols (London, 1841–50), III, 349; *Rotuli litterarum patentium in turri Londinensi asservati*, ed. T. Duffus Hardy, Record Commission, 1835, I, 194b; R. A. Brown, *English Castles*, 199).

[59] On ravaging see M. J. Strickland, *The Conduct and Perception of War under the Anglo-Norman and Angevin Kings, 1075–1217* (unpublished Ph.D. thesis, Cambridge, 1989), 237–79.

[60] Richard of Hexham, 105. In 1139, Stephen ceded Earl Henry the county of Northumberland except the castles of Bamburgh and Newcastle.

[61] Fantosme ll. 271–420.

[62] Richard of Hexham, 71–2. As Matilda's uncle, and having been the first among the magnates to swear homage to her as Henry's successor in 1126, David was in a strong position to attempt to assert Angevin claims in the north. His intervention had been very swift; Henry I had died on December I, 1135, Stephen was crowned on December 22, and David moved into Northumbria in January (R. H. C. Davis, *King Stephen* (London, 1967), 16–18, 21). Huntingdon, 258–9, says David took the border castles by guile, but the ease and speed with which this series of great fortresses surrendered strongly suggests that their garrisons initially accepted David's overlordship on his niece's behalf. Richard of Hexham, 72, says that he took '*fidelitates quoque et obsides de potentioribus et nobilioribus ejusdem regionis, ad conservandam fidem imperatrici nepti suae*'. The arrival of Stephen's army by February forced David to return all these castles save Carlisle, which Stephen granted to Earl Henry along with the honors of Huntingdon and Doncaster, promising also to consider Henry's claim to the county of Northumberland (Richard of Hexham, 72).

[63] Richard of Hexham, 82–3, 84–5, 94–5, 99–100; John of Hexham, 117–8. David was so determined on the destruction of Wark that he specifically exempted its siege from the cessation of hostilities negotiated by the legate Alberic at the end of 1138 (Richard of Hexham, 99).

Fantosme reveals that the capture of the Cumbrian and Northumbrian castles was William the Lion's overriding concern. In 1173, he had approached Wark, Alnwick, Newcastle, Prudhoe and Carlisle, but with a singular lack of success.[64] His campaign the following year, however, brought him initial gains in Cumbria, with his army taking Liddell, Appleby, Brough and Harbottle, and reducing the garrison of Carlisle to desperate straits.[65] Much of the ravaging carried out by the Scots, indeed, must be seen as preparation for investing these border castles.[66] In 1138, for example, David laid waste the crops in the vicinity of Wark before enforcing its blockade, while in a well-known passage in Jordan Fantosme, Philip of Flanders is made to equate ravaging with the necessary prelude to siege: 'Let him not leave them, outside their castles, in wood or meadow, as much as will furnish them a meal on the morrow. Then let him assemble his men and lay siege to their castles. They will not get help or succour within thirteen leagues around them.'[67]

The need to invest castles forced the Scots to abandon a war of movement to which the majority of their troops were best suited and made their armies vulnerable to attack by a relieving army. In 1173, William the Lion narrowly avoided being caught by an English force under Richard de Lucy while besieging Carlisle.[68] His siege of Bowes in 1174 made him the target of an army led by Geoffrey Plantagenet, bishop elect of Lincoln, and later in that same campaign it was while his army lay dispersed before the walls of Alnwick that William was attacked and captured by an English relief force.[69] Such instances, I suggest, provide the key to understanding Anglo-Norman defence strategy and the function of the border fortresses. For castles were never intended to bear the brunt of enemy attack in isolation, but rather to operate in conjunction with the deployment of the Anglo-Norman field armies.

No doubt acutely aware of the inability of the frontier castles to prevent major invasion, Anglo-Norman kings or their commanders instead relied first and foremost on containing Scottish incursions by fielding the feudal host as quickly as possible. Hence Malcolm III's invasion of May 1091 was rapidly halted at Durham by the concentration of an English force just south of the city, while a punitive counter-raid may have been launched shortly afterwards by Nigel d'Aubigny.[70] Rufus himself returned from Normandy in July of that year, and by September was leading a joint land and naval force against Scotland.[71] In early 1136, David I had seized the four great border fortresses of Alnwick, Norham,

---

[64] Fantosme ll. 477–668.

[65] Fantosme ll. 1455–1507; *Gesta Henrici* I, 64–5.

[66] Hence in 1138, David laid waste the crops around Wark before enforcing its blockade. His main army then marched to the Tyne, burning the crops around Bamburgh, Mitford and other sites as they went (Richard of Hexham, 84–5). A raid on Belford and the surrounding area was a prelude to William the Lion's assault on Wark in 1174, while the previous year he had harried the Northumbrian coastal strip as part of his attack on Alnwick, Warkworth and Newcastle (Fantosme ll. 1149–87, 559–60).

[67] Fantosme ll. 445–8.

[68] Fantosme ll. 705–58.

[69] William's siege of Bowes is mentioned only by Gerald of Wales, *Vita Galfridi*, 367, a sobering reminder of the limitations and lack of comprehensiveness inherent in the major chronicle sources. For Alnwick, *Gesta Henrici* I, 65–7; Newburgh, 182–5; Fantosme ll. 1709–1816.

[70] *De miraculis et translationibus sancti Cuthberti*, in Simeon, II, 338–40; *ASC* 'E' 1091; Simeon, II, 221–2; F. Barlow, *William Rufus* (London, 1983), 288–91.

[71] *ASC* 'E' 1091; Worcester, II, 28; Barlow, *William Rufus*, 291–4.

Wark and Carlisle, but further offensive action was curtailed by Stephen's swift arrival at Durham in February.[72] David's invasion of Northumbria at Easter 1137 was speedily barred by 'the greater part of the earls and barons of England' who had assembled at Newcastle, and David was forced to accept a cessation of hostilities till November and the return of King Stephen from Normandy.[73] The campaigns of 1138 began in a very similar manner to those of 1136. David launched a lightning attack in midwinter and besieged Wark, but he had only reached Hexham before Stephen arrived in the north, again by early February.[74] Thus each of David's initial incursions had been repulsed by the deployment of large field armies within a month of the inception of Scottish hostilities. In 1173 and 1174, tactical commitments elsewhere had delayed the English host from marching north immediately, thereby allowing William the Lion considerable freedom of movement.[75] Yet in both these campaigns the eventual arrival of the English army was the decisive strategic factor, forcing the rapid withdrawal of the Scots, and in 1174 effecting the capture of William himself.

It is thus clear that individual castles or those of a vicinity were not intended to operate in a vacuum. Despite their ability to resist direct assault, even the strongest fortress could not withstand prolonged blockade, and it was therefore imperative that the enemy should not be given the opportunity to press a sustained siege. A crucial factor in John's loss of Normandy was his inability to consistently field a powerful relieving army.[76] The prolonged and heroic defence of their castellans should not disguise the fact that defences like Château Gaillard, for all their sophistication, were never intended to be held in isolation for such extensive periods. William the Lion's successful campaign against the castles of Cumbria in 1174 was only made possible by the preoccupation of the royalist forces with increasing rebel activity further south. In this context, it is significant that in both 1138 and 1174 the Scots did not attempt to garrison the castles they took, but demolished them.[77] This was presumably in order to facilitate subsequent incursions, but must also have been motivated by the recognition that they could not supply or relieve garrisons in the face of a substantial English army.

---

[72] Richard of Hexham, 72.

[73] Richard of Hexham, 76-7.

[74] Richard of Hexham, 77-81.

[75] In 1173, de Lucy's forces had been investing Leicester from 3-28 July. The town was taken but the siege of the castle was raised when he moved north against William (Diceto, I, 376; *Gesta Henrici* I, 58). The following year, the royalist forces were confronted by increasing rebel activity in England; the operations of Earl David of Huntingdon, Earl Ferrers and the garrison of Leicester against Northampton and Nottingham (Fantosme ll. 1107-1130; *Gesta Henrici* I, 68); the forays of Mowbray's garrisons of Axholme, Malzeard and Thirsk, finally curtailed by Geoffrey Plantagenet (*Gesta Henrici* I, 68-9; Diceto, I, 379; *Vita Galfridi*, 364-7); and a fresh landing of Flemings in East Anglia, who under the command of Hugh Bigod burned Norwich (*Gesta Henrici* I, 68; Diceto, I, 381).

[76] John's bold but unsuccessful attempt to relieve Château Gaillard in late August 1203, saw the disintegration of the last field force of any adequate size he was able to muster in Normandy. His lack of support and the treason endemic among the Norman baronage caused him to leave Normandy, while his attempts to assemble an army from England in May 1204 to relieve Rouen met with failure. As a result, Philip was left to reduce the fortifications of the duchy at will (K. Norgate, *John Lackland* (London, 1902), 95-102; W. L. Warren, *King John* (London, 1964 reprint), 84-88).

[77] Thus in 1138, David first had Norham destroyed, then Wark (Richard of Hexham, 83, 100). In 1173, William the Lion's Flemings wanted to demolish Prudhoe, although in the event the Scots did not lay siege to the castle until the following year (Fantosme ll. 559-604). If Jordan is to be believed, William garrisoned Appleby when it fell to him, but demolished Brough (Fantosme ll. 1469-74, 1506).

Finally, it was the field armies which proceeded to carry war into Scotland itself in 1072, 1080, 1091, 1138, 1173, 1209 and 1216.[78] And it was from the northern castles that such forays were launched. Hence Wark was the jumping off point for Stephen's raid into Lothian in 1138, while in 1174, the army that seized William the Lion at Alnwick assembled at Newcastle, launched its strike from there and returned to Newcastle the same night.[79] The offensive role of the castle in occupation and conquest has, of course, long been recognised,[80] and nowhere is this more apparent that on the Scottish march. At each stage in a gradual northerly advance, areas of effective Norman control were deliniated by the foundation of key fortresses. The building of Newcastle in 1080 saw the Tyne replace the Humber as the principal boundary of *de facto* rule, while that of Carlisle in 1092 established the Solway as the frontier of the north-western march and consolidated the annexation of Cumbria.[81] By the early twelfth century, Wark and Norham marked the Tweed as the furthest limits of the Anglo-Norman kingdom.[82] Thus rather than seeing castles as being established in some form of defensive network, their location and purpose is better understood if we regard them as being initially conceived as instruments of offence. They subsequently continued to serve this function by operating in conjunction with deployment of the feudal host.

Effective though the deployment of the Anglo-Norman field army was, however, this mechanism of defence was not without serious flaws. If the army was delayed or committed elsewhere, the Scots might make significant gains or inflict widespread damage. Nor could the feudal host stay in the north indefinitely. Logistics and the term of feudal service were crucially limiting factors.[83] There was, moreover, always the eventuality that the Scots might invade more than once in any given year. In February 1138, Stephen's army had repulsed David's initial invasion. Yet by April, David had again crossed the border, and this time no English force barred his way. He invaded a third time in September, to be met at Northallerton by the feudal host supplemented by the shire levies of Yorkshire.[84] Such frequent hostings are suggestive of the extent of military service that the Scottish kings might command, but in contrast, it is doubtful whether the Anglo-Norman feudal levy, designed to combat armies whose timescale of operations

---

[78] *ASC* 'E' 1072, 'D' 1073; Simeon, II, 195–6; Worcester, II, 9; Simeon, II, 211; *Chronicon monasterii de Abingdon*, ed. J. Stevenson, 2 vols, (RS, 1858), II, 9–10; *ASC* 'E' 1091; Worcester, II, 28; Richard of Hexham, 81; John of Hexham, 117; Fantosme ll. 800–4; *Gesta Henrici* I, 61; *Memoriale fratris Walteri de Coventria* (hereafter Walter of Coventry), ed. W. Stubbs, 2 vols (RS, 1872–3), II, 200; *Matthaei Parisiensis, monachi sancti Albani, chronica majora* (hereafter *Chronica majora*), ed. H. R. Luard, 7 vols (RS, 1872–3), II, 525; *Chronica majora* II, 641–2; Walter of Coventry, II, 229.
[79] John of Hexham, 117; Fantosme ll. 1718–22, 1817–25; Newburgh, 183, 185.
[80] See, for example, J. Le Patourel, *The Norman Empire* (Oxford, 1976), 65–7, 72, 303–18, 351–3 .
[81] Simeon, II, 211; Barrow, 'The Scottish Border', 143–7; W. E. Kapelle, *The Norman Conquest of the North. The Region and its Transformation, 1000–1135* (London 1979), 141–2.
[82] Hunter-Blair, 'Early Castles', 155–7; Simeon, I, 140.
[83] In 1091, many of Rufus's invasion army had died of cold and starvation after his supply fleet was wrecked by storms (*ASC* 'E' 1091; Worcester, II, 28), while in 1138, failure of supplies forced Stephen's withdrawal from Lothian following his punitive expedition against David (Richard of Hexham, 81). In 1137, the English army mustered at Newcastle, fixed a truce with the Scots till November of that year, and 'after forty days they retired to their own quarters' (Richard of Hexham, 76–7). The English were fortunate that the Scots honoured this truce and did not invade once the host was disbanded.
[84] Richard of Hexham, 77–88.

was similarly restricted, made allowance for such recurrent military activity.[85] Particularly for operations into Scotland itself, the standard period of service must have been augmented by the retention of knights for wages, although the proportion of stipendiaries in the English armies of 1138, 1173 and 1174 is unknown. A strong force of Flemish and Norman mercenary knights was present at the Standard under the command of Walter de Gant, while a significant element of John's army of 1216 that harried Lothian was composed of *routiers*.[86] Yet whatever the army's composition, there was little that could be done to prevent the Scots harrying across the border again once the main English force had withdrawn.

Such factors made it imperative to strike a decisive blow against the Scots as quickly as possible. Reprisal raids into the Scottish lowlands were undertaken in 1138, 1173 and 1216, but to remove the threat of subsequent raiding, commanders needed to bring the Scots to battle. Conversely, recognition of the impossibility of any prolonged stay north of the Tyne by English field armies and of the far-reaching limitations of their own troops in pitched battle caused Scottish kings to adopt a policy of non-engagement, deliberately denying combat to the English. Hence in 1138, David retreated with his army into an impenetrable swamp to await the imminent retirement of Stephen's forces. Although he avoided the ambush planned for him by David at Roxburgh, Stephen could only ravage Lothian before once more marching south because, according to Richard of Hexham, 'the king of the Scots and his men dared not give battle'.[87] In April of the same year, a mere rumour of an advancing English army caused David, whose own forces had been thrown into confusion by a Galwegian mutiny, to fly in haste back to Norham, abandoning untouched the supplies he had gathered at Durham.[88] Similarly in 1173, William the Lion was forced into a precipitous withdrawal by reports that an army under the justiciar, Richard de Lucy, was nearly upon him. He withdrew to Roxburgh and declined battle till the English were themselves forced to withdraw by news of Robert of Leicester's invasion of East Anglia.[89] In 1174, it was while beating a retreat north that William was attacked and captured at Alnwick.[90] Alexander II likewise withdrew before John's army in 1216, taking refuge beyond the Forth, prompting Matthew Paris to ascribe to King John the remark, 'so shall we hunt the red fox-cub from his lairs'.[91]

Tactical withrawal in the face of an enemy army was, of course, a commonplace of contemporary warfare, as had been recently emphasized by John Gillingham in his study of William I's generalship.[92] Yet in the case of the Scots, avoidance of battle was less a tactical option than a necessity. Perhaps more than any other army of the twelfth century, the strategy, tactics and military effectiveness of the Scottish

---

[85] For a comprehensive discussion of the feudal host see Hollister, *Military Organization*, 72–135.

[86] *Relatio*, 182, where Ailred also notes that William of Aumâle had knights, presumably stipendiaries, from Ponthieu and the Pas de Calais; *The Chronicle of Melrose* (hereafter *Melrose*), ed. A. O. and M. O. Anderson (London, 1936), 62. Among the other royalist forces at the battle of Fornham in 1173, Humphrey de Bohun led '300 of the king's stipendiary knights' (*Gesta Henrici* I, 61), while Geoffrey Plantagenet, the elect of Lincoln, had many stipendiary knights under his command during his campaign of 1174 against Roger de Mowbray (*Vita Galfridi*, 364).

[87] Richard of Hexham, 81; John of Hexham, 117.

[88] Richard of Hexham, 82.

[89] Fantosme ll. 713–832.

[90] *Gesta Henrici* I, 65–6; Newburgh, 182–3.

[91] *Chronica majora* II, 641–2.

[92] J. Gillingham, 'William the Bastard at War', *Studies ... Presented to R. Allen Brown*, 141–58.

army was profoundly circumscribed by the composition of its forces. In an age when few armies could be said to be truly homogeneous, those of the Scots were markedly hybrid in both racial and military terms. The armies of 1138 and 1173–4 comprised two basic components, an indigenous native levy, itself composed of a multiplicity of tribal elements, and an Anglo-Norman or 'Frankish' element consisting of the royal *familia*, Franco-Norman feudal settlers and other external mercenary units. The composite nature of the Scottish army is clearly revealed by Ailred of Rievaulx's description of their battle formation at the Standard in 1138. In the first rank were the Galwegians. In the second, under David's son Earl Henry, the Cumbrians and the men of Teviotdale along with Henry's knights and archers. The third line was composed of the men of Lothian, the men of the islands, and the men of Aberdeenshire, while the King himself formed the last unit with his *familia*, mercenary knights, the Scots – that is those dwelling north of a line between the Forth and the Tay – and the men of Moray.[93]

The bulk of the Scottish army was composed of native infantry, but the majority of these troops were very poorly equipped.[94] Defensive armour was denied to most by its prohibitive cost. Ailred mentions hides and shields of calf skin, to which could probably be added wicker or wooden targes of some form, but to observers south of the Tweed, they were effectively 'inermes'.[95] Offensive armament consisted of a long spear supplemented by javelins and long knives.[96] The Scots shared this use of the long spear with the tribesmen of North Wales, but in the twelfth century there is no evidence that the Scots had developed the disciplined formations of pikemen known as schiltrons that were to prove so effective against cavalry in the later wars of Independence.[97] Instead, the Scots and Galwegian tribesmen relied on speed and agility, and the terrifying effect of their wild charges, very similar, one may imagine, to the onrush of the Highland clansmen in the battles of the '15 and '45.[98]

Contemporaries were clearly struck by the disparity in arms and armour between the native Scots and the Anglo-Norman knights. Both Henry of Huntingdon and Ailred dwell on this factor at length in the pre-battle orations which they create for Ralph, bishop of Orkney, and Walter Espec respectively prior to the battle of the

---

[93] *Relatio*, 190–1. No such equivalent detail of the composition of the Scots' army survives for William the Lion's campaigns of 1173–4, but in addition to the Galwegians there were contingents from Ross, Moray, Buchan and Angus, as well as the troops led by Earl Duncan II of Fife and Earl Waltheof of Dunbar (Fantosme ll. 300, 471–6; *Gesta Henrici* I, 66).

[94] For the native levy see G. W. S. Barrow, *Regesta Regum Scottorum, II. The Acts of William the Lion, King of Scots 1165–1214* (Edinburgh, 1971), 56–8.

[95] *Relatio*, 186. John of Hexham, 120, says the Scots infantry were '*nudi ipsi et paene inermes*'. Fantosme noted of the Scots' muster at Cadonlee in 1173 '*tant i out de nue gent*' (l. 475), while to Diceto, the Galwegian tribesmen were '*agilem, nudam*' and distinguished by their shaved heads (Diceto, I, 376).

[96] Diceto, I, 376; *Relatio*, 186.

[97] *Giraldi Cambrensis opera* IV, ed. J. F. Dimock (RS, 1868), 177, 181; W. M. Mackenzie, *The Battle of Bannockburn: A Study in Medieval Warfare* (Glasgow, 1913), 47–8; G. W. S. Barrow, *Robert Bruce and the Community of the Realm of Scotland* (Edinburgh, 3rd edn, 1988), 220–1, 226–9. I have avoided using the term 'pike', since it is unlikely that these spears were as yet the immense 16′ weapons of the 16th–17th centuries. The true pike, which could only be handled by well-drilled men, seems to have been introduced to Scotland just prior to the battle of Flodden (W. Seymour, *Battles in Britain*, 2 vols (London, 1975), I, 196, 205).

[98] Cf. *Relatio*, 189–90.

Standard.[99] Yet that such observations were not simply literary *topoi* or the preserve of hostile Anglo-Norman writers is indicated by the corroboration afforded by Guibert of Nogent in his *Gesta Dei per Francos*. Guibert describes the Scots on crusade as 'fierce in their own country, unwarlike elsewhere, bare-legged, with their shaggy cloaks, a scrip hanging from the haunches, coming from their marshy homeland, and presenting the help of their faith and devotion to us, to whom their numerous arms would be ridiculous'.[100]

If ecclesiastical observers were so conscious of this imbalance, then Anglo-Norman commanders must have been still more so. The formation adopted at the Standard, though drawing directly on the experience of Tinchebrai and Brémule, was particularly effective in neutralizing the superiority in Scottish numbers and in exploiting the lack of armour among the native infantry by the use of massed archery.[101] David himself was equally aware of the shortcomings of the majority of his troops, and in his initial deployment had intended to place his knights and better equipped foot in the first rank, so that, in Ailred's words, 'armed men should attack armed men, and knights engage with knights, and arrows resist arrows'.[102] The lessons afforded by his brother-in-law's victories had not been wholly lost on David either, but the Galwegians objected to this formation, claiming it was their time-honoured prerogative to lead the first attack. To avoid bloodshed between the Galwegians and his Normans, David was forced to concede this demand with disastrous results.[103]

The quarrel between these two elements of David's army highlighted a second major weakness that hampered the military effectiveness of the Scottish forces. Bitter enmity existed between the native Scots and the knightly settlers, who exercised a political and cultural influence over the Scottish kings out of all proportion to their small numbers.[104] During David's march south in April 1138,

[99] *Relatio*, 186, 189–90; Huntingdon, 262–3. Huntingdon, 38, had earlier pointed to the superiority of the invading Anglo-Saxons' weapons over those of the Picts and Scots: 'And since they [Picts and Scots] fought with javelins and spears, and they [the Saxons] strove very stubbornly with axes and long swords, the Picts were unable to sustain so heavy an onslaught, but consulted their safety in flight'.
At the Standard, Ralph of Orkney is made to say of the Scots:
Her people have neither military skill nor order in fighting, nor self command. They do not cover themselves in armour in war; you are in constant practice of arms in the times of peace that you may be at no loss in the chances of the day of battle. Your head is covered by a helmet, your breast with a coat of mail, your legs with mail leggings, and your whole body with a shield. Where can the enemy strike you when he finds you are sheathed in steel? What have we to fear in attacking the naked bodies of men who know not the use of armour? (Huntingdon, 262–3).
For a discussion of these passages within the context of the genre of pre-battle orations see J. R. E. Beliese, 'Aelred of Rievaulx's Rhetoric and Morale at the Battle of the Standard, 1138', *Albion* xx (1988).
[100] Migne, *Patrologia Latina* clvi, 686. The translation is taken from A. A. Duncan, 'The Dress of the Scots', *The Scottish Historical Review*, 29, (1950) 210–12, who suggests that the scrip mentioned refers to the sporran.
[101] Cf. J. Bradbury, 'Battles in England and Normandy, 1066–1154', *ante* vi, 1–12. At the Standard, the best knights were placed in the front rank, interspersed with archers and spearmen (*Relatio*, 191; Richard of Hexham, 91). All the English chroniclers agree on the devastating effect of the bowmen against the Galwegians, who finally broke and fled. Their defeat demoralised the rest of the Scots army, who turned in flight (*Relatio*, 196–7; Huntingdon, 263–4; John of Hexham, 210; Richard of Hexham, 92).
[102] *Relatio*, 189–90.
[103] *Relatio*, 189–90.
[104] By the early thirteenth century the Barnwell annalist could write: 'The modern kings of Scotland count themselves as Frenchmen in race, manners, language and culture; they keep only Frenchmen in

the lives of the king and his *familia* had been put at grave risk by a Galwegian mutiny at Durham, while the quarrel between Alan de Percy and Malisse, earl of Strathearn, immediately prior to the Standard threatened to throw the army into confusion only hours before battle was joined with the English.[105] William the Lion's capture in 1174 was followed by a violent anti-feudal reaction particularly in Galloway, which revealed how hated Norman cultural and institutional innovation might be.[106] To exacerbate matters, there was little love lost between the native elements themselves, and old hatreds and separatist feelings were quick to surface once the king's cohesive authority was weakened. Hence in the chaotic retreat from the Standard in 1138, scattered bands of Scots, Galwegians and 'Angles' – that is the English of Cumbria and Lothian – fell upon each other despite the danger from the English pursuit.[107] Once William the Lion had been captured in 1174, Gilbert son of Fergus made strenuous efforts to assert Galwegian independence, which were prevented only by the intervention of Henry II.[108]

The third and most critical limitation inherent in the Scottish armies was the lack of a powerful cavalry arm. In an attempt to supplement the native levy, David I and his successors had embarked on a policy of enfeoffment to create a nucleus of heavy cavalry.[109] Yet though the process of feudalisation was well advanced by the third quarter of the century, the number of knights owed per fee was very small in comparison with *servitium debitum* south of the border. Extant royal charters of enfeoffment record only three fees owing more than five knights (two of ten, one of twenty) while the normal service was one knight, or a fraction of one. The tables of extant enfeoffments compiled by Geoffrey Barrow, although not exhaustive, suggests a *servitium debitum* for the late twelfth century of just over 100 knights.[110] To place this figure in context, it need only be noted that the English force which seized William the Lion outside Alnwick, and which was a special task force not the entire strength of the English host, consisted of about 400 horsemen.[111] To augment these feudal quotas, the Scots kings employed

---

their household and following, and have reduced the Scots to utter servitude' (Walter of Coventry, II, 206). Cf. Fantosme, ll. 383–408, 637–44.

[105] Richard of Hexham, 82; *Relatio*, 190. The unsuccessful attempt by Earl Ferteth and five other native earls to attack Malcolm IV at Perth was attributed by the chronicler of Melrose to their anger that the king had accompanied Henry II on his expedition to Toulouse, an act felt to highlight both unwonted subservience to a foreign monarch and his absorption into an alien political and social world (*Melrose*, 36).

[106] *Gesta Henrici* I, 67–8; Newburgh, 186–7.

[107] Richard of Hexham, 94; John of Hexham, 120. Similarly, following William's capture in 1174, the Scots fell on the 'English' in the army (Newburgh, 186–7).

[108] *Gesta Henrici* I, 79–80. Henry II sent Roger of Howden and Robert de Vaux, the castellan of Carlisle, to gain the submission of Uhtred and Gilbert, joint rulers of Galloway. On their arrival, they found that Uhtred had been murdered by his brother's son, and consequently rejected Gilbert's offer of an annual tribute if Henry would free him from the overlordship of William the Lion.

[109] See G. W. S. Barrow, 'The Beginnings of Military Feudalism', and 'Scotland's Norman Families', both in *The Kingdom of the Scots*, 279–314, 315–336. The Norman settlement of Scotland is the subject of Barrow's subsequent Ford Lectures for 1977 (G. W. S. Barrow, *The Anglo-Norman Era in Scottish History* (Oxford, 1980)).

[110] Barrow, 'The Beginnings of Military Feudalism', 311–14. Barrow notes of this cavalry force: 'It was no doubt useful to deal with rebellion in the remote and ungovernable parts of the kingdom, in the far north and west. But even here, William found it easier on one occasion (1212) to ask for mercenaries from England to supress an insurrection' (Barrow, 'Beginnings of Military Feudalism', 286).

[111] Fantosme ll. 1668–70. Newburgh gives the same figure, but as he drew on Fantosme's poem, it is uncertain whether his estimate is independent (Newburgh, 183).

stipendiary knights.[112] Nevertheless, the Scottish kings could never field sufficient knights to confront the English host on anything approaching equal terms. At the Standard, for example, John of Worcester numbered the knights in the Scottish army at only 200, a figure which must have been greatly exceeded by those of the Anglo-Norman host, judging from the roll call of great lords present at the battle with their retinues.[113] Recognition of this crucial weakness underlay the respective strategies adopted by the Scottish and English armies. As we have seen, the Scots were forced to adopt a policy of non-engagement, while the English sought to exploit this disparity by the deployment of their field armies in a far more confident and aggressive manner than would have been possible in other theatres of war.

Contemporary appreciation of these factors is neatly encapsulated by Jordan Fantosme's description of how William the Lion was taken unawares by the arrival of an English army as he lay before Carlisle in 1173:

> The messenger told them [the Scots] his full story of how he had seen the proud array of knights and men in armour who will launch an attack on them before sunrise. 'The army of de Lucy, that man of wisdom and good sense, will be at grips with your men ere midnight. Look to yourselves by the Divine Majesty, lest you be shamed and dishonoured. ... Take my advice – it is the best that can be given to you – betake yourself to the safety of Roxburgh! If you tarry longer here, a mocking song will be sung of you. Thibault de Balesgué did not trounce the French as badly as you will be trounced by the hardened soldiers from the south, if you and they clash in battle.'[114]

Although William himself wanted to stay and fight, his councillors insisted on the wisdom of withdrawal, so that, as Jordan contemptuously remarks, 'not a single man of his army that had been before Carlisle but scurried in arrant cowardice, without any attack being launched or any hurt inflicted'.[115]

Such a passage, designed as it was for the ears of the Anglo-Norman nobility, conveys the arrogant self-confidence of English arms. Yet that this was no empty rhetoric was fully borne out by the outcome of the engagement at Alnwick in 1174. Despite being largely neglected by military historians, the battle of Alnwick sharply

---

[112] At the Standard, David had a bodyguard of English and French knights (*Relatio*, 192). Huntingdon, 264, says that Earl Henry's line was composed of English and Norman knights from his father's *familia*.

[113] John of Worcester in Worcester, II, 111–12. Among those Norman lords at the Standard were: William of Aumâle, Walter de Gant, Robert de Brus and his son Adam, Roger de Mowbray, Walter Espec, Ilbert de Lacy, William de Percy, Richard de Courcy, William Fossard, Robert de Stuteville, Bernard de Baliol '*cum multitudine equitum*' sent by King Stephen, William Peverel, Geoffrey de Halselin and Robert de Ferrers, together with the knights of Archbishop Thurstan of York (Richard of Hexham, 86–8; John of Hexham, 119; *Relatio*, 182–3). The *servitium debitum* quotas of these lords' baronies for which information is available, calculated chiefly from I. J. Sanders, *English Baronies. A Study of their Origin and Descent, 1086–1327* (Oxford, 1960), gives an (incomplete) total of over 375 knights. In times of war, it seems unlikely that the muster of the feudal host was based closely on such artificial and exact knight service quotas; particularly in times of invasion, lords must have turned up to the host with whatever forces they had at their disposal. Nevertheless, the quotas do provide a rough minimum estimate of the number of knights that may have been at the Standard, to which should be added a substantial number of stipendiary knights.

[114] Fantosme ll. 718–35.

[115] Fantosme ll. 755–8.

reveals the high degree of professionalism of the Anglo-Norman forces. While mustering at Newcastle, the forces led by Rannulf de Glanville received detailed intelligence of the Scottish positions. In particular they learnt that the main Scottish army, including some of William's knights, was widely dispersed and occupied in plundering, leaving the king and his small *mesnie* to blockade the castle of Alnwick.[116] Rather than attacking the outlying foraging parties or attempting to force a pitched battle with the main Scottish forces, the English lords decided on a bold tactical stroke. Abandoning the support of infantry for speed of movement, they formed an assault force of approximately 400 horse and rode for Alnwick at full speed.[117] On arrival in the vicinity, they hid in a copse where they rendezvoused with a scout who provided exact information on William's deployment.[118] Their attack caught the Scots king completely unawares, and he and his retinue, which seems not to have much exceeded sixty knights, were quickly overpowered. The English then beat a hasty retreat with their captives to the safety of Newcastle.[119] As Glanville and his commanders had no doubt calculated, the Scots army rapidly broke up in confusion when deprived of its king and fled north in disarray.[120]

There could be no finer example of the quality of contemporary generalship, utilizing speed and surprise to the full. The incautious deployment of the enemy and the Scots' numerical disadvantage in knights were carefully exploited, yet at the same time careful use of regular intelligence ensured that when the English committed themselves to battle it was with the maximum advantage possible.

---

[116] Fantosme ll. 1718–24; Newburgh, 183. The significance of Alnwick as an engagement has been largely obscured by reliance on William of Newburgh. Although he drew on elements of Jordan Fantosme's poem, his later account, written in or shortly before 1196 (A. Gransden, *Historical Writing in England, c.500–1307* (London, 1974), 263), is substantially different, being elaborated and distorted for greater dramatic and didactic effect. According to Newburgh, the English lords who assembled at Newcastle on 12 July were sharply divided concerning their subsequent course of action. Some urged caution; part of their purpose had already been achieved by the Scots' withdrawal northward on hearing of their muster, and it would be rash to expose their scanty forces – 400 horse and no infantry – to the vast barbarian army of 80,000 men, 'to be devoured like a piece of bread'. Others argued that victory would be assured by the justice of their cause, and finally bolder counsel prevailed. Next morning, therefore, they set off with all haste, all the while being covered by a dense fog which obscured their whereabouts. This caused a crisis of confidence, with some urging withdrawal, but after a spirited reply by Bernard de Baliol, they rode on. Suddenly the fog cleared, and to their joy the English beheld Alnwick castle, which they hoped would afford them refuge if pressed by the enemy. Much to their surprise, however, they also caught sight of William the Lion stationed in the fields below the castle with only a small escort, the rest of his army being dispersed in plundering. The Scots king initially mistook the advancing English for a group of his own knights returning from foraging, but on realizing his error, he rushed into the attack. Heavily outnumbered, however, he was quickly overpowered and seized along with the majority of his retinue (Newburgh, 183–5).

Newburgh thus presents the English victory as a wholly fortuitous happening, brought about not by military skill and human daring, but divine providence. In particular, Newburgh was eager to stress the miraculous correlation of William's capture with Henry II's penance at Becket's tomb (Newburgh, 188). When compared to Fantosme's poem, however, the full extent of Newburgh's embellishment is clear. The fog, so vital for the dramatic impact of Newburgh's tale, is wholly absent from Fantosme, who surely would not have failed to mention so graphic a detail had it been a reality. All references to scouts and intelligence reports are omitted, the indecision and disagreement of the army leaders is heightened; the element of finding William by surprise is wholly invented.

[117] Fantosme ll. 1725–45; Newburgh, 183–4.

[118] Fantosme ll. 1758–61.

[119] Fantosme ll. 1762–1909; Newburgh, 184–5.

[120] Newburgh, 186–7.

Conversely, William the Lion was found consistently wanting in the use of intelligence, and he paid a concomitantly heavy price for the neglect of so crucial a branch of the military art.

At Alnwick, William the Lion had not been given a choice about giving or denying battle – he had effectively been ambushed. Yet what of the Standard, the one principal exception to the otherwise consistently implemented Scottish rule of non-engagement? For the decision to join battle at Northallerton in 1138 was unequivocally David's. He had even rejected the offer of the cession of Northumbria to his son, made by the English commanders in return for his withdrawal.[121] Without a better knowledge of David's ultimate strategic goals, we shall never be certain why he joined battle when twice previously that year he had declined any engagement and retired north. Perhaps he believed that the annihilation of the main English force would enable him to effect a permanent occupation of Northumbria, or less likely, to allow him to thrust further south into England. David was an able commander, who had shown himself cautious and pragmatic on several occasions, and we must presume that he felt the odds to be weighted in his favour. He may have felt that he had the advantage of surprise. John of Worcester notes that 'hoping that he should come upon them unawares, he left many vills untouched, and did not allow his men after their wont to burn anything on that day', taking advantage of a dense mist for cover.[122] In the event Thurstan's army was anything but unprepared, and David's decision to press home the attack must have stemmed from confidence in both numbers and in his original plan of deployment.

Yet for all the valuable recent emphasis on the terrors of battle, its great risk, and the infrequency of pitched battle, the vagaries of human nature and in particular the dictates of glory, honour and reputation cannot be overlooked. Jordan Fantosme's poem provides a graphic account of the pressure placed on William the Lion to declare war in 1173 by *'le gent jeufne et salvage'*, against the advice of his older, more mature councillors.[123] Duby has shown how important young knights as a collective body, the *juventus*, might be as a catalyst for war,[124] and we need look no further than the revolt of Robert Curthose or that of the Young King to see these forces in action. It would be unwise to assume that these pressures were never extended to the battlefield. Henry of Huntingdon gives the distinct impression that Earl Henry and his retinue were itching for battle. Despite seeing the disintegration of the main Scottish army, he 'paid no heed', in Huntingdon's words, 'to what he saw was being done by his side, but yearned solely after glory and valour'.[125] His charge of the English ranks was magnificent, but like that of the Lord Edward at Lewes, it did little to save the bulk of the army from defeat.[126] Similarly, in 1173 it was only with great difficulty that William the Lion's councillors dissuaded him from joining battle with de Lucy's army that was

---

[121] Richard of Hexham, 88; John of Hexham, 119; *Relatio*, 192–5.

[122] John of Worcester in Worcester, II, 111.

[123] Fantosme ll. 362–408. Cf. ll. 637–44.

[124] G. Duby, 'Youth in Aristocratic Society', *The Chivalrous Society*, trans. C. Postan (London, 1977), 112–22.

[125] Huntingdon, 264. Cf. *Relatio*, 197–8.

[126] Huntingdon, 264, says that although his charge was repulsed, Henry withdrew *'gloriose tamen re gesta'*. For Edward's charge at Lewes, see M. Prestwich, *Edward I* (London, 1988), 45–6; D. A. Carpenter, 'Simon de Montfort and the Mise of Lewes', *BIHR* lviii (1985), 4–5.

coming to the relief of Carlisle.[127] The following year, rather than attempt flight when surprised by the English at Alnwick, William snatched up his arms and was first into the fray.[128] William of Newburgh, moreover, describes how on William's seizure at Alnwick, many Scottish knights 'returned presently at full gallop and threw themselves rather than fell into the hands of their enemies, deeming it honourable to share their lord's peril'.[129]

Military or political pragmatism was thus not always the overriding factor in knights' behaviour in the field. For if Anglo-Scottish warfare in the twelfth century serves to reinforce recognition of the professionalism of the Anglo-Norman armies and their commanders, it also reveals the profound dichotomy which confronted the Scottish kings in war. David I had been born and raised as an Anglo-Norman knight and baron, while his grandson William gloried in the chivalric world of north-western France.[130] In war, both kings as individuals adhered closely to the conventions of knightly conduct in operation south of the Tweed.[131] Yet the nature and composition of the forces available to them severely restricted their military capability, compelling them to adopt an astute but inglorious policy of non-engagement. When it was an option, tactical withdrawal could be readily appreciated as shrewd generalship, when an invariable necessity it gravely compromised the Scottish kings' reputation in war. Even Jordan Fantosme, who clearly recognized and had much sympathy for William the Lion's predicament, was not above equating retreat with cowardice – 'mult grant lascheté'.[132] It is not surprising then if the sense of frustration and anger engendered by this military imbalance occasionally found expression in tactical decisions that both kings lived to regret. It was Allen Brown who stressed the crucial importance of understanding the mentalité of the Anglo-Norman warrior aristocracy, and the great importance of status, symbolism and nobility.[133] He would have been the first to recognize that in studying the actions of the knighthood, we ignore such irrational but highly important dictates as glory, shame and reputation at our peril.

To conclude, let us return to Ailred of Rievaulx and the speech he creates for his friend and patron Walter Espec immediately prior to the Standard. 'Why', he has Espec say, 'should we despair of victory, when victory has been given to our race [the Normans] as if in fee by the most High?'[134] He then goes on to list Norman conquests and victories from England to Apulia, and continues:

> Who then would not laugh, rather than fear, when to fight against such men runs the worthless Scot with half-bare buttocks? They are those, and only those, who of old thought not to oppose us, but to yield when William, conqueror of England, penetrated Lothian and Scotland as far as Abernethy,

---

[127] Fantosme ll. 713–50.
[128] Newburgh, 185.
[129] Newburgh, 185.
[130] Ritchie, *Normans in Scotland*, 125 ff.; Duncan, *Making of a Kingdom*, 197, 227–8, 255. As a youth, William was present at Henry II's siege of Toulouse (Fantosme ll. 1250–3), and took part in the tournament circuit of north-west France (*L'Histoire de Guillaume le Maréchal*, ed. P. Meyer, 3 vols (Société de l'Histoire de France, 1891–1901), ll. 1303–41).
[131] See Strickland, *Conduct and Perception*, 65–9.
[132] Fantosme ll. 755–8.
[133] See, for example, R. A. Brown, 'The Status of the Norman Knight', *War and Government*, 18–32.
[134] *Relatio*, 185; '*Cur enim de victoria desperemus, cum victoria generi nostro quasi in feudum data sit ab Altissimo?*'.

where the warlike Malcolm was made ours by his surrender: they oppose their naked hide to our lances, our swords and our arrows, using calf-skin for shields, inspired by irrational contempt of death rather than by strength.[135]

Ailred here indulges shamelessly in the Norman myth.[136] Yet in a very real sense, as the strategy adopted by the twelfth-century Anglo-Norman armies to secure the northern border showed, Norman military supremacy over the Scots was no mere literary creation, but a stark reality.

---

[135] *Relatio*, 186. The translation is taken from A. O. Anderson, *Scottish Annals from English Chroniclers, A.D. 500–1286* (London, 1908), 197.
[136] On the Norman myth see R. H. C. Davis, *The Normans and Their Myth* (London, 1970).

WACE AND WARFARE*

Matthew Bennett

Kar custume est de tel ovrainne	That's the way of this kind of work
Que tels i pert que puis guainne.	Some lose, some gain.
(B 8,866–7)[1]	

The 'work' to which Wace is referring is war. I begin with this pragmatic comment because it sums up his attitude to warfare. The unpredictability of war was a truism apparent to its practitioners. His military, aristocratic audience would have known exactly what he meant.[2] Wace is very knowledgeable about many aspects of warfare. Most of his two largest works, the *Roman de Brut* and the *Roman de Rou*, are concerned with campaigns, battles and brave deeds. This was the contemporary fashion – presumably what his audience wanted to hear – but also part of the poet's popularising and propagandising purpose. His tracing back of legitimate authority from Henry II to Brutus, the legendary Trojan conqueror after whom Britain is named, necessarily involved the description of how successive wars were waged. It does not really matter that Wace was a faithful copyist of earlier sources in this context, for he often has additional and original information to add on military matters. It does not matter that his phoney chronology spans three millennia, for he makes almost no attempt to look beyond his experience of contemporary warfare.[3]

I use the word 'experience' deliberately. Recently, it has been suggested that his use of the word 'vaslet' to describe himself may indicate that Wace had a military training in his youth. Certainly, we know very little about his early life. If he was born around 1100 and produced his literary works c. 1150 to c. 1175, we only have an insight into the last third of his life. What did he do for the other 50 years? He certainly lived, in the words of the Chinese curse, in 'interesting' times. In his mid-thirties began the sporadic but long-drawn-out civil war for the English Crown, which led to the conquest of Normandy by her

* Thanks are due to RAB for setting me to read Wace in 1980 and Professor Bernie Bachrach for suggesting this particular topic – in the suitable setting of the castle at Caen in 1987.
[1] Ed. I. Arnold, 2 vols SATF Paris, 1938, 1940. The sentiment is utterly conventional. Cf. the words of a knight to the Countess of Leicester when pulling her out of a ditch at the battle of Fornham St Genevieve in 1174, from *Jordan Fantosme's Chronicle* ed. R. C. Johnston. Oxford 1981, l. 1,071. The translations of the *Brut* are my own. Those of the Rou which follow often owe much to Edgar Taylor, *Master Wace, his Chronicle of the Norman Conquest*, London 1837, although this only covers the section from the Third version concerning William's life.
[2] See my article 'Poetry as History? The Roman de Rou of Wace as a source for the Norman Conquest', *ante* V, 1982, 21–39, for Wace's potential audience.
[3] Except, perhaps, when describing the Normans' adoption of French horses and weaponry as better than their own (Wace II 555–6).

old enemy, Anjou. What did he see of warfare? What did he know of it? Did he do any soldiering himself? Did he suffer the pangs of hunger, blows in battle, the elation of victory and the humiliation of defeat he describes so vividly? Had he seen lands burnt and devastated, villages left smouldering ruins, peasants scattered and townsmen massacred? Had he taken part in such commonplace but gruesome activities in the course of war? Well, I don't know, perhaps he had just an academic interest in warfare – as I do – but which nevertheless enabled him to write most convincingly about it.[4]

What does Wace have to tell us about warfare? Well, there is a mass of material to be mined from both his main works. Admittedly this is based largely on other authors: his *Brut* on Geoffrey of Monmouth, the *Rou*, much more a work of synthesis, on several Anglo-Norman historians writing from immediately after the Conquest into his own times. I am not attempting to compare his account with his sources to show exactly where he left them for his own invention. His 'inventing' used to be held against him, but if we see it rather as a contribution to the history of his own period, then it becomes valuable information. Of course, it is in the nature of Wace's kind of poetry to indulge in conventional expressions and descriptions which can detract from a real appreciation of warfare. But, nonetheless, he has some genuine insights to give us.[5]

Wace's knowledge will be examined under four main headings. First, strategy: involving a discussion of geography, time spent travelling; the descriptions, sites and garrisons of castles; and sieges by which strategic goals were largely achieved, including how long they took and methods employed. Closely associated with strategy is the second topic of logistics, that is, getting the necessary men, horses and materiel to the point where they are needed. Wace is very interested in ships and the sea, which played such a large part in the warfare of Britain, and keen to display his knowledge on the subject. The poet's vocabulary boasts his arcane knowledge as much as his graphic descriptions of fleets and tempests. Wace's language of warfare forms the third topic. It is rich and often idiosyncratic in the stress it lays upon aspects of warfare not often encountered in contemporary epic poetry. Which leads on to the final section on tactics: the organisation of the army on the march and in battle; the deployment of forces; tricks and stratagems employed; and descriptions of the mêlée and the weaponry used. Especially interesting is the attention Wace pays to infantry tactics, although writing in a genre which usually concentrates on chivalric achievement.

An understanding of geography is essential to a proper appreciation of military strategy. It must be said that Wace rarely gives details of topography or the movement of armies that would allow us to reconstruct campaigns from his evidence alone. This is partly because such details were not considered necessary in the poetic genre within which he worked. Partly because he probably knew little of British geography, or indeed that of France south of

---

[4] This whole paragraph must be speculative. Bennett, *ante* 1982, 22 provides a conventional biography, Dr Elisabeth van Houts makes the suggestion that because Wace calls himself 'vaslet', he had received a military education, in 'The Ship List of William the Conqueror' *ante* X, 1987, 159–83, esp. 163 & fn. 22.
[5] See Wace, 3, 99–117–168 for Holden's comments on his use of sources.

Paris.[6] He is largely dependent on his sources except where he occasionally brings them up to date, preferring Dover to Richborough as the most desirable point to enter Britain, for example.[7] But in his account of Belin and Brenne's campaign in Italy he gives a reasonable itinerary, entirely missing from his source. Their route is along the old Via Flaminia to Bologna where they turn south to cross the River Arno on their way to Rome (B 2,865-74).[8] Later the brothers use spies and peasant guides – a realistic touch, especially in mountainous areas – to outwit the Romans (B 2,985-94). Elsewhere Wace makes reference to the importance of spies in finding out an enemy's strategic intention. So, the pagan pirates Wanis and Melga are aware of how poorly Britain is defended when they make their attack (B 6,076-94). Rollo sends spies (or scouts) to gather information on the desirability of invading the Bessin: and the defenders reply in kind, enabling them to surprise the Normans (Wace II 567-82).

On this, his home territory Wace displays far wider knowledge. His account of the young duke William's rapid response to the rebellion of William of Arques provides both a realistic route and motivation. Receiving the news while hunting near Valognes (not far from Cherbourg) he takes the shortest possible route across the mouth of the Vire. Riding on through Bayeux and Caen he makes as if to go to Rouen: but this is a feint. At Pont Audemer, on the Risle, he swings left, crosses the Seine at Caudebec, and gallops via Ivetot on to Arques. William of Poitiers has a similar headlong ride, but with none of these details.[9] Wace's knowledge of Norman geography is used to good effect in his descriptions of the campaigns and actions of Val-ès-dunes, Varaville, and at Caen before 1106. He details the route of the French army in 1057, as it devastated the lands of the Bessin, for example.[10]

This sort of intentional devastation was a key part of mediaeval strategy, designed to cause widespread economic damage and to undermine a lord's political authority.[11] If he was unable to protect his subjects, they were incapable of providing his wealth. Like many of his contemporaries, Wace was keenly aware of this. When count Helias of Maine attacks Normandy in 1101, he drives the peasants from the fields and the merchants from the roads (Wace III 11,135-42). Cassibelan ravages the lands of an unlucky subject, so that

[6] Rosemary Morris, 'Aspects of Time and Place in French Arthurian Verse Romances', *French Studies* XLII, 1988, 257-77, outlines the romancers' approach to geography. Their tendency to transport their characters from Britain to Brittany, without mentioning the sea, is, of course, not indulged in by Wace.

[7] Cf. *Brut* (hereafter, B), 5,109-13 and Geoffrey of Monmouth *Historia Regum Britanniae*, ed. A. Griscom, London 1929, trans. L. Thorpe, Penguin 1966, 115 etc.

[8] They cross the Alps at Mt Genevre and Mt Cenis, capture Turin and Ivrea and then advance by way of Vercelli, Pavia and Cremona, Milan, Piacenca and Bologna, which sounds a bit confused unless this represents two separate lines of advance. The demands of metre and rhyme may also have distorted a reasonable itinerary.

[9] Wace III, 3,529-48: cf. *Gesta Guillelmi* 56-7, which gives no route, though emphasising the speed of William's movement. Wace has this episode out of chronological order, possibly in order to show the young duke triumphing over increasingly dangerous foes. A discussion of Wace's knowledge of geography may be found in M. de Boüard, 'A propos des sources du "Roman de Rou"', *Recueil de travaux offert à M. Clovis Brunel*, Paris 1955, i, 178-82 (Memoires et documents publiés pas la Société de l'Ecole des Chartes, xii).

[10] See below for a discussion of Varaville and Mortemer.

[11] C. Allmand, *The Hundred Years War* CUP, 1988, 54-6 provides a neat summary of *chevauchée* and its impact.

seeing the destruction Androgeus calls on Caesar for aid (B 4,383–95). King Arthur leaves nothing outside castle walls during his invasion of France (B 10,126–8). (I make no excuse for the confusion of chronology that must result from choosing examples so widely separated in time. Wace is describing the same type of warfare, irrespective of the era. For the same reason I use his names rather than their 'historical' counterparts, because many inhabit an imaginary world.) Rollo ravages around Bayeux to force the city's submission (Wace II 575–9); the English ravage the Cotentin, with dire results for themselves (Wace III 1,103–10); the Danes ravage Yorkshire, with King Aethelred powerless to hinder them (Wace III 1,249–56). It is an activity as commonplace as war itself.

All this devastation is far from senseless, and Wace is aware of its more immediate strategic goals. Duke William puts pressure on the French in 1054 by driving off the flocks and herds and dispersing their foragers (Wace III 4,832–40). King Harold, on the other hand, refuses his brother Gyrth's advice to pursue a scorched-earth policy during the Norman invasion. Instead, anger at the destruction of his lands leads him into overhasty battle – and defeat – just as William intended (Wace III 6,925–48). That an entire Christian society can be destroyed by such activities, is exemplified by Wace in the story of Gurmund, King of the Africans. The Saxons invite him to bring his army of 160,000 [sic] men over from Ireland. His ravages largely eradicate British Christianity.

Dunc pristent la terre a destruire;

Deus, quel dolur e quel injuire
De bone terre e de gentil,

Que turné esta tel issil!
Saisne les Alfricans cunduient,
Maisuns ardent, viles destruient;
Les chevaliers e les vilains,
Les clers, les muines, les nuneins,
Batent e chacent e ocient;
La lei Damnedeu cuntralient.

Mult veïssiez terre eissillier,

Femmes hunir, humes percier,
Enfanz en berz esbüeler,
Aveirs saisir, preies mener,
Turs abatre, viles ardeir.
(B 13,473–87)

They they took charge of the land and destroyed it,

God, what sorrow and what injury they did to the fine folk and good land,

What a blow of fate was this ravaging,
The Saxons led the Africans,
burning houses and destroying towns.
Knights and villains,
clerics, monks and nuns
they hunted, beat and murdered.
They did great damage to the Christian faith.

There you might see many lands devastated,
women violated, men speared,
babies disembowelled in their cradles,
riches seized, flocks led off,
towers brought low and towns burnt.

Significantly, Wace tells us, the name of the island was now changed from Britain to England, after its new rulers. The poet knows that war is a terrible thing.[12] Indeed, wise and strong generals like King Arthur have the power to

---

[12] Compare *Historia Regum Britanniae* where Cirencester is just captured and burnt, 264, with Wace's dramatic account: 13,533–624. The poet also makes the scene in which the mother of Belin

restrict plundering (B 9,897–904). And a Norman expedition led by Richard II
pays for all food and fodder taken in the lands of his ally, the king of France
(Wace III 2,169–76).

Destruction and harrying cannot hold a land, merely reduce it to obedience.
The instruments of successful rule are castles. Even centuries before Christ,
Belin holds Northumberland by controlling its castles and its ports (B 2,423–
30). This is not meant to be a radical redefinition of when the castle first
appeared in England. It is, rather, another example of the timelessness of the
realities of war according to Wace. Indeed, he tells us that Swein of Denmark
conquered England precisely because there were no castles, in contrast to
Normandy which was well protected with them (Wace III 1,289–1,300). This
might seem strange, since earlier British kings had defended London well.
According to the *Brut*, Elidur built the Tower and Lud the city walls (B
3,585–6 and 3,745–50).[13] Caesar constructed the Tour d'Odre at Boulogne,
where he cowered for two years secure from the Gauls (B 4,201–24). In
contrast, Brutus is able to construct a tower at Tours (hence the city's name) in
a mere dozen days (B 931–53). That this is not mere exaggeration is witnessed
by the building of Hastings castle in a week in 1066. Wace imagines this as a
prefabricated castle in barrels, reflecting the historical reality not of the
Conquest, but of his own time.[14] The point is, that to Wace warfare was
inconceivable without the castle. He also knew well how this fortification
should be used.

He stresses that a well-defended castle is a well-provisioned one: such as
Tillières, constructed by Richard II.

juste l'ewe ki Arve ad nun	near to the river called the Avre
fist e ferma une maisun.	he had a hall built and fortified.
Tant i ad fait e tant ovré,	Much was done here, much work
ke de paliz, que de fossé	of palisading, and ditching
que de mortier, que de quarel,	of masonry and mortar
ke il i ad fait un fort chastel,	until there was a strong castle
ne crient mangunel ne perrieres,	invulnerable to all kinds of
	stonethrowers,
metre li fist cest nun: Tuillieres.	constructed there with the name of
	Tillières.
Quant Ricard dut d'iloec partir	When Richard had to leave that
	place,
e le chastel out fait guarnir	the castle was well provisioned
de blé e de char e de vin. . . .	with wheat and meat and wine
(RIII 1,459–69)	

It is also garrisoned with brave knights who drive off an attack by Odo, count
of Blois, with great élan.[15] This is part of the offensive use of the castle, which
is best represented by Duke William's *Gegenburg* at Arques:

---

and Brenne prevents a battle between them into a real purple passage, which seems to express a
genuine horror of civil war (B 2,712–830).
[13] This seems to be Wace's original observation.
[14] See Bennett, 1982, *ante* 37, fn. 81 citing *Pipe Roll 17 Henry II*, 29.
[15] The Brut has a parallel passage when King Arthur constructs a 'chastelet' on the Aube,
11,640–6. Wace is fond of attributing similar military actions to his heroes.

de fossé et de heriçun
e de pel fist un chasteillun,
al pié del tertre en la valee,
ki garda tute la cuntree;
n'i pristrent puis cil del chastel

ne buef ne vache ne veel.
(RIII 3,443-8)

from a ditch and barrier
of stakes made a small fort
at the foot of the hill in the valley,
which protected the whole country.
Then those in the castle could take
    nothing,
not a bull, cow or calf.

'The finest knights in Normandy' are gathered for this little castle's defence
and to enforce the blockade.

However well defended, castles are susceptible to siege, of course. Legend-
ary Tintagel is accessible only through Merlin's magic which disguises Uther
Pendragon as its real lord (B 8,621-32, 8,691-736). Those commanders
without the great wizard's assistance have to resort to battering and assault.
This can be a very long-winded business, though, as Gurmund discovers at
Cirencester.

Perieres firent e berfreiz

Sis asaillirent plusurs feiz,
Lur enginz as murs traire,
Mes ne poient engin faire
Que cil dedenz ne cuntrefacent,
Mariens e cleies entrelacent,
Kernels refunt, portes afaitent,

Le jor ovrent, la nuit se guaitent;

Bretesches e murs apareillent.

Quant li un dorment, li un veilent.

As defenses pieres atraient,

E nequedent forment s'esmaient,
Kar il ne sevent ne ne veient

Engin par quei defendu seient.

Cil defors suvent les assaillent
E pur els prendre se travaillent,
mes cil se peinent del defendre;

Nes pot Gurmund par force prendre,
(B 13,541-58)

They construct stonethrowers and
    siege towers,
and make many assaults.
Their engines shoot at the walls;
but they cannot make one,
which those inside do not defeat.
Wood and wattle are well interlaced,
crenellations repaired, doors
    constructed,
open during the day, watched at
    night;
the walls are well provided with
    wooden covers.
When one (guard) sleeps another
    remains alert.
Stones provide materials for the
    defenders.
All the same, they were much afraid,
because they do not know, nor can
    they see,
how they can engineer the place's
    defence.*
Those outside attack often,
and strive to take the town,
but no effort can overcome the
    defence,
nor can Gurmund take it by force.

---

* There is a pun here on 'engines' and trickery or ingenuity which does not quite come off in
English.

Very rarely does an assault succeed. Duke William's capture of Alençon in this way is exceptional.

Lores fist venir esquiers	Then he had the squires come up,
e les homes as chevaliers	together with the knights,
les uns fist aler assaillir,	the latter to conduct the assault,
les altres le fossé emplir:	the former to fill the ditch.
les covertures des maisons	The coverings of houses,
e les lates e les chevrons	planks and pieces of wood
e quantque il ont prof trové	and anything that could be found
ont el fossé amoncelé,	to pile into the ditch,
pois mistrent feu devers le vent,	were set on fire before the wind.
li bois fu secs, li feu esprent.	The wood was dry, the fire flamed,
Que par le feu qu'il aluma,	So by the fire which blazed
que par l'assaut qu'il lor dona,	and which attacked them
li uns sont ars, li altre pris,	here one was burnt, another taken,
e tels i a, honte ocis.	and those caught up in it died a miserable death.

(Wace III 4,333–46)

Here the non-noble troops have a valuable rôle to play; and this emphasis on their importance is something that is peculiar to Wace, and which I shall return to. Taking a castle 'Sanz periere e sanz mangonel' as Richard II does at Mirmande is an extraordinary circumstance (Wace III 2,177). The best, and most usual plan, is to starve the defenders out. This is how Arthur forces the Parisians to come to terms (B 9,976–10,008).

Here we touch on the next topic of my talk: logistics. Even an army in the field, if surrounded and cut off from supplies, is driven to surrender, like Cassibelan's Britons to Caesar.

Quant faim e sei tant les destreint	Weakened by hunger,
Que senz arme e sanz fer les veint?	what could they do without weapon or blade?
Ja ne verrez tel fortelesce,	In truth no fortress,
Tant i ait gent de grant prüesce,	full of men of great valour,
Ki tant seit fort e grefs a prendre.	strongly defended and hard to take,
Que famine vient de vitaille	brought to famine by lack of food,
N'i estuet altre kis assaille.	needs any other assault.

(B 4,675–82)

Wace was aware that hunger is the greatest weapon in war. Whether he knew his Vegetius or not, he certainly understood the practical application of the Roman theorist's ideas.[16] So Arthur, on his Irish campaign, sweeps up all the cows and oxen in the country to feed his men and to deprive the enemy of

---

[16] Both episodes appear in the *Historia* but Wace expands them greatly. The application, by mediaeval commanders, of Vegetius' time-honoured principle of starving the enemy rather than fighting him, is succinctly described in John Gillingham, 'Richard I and the Science of War in the Middle Ages' in *War and Government in the Middle Ages. Essays in Honour of J. O. Prestwich*, ed. John Gillingham and J. C. Holt, Ipswich 1984, 78–91, citing the valuable comments of Wace's vernacular contemporary, Jordan Fantosme, ed. Johnston 83–5.

sustenance (B 9,669–72).[17] Knowing how many mouths he has to feed is of key importance for a general, of course, but Wace does little better than most mediaeval authors when dealing with numbers. He is vague on the size of hosts, saying that he does not know whether Arthur raised 400 or 4,000 Danish warriors from that country (B 9,990–2). Sometimes he does give a total for the knights in an army, though. There were apparently 2,000 in the army of Angusel, king of Scots, Arthur's opponent, but they were accompanied by 'numberless foot' (B 11,038–40). Sometimes his numbers reach the ubiquitous mediaeval 60,000 = a great many. It simply was not fashionable to count. Even his figures of seeming exactitude, like the 696 ships of Duke William's invasion fleet, supposedly passed down from Wace's father, are dubious (Wace III 6,423–6). But the lack of 'accurate' numbers does not affect the poet's ability to describe logistical operations clearly, especially those involving ships, sailing and amphibious landings.

Wace has a knowledge of ships and an expert's vocabulary which he is eager to share, regarding sails and sheets, halliards and hawsers. Clearly fleets play a big part in getting armies to and from Britain (or England). His interest ranges from Caesar's invasion attempts through Arthur's invasion of France, to, of course, the 1066 landings. He gives the correct number of ships (according to *De Bello Gallico*) for Caesar's first invasion, and underestimates for his second. The size of the fleets does not interest Geoffrey of Monmouth, though Wace borrows his vivid description of the holing of vessels by shore defences (B 4,243–59). In most sources little time is spent discussing how ships get from A to B. Not only does Wace provide vivid descriptions of embarking and disembarking, but also of storms which made sea travel so perilous. First, here is Arthur's army embarking for the conquest of Gaul:

Puis vint passer a Suthamtune;	Then they went to Southampton;
La furent les nefs amenees	there the ships were brought together,
E les maisnees assemblees.	and the households assembled.
Mult veïssiez nes aturner,	There you might see many ships made ready,
Nés atachier, nés aancrer,	ships tied up and ships at anchor,
Nés assechier e nés floter,	beached ships and ships afloat,
Nés cheviller e nés cloer,	pegged ships and tarred ships,
Funains estendre, maz drecier,	ropes stretched and masts raised.
Punz mettre fors e nés chargier,	Gangplanks are brought out and the ships loaded.
Helmes escuz, halbercs porter,	Helmets, shields and hauberks are carried,
Lances drecier, chevals tirer,	lances raised and horses drawn aboard.
Chevaliers e servanz entrer.	Knights and their servants enter,
E l'un ami l'altre apeler,	each friend calling to another,

---

[17] Wace also displays his knowledge of the reality of Irish warfare – as essentially a cattle raid – just as he accurately describes their warriors' vulnerability (see below). See Robin Frame's account of 'War and peace in the medieval Lordship of Ireland' in *The English in Medieval Ireland*, ed. James Lydon, Dublin 1984, 118–41.

Mult se vunt entresaluant	wishing to exchange greetings,
Li remanant e li errant.	those remaining and those leaving.
Quant as nés furent tuit entré	When the ships were all loaded,
E tide orent e bon oré,	and the time and tide were right,
Dunc veïssiez ancres lever,	then you might see anchors raised,
Estrens traire, hobens fermer,	painters pulled in and haliards made fast,
Mariniers saillir par cez nés,	the sailors leap about the boats,
Deshenechier veilles e trés;	loosing sails and canvas,
Li un s'esforcent al windas,	some set about the capstan,
Li altre al lof e al betas;	others see to the sheets and luffing.
Detriés sunt li guverneür,	In the stern stand the captains,
Li maistre esturman li meillur.	the best master steersmen.
(B 11,190–214)	

There are several descriptions of landings, but none so full or effective as the disembarkation of the Normans in 1066.

Li dus out grant chevalrie	The duke had a great chivalry
e mult out nes en sa navie,	and many ships in his fleet;
moult out archiers, mult out servanz,	many archers, many sergeants,
homes hardie e combatanz,	brave and warlike men,
carpentiers e engigneors,	carpenters and engineers,
boens fevres e boens ferreiors,	good smiths and metalworkers.
les nes sunt a un port tornees,	The ships steered to one port
totes sunt ensenble aunees,	and reached shore together.
toutes sont ensemble acostees,	All lay together,
toutes sont ensemble aanchres,	all anchored together,
ensemble totes asechierent	all beached together,
e ensenble les deschargierent,	and were all unloaded together.
. . .	. . .
Donc veïssiez boens mariniers,	Then you might see good sailors,
boens servanz e boens esquiers	good sergeants and good squires,
sailir fors e nes deschargier,	sally forth and unload the ships,
ancres jeter, cordes sachier,	cast the anchors and haul the ropes,
escuz e seles fors porter,	bear out shields and saddles,
destriers e palefreiz tirer.	lead out the warhorses and palfreys.
Li archier sunt issu,	The archers disembarked,
al terrain sunt primes venu,	the first to set foot on land,
donc a chascun son arc tendu,	each with his bow bent,
coivre e tarchais al lez pendu;	his quiver and bowcase hanging at his side.
tuit furent res e tuit tondu,	all were shaven and shorn,
de corz dras furent tuit vestu,	and all clad in short tunics,
prez d'assaillir, prez de fuïr,	ready to attack, ready to flee,
prez de torner, prez de gandir;	ready to turn about and ready to skirmish.
le rivage ont tuit poralé,	They scoured the whole shore,
nul home armé n'i ont trové.	but not an armed man could they find there.

Quant issu furent li archier / When the archers had gone out,
donc issirent li chevalier, / then the knights disembarked,
tuit armé et tuit haubergé, / all armed and armoured,
escu a col, elme lacié; / their shields at their shoulder and helmets laced,

ensenble vindrent al gravier, / they formed up on the shore,
chascun armé sor son destrier, / each mounted on his warhorse.
tuit orent ceintes les espees, / All had their swords girded on,
al plain vindrent, lances levées. / and rode onto the plain with lances raised.

Li baron orent gonfanons, / The barons carried gonfanons,
li chevalier orent penons; / the knights had pennants.
joste les archiers se sunt mis, / They placed themselves next to the archers,
le terrain ont avant porpris. / on the ground which had been seized.
(RIII 6,465–76: 481–508)

The details of this account, the sort of information entirely omitted from William of Poitiers, are not, of course, historical. But they bear witness to Wace's powers of observation and ability to interpret military activity.

Not all sea crossings were as fortunate as Duke William's. It is another mark of Wace's attention to detail that he re-creates some ferocious storms.

Une turmente grant leva; / A great tempest arises,
Li tens mua, li venz turna, / the weather changes, the wind shifts,
Tona e plut e esclaira; / – thunder, rain and lightning –
Li ciels neirci, li airs trobla; / the heavens darken, the starlight fades,

La mer mella, undes leverent, / the sea heaves, winds rise,
Wages crurent e reverserent. / waves swell and crash.
Nefs commencent a perillier, / Now ships are in peril,
Borz e chevilles a fruisser; / timbers and pegs break,
Rumpent custures e borz cruissent, / joints burst and timbers creak,
Veilles depiecent e mast fruissent; / sails tear and masts snap.
Ne poeit hom lever la teste, / No man might raise his head,
Tant par esteit grant la tempeste. / so great was the storm.
Les nefs furent tost departies / The ships were all scattered,
E en plusurs terres fuïes. / and fled to many different shores.
(B 2,479–92)

Wace conjures this storm for the Danish fleet which is pursuing Brenne back to Northumbria. The passage shows both his knowledge of technical terms and of the effects of bad weather on ships of his time.[18]

On land Wace makes frequent reference to horses. Warfare is inconceivable without them. First there are the destriers – warhorses – essential for chivalric warfare. Rollo, on his arrival in Gaul, is quick to adapt to cavalry tactics (Wace II 555–6). The English at Hastings are derided for their ignorance of

---

[18] For literary influences see J. Griswald 'A propos du théme descriptif de la tempête chez Wace et chez Thomas d'Angleterre', in *Mélanges de langue et de litterature du Moyen Age et de la Renaissance offerts à Jean Frappier*, 2 vols 1970, i, 375–89.

mounted warfare (Wace III 8,603–5). Horses have a valuable rôle in logistics too, carrying provisions and all the army's gear. The best descriptions of this are in the passages on the French forces at Varaville in 1057 and at Mortemer, three years earlier. In the first case Wace uses the evocative word 'coe' or tail to depict the long, straggling line of march that the baggage train creates (Wace III 5,191–8).[19] When King Henry of France hears of the defeat of the other half of his pincer movement at Mortemer, all is confusion as his men break camp.

pernent palefreis e destriers,	They seized the palfreys and warhorses,
trossent roncins, chargent sommiers,	harnessed the hacks and loaded the packhorses,
loges alument e foillies,	burnt their shelters and bivouacs,
mult les aveient tost voïes;	emptied them of everything,
les herneis enveient avant,	and sent the gear on ahead,
detriés les vait li reis gardant.	– the king went forward with caution.
(Wace III 4,959–64)	

Above all, Wace is aware that money provides the sinews of war. He attributes the success of Henry I over Robert Curthose in the fight for Normandy, rather bitterly, to its power. Money means men: 'moult out deniers, grant gent mena' and Henry's huge wealth is carried 'od grant tonels, od grant charei' (Wace III 10,854/7). In contrast:

Li dus n'aveit gaires deniers,	The duke had hardly any money,
ker il despendeit volentiers,	because he spent it so freely,
tot erent ses rentes faillies	all his rents were exhausted
e despendues ses aïes;	and his feudal dues expended.
n'i poeient pas foisoner	They could not possibly suffice
a bien despendre e a doner.	a generous expenditure and gift-giving.
(Wace III 10,883–8)	

Money provides for provisions, troops and transport, buys off the duke's 'soldeiers' (Wace III 10,899–904) and eventually undermines all his support. Robert has nothing to give but promises.

Quant li dus doner ne poeit,	When the duke could give no more,
ou ne poeit ou ne voleit,	– couldn't or wouldn't –
par pramesses se delivrout,	he delivered himself of promises.
mult pramateit e poi donout.	He promised much and gave little.
(Wace III 10,931–6)	

Wace, ever the realist, assesses that Henry won because 'most of the knights and the best of the barons' defected to the better paymaster (Wace III 11,159–62).

---

[19] The image of an animal's tail dragging behind is one that might strike anyone who had seen a line of march. The modern British Army uses the term 'teeth' to describe frontline troops and 'tail' their innumerable, essential supports.

This idea, of 'gain' as the chief motivation for war, leads us on to the section I have called the language of warfare. We have already seen distinctive uses of vocabulary specific to warfare. Some would claim, Hans-Erich Keller amongst them, that a great deal of this vocabulary is specific to Wace.[20] Certainly the poet lays great emphasis on ransoms, booty and on pay for the 'soldeier'. This word has caused controversy when translated as mercenary owing to the modern, derogatory connotations of the term. To men of rank and status it could be insulting, as Robert Curthose made clear to his father. But it need not be, for lesser men, and its literal translation of soldier serves us well.[21] A wise general, like duke William, ensures that pay and gifts are kept up to such men, during periods of inaction. The long wait for a good wind at St Valéry epitomises the problem.

Donc vindrent soldeier a lui,	Then soldiers came to him
e uns e uns, e dui e dui,	one by one, and two by two,
e quatre e quatre, e cinc e siés,	and four by four, by fives and sixes,
or set, or oit, or nof, or diés;	by sevens, eights, nines and tens;
e li dus toz les reteneit,	and the duke retained them all,
mult lor donout et pramateit.	giving them much and promising more.
Plusors vindrent par covenant	Many came according to an agreement
que il aveient fait avant;	which they had made beforehand.
plusors del ducs terres voleient	Many wished for the duke's lands,
s'Engleterre prendre poeient;	should he conquer England.
alquanz soldees demandoent,	Some required pay,
livreisons e dons coveitoent,	and allowances and gifts.
sovnet les estoveit despendre,	Often it was necessary to distribute these,
ne poeient longues atendre.	to those who could not afford to wait.
(Wace III 6,403–16)	

Wace celebrates the great booty following Richard I's defeat of the Germans at Rouen (Wace II 3,291–9; 3,357–62). Horses and equipment are the immediate prizes; their masters languish in prison awaiting ransom. This gleeful passage following Mortemer sums up the poet's attitude:

N'i out gaires si vil garçon	There was hardly a boy, no matter how lowly,
que n'en menast Franceis prison	who did not lead a Frenchman to prison,
e bes destriers, ou dous ou treis,	with a fine warhorse, or two, or three,

---

[20] *Étude descriptive sur le vocabulaire de Wace*, Deutsche Akadamie der Wissenschaften zu Berlin, Veroffentlichungen des Instituts fur Romanische Sprachwissenschaft Nr. 7, Berlin 1953. See also A. Bell. 'Notes on Gaimar's military vocabulary' in *Medium Aevum* XL, 1971, 93–104, who concludes that Wace's military vocabulary is much richer but not as exceptional as Keller believes.

[21] Orderic, V, 98 uses the term 'Mercennarius' as a derogatory one. Cf. the French 'soldeier' at Hastings who overcomes his fear to dispatch two opponents (Wace III 8,295–328).

estre l'autre menu herneis;
n'out chartre en tote Normendie

que de Franceis ne fust emplie.
(Wace III 4,909–14)

apart from all the lesser gear.
Nor was there a dungeon in all
        Normandy,
which was not full of Frenchmen.

Even when prisoners are ransomed, their equipment was kept by their captors. This provided an incentive – especially for the lower ranks in the host. These 'non-noble' warriors include squires, sergeants and footsoldiers of all sorts. Wace lays especial emphasis on the value of infantry, whom he often calls the 'gelde'. This word has the dual implication of someone who is a paid warrior and also suggests a sense of corporate identity.[22] He includes the English, fighting on foot in their traditional manner at Hastings under this heading. And, although some of his characters make derogatory reference to such troops, on the whole they are shown to play an important part in war and battle. Richard I's victory over the French on the Rive Béthune (arr. Seine-Maritime) is achieved through their efforts:

Franchoiz furent plusor et cil de Normandie.
mez a l'eve se tindrent, quer de gelde iert garnie,
d'archiers et d'escuiers qui n'espernerent mie; . . .
Archiers trove et villainz donc la terre est planiere,
a chenz et a milliers garnissent la riviere,
qui porte arc et qui hache, quil grant lance geldiere;
moult occient chevauls et devant et derriere. . . .
Li roi vit son damage, puiz retrait sa baniere.
(Wace II 3,928–30; 37–41; 45)

The French were in greater numbers than the Normans,
but they were checked at the stream, because the footmen defended it,
with archers and squires, who gave them no mercy . . .
There were archers and peasants on the level ground,
in their hundreds and thousands lining the riverbank,
here a man carried a bow, here an axe, here a long pike,
they killed so many horses in the front and rear ranks . . .
When the king saw his losses, he led off his troops.

In the same battle, esquires are described as armed with pikes, coming to the rescue of the knights (Wace II 3,898). There are lesser men yet; 'li garçon et l'autre frapaille' who appear at Hastings and are used by Arthur in a battle against the Romans, made to stand on a hill and to look more warlike than they actually are (Wace III 7,941–94; B 12,309–14).[23]

Wace also uses some interesting vocabulary associated with the organisation and command of an army. A large force is described as an 'ost' or 'esforz'; a smaller group as a 'compagnie' or 'maisniee' (both having connotations of

---

[22] See F. Godefroy *Lexique de l'Ancien Français*. Paris 1901, 255, where 'gelde' can mean either a unit of soldiers or a craft association, and 'geldon' a spearman or a peasant levy.
[23] This is another example of paralleled behaviour between two great commanders. Either that, or a good idea used twice.

group loyalty); tactical units are the 'conrei' (squadron) and 'conestablie' (troop). This is effectively a hierarchy of units and Wace stresses the importance of leadership. 'Chevetaines' (captains) command companies and below them are constables. Unlike his Latin sources he sees no need to employ archaic and anachronistic terminology like legions, cohorts and centuries to describe his 'contemporary' warfare. In fact, he only uses the word 'legiun' in the context of a Roman force (B 3,179–83; 5,275). Wace employs a wide range of words to describe deployment for battle and manoeuvres of the opposing troops. Alexander Bell has pointed out the relative paucity of Gaimar's language in this area. This greater variety may be indicative of greater poetic skill; but I consider it to be a product of a greater interest in the subject and a wider knowledge.

Finally, there is another group of words which ties in the last topic: description of weaponry, especially non-chivalric equipment. He describes axes: 'hache', often 'noresche' (Scandinavian) and 'besague': pikes, 'gisarme' and 'truble' which is a combination of these two (rather like a halberd). He uses many words associated with an archer's equipment: 'coivre' and 'tarchais' to carry their arrows, and the 'talevas', a shield to keep them out. He has also other missile weapons, the 'funde' or sling and 'plumee' (which may be a lead-weighted javelin) both associated with siege and street fighting.

Before we leave this section on the language of warfare I would like to include a passage in which Wace sets out the ethos of the chivalric warrior. This is largely through the words he puts into the mouth of Neél (Nigel) vicomte of the Cotentin when repelling a Breton invasion in 1033, during the reign of Robert the Magnificent.

Neel e Auveré oïrent	Nigel and Alfred heard
l'asemblee ke Bretun firent,	of the Breton muster
cels de Avrencein asemblerent	and assembled the men of the Avrencin,
e tuz cels k'il porent manderent,	and anyone else they could call upon,
gent a pie e gent a cheval.	men on foot and on horse.
'Baruns,' funt il, 'franc natural,	'Barons,' he cried, 'freeborn men,
or verrum ki bein le fera	it is well known that you fight well,
e ki sun seignur amera;	and love your lord.
gardez ui cest jurn vostre honur,	Look to your honour this day
gardez le pru vostre seignur.	and protect your lord's reputation.
Pur malvaise gent cil nus tienent,	They will hold us cheap,
ki pur le lostre el nostre vienent;	those who come to take our reputation from us,
de la preie acoillir se peinent,	Who strive to gather and carry off the flocks.
se il, noz oilz veant, l'en meinent,	If this robbery happens before our eyes,
ke nus ne escuums noz aveirs,	and we do not recover our riches,
grant reprovier iert a nos eirs.	great blame will attach to our heirs.
Fierement les envaïssiez,	Attack them fiercely,
sis avrez tost estolteiez;	if you wish to rout them utterly.
ferez chevaliers e chevals,	Strike knights and horses,

ferez seignurs, ferez vassals,	strike lords, strike vassals,
tuez quanque tuer porreiz,	kill all of them which you may kill,
je mar humme i esparnierez.'	woe to any man of you who shows mercy.'
E cil crient: 'Alum, alum!	And they cry, 'Let's go, let's go!
Ke faites vu? Trop demorum!'	What are you doing? We have waited long enough!'

(Wace III 2,641–64)

All Neel's rousing speech seems to suggest is that 'Up and at 'em' is sufficient instruction to conduct a battle. In fact, as Wace shows, orders, and the co-ordination of forces known as tactics, are vitally important. He has clear ideas of how best to set out men for a battle. (I know battles were rare in reality; but they are very common in poetic description.) As I have already pointed out he is interested in the arms and armour of footmen, which has tactical implications. For example, there are the 'Haches, darz, gavelocs, gisarmes' of Arthur's infantry (B 11,140). These are similar to the 'English arms' which Harold describes at Hastings, when encouraging his men:

'e vos avez haches agues	'and you have sharp axes,
e granz gisarmes esmolues;	and large, glittering halberds;
contre vos armes, qui bien taillent,	against your arms, which cut so well,
ne qui que les lor gaires vaillent;'	they will hardly avail;'

(Wace III 7,771–4)

Wace makes the point that 'the English did not know how to joust, nor to carry arms on horseback' (Wace III 8,603–4) – something which clearly counted against them at Hastings. He follows this fairly conventional comment with a most original observation. 'It seems to me that it is not possible for a man to strike good blows with a two-handed axe and protect himself at the same time' (Wace III 8,607–13). Both remarks show that Wace really thought about warfare at the basic level of hand-to-hand fighting. Infantry weapons were good in the hands of brave, well-trained men, even those of low social rank; cavalry tactics were better but could be thwarted by good foot. I can think of no contemporary who expresses this conflict so clearly.

William wins at Hastings, according to the Norman sources, by a combination of the feigned flight of his knights (of which more later) and his powerful archers. Wace is aware of the significance of the missilemen, and not just at Hastings. In Arthur's battle against the emperor Lucius, arrows 'fall like hail' (B 12,547–8). His conquest of Ireland is made easier by the natives' ignorance of the weapon, while his own archers shoot most thickly. The Irish are further hampered by their lack of armour (B 9,681–8) and indeed are quite unaccustomed to battle (B 8,113–14).[24] Wace naturally assumes that his heroes – Briton or Norman – do have that advantage. He says very little about military training, although he is not unusual in that. When knights are in mock battle at Cassibelan's court, in celebration of his recent defeat of Julius Caesar, his

---

[24] Wace's assessment of the Irish is supported by the *Song of Dermot and the Earl*, ed. G. H. Orpen, Oxford 1892. This vernacular text of a generation later describes their lack of armour most tellingly in their first battle against the English, ll. 664–85, esp. 672–5.

nephew Hireglas is accidentally killed. Now, Wace distinguishes the 'bohorde', a safer form of mounted joust between the chevaliers, from the 'escrimie' or fencing, which the younger warriors ('bachelers' and 'damoiseaux') take part in. The day ends with a fencing match in which Hireglas' opponent loses his temper and kills him (B 4,334–62).[25]

These are individual exercises in arms, of course. What is missing from Wace, as from most mediaeval sources, are descriptions of training in a body. Knights were accustomed to acting in concert in the hunting-field from an early age. In the twelfth century we first have evidence for tournaments, including the mass mêlée which involved manoeuvre by troops of horse and foot.[26] Clearly such expertise must have been required for such a ruse as the feigned flight. Wace describes this on several occasions, not just at Hastings, and although the feasibility has recently once again been doubted, he obviously believed it possible.[27]

Another favourite ploy of the author's is the ambush. These are usually mounted from woods, as the word 'enbuschement' suggests. They occur frequently in the *Brut*, with some influence from Geoffrey of Monmouth, as in the case of Androgeus' treacherous attack on Cassibelan (B 4,596–8; 608–14). The French knights accompanying a supply train destined for rebellious Arques is lured into ambush by a feigned flight (Wace III 3,475–98). Or a valley may serve as a hiding-place, as it does for vicomte Nigel's attack on the Bretons already cited (Wace III 2,669–70).

Wace's finest description of an army-sized ambush is Duke William's attack on the French rearguard at Varaville.

Li reis aveit Dive passee,	The king had crossed the Dive,
l'eve qui cort par la contree,	the river which runs through that country,
ensemble od lui le plus de l'ost,	together with the majority of his army,
qui se penoent d'aler tost,	which had taken care to move quickly.
mais longue esteit la rote arriere,	But line of march behind was long
continuel tote et entiere.	and all together.
Li dus vit que la force ert soe	The duke saw that he could gain an advantage,
vers cels qui erent en la coe;	over those in the army's tail.
quant il entra en Garavile,	He pressed his men on from village to village,
sa gent enprés de vile en vile,	and when he came to Varavile,
Franceis trova qui se teneient,	he found those of the French there
qui la rieregarde faiseient.	who formed the rearguard.

[25] See *Orderic* ii, 29 for the 'real-life' death of Hugh de Giroie in javelin practice.
[26] Juliet Vale. *The Tournament 1100–1300*, Boydell & Brewer, 1986.
[27] J. M. Carter doubts the likelihood of the feigned flight in the eleventh century but will admit it in the twelfth. See: *The Anglo-Norman Anonymous*: The newsletter of the Haskins Society, 6, 1988, 7–8. Certainly Wace believed it possible, since he used it often eg. II 161–4, 3,231–5 etc. He makes the feigned flight at Hastings a tactic the Normans were so well versed in that they are able to put it into operation as it suits them (Wace III 8,175–88).

La veïssiez fiere assemblee,
maint colp de lance e d'espee,
de lances fierent chevaliers
e od les ars traient archiers,
e od les pels vilains lor donent,

mult en confundent e estonent,
en la chaucie les enbatent,
mult en i tuent e abatent,
e li Norman tot tens creisseient,
qui grant torbes acoreient.
Donc veïssiez rote haster,

l'un Franceis l'autre avant boter,
Mult lor ennoie la chaucie
qu'il trovent longe e enpeirie,
e il esteient encombré,
de co qu'il aveient robé;
mult en veissiez desroter
e trebuchier e fors voler,

qui pois ne porent relever
ne en la dreite veie entrer;
al pont passer fu grant la presse

e la gent d'aler mult engresse.
Viez fu li pont, grant fu li fais,

plances trebuchent, chient ais;
la mer monta, li flo fu granz,

sor le pont fu li fais pesanz,
li pont trebucha a chai
e quantqui out desus peri;
maint en chaï enprés le pont,
qui devala el plus parfont.
Al pont chaeir fu la criee,

mult dolerose e esfree,
mult veïssiez herneis floter,
homes plungier e affondrer;
nus ne s'en pout vif escaper
s'il ne fu bien doit de noer.
Qant il orent al pont failli

n'i out si proz ne si hardi

qui n'eust poor de perir,
ker il n'aveient ou gandir;

Then there was a fierce battle –
many blows of lance and sword.
The knights struck with their lances,
the archers shot their bows,
and the peasants gave them what
    with their pikes,
stunning and utterly confounding them,
killing them and driving them
down the causeway in pursuit.
The Normans increased in numbers
hastening to form a large force.
Then you might see the French
    troops routed
pressing one on another.
The causeway hindered them,
being long and in bad repair,
and they were encumbered,
by everything they had plundered.
Many were seen breaking the line,
stumbling and hastily leaving the
    route,
who could not retrace their steps
or get onto the right track again.
On crossing the bridge the press was
    great,
everyone was eager to reach it.
The bridge was old, its burden was
    heavy,
its boards broke, planks split,
the sea rose and the current was
    strong.
The heavy weight on the bridge
caused it to crash and shatter,
and everyone upon it perished.
Many fell in close by the bridge
where the water was deep.
As the bridge collapsed into the
    water there a cry was heard,
of great sorrow and terror.
Much harness was to be seen floating,
men plunging and sinking.
No-one could escape alive,
if he did not know how to swim well.
When they heard that the bridge had
    fallen,
there was no-one, no matter how
    brave or bold,
who did not fear for his own life,
lest he should not be spared.

Normant detriers les vont pernant,	They see the Normans pressing on from behind
n'il ne poent aler avant,	but they may not go forward.
par les rivages vont tastant,	They cast along the river banks,
quez et passages vont querant,	seeking for fords and crossings,
armes e robes vont getant,	throwing away arms and plunder,
co peise lor qu'il en ont trebuchant,	because the weight of it causes them to stumble.
e li uns l'autre traïnant,	One leads another,
e li Normant d'iloc les traient,	the Normans press upon them there
qui nes esparnent ne manaient.	sparing none nor showing any mercy.
Tuit cil qui furent aresté,	All those who were trapped,
qui ne furent al pont passé,	and unable to cross that bridge,
furent retenu e lié,	were captured and bound,
ou ocis furent ou neié.	or killed, or drowned.
(Wace III 5,191–256)	

The vividness of this description is unique to Wace. Only he mentions the broken bridge and its disastrous impact on the fleeing French. It does not matter if this bridge never existed; we still have a powerful and accurate portrayal of an army in rout. And ambushes were important in warfare; they were much feared and often employed. Henry I's decisive victory at Tinchebrai was the result of an outflanking charge by a hidden group of cavalry.[28]

If open fields were more common as battlefields, this was because it was easier to muster men for purposes of control and morale. Wace usually employs the term 'conrei' meaning both an army's deployment and its smaller units to describe a battle line. It is normally composed of three divisions and composed of 'eschielles' (squadrons) commanded by the 'seigneurs' and 'chevetains' and the smaller units of 'conroi' and 'mesnee'. He places great emphasis on the importance of banners on the field of battle. The gonfanon is both a symbol of authority and a guide. So, when in the battle against the Bretons, vicomte Nigel leads the way:

e Auveré serreement	and closely ordered, Alfred
dut mener tute l'autre gent;	led all the other men,
lez lui fist un penun porter	near to him a banner borne,
ou lur gent pussent recuvrer.	upon which their troops could rally.
(Wace III 2,673–6)	

The death of a standard bearer signalled defeat, as Rollo points out when, in fighting the French.

Roullant fu ocis, qui l'enseigne portout,	Roland was killed, he who bore the standard,
qui tenoit les mesnies et les autres quiout.	who commanded the households and led the rest.
(Wace II 547–8)	

[28] The battle has been most recently discussed (and illustrated) by Jim Bradbury, *The Medieval Archer*, Woodbridge 1985, 42–3.

Wace makes a great point of the importance of Turstan fitz Rou's exemplary behaviour with William's standard at Hastings (Wace III 8,673–80 etc.).[29] Other field commands are given by horns (B 452) and trumpets (Wace III 7,999–8,000). The latter instrument is used to recall Brutus' forces from pursuing the 'French' (B 1,044–5). This suggests that Wace envisaged commanders having a tighter control over their knights than is normally supposed (unless we presume this mythical exaggeration). At night no sound is to be made until the battle cry for attack is shouted (B 9,085–8). This again speaks volumes for the control Wace thought commanders could exercise.

In battle the poet also stresses control, disciplined manoeuvre and good close order to fight effectively. He is not alone in this; many contemporary works recognise these military virtues, although they are often best expressed in the vernacular.[30] Harold exhorts the English at Hastings to keep good, close order to prevent the Normans from penetrating their ranks (Wace III 7,757–69). So much are his Latin sources agreed upon, but Wace adds a barricade, of which more later. William's forces are also carefully arrayed:

Cil a pié aloent avant,	Those on foot led the way
sereement, lor ars portant,	in serried ranks, bearing bows.
chevaliers emprés chevalchoent,	The knights rode close,
qui les archiers aprés gardoent;	protecting the archers from behind.
cil a cheval e cil a pié,	Those on horse and those on foot,
si com il orent commencié,	just as they had begun,
tindrent lor eirre e lor compas,	kept their order and the same pace,
sereement, lor petit pas,	in close ranks and at a slow march,
li un l'autre ne trespassout	So that no-one might overtake another,
ne n'apreismout ne n'esloignout,	nor get too close nor too far apart.
tout aloent serreement	All advanced in close order;
e tuit aloent fierement;	and all advanced bravely.
(Wace III 7,685–96)	

For the final Norman charge at Hastings, with Duke William closely surrounded by his knights, Wace provides a classic description.

jost lui vit son gonfanon,	You might see near to him, his banner,
plus de mil armez environ,	and more than a thousand armed men around him,
qui del duc grant garde perneient	who took good care of the duke,
e la ou il poigneit poigneient	and struck where he struck.
sereement, si com il durent,	In the closest order they could achieve,
vers les Engleis ferir s'esmurent.	they hurled themselves against the English.
Od la force des boens boens destriers	With the weight of the good warhorses,

---

[29] See my more detailed comments on this in *ante* 1982, 33.
[30] See the comments of J. F. Verbruggen, *The art of warfare in western Europe during the Middle Ages*, Oxford 1977, 16–17.

e od cels cols des chevaliers, — and the blows of the knights,
la presse ont tote derompue — they broke the enemy ranks
e la turbe avant els fendue; — scattering the mob before them.
li boens dus avant les conduit, — The good duke led from the front.
maint en chaça e maint s'en fuit — Many fled and many pursued.
(Wace III 8,759–70)

What happened if close order was given up is exemplified in the *Brut*. A group of British knights charge out of a wood, surprising the emperor Lucius' men; but overtaken by enthusiasm they are thrown back by Romans in good order.

Breton puineient a desrei, — The Bretons charged in disorder
Ne vuleient estre en cunrei, — they did not wish to retain their formation.

. . . — . . .

Petreïeus fu mult engrés, — (The Roman commander) was unrelenting,

Ses bons humes tint de sei pres. — He kept his good men very close to him.
(B 11,957–8; 65–6)

I shall close this section with what I suspect is, to Wace, a perfect battle array. It is the one Belin and Brenne adopt in their final battle against the Romans, when they have to reorganise their men for the decisive blow.

Lur gent firent raseürer, — Their troops were allowed to recuperate,

Chevals restreindre, homes armer, — to harness horses and arm the men.
Puis unt fait conreiz de lur gent — Then to form up in battle array,
Par mil, par cinquante, par cent; — by thousands, by fifties and by hundreds.

de plus hardiz, des plus aidables — The toughest and most useful men
Firent maistres e conestables — were made leaders and constables
A chescune eschielle par sei, — over each of their squadrons
Quis face tenir en conrei. — which take their place in the battle line.

Les plus hardiz combateors — The best fighters
Mistrent avant as fereors; — were placed in front as strikers.
lez cels firent destre e senestre — Those on the right and left flanks
Arbelastiers e archiers estre. — were crossbowmen and archers.
Le mielz de lur gent e le plus — The better and the larger part of their army

Descendirent des chevals jus, — dismounted from their horses[31]
En mi le champ furent a pied — and, in the middle of the field, on foot

Ordeneement e rengied. — drew up their ranks in good order.
Cil unt par mi trenché lur lances — They cut their lances down,

---

[31] The tactical significance of dismounting knights to fight on foot in the twelfth century is best expressed and discussed by Bradbury, *The Medieval Archer*, 39–57. The battle of Lincoln, where King Stephen fought on foot with a Scandinavian axe, and the Welsh foot played a large part in his defeat, seems directly relevant to Wace's interpretation of Hastings and other battles. Orderic vi, 542.

E querpies lur conuaissances,	and abandoned their heraldic devices.
Cil en irrunt le petit pas	They advanced at a slow march
Ferir sur la grant presse el tas,	to fight through the mêlée in a body.
Ja uns d'els ne desrengera	So that no one should lose his place
Ne pur home guenchira.	nor any man turn in flight.
Dunc unt grailles e corns soné	Then trumpets and horns were heard to sound
Si sunt al ferir aturné.	as they set themselves to fight.
(B 3,115–38)	

I hope I have shown that Wace had a profound knowledge of warfare, which he was eager to share with his audience. True, there is much that is conventional in his descriptions, which we can find in the *chansons de geste* and elsewhere. But there is a great deal of unique material and significant insights in the poet's work which make them worthy of careful study for the military information they contain. His vision of how war should be pursued in the mid- to late twelfth century is comprehensive and packed with relevant detail. Without forgetting the main purpose of his mythical and historical epics, is there an element of didacticism in his work?

I have already stressed Wace's interest in the non-knightly component of contemporary armies. He has much to say about the value of infantry – at Hastings and Val-ès-Dunes, in the numerous defences of Normandy and in the many battles of the *Brut*. He is also interested in defences which make them more effective in battle: the river Semillon, the barricade at Hastings, the 'plashing' of woods by the Irish.[32] Indeed there are themes which suggest that he had a great interest in 'li communes', troops raised from town and villages, such as his own Caen. It is the term used for the peasant rebellion against Richard I, and it is as though Wace wants to make the point of the military viability of such troops.

Admittedly, the fighting he describes at Caen is a classic chivalric encounter (Wace III 10,945–11,054); but he sets the French defeat at Mortmer in a town. The French are depicted as being trapped in their lodgings, barricaded in and smoked out by the Norman forces (Wace III 4,867–902). Seen in this light, the barricade at Hastings makes more sense. After all, it is composed of window frames and other bits of wood (Wace III 7,793–805). Where were these to be found on an open battlefield? Rather they represented the materials to hand in a built-up area. Did Wace's knowledge of warfare have something to do with a town militia? Had he witnessed the attack on Bayeux and Caen by Robert of Gloucester in 1138?[33] This is mere speculation, of course, but it is worth speculating to try to identify the source of Wace's military knowledge. We do not know that he was a fighter, whether as a knight serving in a household or playing a rôle with the night watch. But he certainly knew his military onions; something that his audience, then and now, should appreciate.

---

[32] The technique of 'plashing' or cutting trees to make the edge of woods into an impenetrable defence was a peculiarly Irish activity. Wace's use of the word 'plaissier' is, as far as I know, the earliest description of this activity. Cf. *Song of Dermot and the Earl*, 1,588–97, where ditches are also used to impede the English army's movement.

[33] *Historia Novella*, 73.

War and Chivalry in the *History of William the Marshal*

John Gillingham

Ever since the *History of William the Marshal* was discovered in the late nineteenth century it has been universally recognized as a document of the very greatest importance: the earliest vernacular life of a layman in European history.[1] In Antonia Gransden's words, 'just as Jocelin of Brakelond gives a unique account of the life in the cloister', so the *History* offers 'a unique picture of the chivalric society'.[2] Thanks to the work of Paul Meyer, Sidney Painter, Jessie Crosland and now Georges Duby, there can be little doubt that, leaving aside kings and clerics, William the Marshal is better known than any other figure of the twelfth or thirteenth centuries. Yet, despite its fame, the *History* remains in some ways a curiously neglected source. This is because historians have come to the *History* knowing what they were looking for and confident that they would find it. For Painter it was the portrait of a 'typical feudal baron', the knight-errant who after years on the tournament-circuit finally settled down with his heiress wife to the life of the great landowner and, ultimately, elder statesman.[3] For Crosland it offered a literary atmosphere reminiscent of the *chansons de geste*, 'when physical courage and loyalty were the two qualities most to be admired in a knight, and romantic adventure and the cult of the woman had no place'.[4] For Duby it provided welcome confirmation of his views on the patterns of inheritance and marriage, and on the role of the *juvenes* in the shaping of aristocratic society.[5] In Duby's case, indeed,

[1] *L'Histoire de Guillaume le Maréchal*, ed. P. Meyer (Société de l'Histoire de France, 1891 – 1901). Quotations from the text, and references to this edition will be given as *HGM* hereafter. I would like to thank Maurice Keen and Malcolm Vale for their kindness and generosity in reading and commenting on this paper. Although *The Poem of the Cid* is earlier, it contains far too many fictional elements to be regarded as a genuine biography.
[2] A. Gransden, *Historical Writing in England c. 550 to c. 1307* (London, 1974), 345.
[3] S. Painter, *William Marshal* (Baltimore, 1933), viii.
[4] J. Crosland, *William the Marshal* (London, 1962), 13 – 14. While it is true there is no 'cult of the woman' in the *History*, nonetheless William did go out of his way to help, not a damsel, but an old woman in distress during the fire at Le Mans which threatened to engulf her and her property: *HGM* 8753 – 72. Indeed it is worth noting that, as the *History* tells the story, conspicuous gallantry in the service of great ladies was crucial to the social ascent of both William and his father, John Marshal — William as escort to Eleanor of Aquitaine in 1168, and his father as escort to the Empress Matilda in 1141. William may not have performed prodigies of prowess 'for love of a fair lady'; nonetheless, the chief reward for his good service was the hand of a great heiress, 'la pucelle' who, in the words of the poem, 'fu bone et bele': *HGM* 8303 – 4.
[5] G. Duby, *Guillaume le Maréchal ou le meilleur chevalier du monde* (Paris, 1984). An English translation with the sub-title, *The Flower of Chivalry*, was published in the USA in 1985 and in the UK in 1986, but since the translation is a particularly poor one, I shall refer only to the French edition.

there is one occasion when, on reading the *History* and not finding what he expected to find, he simply invented it.

He expected to find that the day when William was made a knight was given its due prominence, and so he argues that the poet decided to make his narrative of a real battle — the fight at Drincourt — do service as a description of the chivalric exercise which must have been held to celebrate so great a day in the young warrior's life. The fact, Duby tells us, that the poet wrenched an engagement which really occurred in 1173 out of its proper place in the sequence of events, and put it instead in 1167, at about the time of the knighting, reveals very clearly just how determined the poet was to provide the proper setting for, and so emphasize the crucial importance of, the young man's entry into knighthood.[6] Unfortunately, however, Duby got it wrong. The fight at Drincourt, as the poet describes it in 360 lines of verse, was between, on the one side, a party of Normans led by William de Mandeville and the young William's own lord, the chamberlain of Tancarvile (who were defending the town of Drincourt), and, on the other, an invading force led by the counts of Flanders, Boulogne and Ponthieu.[7] Now, if this fight really had taken place in 1173, as Duby asserts, then William the Marshal, by that time in the service of the Young King (Henry II's eldest surviving son), should have been fighting on the side of Philip of Flanders, the Young King's ally in the revolt against his father. In 1173 William would have been attacking the town, not defending it.[8] The fact is that Duby's date, 1173, is the one year in which this particular fight could *not* have occurred. The evidence, such as there is, suggests that it actually happened in 1167, a minor incident — minor in the sense of not being noticed by any surviving chronicle — in a campaign noticed only by Gervase of Canterbury.[9] In that case, of course, it occurred precisely at the point in time at which the poet's narrative suggests it occurred. In other words there was no deliberate chronological dislocation on the part of the poet, and equally, therefore, no peculiarly revealing insight into the chivalrous mentality.

There is, however, a revealing insight into the mentality of modern historians. Few of us, I hope, go quite as far as Duby, but we all tend to see in the *History* what we want to see. Quite rightly, we see William as a model of chivalry: that, after all, is how he is presented. He had been, said the archbishop of Canterbury, at his funeral, 'the best knight in the world', and, says his thirteenth-century biographer, 'the story of his life ought to encourage all good men who hear it'.[10] Knowing perfectly well what a model of chivalry should be like, that is what we read into the *History of William the Marshal*, and in consequence we leave a great deal out. As an example of what I mean, let me cite the treatment of the work by one of the finest

---

[6] Duby, 86 – 8. Here Duby re-interprets Meyer's view that at this point the poet's narrative had simply become hopelessly confused: *HGM* iii. 16, n. 2, and 34, n. 2. Also following Meyer, yet moving in a different direction, G. H. White dated William's knighting to 1173: *GEC* x. 358. On the other hand, Duby's suggestion that William may have been knighted 'anonymously', as just one of a group, is a very reasonable speculation.

[7] *HGM* 805 – 1166.

[8] As pointed out long ago by Kate Norgate, *The Minority of Henry III* (London, 1912), 64, n. 2; and then, following her, by Painter, 20, n. 19. For Duby's own assessment of his use of Painter, Duby, 47.

[9] *The Historical Works of Gervase of Canterbury*, ed. W. Stubbs (RS, 1879 – 80), i. 203.

[10] *HGM* 19,072, 19,162 – 4. And whatever Henry III, that fine judge of men, may have thought, this is how he continued to be perceived. But, as Richard Marshal may have discovered to his cost, it is not always an advantage to have a father who is a hero-figure. See Paris, *CM* iii. 43, 273 – 6; iv. 157.

historians of chivalry, Maurice Keen. After summarizing William's early career, his tournaments, his role as the Young King's 'tutor' in chivalry, and his journey to the Holy Land — all of this brings us to 1187 when William was about forty years old — Keen goes on to write that 'the details of William's subsequent career need not detain us'.[11] Why need they not detain us? After all, in one of Keen's favourite texts, the *Livre de Chevalerie* of Geoffrey de Charny, we are explicitly and emphatically told that those who distinguish themselves in 'the great business of war' deserve higher praise than those who shine in jousts and tournaments, for 'war passes all other manner of arms'.[12] So why do we not hear of William's subsequent career in the highest arena of chivalry, of his role in the Angevin-Capetian struggle — 'the great war', as the poet calls it (*HGM* 7365), which started in 1188 —, of his role as *rector regis et regni* in the civil war of 1216 – 17?[13]

Reading modern authors, one might be forgiven for believing that the *History* has little to say about war, so little attention do they pay to it. Thus Gransden describes the *History* as a work which 'belongs to the artificial world of the knights errant', 'less concerned with heroism in real battles aimed at actual military advantage than with displays of bravery at tournaments'.[14] But this is not so. On my count, in a poem of 19,214 lines there are about 3150 lines dealing with tournaments, compared with some 8350 dealing with war — of which about 6800 describe the warfare of 1188 and after; they therefore belong to the details of William's subsequent career. Of course, it is true that those verses on tournaments possess rarity value. Other vernacular works describe warfare — Jordan Fantosme's *Chronique*, for example, or Ambroise's *Estoire de la Guerre Sainte*, or the *Histoire des ducs de Normandie* — but none contains anything remotely approaching the *History*'s detailed account of tournament after tournament. So it is perhaps only natural that historians should have been bowled over by the passages concerning tournaments and in consequence think of William chiefly as a bachelor knight, a tournament champion.[15] But they should not have forgotten to count what can be

[11] M. Keen, *Chivalry* (New Haven, London, 1984), 20 – 1.

[12] Charny's *Le Livre de Chevalerie* was printed by K. de Lettenhove in his *Oeuvres de Froissart*, I, parts 2 – 3 (Brussels, 1872), 463 – 533. 'ainsi comme l'on doit honorer bonnes gens d'armes et ainsi comme il appartient a eulx de si tres-noble oevre comme de fait d'armes de guerre qui passe tous autres, excepte Dieu servir' (p. 466). Charny goes on to distinguish jousts (individual encounters between *gens d'armes*), tournaments (encounters between teams of *gens d'armes*), and war: 'Et pour ce doit – l'en priser plus et honorer gens d'armes pour la guerre que nulles autres gens d'armes qui soient'; and this is because 'ces deux mestiers d'armes [i.e., jousts and tournaments] sont tous compris ou fait d'armes de guerre'. (Charny, 466; cf. 473).

[13] Concentrating on the years before 1188 has the effect of emphasizing that period in William's life when he was the ideal young knight and minimizing that even longer period when he was the ideal mature knight. In general, historians of chivalry have been attracted to the type of behaviour appropriate to the young man — the knight errantry and the individualism — and in consequence have tended to neglect the more prudential behaviour of the knight with responsibilities. What the *History* makes clear is that although good knights were expected to behave differently at different stages of their career (*HGM* 11,247 – 56), nonetheless they all belonged to a single military society governed by a single code of honour. Within that society it was the experienced knights who wielded power and who, not surprisingly, were the ones to be listened to. Charny, 475: 'Car par raison ils en doivent miex parler, aprendre et conseiller que li autre, car ils ont veu et sceu, fait, este et essaie en toutes manieres d'armes'.

[14] Gransden, 345.

[15] On the basis of these passages Duby, 111 – 37, provides a fine analysis of tournaments. Cf. G. Duby, *Le Dimanche de Bouvines* (Paris, 1973), 111 – 28. It is as a tournament champion that the Marshal leaves his mark in R. Barber, *The Knight and Chivalry* (London, 1970).

counted, and the fact is that the *History* gives well over twice as much space to war as it does to tournaments. Thus Duby is quite right to say that the stage on which William and his fellows move is the theatre of war.[16] Yet, though he then offers us a long and excellent analysis of tournaments, he says very little about war, and that little, as I shall make clear, is mostly rubbish.[17]

But if the historian of chivalry takes Geoffrey de Charny's order of priorities seriously, then should he not look carefully at the paragon of chivalry at war? As Maurice Keen writes, 'if ever a knight lived up to Geoffrey's principle of chivalrous prowess, it was surely William Marshal'.[18] Yet, so far as I know, no historian of chivalry has tried to do so. Perhaps, it might be thought, because they have left that side of William's life to the specialists, to the historians of war. But if we look at Contamine, at Verbruggen, at Lot, at Oman, we find that they have not done so either.[19] So we reach the curious conclusion that neither the historians of war, nor the historians of chivalry, nor indeed the modern biographers of William the Marshal have made any real attempt to investigate the Marshal's military career. It is all the more curious in view of the traditional opinion that medieval warfare was, in essence, knightly warfare.[20] All the more curious, too, in view of the considerable interest in the relationship between war and chivalry.[21] For where could we hope to find out what a thirteenth-century writer thought knightly warfare was, or chivalry was, if not in the pages of the *History of William the Marshal*? This, then, is my intention in this paper: to see how war was perceived by an extraordinarily well-informed vernacular author, writing in the 1220s, and writing, I imagine, for an audience who themselves knew a great deal about war. Thus I am not so much concerned with what really happened as with what this author said had happened. Naturally, I too shall see in the *History of William the Marshal* exactly what I want to see.

I begin where Maurice Keen left off. The year is 1188. William has returned from the Holy Land and has entered the service of King Henry II: 'De sa maisne le

---

[16] 'Ce fut entouré de guerriers que Guillaume vécut et agit. Ils occupent tout son souvenir': Duby, *Guillaume*, 68 – 9.

[17] All we get are passing references to Montmirail, Arras and Milli (out of the 1400 lines which the poet devoted to the war of 1192 – 9), and a page on the battle of Lincoln, mostly taken up by William's pre-battle speeches (out of more than 2500 lines on the war of 1215 – 17).

[18] Keen, 21. Charny's oft-repeated principle was 'Qui plus fait, miex vault.'

[19] The only reference to William in P. Contamine, *War in the Middle Ages* (trans. M. Jones, London, 1984), 216, is to the tournaments of his day. According to J. F. Verbruggen, *The Art of Warfare in Western Europe during the Middle Ages* (trans. S. Willard and S. C. M. Southern, Amsterdam, 1977), 14, the *History* is 'very useful', but he attempts no analysis of it and uses it chiefly to illustrate tournament practice. He also claims (p. 16), on grounds which are not clear to me, that the author of the *History* failed to understand what happened at Fréteval (1194), when William was in command of a force which Richard I held in reserve. So far as I can see there is only one brief footnote reference (on Bouvines) in the whole of F. Lot, *L'Art Militaire et les Armées au Moyen Age* (Paris, 1946), i. 229, n. 8. As might be expected, C. W. Oman, *The Art of War in the Middle Ages* (London, 1898), 407 – 13, merely used the *History* in his reconstruction of the battle of Lincoln. So did T. F. Tout, 'The Fair of Lincoln and the "Histoire de Guillaume le Maréchal" ', *EHR* xviii (1903), 240 – 65.

[20] E.g., the title of M. Howard, *War in European History* (Oxford, 1976), ch. 1, is 'The Wars of the Knights'.

[21] See M. Vale, *War and Chivalry* (London, 1981). However, as its subtitle — 'Warfare and Aristocratic Culture in England, France and Burgundy at the End of the Middle Ages' — indicates, this is principally concerned with a different period.

retint / de ses hals consels le fist mestre'.[22] Presumably it was his new position in the royal household which allowed William, in his turn, to recruit new servants, among whom was John of Early, the man whose memories or *mémoires*, or both, served as the basis around which a professional *trouvère* composed our history.[23] So, for several reasons, the year 1188 is an important one in the life of the Marshal. It is also the year in which he gave his first recorded advice on how to make war.

King Philip II of France has launched an attack on the castle and town of Gisors. It failed; indeed, in the course of it a charge of the supposedly invincible French knights, lances lowered, was twice beaten off by the spears of Henry's 'boen servant' — not the kind of thing that is supposed to happen in medieval warfare before the battle of Courtrai in 1302 — and the disgruntled Capetian army, after demonstrating its prowess by chopping down the famous elm of Gisors, withdrew into Capetian territory and dispersed.[24] As soon as he heard this news, William goes to speak to his lord:

> Listen to me sire. Philip has divided and disbanded his troops. I advise you to disperse your men too, but to give them secret orders to re-assemble at a given time and place. From there they are to launch a *chevauchée* into the territory of the king of France. If this is done in force, prudently and promptly, then he will find he has to suffer far greater damage than the loss of one elm. This will be a better and a finer deed.

'By God's eyes', said the king, 'Marshal, you are most courteous ('molt corteis') and have given me good advice. I shall do exactly as you suggest.' And he did. He ordered his army to disband and then quietly to muster again at Pacy. It crossed the frontier and burned and ravaged all the land between there and Mantes. William des Barres and some other knights of the French king's household, then based at Mantes, did their best to prevent it, but they had been deceived by the initial manoeuvre and were hopelessly outnumbered. At the end of the day Henry's men marched into Ivry, loaded down with plunder and well-satisfied with themselves. The poet then reports a conversation between Henry and his warlike son Richard, in which they agree to give all the credit for this day's work to the Marshal's good advice.[25]

In the very next episode, later that same year, Henry decided to surprise his enemies by launching a mid-winter attack from Chinon. His orders to his men were that they should ride day and night until they reached the vicinity of Montmirail; then they were to burn and destroy everything in sight, sparing nobody, seize the town, sack it and burn it. And, led by the Marshal, that is exactly what they did. On

---

[22] *HGM* 7308–9.
[23] *HGM* iii. vii–xiv; Gransden, 346; M. D. Legge, *Anglo-Norman Literature and its Background* (Oxford, 1963), 306–8.
[24] *HGM* 7436–781, esp. 7738–69. The dispersal of the French troops is confirmed by William the Breton in *Oeuvres de Rigord et de Guillaume le Breton*, ed. H-F. Delaborde (Paris, 1882–5), i. 189.
[25] *HGM* 7782–852.

their return the Old King declared himself well-pleased with the results of their *chevauchée*.[26]

And so it goes on. Sometimes it is William who is on the receiving end, as in 1218 when the Welsh prince, Morgan of Caerleon, ravages the Marshal's lands, burning (we are told) twenty-two churches in the process.[27] Whether, as on these occasions, we are given details, or whether we get no more than a casual, passing reference to the 'doing of damage', it is clear that the poet, like the authors of *chansons de geste*, regards these ravaging expeditions as the normal business of war.[28] It is clear, too, that the poet understood the dual function of the raid: to gain plunder and to put pressure on the enemy. In his own words, 'for when the poor can no longer reap a harvest from their fields, then they can no longer pay their rents and this, in turn, impoverishes their lords'.[29] It is clear, too, from the way he tells the stories of the Gisors and Montmirail episodes, that the well-organized *chevauchée* was one which took the enemy by surprise. The intention was not to seek out the enemy's knights and meet them in a head-on clash of arms. On the contrary, the aim was to send his armed forces in the wrong direction, and then, in their absence, to destroy his economic resources, the fields and flocks of his people. This was how the Marshal made war, and this is how the Marshal said war should be made. And note the poet's language. When the Marshal offered this good advice, he was 'molt corteis'.[30] This, in other words, is chivalrous warfare.

How does the Marshal's advice fit in with Duby's view that William 'was blessed with a brain too small to impede the natural vigour of a big, powerful and tireless physique'?[31] It does not, of course, and Duby nowhere mentions this example of William's military advice. On the other hand, he does cite another case in which William had advice to offer. In 1197 Count Baldwin of Flanders was laying siege to a town (probably Arras) when King Philip approached with a relieving army. The Flemish barons recommended using the communal carts together with their militias as a kind of barrier fortress, a retreat before which the knights could safely offer battle to the French. William, however, opposed this. In his view the carts should be left behind while the knights moved out in battle array, ready to confront the enemy in open field.[32] This, claims Duby, was the characteristic attitude of the true knight: temerity has dethroned prudence.[33] But this is a hopelessly one-sided

---

[26] *HGM* 7872 – 8048. Note the use of the word 'chevalchie' (line 8047, as earlier in line 7792) and the verbal form 'chevacha' (line 7835) and 'chivalchiez' (line 7886).

[27] *HGM* 17,748 – 864.

[28] I doubt if a line recurs more frequently than variants of 'maint ennui li fist et maint mal' (*HGM* 148, 282, 367, etc.). That the authors of *chansons de geste* also regarded ravaging as commonplace was pointed out by M. Bennett, 'The Status of the Squire: the Northern Evidence', in *The Ideals and Practice of Medieval Knighthood*, ed. C. Harper-Bill and R. Harvey (Woodbridge, 1986), 4. For further comment on the function of ravaging, see J. Gillingham, 'Richard I and the Science of War in the Middle Ages', in *War and Government in the Middle Ages. Essays in Honour of J. O. Prestwich*, ed. J. Gillingham and J. C. Holt (Woodbridge, 1984), 78 – 91.

[29] *HGM* 659 – 69.

[30] *HGM* 7800.

[31] Duby, *Guillaume*, 186. This judgment is at the heart of Duby's summing-up of the Marshal's career and reputation.

[32] *HGM* 10,783 – 840.

[33] Duby, *Guillaume*, 107. He made the same point, on the evidence of the same episode, in Duby, *Dimanche*, 136.

interpretation of this incident. For one thing, leaving the carts behind is presented not as a bold gesture of defiance but as a tactical device; the role of the carts and their troops is to prevent the townspeople making a sortie and taking the besiegers in the rear. For another, when Philip's scouts reported the reception which Count Baldwin, in conformity with William's advice, had prepared for him, he decided to withdraw and leave Arras to its fate.[34] So is this an episode which illustrates chivalrous temerity? Or is it one which emphasizes knightly caution? The poet, incidentally, approved Philip's decision. For him, too, there was no wisdom in risking battle where one had no clear-cut advantage.[35] There is further evidence of the poet's own attitude to battle in his account of Bouvines. Once again we find the French under Philip retreating in order to avoid an engagement, and if this time they win the day it is only because the over-confident allies forced a battle before the bulk of Otto IV's forces had had time to come up. In doing this they had gone against the count of Boulogne's advice. 'Let them go', he had said, 'for the land will then be ours for the taking', and it is clear that the poet agreed. 'If they [i.e. the allies] had only waited until the morrow', he writes, 'then they would have won great honour.'[36] Contrast this with Duby's dictum on the knight: 'Honour compelled him to appear intrepid, even to the point of folly.'[37] One of the odd things about Duby's view of the knight at war is that it is at odds with his own analysis of the knight in training for war. For he points out that in tournaments victory was the reward not of ardour but of discipline.[38] Not that he seems to be aware of this contradiction; sadly, these days, Duby seems to be blessed with a brain too small to impede the natural facility of his tireless pen.[39]

An episode which is peculiarly revealing of the pre-occupations of modern historians is the *History*'s account of Richard I's campaign in the Beauvaisis in 1197. What all modern writers seize upon is the moment when the Marshal threw himself into the assault on the castle of Milli and went up the scaling-ladder like a young man.[40] Duby uses this remarkable display of courage and prowess by a man in his fifties and, in Duby's words, 'already creaking at the joints', in order to characterise the Marshal's good service in Richard's wars.[41] But what he does not

---

[34] *HGM* 10,827 – 32, 10,867 – 81.

[35] *HGM* 10,882 – 90.

[36] *HGM* 14,746 – 800.

[37] Duby, *Guillaume*, 107. When medievalists say this kind of thing it is hardly surprising that a modern historian should write of the 'old chivalry of the feudal host in which every man charged for himself, concerned as much with personal honour as with victory': Howard, 16.

[38] Duby, *Guillaume*, 123. It is, of course, now conventional to emphasize the close similarity between tournaments and real engagements, and, therefore, the value of the sport as training for war — a point made by Roger of Howden in the twelfth century, Geoffrey de Charny in the fourteenth and, most recently, by Juliet Barker in the twentieth. See J. R. V. Barker, *The Tournament in England 1100 – 1400* (Woodbridge, 1986), esp. 17ff. One additional point could perhaps be made: that tournaments trained men to fight together in small groups of friends. For the importance of this in war, see J. Keegan, *The Face of Battle* (London, 1976), 51 – 2, 71 – 2, citing the findings of the study of human behaviour in combat made by the US Army Historical Service.

[39] Harsh words perhaps, but no harsher than his own judgment on William Marshal, who is in no position to answer back. And given the astonishing achievement of Duby's early writings, the relatively poor quality of his recent works is doubly distressing.

[40] *HGM* 11,169 – 231.

[41] Duby, *Guillaume*, 171.

point out is that William's actions were criticized as being foolhardy and inappropriate — and criticized by none other than Richard I, the king whom the poet calls 'le meillor prince del monde'.[42] At least both Painter and Crosland, in their much fuller accounts of this incident, do find space for Richard's criticism, yet neither they, nor (so far as I can see) anyone else has thought it worthwhile to set the incident in the context of the campaign.[43] And yet, again, the context is one of secret orders, an undercover muster and then a sudden attack, in this case by two columns operating in tandem. One column, under Richard's personal command, having taken Milli by surprise, was able to capture it by assault; the other column, consisting of the *routiers* under Mercadier's command, succeeded in capturing one of Richard's great enemies, the bishop of Beauvais, and took so many other prisoners that, according to the poet, there was no room anywhere to put one's feet.[44] Now the *History* reports all of this, but not modern historians. This suggests that the thirteenth-century view of knightly warfare was both more complex and more comprehensive than that of modern writers. Clearly, like modern scholars, our thirteenth-century author was drawn to the compelling image of the middle-aged knight on the scaling ladder, but unlike them, he did not allow that image to fill his mind to the exclusion of everything else.

As in these episodes, so also in many others. Time and again we hear of one commander trying to surprise his opponent. Indeed, the first military action in the *History* occurs when King Stephen raced to the relief of Winchester in 1141 and took the empress Matilda so much by surprise that she was forced to 'hitch up her skirts' and ride like a man.[45] According to the poet, Stephen's next coup was to surprise the garrison of Newbury. Here, indeed, the word 'surprise' occurs three times in the space of twelve lines.[46] Time and again the author emphasizes the rapidity of troop movements. A commander in a hurry might persuade his troops to press on after dinner, as when King Richard rode to the relief of Verneuil in 1194.[47] We hear, too, of night marches, as in the attack on Montmirail, and as used by William's father, John Marshal, to ambush Patrick of Salisbury's men outside Winchester in 1141.[48] Or by Henry II when, in 1173, he strove to capture his rebellious eldest son. Although Henry's swoop failed to capture the Young King, it created such a state of panic in the rebels' camp that they had to resort to the emergency measure of having him hastily knighted by the best man immediately to

---

[42] *HGM* 11,247 – 56, 11,766. Curiously, Duby refers to Richard's reproach at Milli elsewhere in his book (p. 124) in his discussion of tournaments. But, as already noted, Duby allows discipline and self-discipline a far greater place in tournaments than in war. Similarly, although Duby mentions another occasion when William's rash actions (on the bridge at Montmirail) were criticized by the best knights present, Baldwin de Béthune and Hugh de Hardincourt (*HGM* 7996 – 8003), he goes on to draw conclusions which do not require him to modify his view of what constitutes 'proper knightly behaviour': Duby, *Guillaume*, 109.

[43] Painter, 111; Crosland, 78.

[44] *HGM* 11,106 – 280.

[45] *HGM* 183 – 225.

[46] *HGM* 200 – 11.

[47] *HGM* 10,453 – 63.

[48] *HGM* 299 – 354. In consequence Earl Patrick's men were not wearing armour when attacked and were routed, losing a great deal of baggage. But twenty-seven years later this lesson seems to have been forgotten, this time with fatal consequences for the earl. See below, 11.

hand, that is our hero.[49] All this was in accord with the maxim of Vegetius: 'courage is worth more than numbers, and speed is worth more than courage'.[50]

Inevitably, then, we constantly find commanders haunted by the fear of being taken by surprise.[51] Naturally, in these circumstances, the competent commander was acutely aware of the importance of good reconnaissance. The *History* contains several object lessons on how to carry out effective reconnaissance. In 1189, for example, Henry II, at bay at Le Mans, sent William out on patrol in the early morning mist; the Marshal made sure they got close enough to the Capetian forces to obtain accurate information about their numbers and disposition, and he resisted the temptation to pick up easy plunder so as not to jeopardise what was essentially a news-gathering mission.[52] In another example we hear how in 1202 William Marshal and the earls of Salisbury and Warenne, having ridden out themselves to check information which their scouts had brought them — that Philip Augustus had given up the siege of Arques — at once decided that discretion was the better part and beat a hasty retreat when they realised that the Capetian, taking advantage of a concealed valley, had sent against them a well-armed intercepting force under the command of William des Barres.[53] One of the other lessons of that episode — that a good commander should check the accuracy of information coming in — is further developed in the account of how Richard the Lionheart, by good reconnaissance, using both local knights and his own eyes, was able to take Philip by surprise at Gisors in 1198 and come within a hair's breadth of capturing him.[54]

It is against a background of assumptions like this that the poet tells the story of the climax of William's career, the war of 1216 – 17. When, on the very day of the child Henry III's coronation, William is informed of a threat to his own castle at Goodrich, he at once sends a force of knights, sergeants and crossbowmen on a night march to its relief.[55] During their march to Winchester in the spring of 1217, the earl of Salisbury and the young Marshal — for whom, of course, the *History*

[49] *HGM* 2024, 2038 – 9, 2161 – 2.

[50] Cited by Contamine, 252. On the use of Vegetius see Contamine, 210 – 11, and Gillingham, 'Richard I', 82 – 7, and the works cited there. Thus Ross was wide of the mark when he suggested that, even at the time of writing, 'Vegetius was hopelessly out of date': D. J. A. Ross, 'The Prince Answers Back: ''Les Enseignements de Theodore Paliologue'' ', in *Ideals and Practice*, ed. Harper-Bill and Harvey, 165. Eternal common-sense principles — R. C. Smail's description of Vegetius's strategic maxims — do not date.

[51] *HGM* 524, 12,235 – 40, 14,746. These lines refer to Stephen at Newbury in 1152, to Philip Augustus when withdrawing from Arques in 1202, and to Philip again on the eve of Bouvines. See also below, 10.

[52] *HGM* 8381 – 478.

[53] *HGM* 12,251 – 314.

[54] *HGM* 10,924 – 11,012. Note also that William of Poitiers, himself an old soldier, in his life of William the Conqueror compares William favourably both with the great generals of antiquity and with modern commanders in that William was prepared to go out on reconnaissance patrol himself, instead of leaving it all to subordinates. Obviously there were risks, but accurate information was all-important. 'Fuit illorum et est ducum consuetudinis, dirigere non ire exploratores: magis ad vitam sibi, quam ut exercitui providentiam suam conservarent. Guillelmus vero cum viginti quinque, non amplius militum comitatu promptus ipse loca et incolas exploravit': Guillaume de Poitiers, *Histoire de Guillaume le Conquérant*, ed. R. Foreville (Paris, 1952), 168. Even in a tournament 'scouts' were useful, as when at the great tournament of Lagny (1180) the seneschal of Flanders kept a squadron of thirty knights clear of the *melée* until a knight sent him word of the precarious plight of the Young King: *HGM* 4935 – 51.

[55] *HGM* 15,352.

was written — take good care to avoid being ambushed.[56] Later that year, Prince Louis of France, because he feared a sudden attack on London, hastily abandoned his siege of Dover.[57] And as for the two critical battles of 1217, one of them, Lincoln, may have reminded the old man of his tournament years, but even a work in praise of the Marshal makes it clear that it was the brilliant reconnaissance work of Peter des Roches which created the decisive advantage. By finding a hidden entrance the bishop of Winchester enabled the royalists to take the French so much by surprise that their master of artillery was killed by men he believed to be on his own side.[58] The old man's last charge captures the imagination, but it was only the icing on the cake.[59] Incidentally, so far as I can see, it was also the first time since Drincourt in 1167 — exactly fifty years earlier — that William had charged into battle, so rare an event was the battle charge of the heavily-armoured knight. No wonder the old fellow was so out of practice that he forgot to put on his helmet.[60] Similarly, at least the way the *History* tells it, it was not audacity but deviousness which won the battle of Sandwich in 1217. By ensuring that his cog was lightly laden and therefore rode high in the water, William enabled his sergeants to throw potfuls of blinding chalk-dust into the eyes of the unfortunate French.[61]

The use of this method, clearly with the poet's approval, raises the question of what was, or was not, considered unchivalrous. Just as the kinds of tournament tricks which Philip of Flanders employed seem to have been regarded as perfectly respectable behaviour,[62] so also in war there was clearly nothing dishonourable about deceiving the enemy, particularly if it permitted one to ravage his lands without interruption.[63] Was anything unchivalrous? In a tournament it would appear that it was unchivalrous to make off with the prize which another knight had taken, especially when that other knight was William — though even this seems to have been a debatable point of honour.[64] And what about in war? In passing, the poet makes it clear, as one would expect, that it was dishonourable to surrender a castle all too readily, as the defenders of Carrickfergus did in 1210, and honourable to resist stoutly, as William de Silli did at Le Mans in 1189, and William Mortimer at Verneuil in 1194 and at Arques in 1202.[65] Equally to be expected is his disapproval of the anxiety of some of the French knights at Gisors in 1198 to save their own necks — behaviour all the more reprehensible because it jeopardised the safety of

---

[56] *HGM* 15,920 – 4.

[57] *HGM* 17,069 – 84.

[58] *HGM* 16,629 – 42.

[59] In his account of Lincoln, Duby, *Guillaume*, 182 – 3, goes straight from the Marshal's speech to the Marshal's charge. In this version there is no room for Peter des Roches, 'qui fu mestre cel jor de conseillier nos genz': *HGM* 16,998 – 9.

[60] *HGM* 16,597 – 604. More generally, on the rarity of the charge in a pitched battle, see Gillingham, 'Richard I', 80 – 1, 91.

[61] *HGM* 17,381 – 404.

[62] *HGM* 2723 – 9, 4821 – 916.

[63] For an explicit justification of both deception and ravaging by a fourteenth-century canonist, see Honoré Bonet, *The Tree of Battles*, ed. G. W. Coopland (Liverpool, 1949), 154 – 5. And as he puts it (p. 154), 'if sometimes the humble and innocent suffer harm and lose their goods, it cannot be otherwise'.

[64] *HGM* 3965 – 4284. For similar quarrels after real fights see M. Keen, *The Laws of War in the Late Middle Ages* (London, 1965), 164 – 6.

[65] *HGM* 14,276 – 8, 8878 – 86, 10,468 – 80, 12,044 – 55.

their king.[66] But there are only two occasions when the poet goes out of his way to call a course of action shameful. One was the killing of Earl Patrick in 1168, struck down from behind when he himself was unarmed.[67] The other takes us back once again to 1167 and to Drincourt — to William's first experience of war. As the count of Flanders moved up to attack the town, so the constable of Normandy prepared to move out. Seeing him go, the chamberlain, William's lord, called out, 'Sire, it would be great shame on him who lets this town burn.' Later on, the poet describes the constable's departure as 'villainous', and says why — because it put the town in great danger of being plundered and burned to the ground.[68] Undoubtedly it is true that the ensuing fight at Drincourt is described in language very like that used to describe a tournament — as Meyer, Crosland and Duby have all emphasized[69] — but it clearly was very much more than two teams of knights having fun by playing at war. A town and its inhabitants were to be saved from destruction, and it was this purpose which made the fight a notably honourable one. Equally, of course, there was nothing dishonourable about the intentions of the attackers. In a similar situation William would do exactly the same.[70] What was shameful was for the knight whose role it was to defend the people to fail to do so when the moment came.[71] Fortunately no one behaved shamefully at Lincoln, but the message, made explicit in William's two speeches to his men, was still essentially the same one. They were fighting not only for their honour but also for their wives,[72] their children and their land, even for the very existence of their country.[73] Thus, in William's last war, as in his first, we find the same message: war is not fought for the sake of individual gain, whether glory, reputation or material reward, but for

---

[66] *HGM* 11,025 – 30. Their headlong flight when Richard attacked 'like a ravenous lion' (*HGM* 10,993) was not what Charny called 'du beau retraire seurement et honorablement', in his section on 'comment l'en met sus une chevauchee pour guerrier et courre sus a ses ennemis': Charny, 473.

[67] *HGM* 1636 – 52. Contrast this with William's own behaviour when confronted by an unarmed Lionheart in 1189. 'By the legs of God, Marshal, do not kill me. That would be wrong for I am not in armour.' 'No, I will not kill you. I leave that to the Devil', replied the Marshal, running the future king's horse through with his lance and killing it on the spot. 'That was a fine blow', concludes the poet: *HGM* 8839 – 50.

[68] *HGM* 854 – 5, 1124 – 8.

[69] *HGM* iii. 18, n. 4; Crosland, 24 – 5; Duby, *Guillaume*, 88.

[70] What mattered was that the war should be a legitimate one. 'If on both sides war is decided upon and begun by the Councils of the two kings, the soldiery may take spoil from the kingdom at will': Bonet, 154.

[71] E.g. Charny, 465, 512. For Ramon Lull's view that chivalry was instituted to discipline and defend the people, see Keen, 8 – 11; Vale, 22f.

[72] One of the ways in which Duby minimizes the (admittedly small) role of women in the *History* is by consigning William's wife to the margins: Duby, *Guillaume*, 49, 167. But this is to ignore totally her role in William's council, particularly important when matters involving her own inheritance, notably in Ireland, were being considered: *HGM* 13,386 – 9, 14,095 – 100 (an interesting reversal of traditional male-female roles). And even in a vital affair of state — when William is deciding who should succeed him as Henry III's guardian — he calls the countess to counsel him: *HGM* 18,032. On the subject of the wife's role as adviser in *chansons de geste*, see P. S. Gold, *The Lady and the Virgin* (Chicago, London, 1985), 8 – 18.

[73] *HGM* 16,137 – 96, 16,277 – 310. And it was in the middle of the battle of Lincoln, as Duby, *Guillaume*, 68 – 9, rightly points out, that the poet places his profession of faith in the worth of chivalry. 'Que est donques chevalerie? / Si forte chose et si herdie / e si tres costos a aprendre / Que nuls malveis ne l'ose enprendre': *HGM* 16,859 – 62.

the common good — a thoroughly conventional message, and one which the *History* shares with the didactic treatises on chivalry.

If the proper purposes of knightly war were thoroughly conventional, so too, I believe, were the methods of knightly war. The kind of war William fought — and by definition this was the kind of war the best knights fought — was a war full of ravaging, punctuated quite often by attacks on strong-points but only rarely by pitched battles.[74] The *History* describes seventeen sieges but only three or four battles. Moreover, William in a remarkably long lifetime of warfare was present at only two battles.[75] If you had to fight then you fought hard, but always before you fought you tried to catch your enemy offguard, and often you preferred not to fight at all. This, of course, is not at all the impression which, as we have seen, continues to be fostered by the kind of nonsense that Duby writes on the subject. In reality, knights like William Marshal saw themselves as engaged in a deliberately destructive type of warfare, a warfare characterized by watchfulness, deviousness and sudden swoops. These are not the methods that we are inclined to associate with the word 'chivalrous'. We are inclined to assume that there is a contradiction, an inherent tension, between the ideals of chivalry and the nasty reality of war, and to sympathise, I suppose, with the words of the Limousin troubadour Girart de Bornelh, a contemporary of the Marshal:

> I used to see the barons in beautiful armour, following tournaments, and I heard those who had given the best blow spoken of for many a day. But now honour lies in stealing cattle, sheep and oxen, or pillaging churches and travellers. Oh, shame upon the knight who drives off sheep, robs churches and travellers, and then appears before a lady.[76]

But, with the exception of robbing churches, these are precisely the methods of making war which the *History* advocates. Read, for example, William the Breton's account (in other words, the victim's account) of precisely that raid which William Marshal advised Henry II to undertake in 1188.[77] If, as Malcolm Vale has pointed out, there is no sign of any tension between ideal of chivalry and reality of war in the mid fifteenth-century writings of Oliver de la Marche, equally there is no sign

---

[74] Cf. C. Gaier, *Art et organisation militaires dans la principauté de Liège et dans le comté de Looz au Moyen Age* (Brussels, 1968), 216.

[75] The sieges are Winchester (1141), Newbury (1152), Limoges (1184), Le Mans (1189), Windsor, Nottingham and Verneuil (1194), Arras (?1197), Milli (1197), Arques and Mirebeau (1202), Kilkenny (1207 – 8), Rochester (1215), Winchelsea, Winchester, Mountsorrel and Lincoln (1217). The battles are Bouvines (1214), Lincoln and Sandwich (1217), and possibly, on the grounds that it might well have involved the greater part of the forces active in a particular theatre of war (i.e. eastern Normandy in 1167), Drincourt. I do not count Fréteval (1194) or Gisors (1198), since on both occasions Philip ran for cover and made no effort to fight. Nor do I count Gisors (1188), since neither Henry II nor Philip allowed the greater part of their forces to get involved in the fighting. See above, 5. Thus whether William was present at one or two battles depends on whether or not one counts Drincourt as a battle — and most historians seem to regard it as only a skirmish.

[76] *Sämtliche Lieder des Trobadors Giraut de Bornelh*, ed. A. Kolsen (Halle, 1910) n. 65, pp. 414 – 15; cited by Keen, *Chivalry*, 233 – 4.

[77] Guillaume le Breton, *Philippidos*, Book 3, lines 286 – 309.

of it in the *History* either. There is really no question, as is sometimes suggested, of the chivalric ethic being gradually eroded in the later Middle Ages by the increasing savagery of war.[78] Of course, this is what contemporaries believed. In the words of the fourteenth-century canonist Honoré Bonet,

> In these days all wars are directed against the poor labouring people and against their goods and chattels. I do not call that war, but it seems to me to be pillage and robbery. Further that way of warfare does not follow the ordinances of worthy chivalry or of the ancient custom of noble warriors who upheld justice, the widow, the orphan and the poor. And nowadays it is the opposite that they do everywhere, and the man who does not know how to set places on fire, to rob churches and usurp their rights and to imprison priests, is not fit to carry on war. And for these reasons the knights of today have not the glory and the praise of the old champions of former times.[79]

But the *History of William the Marshal* makes it crystal clear that, when on the offensive, at least one much-praised champion of former times went to some trouble to ensure that his wars were 'directed against the poor and labouring people and against their goods and chattels'.

All this, it seems to me, is to reinforce Maurice Keen's point that the tendency of chivalry was not to limit the horrors of war, but 'rather to help make those horrors endemic'.[80] This is partly because, as he says, chivalry presented knightly conduct in an idealizing light, and this therefore had the effect of prompting men to seek wars. In this interpretation the horrors of war are looked upon as an inevitable and regrettable side effect of going to war. But is it entirely right to treat them merely as side effects? Surely, what the *History* shows is not just that the chivalric ethic of the thirteenth century already took the horrors of war for granted. What it also shows is that 'pillage and robbery' were central to chivalrous war-making. The good knight regretted them only when it was his dependants who were the victims. When he was on the attack then pillage and robbery were not simply taken for granted, rather they were actually approved of as the right, the proper, the courteous way to make war by 'the best knight in the world', the man whose life was held up as a model for all good men to follow. Since these were the methods advocated by the 'patron saint' of chivalry, it is perhaps not after all surprising that, as Matthew Paris reports, when William's tomb in the New Temple was opened in 1240, his body was found to be 'putrid and, so far as could be seen, detestable'.[81]

---

[78] Vale, 157–61. Similarly, *c.* 1200, troubadour poetry cultivated at the court of Montferrat expressed a knightly ethos in which courtly and martial values were felt to be in harmony — and the latter dominant. See A. Barbero, 'La Corte di Montferrato allo specchio della poesia trobadoura', *Bolletino Storico Bibliografico Subalpino* (Turin, 1983), 641–703, esp. 664–89. I owe this reference to the kindness of Maurice Keen.

[79] Bonet, 189.

[80] M. Keen, 'Chivalry, Nobility and the Man-At-arms', in *War, Literature and Politics in the Late Middle Ages*, ed. C. T. Allmand (Liverpool, 1976), 45.

[81] Paris, *CM* iv. 495.

SELECT BIBLIOGRAPHY

The following bibliography is by no means exhaustive, but is rather intended as a general guide. Its focus is chiefly on material concerning warfare and military organization in England and north-west France in the eleventh and twelfth centuries, although the section on Anglo-Saxon military matters has been given a wider chronological span. Comprehensive bibliographies on medieval warfare are furnished by P. Contamine, *War in the Middle Ages* (London, 1984) and by E. Crosby, *War in the Middle Ages: A Bibliographical Guide* (New York, 1990).

GENERAL SURVEYS

Beeler, J. H., *Warfare in England, 1066–1189* (Ithaca and New York, 1966).
———, *Warfare in Feudal Europe, 730–1200* (Ithaca and London, 1971).
Contamine, P., *La Guerre au Moyen Âge* (Paris, 1980), tr. M. Jones as *War in the Middle Ages* (London, 1984).
———, 'L'histoire militaire et l'histoire de la guerre dans la France médiévale depuis trente ans', *Actes du C^e Congrès national des Sociétés savantes, Paris, 1975, Section de philologie et d'histoire jusqu'à 1610* (Paris, 1977), I, 71–93.
Delbrück, H., *History of the Art of Warfare Within the Framework of Political History*, tr. W. J. Renfroe Jnr, 4 vols. (Connecticut and London, 1975–82).
Keegan, J., *The Face of Battle* (London, 1976).
Lot, F., *L'art militaire et les armées au Moyen Âge, en Europe et dans le Proche-Orient*, 2 vols. (Paris, 1946).
Oman, C. W. C., *A History of the Art of War in the Middle Ages, 378–1485*, 2 vols. (London, 1924: repr. Ithaca, 1960 and Oxford, 1991).
———, *The Art of War in the Middle Ages*, rev. and ed. J. Beeler (Ithaca and New York, 1953).
Powicke, F. M., *The Loss of Normandy, 1189–1204* (Manchester, 1913; 2nd ed., 1963).
Smail, R. C., 'The Art of War', *Medieval England*, ed. A. L. Poole (Oxford and New York, 1958), I, 128–67.
Verbruggen, F., *De Krijkunst in West-Europa in de Middeleeuwen (IXe tot begin XIVe eeuw)* (Brussels, 1954), tr. S. C. M. Southern and S. Willard as *The Art of Warfare in Western Europe During the Middle Ages, From the Eighth Century to 1340* (Amsterdam and New York, 1976).
———, 'L'art militaire en Europe occidentale du IXe au XIVe siècle', *Revue internationale d'Histoire militaire* (1953–55), 486–96.

ANGLO-SAXON WARFARE

Abels, R. P., 'Bookland and Fyrd Service in Late Anglo-Saxon England', *Anglo-Norman Studies*, vii (1985), 1–25.

————, *Lordship and Military Obligation in Anglo-Saxon England* (Berkeley, 1988).

————, 'English Tactics, Strategy and Military Organization in the Late Tenth Century', *The Battle of Maldon, AD 991*, ed. D. Scragg (Oxford, 1991), 143–155.

Brooks, F. W., *The Battle of Stamford Bridge* (York, 1956).

Brooks, N. P., 'The Development of Military Obligations in Eighth- and Ninth-Century England' in *England Before the Conquest*, ed. P. Clemoes and K. Hughes (Cambridge, 1971), 69–84.

————, 'Arms, Status and Warfare in Late Anglo-Saxon England' in *Ethelred the Unready*, ed. D. Hill (*British Archaeological Reports, British Series*, lix (1978)), 81–103.

————, 'Ninth-Century England: The Crucible of Defeat', *TRHS*, 5th ser., xxix (1979), 1–20.

————, 'Weapons and Armour', *The Battle of Maldon, AD 991*, ed. D. Scragg (Oxford, 1991), 208–219.

Brooks, N. P., and Walker, H.E, 'The Authority and Interpretation of the Bayeux Tapestry', *Anglo-Norman Studies*, i (1979), 1–34.

Clapham, J. H., 'The Horsing of the Danes, *EHR*, xxv (1910), 287–93.

Cross, J. E., 'The Ethic of War in Old English', *England Before the Conquest*, ed. P. Clemoes and K. Hughes (Cambridge, 1971), 269–282.

Duncan, A. A. M., 'The Battle of Carham, 1018', *Scottish Historical Review*, 55 (1976), 1–28.

Fleming, R., 'Monastic Land and England's Defence in the Viking Age', *EHR*, c (1985), 247–265.

Glover, R., 'English Warfare in 1066', *EHR*, 67 (1952), 1–18.

Hawkes, S. C. (ed.), *Anglo-Saxon Weapons and Warfare* (*Oxford Archaeological Committee*, Monograph no. 21, Oxford, 1989).

Hollister, C. W., *Anglo-Saxon Military Institutions on the Eve of the Norman Conquest* (Oxford, 1962).

Hooper, N., 'Anglo-Saxon Warfare on the Eve of the Conquest: A Brief Survey', *Anglo-Norman Studies*, 1 (1979), 84–93.

————, 'The Housecarls in England in the Eleventh Century', *Anglo-Norman Studies*, vii (1985), 161–76.

John, E., 'War and Society in the Tenth Century: The Maldon Campaign', *TRHS*, 5th ser., xxvii (1977), 173–195.

Kiff, J., 'Images of War: Illustrations of Warfare in Early Eleventh Century England', *Anglo-Norman Studies*, vii (1985), 177–194.

Reynolds, S., 'Eadric Silvaticus and the English Resistance', *BIHR*, liv (1981), 102–105.

Woolf, R., 'The Ideal of Men Dying with their Lords in the "Germania" and the "Battle of Maldon" ', *Anglo-Saxon England*, v (1976), 69–81.

BATTLE, STRATEGY AND TACTICS

Bachrach, B. S., 'The Feigned Retreat at Hastings', *Mediaeval Studies*, xxxiii (1971), 264–7.

Baring, F., 'The Battlefield of Hastings', *EHR*, lxxvii (1905), 65–70.

Barlow, F., 'Military Society and the Art of War', in his *William I and the Norman Conquest* (London, 1965), 26–34.

Beeler, J. H., 'Castles and Strategy in Norman and Early Angevin England', *Speculum*, xxi (1956), 581–601.

———, 'A XIIth Century Guerilla Campaign', *Military Review*, 42 (1962), 39–46.

Bell, A., 'Notes on Gaimar's Military Vocabulary', *Medium Aevum*, lx (1971), 93–103.

Bennett, M., '*La Règle du Temple* as a Military Manual, *or* How to Deliver a Cavalry Charge', *Studies in Medieval History Presented to R. Allen Brown*, ed. C. Harper-Bill, C. Holdsworth and J. Nelson (Woodbridge, 1989), 7–20.

Bradbury, J., 'Battles in England and Normandy, 1066–1154', *Anglo-Norman Studies*, vi (1983), 1–12.

Brown, R. A., 'The Battle of Hastings', *Anglo-Norman Studies*, iii (1980), 1–21.

Carter, J. M., 'The Feigned Flight at Hastings Re-considered', *The Anglo-Norman Anonymous*, vi (1988).

Chevalier, C. T., 'Where was the Malfosse? The End of the Battle of Hastings', *Sussex Archaeological Collections*, ci (1963), 1–13.

Cook, D. R., 'The Norman Military Revolution in England', *Proceedings of the Battle Conference (Anglo-Norman Studies)*, ii (1979), 94–102.

Delpech, H., *La tactique au XIIIe siècle*, 2 vols. (Paris, 1886).

Drummond, J. D., *Studien zur Kriegsgeschichte Englands im 12. Jahrhundert* (Berlin, 1905).

Duby, G., *27 Juillet, 1214. Le dimanche de Bouvines* (Paris, 1973), trans. C. Tihanyi as *The Legend of Bouvines. War, Religion and Culture in the Middle Ages* (Cambridge, 1990).

Gaier, C., 'La cavalerie en Europe occidentale du XIIe au XIVe siècle: un problème de mentalité', *Revue internationale d'Histoire militaire* (1971), 385–96.

Gaier, C., 'Relire Verbruggen . . .', *Le Moyen Âge*, lxxxv (1979), 105–12.

Gillingham, J., 'Richard I and the Science of Warfare', *War and Government. Essays in Honour of J. O. Prestwich*, ed. J. Gillingham and J. C. Holt (Woodbridge, 1984), 78–91.

———, 'William the Bastard at War', *Studies in Medieval History Presented to R. Allen Brown*, ed. C. Harper-Bill, C. Holdsworth and J. Nelson (Woodbridge, 1989), 141–158.

Hill, R., 'The Battle of Stockbridge, 1141', *Studies in Medieval History Presented to R. Allen Brown*, ed. C. Harper-Bill, C. Holdsworth and J. Nelson (Woodbridge, 1989), 173–178.

Hollister, C. W., 'The Campaign of 1102 against Robert of Bellême', *Studies in Medieval History Presented to R. Allen Brown*, ed. C. Harper-Bill, C. Holdsworth and J. Nelson (Woodbridge, 1989), 193–202.

Lemmon, C. H., 'The Campaign of 1066', in *The Norman Conquest, its Setting and Impact*, ed. D. Whitelock *et al.* (London, 1966), 79–122.

Spatz, W., *Die Schlact von Hastings* (Berlin, 1896).

Stevenson, W. H., 'Senlac and the Malfosse', *EHR*, xxviii (1913), 292–303.

Tout, T. F., 'The Fair of Lincoln and the *Histoire de Guillaume le Maréchal*', *EHR*, xvii (1903), 240–65.

268 SELECT BIBLIOGRAPHY

Turner, C. J., 'William the Conqueror's March to London', *EHR*, cvi (1912), 209–25.
Verbruggen, F., 'La tactique militaire des armées des chevaliers', *Revue du Nord*, 29 (1947), 161–80.
Waley, D. P., 'Combined Operations in Sicily, AD 1060–78', *Papers of the British School in Rome*, 22 (1954), 118–25.

LOGISTICS AND SUPPLY

Bachrach, B., 'On the Origins of William the Conqueror's Horse Transports', *Technology and Culture*, xxvi (1983), 505–31.
———, 'The Military Administration of the Norman Conquest', *Anglo-Norman Studies*, viii (1986), 1–25.
Gilmor, C., 'The Naval Logistics of the Cross Channel Operation, 1066', *Anglo-Norman Studies*, vii (1984), 105–131.
Graindor, M., 'Le débarquement de Guillaume en 1066: un coup de maître de la marine normande', *Archaeologia*, xxx (1969).
Laporte, J., 'Les opérations navales en Manche et Mer du Nord pendant l'année 1066', *Annales de Normandie*, xvii (1967), 3–42.
J. W., 'The Rate of March of Crusading Armies in Europe, *Traditio*, 19 (1963), 167–81.
Pryor, J. H., 'The Transportation of Horses by Sea during the Era of the Crusades: Eighth Century to 1285 AD', *Mariner's Mirror*, lxxviii (1982).

ARMS, ARMOUR AND EQUIPMENT

Bachrach, B., 'Animals and Warfare in Medieval Europe', in *L'uomo di fronte al monde animale nell' alto medioevo*, in *Settimane di studio del Centro italiano di studi sull'alto medioevo*, xxx1. i (Spoleto, 1985), 707–64.
Blair, C., *European Armour* (London, 1958).
Bradbury, J., *The Medieval Archer* (Woodbridge, 1985).
Burgess, E. M., 'The Mail Maker's Technique' and 'Further Research into the Construction of Mail Garments', *Antiquaries Journal*, xxxiii (1953), 48–55, 193–202.
Clark, G. 'Beowulf's Armour', *Journal of English Literature and History*, 32 (1965), 409–41.
Davidson, H. R. E., *The Sword in Anglo-Saxon England. Its Archaeology and Literature* (Oxford, 1962).
Davis, R. H. C., 'The Medieval Warhorse', *Horses in European Economic History*, ed. F. M. L.Thompson (London, 1983).
———, 'The Warhorses of the Normans', *Anglo-Norman Studies*, x (1987), 67–82.
———, *The Medieval Warhorse: Origin, Development and Redevelopment* (London, 1989).
Dufty, A. R., *European Armour in the Tower of London* (London, 1968).
———, *European Swords and Daggers in the Tower of London* (London, 1974).
Gaier, C., *Les armes* (*Typologie des sources du Moyen Âge occidental*, 10, Turnhout, 1979).
Hardy, R., *Longbow. A Social and Military History* (London, 1976).

Legge, D. M., ' "Osbercs doublez." The Description of Armour in Twelfth Century Chansons de Geste', *Société Rencesvals. Proceedings of the Fifth International Conference* (Oxford, 1970), 132–42.

Manley, J., 'The Archer and the Army in the Late Saxon Period', *Anglo-Saxon Studies in Archaeology and History*, iv (1985), 223–35.

Nichol, D., *Arms and Armour of the Crusading Period, 1050–1350*, 2 vols. (New York, 1988).

Oakeshott, R. Ewart, *The Archaeology of Weapons. Arms and Armour from Prehistory to the Age of Chivalry* (London, 1960).

———, *The Sword in the Age of Chivalry* (London 1964, 2nd ed. 1981).

———, *Records of the Medieval Sword* (Woodbridge, 1991).

Payne-Gallwey, R., *The Crossbow, Medieval and Modern, Military and Sporting* (London, 1903, repr. 1958).

Peirce, I., 'The Knight, his Arms and Armour in the Eleventh Century', *The Ideals and Practice of Medieval Knighthood. Papers from the First and Second Strawberry Hill Conferences*, ed. C. Harper-Bill and R. Harvey (Woodbridge, 1986), 152–164.

———, 'Arms, Armour and Warfare in the Eleventh Century', *Anglo-Norman Studies*, x (1987), 237–258.

KNIGHTHOOD AND CHIVALRY

Barber, R., *The Knight and Chivalry* (London, 1970).

Barber, R. and Barker, J. R. V., *Tournaments. Jousts, Chivalry and Pageants in the Middle Ages* (Woodbridge, 1989).

Barker, J. R. V., *The Tournament in England, 1100–1400* (Woodbridge, 1986).

Batanay, J., 'Du *bellator* au *chevalier*, dans le schema des 'trois ordres' (étude sémantique), *Actes du CIe Congrès national des Sociétés savantes, Lille 1976, Section de philologie et d'histoire jusqu'à 1610, La Guerre et la paix* (Paris, 1978).

Bennett, M., 'The Status of the Squire: the Northern Evidence', *The Ideals and Practice of Medieval Knighthood. Papers from the First and Second Strawberry Hill Conferences*, ed. C. Harper-Bill and R. Harvey (Woodbridge, 1986), 1–11.

Benson, L. D., 'The Tournament in the Romances of Chrétien de Troyes and *L'Histoire de Guillaume le Maréchal*', *Studies in Medieval Culture*, xiv (1980), 1–24.

Chibnall, M., 'Feudal Society in Orderic Vitalis', *Anglo-Norman Studies*, 1 (1979), 35–48.

Crosland, J., *William the Marshal* (London, 1962).

Crouch, D., *William the Marshal. Court, Career and Chivalry in the Angevin Empire c. 1147–1219* (London, 1990).

Duby, G, 'Guerre et société dans l'Europe féodale: la morale des guerriers', *Concetto, Storia, Miti e Imagini del Medio Evo, Atti del XIV Corso internazionale d'alta cultura*, ed. V. Branca (Florence, 1973), 449–459.

———, 'The Origins of Knighthood' in *idem, The Chivalrous Society*, tr. C. Postan (Berkeley, Los Angeles and London, 1977).

———, *Guillaume le Maréchal ou le meilleur chevalier du monde* (Paris, 1984), tr. R. Howard as *William the Marshal, The Flower of Chivalry* (London, 1986).

Flori, J., 'Qu'est-ce qu'un *bacheler*? Étude historique du vocabulaire dans les chansons de geste du XIIe siècle', *Romania*, xcvi (1975), 289–314.

——, 'Chevalerie et liturgie. Remise des armes et vocabulaire 'chevaleresque' dans les sources liturgiques du IXe au XIVe siècle', *Le Moyen Âge*, lxxxiv (1978), 147–78.

——, 'Sémantique et société médiévale. Le verbe adouber et son évolution au XIIe siècle', *Annales* (1976), 915–40.

——, *L'essor de la chevalerie* (Geneva, 1986).

Gillingham, J., 'War and Chivalry in the History of William the Marshal', *Thirteenth-Century England. Proceedings of the Newcastle-upon-Tyne Conference*, II (1987), 1–14.

Guilhiermoz, P., *Essai sur l'origine de la noblesse en France au Moyen Âge* (Paris, 1902; repr. New York, 1960).

Keen, M., *Chivalry* (New Haven and London, 1984).

Painter, S., *William Marshal* (Baltimore, 1933).

——, *French Chivalry* (Baltimore, 1940).

STIPENDIARY FORCES, MERCENARIES AND ROUTIERS

Boussard, J., 'Les mercenaires au XIIe siècle. Henri II Plantagenet et les origines de l'armée de métier', *Bibliothèque de l'École des Chartes*, cvi (1945–46), 189–224.

Brown, S., 'Military Service and Monetary Reward in the Eleventh and Twelfth Centuries', *History*, ccxl (1989), 20–38.

Chibnall, M., 'Mercenaries and the Familia Regis under Henry I', *History*, lxii (1977), 15–23.

Duby, G., 'Guerre et société dans l'Europe féodale: la guerre et l'argent', *Concetto, Storia, Miti e Imagini del Medio Evo, Atti del XIV Corso internazionale d'alta cultura*, ed. V. Branca (Florence, 1973), 461–471.

Geraud, H., 'Les routiers au XIIème siècle', *Bibliothèque de l'École des Chartes*, iii (1841–2), 125–47.

——, 'Mercadier. Les routiers au XIIIème siècle', *Bibliothèque de l'École des Chartes*, iii (1841–2), 417–43.

Grundmann, H., 'Rotten und Brabazonen: Soldner-Heere im 12. Jahrhundert', *Deutsches-Archiv für Geschichte des Mittelalters*, v (1941–2), 419–492.

ORGANIZATION, TENURE AND MILITARY SERVICE

Audouin, E., *Essai sur l'armée royale au temps de Philippe Auguste* (Paris, 1913).

Bachrach, B., 'Angevin Campaign Forces in the Reign of Fulk Nerra, Count of the Angevins, 987–1040', *Francia*, xvi (1), (1989), 67–84.

Beeler, J. H., 'The Composition of Anglo-Norman Armies', *Speculum*, xl (1965), 398–414.

Boussard, J., 'L'enquête de 1172 sur les services de chevalier en Normandie', *Recueil de travaux offert à Clovis Brunel* (Paris, 1955), I, 192–208.

——, 'Services feodaux, milices et mercenaires dans les armées en France aux Xe et XIe siècles', *Ordinamenti militari in Occidente nell'alto Medioevo*, 2 vols. (*Settimane di Studio del Centro Italiano di studi sull'alto Medioevo*, Spoleto, 1968), I, 131–68.

Brooks, F. W., *English Naval Forces, 1199–1272* (London, 1933).

Brown, R. A., *Origins of English Feudalism* (London and New York, 1973)

Chew, H. M., *The English Ecclesiastical Tenants-in-Chief and Knight-Service* (Oxford, 1932).

Dodwell, B., 'East Anglian Commendation', *EHR*, lxiii (1948), 289–306.

Douglas, D. C., 'The Norman Conquest and English Feudalism', *Economic History Review*, ix (1939), 128–143, reprinted in *idem, Time and the Hour* (London, 1977), 161–175.

Gillingham. J., 'The Introduction of Knight-Service into England', *Anglo-Norman Studies*, iv (1982), 53–64.

Harvey, S., 'The Knight and the Knight's Fee', *Past and Present*, xlix (1970), reprinted in *Peasants, Knights and Heretics*, ed. R. Hilton (Cambridge, 1976).

Hollings, M., 'The Survival of the Five-Hide Unit in the Western Midlands', *EHR*, lxiii (1948), 453–487.

Hollister, C. W., 'The Significance of Scutage Rates in Eleventh and Twelfth Century England', *EHR*, lxxv (1960), 417–36.

———, 'The Annual Term of Military Service in Medieval England, *Medievalia et Humanistica*, xiii (1960), 577–88.

———, 'The Five-Hide Unit and the Old English Military Obligation', *Speculum*, xxxvi (1961), 61–74.

———, 'The Norman Conquest and the Genesis of English Feudalism', *AHR*, lxvi (1961), 641–664.

———, *The Military Organizaton of Norman England* (Oxford, 1965).

———, 'Military Obligation in Late Saxon and Norman England', *Ordinamenti Militari in Occidente Nell'Alto Medioevo*, Settimane di Studio del Centro italiano di studi sull'alto medioevo, xv (1968), 168–186.

———, '1066: The "Feudal Revolution" ', *American Historical Review*, lxxiii (1968), 708–723.

Holt, J. C., 'Feudalism Revisited', *Economic History Review*, 2nd. ser., xiv (1961).

———, 'The *Carta* of Richard de la Haye, 1166. A Note on 'Continuity' in Anglo-Norman Feudalism', *EHR*, lxxxiv (1969), 289–297.

———, 'The Introducion of Knight Service in England', *Anglo-Norman Studies*, vi (1983), 89–106.

John, E., *Land Tenure in Early England* (Leicester, 1960).

———, 'English Feudalism and the Structure of Anglo-Saxon Society', in his *Orbis Britanniae* (Leicester, 1966), 128–153.

Keefe, T. K., *Feudal Assessments and the Political Community under Henry II and his Sons* (Berkeley, Los Angeles, London, 1983).

King, E., 'The Peterborough *Descriptio Militum* (Henry I)', *EHR*, lxxxiv (1969), 82–101.

———, *Peterborough Abbey, 1086–1310* (Cambridge, 1973).

Lyon, B., 'The Money Fief under the English Kings', *EHR* lxvi (1951), 161–93.

———, *From Fief to Indenture* (Cambridge, Mass., 1957).

Miller, E., *The Abbey and Bishopric of Ely* (Cambridge, 1951, repr. 1969).

Powicke, M. R., *Military Obligations in Medieval England* (Oxford, 1962).

Prestwich, J. O., 'Anglo-Norman Feudalism and the Problem of Continuity', *Past and Present*, xxvi (1963), 39–57.

Round, J. H., 'The Introduction of Knight Service into England', in his *Feudal England* (London, 1895), 225–316.

———, 'Military Tenure before the Conquest', *EHR*, xii (1897), 492–494.

Sanders, I. J., *Feudal Military Service* (Oxford, 1956).

Schlight, J., *Monarchs and Mercenaries* (Bridgeport, Conn., 1968).

Stenton, F. M., *The First Century of English Feudalism, 1066–1166* (Oxford, 2nd ed., 1961).

Stevenson, W. H., 'Trinoda Necessitas', *EHR*, xxix (1914), 689–702.

Tabuteau, E., 'Definitions of Feudal Military Obligations in Eleventh-Century Normandy', in *On the Laws and Customs of England: Essays in Honour of Samuel E. Thorne*, ed. M. S. Arnold *et al.* (Chapel Hill, North Carolina, 1981).

Van Luyn, P., 'Les *milites* dans la France du XIe siècle. Examen des sources narratives', *Le Moyen Âge*, lxxvii (1971), 5–51, 193–238.

Notes

The Battle of Hastings   R. Allen Brown

[1] R. Allen Brown, *The Normans and the Norman Conquest*, London 1969.
[2] The principal modern accounts and discussions of the Battle of Hastings are those of
   E. A. Freeman, *The Norman Conquest*, iii, Oxford 1869, Chapter xv, 377–507 (Cf.
   J. H. Round, 'Mr Freeman and the Battle of Hastings', *Feudal England*, London
   1909, 332–98); W. Spatz, *Die Schlacht von Hastings*, Berlin 1896; F. H. Baring,
   Domesday Tables . . ., London 1909, Appendix B, 217–32; H. Delbrück, *Geschichte
   der Kriegskunst im Rahmen des Politische Geschichte*, iii, Berlin 1923, 150ff; Sir
   Charles Oman, *A History of the Art of War in the Middle Ages*, 2nd. ed., London
   1924, 151–66; F. Lot, *L'art militaire et les armées au moyen âge en Europe et dans le
   proche Orient*, Paris 1946, i, 282–5; F. M. Stenton, *Anglo-Saxon England*, 2nd. ed.,
   Oxford 1947, 583–8; A. H. Burne, *The Battlefields of England*, London 1950, 19ff;
   Richard Glover, 'English Warfare in 1066', *EHR* lxvii, 1952; G. H. White, 'The
   Battle of Hastings and the Death of Harold', *Complete Peerage*, xii, London 1953, Pt.
   i, Appendix L; J. F. C. Fuller, *The Decisive Battles of the Western World*, London
   1954, i, 360ff; D. C. Douglas, *William the Conqueror*, London 1964, 194–204; C. H.
   Lemmon, 'The Campaign of 1066' in *The Norman Conquest, its setting and impact*,
   ed. D. Whitelock and others, London 1966; John Beeler, *Warfare in England
   1066*–1189, Cornell U.P. 1966, 11–33; Brown, *Normans*, 158–76.
[3] One thinks especially, in this country, of the work of R. C. Smail, notably *Crusading
   Warfare*, Cambridge 1956; and, on the continent, of J. F. Verbruggen, especially his
   brilliant summary article, 'La tactique militaire des armées de chevaliers', *Revue du
   nord* xxix, 1947. Examples could and should be multiplied if this were a full
   bibliographical note.
[4] London 1960; Fontana paperback 1967.
[5] 2nd. ed., London 1924.
[6] Ed. John H. Beeler, Ithaca, New York, 1953.
[7] Ed. Beeler, 58.
[8] *Die Schlacht von Hastings.*
[9] *Geschichte der Kriegskunst.*
[10] F. W. Maitland, *Domesday Book and Beyond*, Fontana paperback 1960, 363.
[11] *EHR* lxvii, 1952.
[12] *Carmen*, especially Appendix B.
[13] *EHR* xciii, 1978. Cf. *ante* ii, 1979, 1–20.
[14] *The Chronicle of Battle Abbey*, Oxford Medieval Texts, Oxford 1980, 17–23; *ante* ii,
   1979, 155–6.
[15] I wish in this note to do public penance and make amends to bishop Odo. I do not

273

believe he *fought* at Hastings, any more than did Geoffrey, bishop of Coutances. In the famous pl.68 of the *BT* the mace he carries is not an offensive weapon but evidently the eleventh-century equivalent of the field marshal's baton (cf. pls.21, 55–6), and the garment he is wearing is not a hauberk (cf. pl.21).

[16] Wace, *ll.*6423–5. The number given is 696.

[17] *Battle Chronicle*, 44, 45.

[18] *Battle Chronicle*, 40.

[19] For the sources and some commentary upon what follows, see Brown, *Normans*, 145ff.

[20] In a private discussion after this paper had been read, Dr Marjorie Chibnall suggested to the writer that the long delay of the invasion force may even have been at least in part a deliberate feint by William to confuse his adversary.

[21] 'Evidence for a pre-Conquest origin for the chapels in Hastings and Pevensey castles', *Château-Gaillard, European Castle Studies* iii, 1966, London 1969, 144–51.

[22] *ASC*, 142.

[23] *ASC*, 142, 143.

[24] *ASC*, 'C', 143-4; Brown, *Normans*, 156–7.

[25] Glover, *EHR* lxvii.

[26] R. Allen Brown, *The Origins of English Feudalism*, London 1973, 34-43; *Normans*, 94–8.

[27] Freeman, *Norman Conquest*, ii, 2nd. ed., London 1870, 126–7. 'Shield-wall to shield-wall, sword to sword or axe to axe, had men waged the long warfare which had ranged from the fight of Reading to the fight of Assandun.'

[28] *Normans*, 158.

[29] Below, p. 00

[30] *Normans*, 158–60.

[31] Jumièges, 134; *Gesta Guillelmi*, 180; Orderic, ii, 172.

[32] *Gesta Guillelmi*, 180; Orderic, ii, 172; *Carmen*, *ll.*319–20.

[33] *ASC*, 141.

[34] Worcester, i, 227.

[35] *Gesta Guillelmi*, 180.

[36] Jumièges, 135.

[37] Ed. Eleanor Searle, 15, 36; Baring, *Domesday Tables*, 225–6.

[38] *Gesta Guillelmi*, 186–8, 208; Jumièges, 135; Worcester, i, 227. One should perhaps add Freeman's comment here (*Norman Conquest*, ii, 1969, 477 n.2), 'I cannot help noticing the tendency to make the hours of the battles and of other great events coincide with the hours of the Church'.

[39] Eg. Morton and Munz in *Carmen*, 74, 76–7.

[40] Eg. *De Gestis regum* ii 302; Wace, *ll.*7323 *et seq.*

[41] Jumièges, 134.

[42] *BT* pl.58.

[43] Freeman, iii, 1869, 438ff; C. H. Lemmon, 'The Campaign of 1066' in *The Norman Conquest* . . ., 79–122; Morton and Munz, *Carmen*, 76 n. 3.

[44] *ASC*, 'D', 143.

[45] Worcester, i, 227.

[46] Worcester, i, 227. For desertions see also *De gestis regum*, i, 281–2, ii, 300; Brown, *Normans*, 161; and *ASC*, 'D', 143 ('the king nevertheless fought hard . . . with the men who were willing to support him').

[47] *EHR* lxvii, 2–4.

48 *Gesta Guillelmi*, 180.
49 Cf. Freeman, iii, 411–2; D. C. Douglas, *William the Conqueror*, 197. Intentional provocation was accepted by Spatz (*Hastings*, 23, 25) but rejected by Delbrück (*Kriegskunst*, iii, 160). The concentration of Harold's patrimony, *i.e.* the lands of the house of Godwin, in Sussex, however, as shown by Dr Williams (pp. 176–7, 185–6 below), gives a new dimension to this hypothesis of the Conqueror's strategy, for what was at issue in contemporary terms was very much more than the modern and anachronistic concept of the defence of subjects by the king. One wonders, indeed, if William's first intention was to cross from Dives-sur-Mer to Bosham, the eventual crossing from St Valéry to Pevensey (where there were also Godwinson lands) being later substituted.
50 Brown, *Normans*, 150 n. 47.
51 I shall continue to use the term until such time as Mr Nicholas Hooper of King's College, London, currently working on pre-Conquest English warfare, tells us what we should mean by it.
52 Wace, 1.8257; *Chroniques Anglo-Normandes*, ed. F. Michel, i, Rouen 1836, 201.
53 *De gestis regum*, i, 282.
54 *Gesta Guillelmi*, 186. Cf. Sten Körner, *The Battle of Hastings, England, and Europe 1035–1066*, Bibliotheca Historica Lundensii xiv, Lund 1964, 220.
55 Above, p. 3.
56 *De gestis regum*, ii, 302. 'Rex ipse pedes juxta vexillum stabat cum fratribus, ut, in commune periculo aequato, nemo de fuga cogitaret.'
57 *BT*, pls. 64–5.
58 Thus Freeman, iii, 472–6; Spatz, 40–1; Fuller, *Decisive Battles*, 376. For Freeman's dispositions, cf., of course, J. H. Round, *Feudal England*, especially 359ff.
59 See Brown, *Normans*, 167 n.127, and especially Baring, *Domesday Tables*, 217–20.
60 Thus William of Poitiers, *Gesta Guillelmi*, 186—'Protinus equorum ope relicta, cuncti pedites constitere densus conglobati'. In the later sources the note of contempt by cavalry for flat-footed infantry already comes echoing across the ages—thus the *Carmen*, *ll*.369–70.
    'Nescia gens belli solamina spernit equorum,
    Viribus et fidens, heret humo pedibus'
and Wace, *ll*.8623–6
    'Engleis ne saveient ioster,
    Ne a cheval armes porter,
    Haches e gisarmes teneient,
    Od tels armes se combateient,'
61 Only one English archer is shown on the Tapestry (Pl. 63), though it should be noted that in the Song of Maldon 'bows were busy' (trans. in *EHD* i, 295).
62 *Gesta Guillelmi*, 192, 194.
63 *EHD* i, 294.
64 Wace, *ll*.8627–30.
65 The least ambiguous references to crossbows unfortunately occur in the *Carmen* (*ll*.337–8, 381–2, 411, and see Appendix C, 112–15). Cf. *Gesta Guillelmi*, 184—'Pedites in fronte locavit, sagittis armatos et balistis.' No crossbow is shown on the Tapestry.
66 Cf, Burne, 28–9, 30–1; Fuller, 378–9; Lemmon, 106, 108.
67 *Gesta Guillelmi*, 184.

68 *Gesta Guillelmi*, 184 ('ipse [Guillelmus] fuit in medio [equitum] cum firmissimo robore, unde in omnem partem consuleret manu et voce'), 190 ('Britanni, et quotquot auxiliares erant in sinistro cornu'). There were, however, also Normans on the right with the French, *e.g.* Robert de Beaumont and his contingent (192). Those modern commentators who place William in some rear 'headquarters' or 'command post' are obviously ignorant of the facts as well as of the spirit of the age and the man (Spatz, 67; Burne, 34; Fuller, 378–9; Lemmon, 104, 106).

69 Oman, ed. Beeler, 63–4.

70 *Gesta Guillelmi*, 194.

71 *Gesta Guillelmi*, 186–8.

72 'English Warfare in 1066', *EHR* lxvii, 1952.

73 *BT*, pls. 70–1.

74 *Gesta Guillelmi*, 198.

75 'L'originalité de "Turoldus": le maniement de lance', *Cahiers de civilisation médiévale* vi, 1963.

76 Orderic, ii, 30. Cf., perhaps, 132.

77 The only certain instance I can find, *i.e.* of a lance or spear detached from any (Norman) hand and going in the right direction, occurs in Pl. 62. Cf. perhaps, 64. The circumstance of the attack on the castle of Dinan (pl. 25) is, of course, different.

78 Eg. pls. 63, 64, 65.

79 Eg. pl. 62.

80 *The Alexiad of Anna Comnena*, ed. and trans. E. R. A. Sewter, Harmondsworth 1969, 416.

81 Eg. pls. 62, 65, 67.

82 Eg. pl. 55.

83 Eg. pls. 55, 59, 60, 61.

84 Pls. 12, 53 and *passim*.

85 *Gesta Guillelmi*, 202.

86 *Gesta Guillelmi*, 188–90.

87 It is generally assumed that they broke orders in advancing, though it is only Wace who makes Harold specifically order his forces to stand firm no matter what (ll.7757 *et seq*).

88 Pl. 68.

89 Cf. n. 15 above.

90 *Gesta Guillelmi*, 192.

91 *Gesta Guillelmi*, 194.

92 For the possibility that *BT* pls. 66–7 represent this incident, see p. 20 below.

93 *De gestis regum*, ii, 302, 303.

94 *Gesta Guillelmi*, 194.

95 Thus Spatz, 55ff, 61–2, 67; cf. Delbrück, 165; Burne, 31, 42–3; Lemmon, 108–10; Beeler, 21–2. Fuller (380) is an honourable exception in this company.

96 Jumièges, 120; D. P. Waley, 'Combined operations in Sicily, AD 1060–1078'. *Papers of the British School at Rome* xxii, 123; A. Fliche, *Le règne de Philippe I, roi de France*, Paris 1912, 258–9.

97 *Histoire des fils de Louis le Pieux*, ed. P. Laver, Classiques de l'Histoire de France au Moyen Age, Paris 1964, 110–12; *De moribus et actis primorum Normanniae ducum*, ed. J. Lair. Soc. des Antiquaires de Normandie, Caen 1865, 143. In Nithard the two sides at a kind of review or tattoo before Charles the Bald and Louis the German are evidently on foot in spite of current published translations. I owe the first reference to

my son G. P. A. Brown and the second to Professor Eleanor Searle. One suspects that others could be found if looked for.

[98] Here, therefore, cf. Delbrück, 165 and Stenton, p. 587. In general, see J. F. Verbruggen, 'La tactique militaire des armées de chevaliers', *Revue du Nord* xxix, 1947.

[99] *Gesta Guillelmi*, 194.

[100] Huntingdon, 203; Wace, ll.8139 *et seq.* It should perhaps be mentioned that some of the archers in the lower border of the Tapestry hereabouts (pls. 70–1) are apparently shooting high. This is very slender evidence but might conveivably be the source of a legend.

[101] *Gesta Guillelmi*, 200–2.

[102] Jumièges, 135; Orderic, ii, 177 (and in his edition of Jumièges).

[103] *Battle Chronicle*, 38.

[104] *BT*. pls. 71–2.

[105] *Ante* i, 23ff.

[106] *Les Oeuvres Poétiques de Baudri de Bourgueil*, ed. P. Abrahams, Paris 1926, 209, ll.461–4; *De gestis regum*, ii, 303; Huntingdon, 203; Wace, ll.8161 *et seq.*

[107] *Carmen*, 34–6 and Appendix D.

[108] Thus *e.g.* W. H. Stevenson, 'Senlac and the Malfosse', *EHR* xxviii, 1913, 292–303; also the most recent discussion of the Malfosse and its location by C. T. Chevalier, 'Where was the Malfosse? The End of the Battle of Hastings', *Sussex Archaeological Collections* ci, 1963, 1–13.

[109] *Gesta Guillelmi*, 202–4.

[110] Elizabeth M. C. Van Houts, 'Quelques remarques sur les interpolations attribuées à Orderic Vital dans les *Gesta Normannorum Ducum* de Guillaume de Jumièges', *Revue d'Histoire des Textes* viii, 1978, 213–22.

[111] Jumièges, 197.

[112] Orderic, ii, xv.

[113] Orderic, ii, 176–8.

[114] For Engenulf see Dr Chibnall's note 4 to Orderic, ii, 177.

[115] Ed. Searle, 38. See also 8, 15–16.

[116] See above.

[117] *BT* pls. 66–7.

[118] Above, p. 16.

[119] *Anglo-Saxon England*, 584.

[120] The Tapestry's depiction of the terrain on the right of pl.66 is very similar to that of the bay of Mont St Michel in pls. 21–2, with the addition of tufts of marsh grass or other vegetation.

[121] *De gestis regum* 303 and cf. p. 18 above.

[122] Huntingdon, 203.

[123] Wace, ll.6969–72, 7847–8, 8079 *et seq.*

[124] Ed. F. Michel, *Chroniques Anglo-Normandes*, i, Rouen 1836, 197ff.

[125] *Chroniques Anglo-Normandes*, i, 6ff.

[126] Ed. J. A. Giles, *Scriptores Rerum Gestarum Willelmi Conquestoris*, London 1845, 7–8. See Searle, *Chronicle of Battle Abbey*, 19–20.

[127] Ed. Phyllis Abrahams, cxcvi, 207–9, 232. The date is 1099–1102.

[128] Freeman, perhaps characteristically, took both (iii, 490–1, 502–3).

[129] See *Feudal England*, 'Mr Freeman and the Battle of Hastings', 332ff, especially 374ff.

[130] *De gestis regum*, i, 282.